DO
DEFICITS
MATTER?

DO DEFICITS MATTER?

DANIEL SHAVIRO

The University of Chicago Press / Chicago and London

DANIEL SHAVIRO is professor of law at New York University
and a former legislation attorney with the Joint Committee
on Taxation of the United States Congress.

The University of Chicago Press, Chicago 60637
The University of Chicago Press, Ltd., London
© 1997 by Daniel Shaviro
All rights reserved. Published 1997
Printed in the United States of America
06 05 04 03 02 01 00 99 98 97   1 2 3 4 5

ISBN: 0-226-75112-0 (cloth)

Library of Congress Cataloging-in-Publication Data

Shaviro, Daniel
    Do deficits matter? / Daniel Shaviro.
      p.   cm.
    Includes bibliographical references and index.
    ISBN 0-226-75112-0 (alk. paper)
    1. Budget deficits—United States.   2. Government
spending policy—United States.   3. Fiscal policy—United
States.   I. Title.
HJ2051.S475   1997
339.5′23′0973—dc20   96-33370
                                                    CIP

♾ The paper used in this publication meets the
minimum requirements of the American National Standard
for Information Sciences—Permanence of Paper for
Printed Library Materials, ANSI Z39.48-1984

To Patricia Ludwig, with all my love

Contents

Acknowledgments

For their comments on earlier drafts or portions thereof, I am grateful to Anne Alstott, David Bradford, Richard Craswell, Robert Eisner, Daniel Farber, David Friedman, Beth Garrett, Laurence Kotlikoff, Thomas LaWer, Michael McConnell, Mark Ramseyer, and Sol Shaviro.

I also received valuable comments at faculty workshops at the University of Chicago Law School, Columbia University School of Law, New York University Law School, and the Public Choice Society.

Above all, however, I wish I could thank the late Walter J. Blum for inspiring this project.

ONE

Introduction

$\mathbf{F}$ew topics in American politics are more discussed and less understood than the federal budget deficit. We frequently hear that deficit reduction is vital to our prosperity, but we rarely hear why this might be so. The deficit is blamed for all manner of economic ills, ranging from high interest rates to unemployment to the trade deficit to the low rate of national saving to low productivity growth—whichever seems most crucial at the moment—but little attention is paid to why it might have any of these effects.

The near unanimity in public discourse about the evil of deficits might seem to suggest that economists are similarly unanimous. In fact, however, they disagree fundamentally about whether deficits matter and, if so, then why. They have been debating these issues for more than two centuries, with consensus occasionally emerging but not persisting. Over the past twenty-five years, the deficit debate among economists has grown increasingly discordant, reflecting the issue's increased prominence, the growing size of reported deficits, and the collapse of 1960s Keynesianism.

Despite the scope and intensity of this debate, no one has ever published a serious, comprehensive study of budget deficits' economic and political significance. Economists generally do not focus on more than one or two of the main issues that we will see deficits pose, nor do they explore the relationships between the issues. They also mainly ignore the question of how deficits affect the level of federal spending, although this is a key part of the national political debate. Moreover, their work is sometimes marred by partisanship of the Left or the Right, or by the impulse to stake out a public stance like a cam-

1

paigning politician—often as the foundation of one's academic career—and then to stick to it at all costs, ignoring or disparaging all contrary arguments and evidence.

For the first time in two centuries of deficit debate, this book unifies the varied strands of the economic and political science literature and draws definite, balanced, and interrelated conclusions regarding all of the main issues that budget deficits present. The journey has many stages and will take us in a number of different directions. I therefore offer the following summary of my analysis and conclusions.

1. *Purely as a descriptive matter, why do Americans care so much about budget deficits?* The United States has a history of unusual concern about federal (although not state) budget deficits, going back to the earliest days after adoption of the Constitution. Other industrialized nations generally have not shown similar levels of concern, even when they have had comparable or greater budget deficits (or outstanding national debt) relative to their economies.

Our deficit fixation results in part from equating government debt with an individual's or household's debts, which generally could not grow for decades at a time without raising a serious prospect of default. In addition, deficits are a deeply rooted symbol in American history, the meaning of which has changed over time but which continually relates to distrust of the national government. The historical lineage from Thomas Jefferson's denunciations of the deficit to those of H. Ross Perot should alert us to the cultural conditioning that needs to be left to one side for purposes of clear analysis.

2. *Are the national government's debts properly analogized to those of an individual or household?* People often exaggerate the analogy, although it is not wholly misplaced. The main distinction is that the federal government, with its power to raise taxes and print money, faces less default risk than would a household that regularly spent more than it took in. In addition, our debt is mainly internal, owed by American taxpayers to American bondholders (two groups that overlap).

While the prospect of involuntary default is remote in the United States at present, we face a problem that is a lesser version of it: *policy sustainability,* or our ability to meet current commitments that are not quite as definite as the pledge to honor government bonds. Current fiscal policy is likely to prove hard to sustain—not only because of the growing national debt but also because of the expected long-term insolvency of Social Security and Medicare. Fiscal policy changes may result in disappointing expectations that our present fiscal policy encourages people to hold. Yet more and more people realize that our fiscal policy must and will change. The main problem posed by policy unsustainability is the shock and dislocation that result when expectations must change too fast.

3. *What issues do federal budget deficits raise, apart from concern about default and policy sustainability?* The first issue is *generational equity*, or concern about unduly benefiting current generations at the expense of future generations. The second issue is what *macroeconomic effects* deficits generally have. At one time, they were lauded by Keynesians as the cure for recession or even significant unemployment, based on the claim that they increased current consumer spending and thereby stimulated the economy. Today, the same causal claim leads many to condemn deficits as a cause of the low rate of national saving. The third issue concerns their effects on the *size of the national government*. Some supporters of limited government identify deficit spending as a major cause of undesirable government growth and therefore advocate the adoption of a balanced budget amendment to the U.S. Constitution.

Each concern rests on a common causal claim: that deficit spending reduces the perceived (whether or not the actual) cost of government spending to current consumers and voters, thus inducing them to feel wealthier. They therefore consume more, leave less for subsequent generations, and accept a higher level of government spending than they would have otherwise. Before discussing the accuracy and significance of this causal claim, we must look more carefully at how deficits are defined and measured.

4. *Is the budget deficit a meaningful economic measure?* The budget deficit would seem most likely to have these claimed effects if it were a meaningful economic measure. Unfortunately, it is not—although there *is* a meaningful underlying phenomenon, which it mismeasures, about which the above claims can be made.

The budget deficit's main shortcoming is that it is calculated on the basis of cash flow rather than economic accrual. Suppose that an individual kept his books under the rules that the federal government uses to measure the budget deficit. If he managed to buy a million-dollar home for only a thousand dollars, he would seem to have acted imprudently, since, in the year of purchase, he would have increased his deficit. This transaction would be treated identically to losing a thousand dollars at the racetrack. If he instead sold a million-dollar home for a thousand dollars, or agreed to pay someone a million dollars next year in exchange for a thousand dollars today (assuming that this was not classified as a loan), he would have accomplished deficit reduction, at least under some versions of the measure, and thus would seem to have acted prudently.

While inaccuracies of this kind may have mattered little at one time in American history, that time has passed. Today, a cash-flow measure creates systematic, not just random, bias, for three main reasons. First, it encourages ignoring the approach of unfunded future spending commitments, as under Social Security and Medicare. Second, it encourages legislative responses that, over the long term, are meaningless or even make the government's fiscal posture worse. "Smoke and mirrors" policy changes, or those that reduce deficits in the short term while increasing them for "out years" beyond the estimating window, have been a feature of all major deficit reduction initiatives in Washington. Third, to the extent that fiscal policy affects economic behavior via its impact on perceived wealth, the long-term elements of such policy that the deficit ignores may matter. Unless people are highly myopic, their expectations regarding how much the government will pay or take from them in the future should affect their current behavior.

5. How could we better describe the underlying fiscal policy that deficits mismeasure? Given the deficit's economic inaccuracy as a cash-flow measure, we need a new vocabulary to describe the underlying phenomenon of having spending accrue before taxes. I will use the term *tax lag* to describe a fiscal policy (such as our present one) in which, over the long term, (a) tax revenues will be inadequate to pay for government spending absent a policy change, and/or (b) younger individuals and future generations will end up paying for government spending on behalf of older individuals and current generations. The word *lag* is appropriate because, over the long term, no government spending is free; it all must and will be paid for by someone. Even if the national debt is never repaid, taxpayers bear it economically over time by perpetually paying interest on the debt. Nor would defaulting on our debt obligations eliminate the cost of paying for government spending. Default would merely shift the cost from taxpayers to bondholders—functioning, in effect, as a one-time tax on the latter.

When I use the term *tax lag*, the reader should keep in mind that I am describing the *relative* timing of taxes and spending, rather than anything absolute about taxation. I could just as easily refer to *spend-*

ing acceleration. Tax lag can be reduced through policy changes either on the tax side or on the spending side of the federal budget. On the tax side, one can increase the extent to which necessary future taxes are specified and/or increase taxes on current generations and older individuals. On the spending side, one can reduce planned present or future spending, in particular that on behalf of current generations and older individuals.

The most intuitively obvious way to measure changes in tax lag would be through what I call the *economic accrual budget deficit* (as distinct from the cash-flow budget deficit currently used). This measure—which I mean only as a thought experiment—would focus on economic accrual over time, rather than cash flow, by taking account of expected future revenues and outlays at their interest-adjusted present value. Suppose that at the beginning of the fiscal year, the national debt stood at $2 trillion and the present value of all expected future budget deficits stood at $3 trillion. Tax lag would therefore total $5 trillion in present-value terms at the start of the year. (This would be the "economic accrual national debt.") Next, suppose that during the fiscal year, there was a $100 billion cash-flow budget deficit and the present value of all expected future deficits rose by $150 billion. The economic accrual budget deficit would equal the sum of these two amounts, or $250 billion, as the present value of our tax lag would have increased by that amount to $5.25 trillion in the course of the fiscal year.

The measure, as I have described it thus far, would still be too cash-flow-oriented in a critical respect. It would fail to distinguish between expenditures that create durable government assets and those that are immediately consumed. Recall my earlier point that spending a thousand dollars to buy a house is quite different from spending that amount at the racetrack. To the extent feasible, one would want to adjust the economic accrual budget deficit to use standard principles of accrual accounting for government expenditures. At a minimum, expenditures that created lasting government assets would be deducted over their estimated useful lives rather than in the year of the expenditure. One might also want to consider adjusting for fluctuations in the value of government assets (at least those plausibly held for sale, if not, say, the Lincoln Memorial) and ignoring government asset sales that merely convert property to cash.

Yet, even if one could make these adjustments, another problem would arise. Suppose that Congress in 1998 enacted a head tax of

$50,000 per year, to apply starting in 2050 to each adult American and remain in force as long as needed to pay off all public debt and eliminate all funding shortfalls in Social Security and Medicare. This enactment probably would not alter one's view of our current fiscal policy, whether because it seemed frivolous or because the bottom line, the fact that taxes ultimately will pay for today's spending, was already implicit. This suggests two problems with the economic accrual budget deficit. The more trivial one is that the set of tax and payment rules currently on the books is less important, for some purposes, than the set of rules that actually, credibly constitute our current policy. The more fundamental problem is that what really matters about taxes and spending, at least distributionally, is *who* pays for and receives them. A tax on younger generations in fifty years may be quite different from a tax on us today, even if the taxes have the same present value.

Responding to these problems in measuring tax lag, economist Laurence Kotlikoff has proposed a new measurement system to replace the cash-flow budget deficit that, while less intuitive than the economic accrual budget deficit, provides more meaningful information. He calls it *generational accounting*. Its most important innovation, beyond employing principles of economic accrual, is that it compares expected taxes to expected outlays by age group rather than providing a single overall measure of tax lag. Generational accounting involves computing the estimated *lifetime net tax payment* and *lifetime net tax rate* for the average member of an age group—those born, say, in 1930, 1960, 1990, or the future—assuming the continuation of current policy (except that future generations are deemed to make up all long-term revenue shortfalls). The lifetime net tax payment is the excess of taxes paid over transfers received, computed on a lifetime basis in present-value terms from birth. The lifetime net tax rate is the lifetime net tax payment, divided by estimated lifetime income.

Generational accounting thus directly addresses which age groups win and lose under fiscal policy and sheds light on such policy's likely sustainability. According to Kotlikoff, lifetime net tax rates have been rising throughout the twentieth century and now stand at astronomical levels for future generations—more than 84 percent under current policy, according to his most recent data.

Unfortunately, any long-term economic accrual measure involves conceptual and computational difficulty. In calculating future years' tax and spending levels, what set of policies should we assume will be followed? How confident can we be in any long-term economic and demographic forecasts? Should mere expectations of benefiting in future years from government spending programs be distinguished from explicit public debt? Can we really determine the incidence, within a multigenerational household, of government taxes and transfers?

While these problems reduce generational accounting's practical value—especially given estimating games in the real world of partisan politics—it remains conceptually superior to the cash-flow budget deficit. Generational accounting requires extensive assumptions, but at least it sets forth a meaningful economic concept. Moreover, it addresses an important gap in current understanding. While political debate has moved in the direction of focusing on long-term economic accrual (as through multiyear deficit forecasts and debate about the long-term solvency of Social Security and Medicare), it has tended to ignore the generational implications of alternative policies.

Still, despite the importance of focusing on long-term accrual and on who pays what, discussion of the cash-flow budget deficit is not wholly without value, as long as we keep its limitations in mind. Major deficit reduction initiatives in Congress often would reduce tax lag, even if they also include smoke-and-mirrors elements. One could even argue that the deficit has particular advantages as a guide for public political discourse, despite its conceptual flaws, because of its greater salience and symbolic heft.

6. What aspects of government policy do even long-term fiscal policy measures ignore? So far, the discussion has been limited to fiscal policy, which concerns cash flows to and from the government. This focus is incomplete, since cash transactions represent only a part of total government activity. Both in-kind benefits from government spending and the various in-kind benefits and burdens resulting from government regulation are similar in principle to cash subsidies and tax levies. Yet they generally are ignored in discussions of fiscal policy, for no better reason than that they are hard to measure and allocate to specific individuals or groups.

One could argue that just as the cash-flow budget deficit is not a true economic measure because it ignores long-term accrual, so generational accounting is not a true economic measure because it ignores the value of in-kind benefits and burdens imposed on different age groups by government policy. Consider Kotlikoff's finding that lifetime net tax rates have been rising over time. If this were wholly an artifact of government growth that could increase the value of in-kind public goods and services, it might have little significance. The claim that one can meaningfully evaluate fiscal policy separately from all other government policy is essentially an "all else equal" claim (or hope)— although perhaps not an unreasonable one.

7. *All else equal, does tax lag actually have the generational, macro-economic, and size-of-government effects that have been attributed to budget deficits?* This is an empirical question, which turns on whether tax lag actually causes people to feel wealthier and regard government spending as less costly than they would if taxes were accruing at the same rate as spending. The argument against tax lag's having this effect begins with the observation that rational private borrowers recognize that borrowing money generally does not make them wealthier but merely gives them current cash against a future, interest-bearing charge. If people generally took this view of public debt—considering it, in the aggregate, a charge on their current wealth since it implies higher future taxes, including interest on the deferral—then tax lag would fail to increase their perceived or actual wealth.

Economist Robert Barro asserts that people actually view tax lag this way. Thus, he would expect a $100 billion current-year tax reduction (holding government spending constant) not to affect current consumption behavior or to have any systematic impact. This claim— called Ricardian equivalence for economist David Ricardo, who first described it—suggests that tax lag is largely irrelevant because people make offsetting adjustments. In effect, they put the amount of any deferred tax in a dedicated bank account to pay the tax when it comes due, rather than regarding it as giving them extra money to spend— even if they do not expect it to come due during their lifetimes. Barro derives this claim from a "rational expectations" framework in which people, acting without systematic error, pursue fixed goals regarding how much wealth to transfer to their children net of deferred taxes and thus achieve whatever end result they prefer without regard to any government policies that fail to alter the "opportunity set."

If Barro were correct, then politicians could, with relative impunity, propose massive current tax increases to eliminate tax lag, leaving the question of spending levels to be debated separately. Yet even the barest familiarity with contemporary politics shows that this is false. Voters generally punish politicians who propose current tax increases, evidently not agreeing with the Ricardian argument that the timing of taxation has no effect on its perceived current level. We also fail to observe other apparent implications of Ricardianism—for example, equal frequency of budget deficits and surpluses, or any tendency of large families to prefer current tax increases based on the view that their share of the tax burden will grow over time as they split into multiple households. All this suggests that increasing tax lag does tend to increase perceived wealth, leading to the claimed generational, macroeconomic, and size-of-government effects.

8. *What should we think of tax lag's generational effects?* Many argue that shifting tax burdens to future generations is immoral. The question is not really one of wealth transfer, which is pervasive and inevitable between generations in any event (as whenever parents spend money on their children or leave bequests). Rather, the issue is better put in terms of rising lifetime net tax rates. Kotlikoff argues that a norm of "generational balance" requires avoiding any increase in the expected lifetime net tax rates for future generations relative to those for current generations.

I find the argument for this norm unpersuasive. The real issue is the overall distribution of lifetime consumption between succeeding generations. This, in turn, depends less on fiscal policy than on the present generation's overall rate of saving and productivity of investment, along with decisions within the household concerning such matters as child care, educational investment, and the rate of divorce. There is no apparent reason for government fiscal policy, which is merely one component of everything we do that affects our descendants, to be generationally "balanced." Even the narrower claim that reducing tax lag, by increasing national saving, would shift lifetime consumption in the right direction may not be correct. For example, if technological advances cause people fifty years from now to be wealthier than we are—just as we are wealthier than people fifty years ago, and they are wealthier than people fifty years earlier still—then changing fiscal policy to benefit future generations would amount to playing Robin Hood in reverse. While per capita societal wealth is not certain to continue increasing, our inability to predict the future makes it hard to know what generational policy would be best.

One might ask: even if *some* increase in lifetime net tax rates is justifiable, isn't a projected 84 percent rate for future generations far too high? The answer might be yes if such a rate were actually possible. Even Kotlikoff agrees, however, that it is not. Rather, this projected rate reflects a computational convention, under which he estimates the implications of current policy (although it may be certain to change) by assigning the entire unprovided-for net tax burden to future generations. He does this both because *some* arbitrary assumption is needed (since current policy does not tell us how tax lag will be addressed) and as a rough indicator of where current fiscal policy is headed. A staggering lifetime net tax rate for future generations mainly indicates a sustainability problem for current policy, suggesting that some of the as yet unprovided-for net tax burden will have to be borne, in the end, by members of present generations.

9. *What should we think of tax lag's macroeconomic effects?* Again, tax lag tends to increase current consumption relative to saving. While many condemn this effect on the ground that the current rate of national saving is too low, it is hard to be sure. What *is* the optimal rate of saving? No one knows. The whole point of saving, rather than consuming, is to make possible greater future consumption. Yet the choice between present and future consumption presents a difficult tradeoff, and neither is to be preferred automatically. In any case, while saving helps to promote long-term economic growth, such growth probably depends more, in the end, on technological developments than on the precise level of capital accumulation.

Tax lag's effect on the choice between current consumption and saving also matters in Keynesian theory, where one can moderate recessions by making people feel wealthier, thus offsetting fear-induced reductions in consumer spending. However, although Keynesianism has rebounded from its apparent intellectual collapse in the 1970s, even most Keynesians now recognize that the case for an actively countercyclical fiscal policy is extremely weak. The main problems are systematic misuse by politicians pursuing short-term political goals and undue lag in implementing fiscal policy changes. Keynesian fiscal policy should be purely automatic rather than discretionary, as when unemployment benefits rise and income tax revenues decline during a recession.

10. *What should we think of tax lag's size-of-government effects?* Again, tax lag tends to increase government spending by reducing its perceived cost. While this does not prove that, on balance, the federal government spends too much, there is much to be said for such a view. Political and regulatory processes often lead to bad and wasteful policy because of their structural problems, such as the power of special interest groups, politicians' and bureaucrats' inappropriate incentives, and voters' limited information.

Nonetheless, even if by reducing tax lag one could reduce the number of dollars the government spends, a smaller and better government might not result. For one thing, the size of government and the level of harm from bad policies correlate only very roughly, if at all, with the number of dollars the government spends. For another, political pressures might mainly lead to a reduction in good rather than bad spending. For a third, reducing tax lag might simply yield changes in the form of government activity, with regulatory mandates replacing explicit taxes and spending. This has already happened to some extent in recent years. Therefore, it is not clear that reducing tax lag would lead either to a genuinely smaller government or to one whose policies, when misguided, did less harm.

The foregoing discussion suggests that while tax lag is important and needs to be better understood, the appropriate response to it is unclear. Only on size-of-government grounds do its effects seem clearly undesirable, and even there reducing it might not accomplish much. This suggests skepticism about enacting a balanced budget amendment (BBA)—the great political issue concerning tax lag in recent years— even disregarding the budget deficit's shortcomings as a measure.

Such skepticism is enhanced when one examines the BBA's likely form, as in the version nearly approved by Congress in 1995. This version of the BBA would probably be grossly ineffective, even on its own terms, for two main reasons. First, it allows a 60 percent supermajority in both houses of Congress to authorize deficits of any size and for any reason. While this flexibility has some virtues, in practice it might lead to *increased* budget deficits. Supermajority requirements may increase the amount of logrolling that is necessary to assemble a winning coalition. Second, the proposed BBA has no built-in enforcement mechanism. It merely states that unauthorized deficits should not occur. Any enforcement legislation that was adopted to fill this gap would lack the constitutional status of the BBA itself and thus would likely fail to provide a binding constraint.

In the end, the most pressing concern raised by current tax lag relates not to the three main long-term issues that I have identified but to the relatively short-term, prudential issue of policy sustainability. If, as seems likely, we cannot long pay for everything that current fiscal policy seems to promise—above all, because of the likely long-term insolvency of Social Security and Medicare—then our policy must change and eventually will change. Along the way, however, there may be disruption and severely disappointed expectations unless the shift to a sustainable policy is made gradually, with broadly distributed impact, and in a reasonable, well-explained fashion. The sooner the shift to a sustainable policy is made, the less disruptive it is likely to prove.

The plan of this book largely follows that of the Introduction. Chapter 2 examines the general and idiosyncratically American reasons for our concern about budget deficits. Chapter 3 looks at the first two hundred years of the deficit debate among economists, extending from David Hume and Adam Smith in the second half of the eighteenth century through the rise and decline of Keynesianism between the 1930s and the 1970s. Chapter 4 examines the deficit debate among economists since the 1970s, focusing on the work of Robert Barro, Martin Feldstein, James Buchanan, Robert Eisner, and Laurence Kotlikoff. Chapter 5 discusses generational policy. Chapter 6 looks at the macroeconomic implications of tax lag and budget deficits. Chapter 7 examines the size-of-government issues, including the merits of the balanced budget amendment and alternative proposals to limit the size of government. Chapter 8 provides a brief conclusion.

TWO

Reasons for the Perceived Importance of Budget Deficits

A. The Analogy between Private Debt and Public Debt

Whatever the ultimate merits of comparing public debt owed by a government to private debt owed by an individual or household, the latter provides a natural starting point for thinking about the former. I begin, therefore, by examining the considerations that might underlie an economically rational private decision to borrow.

When I consider an expenditure that may require me to borrow, I face two main decisions. First, should I make the expenditure to begin with? This involves comparing the value I will derive to the cost. If I am considering an investment, does the expected rate of return exceed the interest rate or opportunity cost? If I am considering a consumption expenditure, will I benefit enough both from making it at all and from forgoing investment opportunities by making it now? Second, assuming the expenditure will be made, how should I finance it? If I own liquid assets, then, in addition to determining which lender offers the best terms, I should compare the opportunity cost of self-financing with the rate of interest that I would pay on a loan.

Both decisions involve attempting to maximize actual, implicit, or psychic returns, while minimizing costs and creating net gain or advantage if possible. However, neither decision relies on or leads to any insights of a general nature about the merits or significance of borrowing. The principles "buy low, sell high" and "consume when you prefer" or, more generally, "make good decisions" are tautologically correct from a self-interested standpoint, but they are uninformative.

Borrowing can, however, have another, more general implication: the creation of potential danger for the risk-averse. Suppose that I borrow money at a fixed interest rate in order to make a more speculative investment. Or, if the loan is used for consumption, suppose that the other transactions I am relying on to permit repayment offer a wide range of possible returns. (For example, if I currently have a job, I might get fired.) Now borrowing gives me downside risk, even if on balance I expect to benefit or profit. In particular, I may be risking default and bankruptcy.

To some borrowers, the prospect of default may encourage borrowing, since default offers the opportunity to use funds and never repay them. Yet, perhaps few borrowers take so blithe a view. Internalized notions of personal success and responsibility can make default a source of guilt or shame. Bankruptcy disrupts one's affairs, can tie one up in court, and impedes future borrowing. Even if one barely avoids default, the prospect of losing a substantial portion of one's assets can be painful if one values certain core assets or attaches declining marginal utility to one's wealth.

In part for these reasons, few themes in literature are as popular and perennial as the plight of the borrower burdened by crushing debts. At times, the borrower is mainly unlucky, like Antonio in Shakespeare's *Merchant of Venice*, a merchant whose ships are lost at sea. Many fictional borrowers, however, are imprudent in their acceptance of risk (as, perhaps, Antonio was) or downright thoughtless and undisciplined, craving short-term consumption that they cannot afford, like Emma in Flaubert's *Madame Bovary*. For their weaknesses—cruelly exploited by cunning or malevolent creditors—they often suffer horribly.

In *Madame Bovary*, Emma's affairs disappoint her—she discovers "in adultery all the platitudes of marriage" (1965, 209)—but her debts humiliate and destroy her. Very near the end, when she is in a "stupor . . . only conscious of herself through the beating of her arteries, that seemed to burst forth like a deafening noise filling all the fields," until "her head seemed to explode at once like a thousand pieces of fireworks" (228), she is responding to financial ruin, not lost love. She swallows rat poison rather than face foreclosure.

Dickens's Wilkins Micawber, perhaps the most famous chronic debtor in literature, fares better in *David Copperfield*, ultimately finding in Australia the elusive field for his "talent." Along the way, however, he exemplifies the type one would rather know than be—plunged frequently into flamboyant despair yet no more able than an infant to act purposefully in his own interest or even to remember his troubles from one moment to the next. The novel's mix of fondness for Micawber and ironic distance from him only sharpen the reader's sense of the desperate practical importance of the qualities of foresight, self-discipline, and sense of purpose that he so sadly lacks.

The cultural perceptions of debt and debtors that these literary sources illustrate will prove important when we turn to the contemporary debate about the budget deficit. For now, I should note that such perceptions underlie the frequent disjuncture between popular and academic views of budget deficits. While members of the public tend to analogize public to private debt and to regard the two as comparably imprudent, economists often question or reject the analogy.

Sometimes private borrowing by individuals or households and public borrowing by governments have much in common. For example, countries without strong economies that must borrow in foreign currencies sometimes fail to meet their loan obligations—although they are not subject to bankruptcy court and may not experience the guilt or shame of a fictional private borrower. Even in societies with sufficient wealth to meet public fiscal needs, governments can become dependent on foreign lenders and ultimately face default and the cutoff of credit if they lack domestic political support. Both the English Revolution of 1640 and the French Revolution of 1789 were triggered by fiscal crises resulting from the monarchies' inability either to impose new taxes or to attract domestic loan capital (Hill 1961, 107; Schama 1989, 62, 71).

Yet in England, by the late eighteenth century, the evolution of a state with more modern fiscal powers and practices had caused the analogy between public and private debt to lose much of its accuracy. England was wealthy enough, and its government sufficiently powerful and popular, to alleviate default risk even when foreign wars created a need for significant expenditure and borrowing. Once the English government had established a well-functioning tax system, it could respond to pressing financial needs by offering bonds to its own citizens, payable with reasonable interest in its own currency. Such public debt was significantly different from private debt, in both the likelihood of default and the significance of repayment. When needed, new taxes could and would be imposed to ensure that promises of repayment would be honored. Bondholders were sufficiently confident of this to lend money to the state at relatively low interest rates.[1] Moreover, because the bonds were largely internal debt held by English subjects, they were in the aggregate self-owed and did not require withdrawing resources from England's economy. Despite these changes, however, the force of traditional thinking, along with the rapid growth and sheer size of the public debt after a century of war, was such that "every politician and political pundit of the era complained" about the government's purportedly imprudent fiscal position (Brewer 1989, 114). David Hume, for example, predicted that England, by reason of its debt burden, would either disavow its debts, thus destroying its credit and ruining its mostly domestic creditors, or else, even more calamitously, succumb to tyranny or foreign invasion (Hume 1764).

The American national government was similarly put on a strong fiscal footing by the U.S. Constitution. Its taxing and money-printing powers, along with the relatively limited demand for federal spending, allowed the national government to use little debt financing (apart from recessionary and wartime debts that were mostly repaid in peacetime) from the enactment of the Constitution until the Great Depression of the 1930s. This accorded with the preferences of most American commentators, who as early as 1820 expressed concern about "burdening our posterity" and who between the 1860s and the 1880s made retiring the Civil War debt a "national obsession" (Savage 1988, 101, 127).

Yet the long American history of practicing or at least preaching budgetary balance, and of abhorring debt financing, cannot be explained solely by concerns of fiscal prudence based on analogizing the national government to a private borrower. The force of that analogy fails to explain the difference between American practice and that in western European countries (including England over the last century), as well as other industrialized nations such as Japan. In these countries, at least until recently, the deficit issue has generally failed to attract significant attention even when deficits larger than our own relative to the size of the economy have been commonplace.

The private borrower analogy also fails to explain the distinction between practice at the national and state levels in this country. State

1. On England's establishment, beginning in the late seventeenth century, of a tax system that functioned sufficiently well to support large public debts, see Brewer 1989, 87–134.

governments are far more like private borrowers than is the national government, since they cannot print money, are more likely to owe debt to outsiders, and have less power to raise revenue given the greater ease of exit by prospective taxpayers. Nonetheless, American concern about budget deficits has often, paradoxically, been focused on the national level, although default has been the exclusive province of state and local governments (106).

The leading historical study of American deficit politics and practice—James Savage's *Balanced Budgets and American Politics*—demonstrates that intense concern about budget deficits is a relatively unique American phenomenon with deep cultural roots that give the issue "symbolic as well as instrumental or economic properties" (1988, 5). The symbolism of deficit versus balance has changed radically over time but has continually related to unease about the national government.

B. American History and the Symbolic Significance of Debt and Deficits

1. From the Colonial Era to the Civil War

America's special abhorrence of debt financing was not instinctive or original. The colonies frequently borrowed or printed money to finance wars and public works programs and to stimulate their economies. In the 1760s, England began restraining these practices, and in so doing added to the grievances that sparked the American Revolution. The American military effort in the revolution was largely financed by debt and paper money, as perhaps befitted what was in part a tax revolt. This debt largely remained outstanding (or fell in arrears) during the 1780s, causing domestic turmoil and international embarrassment, because of the Continental Congress's lack of authority to levy taxes and the states' unwillingness to comply with its funding requests.

Perhaps because the country's capacity to repay the Revolutionary War debt, under different institutional arrangements, was so obvious, the experience of the 1780s did not lead directly to fear of public debt. Instead, it built support for the view, reflected in the Constitution, that the national government needed to be strengthened, in particular by the granting of taxing authority. The decade's hyperinflation, as the continental currency lost value and state currencies proliferated, also helped inspire the constitutional provision barring the states from printing money—a provision they soon learned to evade by selling securities that could circulate like currency but did not legally qualify as such (107).[2]

Abhorrence of debt financing arose shortly after the adoption of the Constitution; however, it expressed not fear of default but the opposite: fear of good credit. Early in the Washington administration, Treasury secretary Alexander Hamilton set in place an ambitious program to secure the Revolutionary War debt, without repaying it immediately, in order to establish firm public credit. Other Hamilton programs, such as establishment of the National Bank, similarly sought to enable the national government to borrow at low cost and without weakening the currency. Hamilton's underlying goal was to establish a strong national government that could actively manage the money supply, promote industry, and undertake ambitious public works programs.

This program became controversial to an extent and in a manner that is difficult to understand today or to express in familiar terminology. One complaint was that honoring at face value the depreciated Revolutionary War debt and continental currency would yield a windfall to well-connected speculators who had bought the notes at steep discount. More generally, however, Thomas Jefferson and other nascent Democrats attacked Hamilton's entire program as corrupt, monarchical, and promoting inequality. Jeffersonians inveighed against the "moneyed aristocracy" that would exploit the financial leverage Hamilton envisioned for both profit and political advancement. They also denounced Hamilton's plan to promote industry, noting the social divisions that it would bring and accusing him of emulating the English model of society.

The emotional attack on "corruption," which was at the center of anti-Hamiltonian rhetoric, is especially difficult to grasp today. The term did not then primarily connote graft, although that was a part of it. More generally, *corruption* referred to subverting the natural balance of society, by empowering the central administration to dole out financial favors that would enable it to dominate the legislature and to achieve, on behalf of itself and its allies in the moneyed aristocracy (as

2. In substance, the only important difference between securities and bills of credit was that the former paid explicit interest.

distinct from the landed or natural aristocracy), a tyrannical preeminence over the rest of society (Wood 1969, 32—36, 107—14).

Fear of corruption in this sense led Jeffersonians to abhor deficit spending and strong public credit. At one point, Jefferson proposed a balanced budget amendment to the Constitution, arguing that even the hardship it would cause in times of war was well worth the benefit of discouraging wars. Similar concerns later led his political heirs, the Jacksonians, to dismantle the National Bank. Yet the conflict was not between advocates of powerful versus limited government (although, of course, all of the era's visions of government were "limited" by modern standards). Rather, it pitted advocates of national government power against those who preferred to locate power in the states.

One might think that the Jeffersonian and Jacksonian Democrats' fears about corruption were at least partly transferable to the state level, where governors conceivably could use debt financing to dominate the legislature and entrench their own moneyed aristocratic friends. The Jeffersonians and Jacksonians did not think so, however. Whether because state power is inherently more limited by geography or because the real question was merely who got to exercise financial and spending power, they consistently lauded state government—regarding it, in Jefferson's words, as "the very best in the world, without exception or comparison" (Savage 1988, 106). They objected neither to debt financing nor to public works programs undertaken by the states. From roughly 1820, when New York successfully completed the Erie Canal, to 1838, when financial panic forced retrenchment, the amount the states *borrowed* was nearly half as great as the amount the national government *spent* (110, 288). The panic of 1837, which largely resulted from an explosion of unsound state bank credit encouraged by the state governments, led many states to default. Faced with higher borrowing costs in the future, most states responded to the crisis by adopting constitutional amendments that limited their borrowing powers or required balanced budgets, but state debt nonetheless continued to grow.

Two further points about the Jeffersonian and Jacksonian aversion to national public debt are worth making. First, it seems to have had a generational component, although concern about corruption and the powers of the national government were plainly paramount. Jefferson himself held the quirky and extreme view that no generation should be able to bind its successors to any set of practices because "the earth belongs always to the living generation." That no public debt should remain outstanding for more than nineteen years—a number he based on elaborate life expectancy calculations for living adults—was one of the tamer implications he derived from this view. More startling was his famous claim that "Every constitution . . . and every law, naturally expires at the end of nineteen years. If it be enforced longer, it is an act of force and not of right" (Malone 1951, 2:179). While James Madison disputed Jefferson's conclusion, not only regarding constitutions (where he thought it dangerous) but also regarding public debt, he accepted the weaker claim that no generation should, on balance, burden its successors. Considering the "living generations" thesis to be useful and important but logically flawed in its proposed applications, Madison argued (as paraphrased by Dumas Malone) that "debts may be incurred for the benefit of the unborn no less than for the living, and that obligations could be rightly inherited along with benefits" (2:291).

Second, aversion to public debt, although it powerfully influenced public policy, was less rigid in practice than in principle. Again, Jefferson provides an illustration. As president, he failed to propose the balanced budget amendment that he had been advocating as the leader of the opposition. Although each of his eight years in office yielded a modest budgetary surplus (reducing the outstanding national debt by about 30 percent), he undertook the Louisiana Purchase in 1802, financed by issuing $15 million of public debt. In 1814, he unsuccessfully urged Madison, who had succeeded him as president, to pay for the ongoing War of 1812 by issuing $200 million in paper money (Kimmel 1958, 14).[3]

2. *From the Civil War to the New Deal*

The second era that Savage identifies began with the Civil War, which gave rise to a federal debt of nearly $2.8 billion, or more than twenty times its highest previous nominal level. A national consensus—viewed with some bemusement by more debt-tolerant European observers—supported paying it off in full as swiftly as was practicable. While this consensus may have owed something to the previous era's suspicion of federal debt (and to the widespread experience of state default), public concern now focused less on corruption, in the Jeffer-

---

3. On the budgetary surpluses while Jefferson was president and their effect on the national debt, see Savage 1988, 287.

sonian sense, than on burdening future generations and forcing current taxpayers to bear heavy interest costs on behalf of wealthy or foreign lenders. Despite the public consensus, the federal debt was never wholly eliminated, but twenty-seven consecutive years of budget surplus (from 1866 through 1892) reduced it by more than 60 percent.

As the Civil War debt gradually shrank and did not cause calamity to the extent it remained outstanding, attention shifted from debt elimination to annual budgetary balance. This norm now denoted not Jeffersonian distaste for the exploitation of financial leverage but modern reformist or progressive notions of administrative efficiency, rationality, and control of corruption in the sense of graft. This new meaning reflected the fact that government debt, from the mid–1860s on, grew principally in the cities, where reformers and progressives attributed it to bossism and machine politics.

Perhaps more important than the Civil War's creation of a huge federal debt was that it changed the dominant national political regime. The Democrats had generally controlled the federal government between 1800 and 1860, but now the Republicans, Hamilton's political heirs, would generally control it until the 1930s. The Republicans were strongly protectionist, and thus supported high tariffs, but they had to pay heed to budget-balancing sentiment and apparently lacked the will or the political power to set tariffs far above the revenue-maximizing level. This gave them a continuing political problem that today's politicians would envy: how to spend enough money to justify taxes (in the form of tariffs) that produced substantial revenue, in an era when the appetite for federal spending was relatively limited.

To be sure, finding ways to spend federal money did not prove impossibly difficult. The Republicans in any case favored reviving Hamilton's program of extensive federal public works programs to promote industry and trade. In Congress, both parties quickly learned to welcome pork-barrel appropriations and bureaucratic expansion that created increased opportunities for patronage. Moreover, an expensive pension program for Union veterans of the Civil War consumed revenue while serving powerful political interests. Still, the political demand for spending remained below the demand for revenue-producing tariffs. Thus, the norm of budgetary balance, by stimulating additional public works projects and bureaucratic expansion in order to justify the tariffs, "led to the greatest enhancement of federal power yet known in the country's history" (Savage 1988, 160).

The long run of post–Civil War budget surpluses finally ended in 1893 in the face of a severe economic depression. Democrats and progressives, believing in budgetary balance but not in higher tariffs or in Jeffersonian limited government, now pushed for new types of taxes—in particular, income taxes on corporations and the wealthy. By 1913, such taxes had become well established legally and politically. Before long, they would make taxation newly obnoxious rather than attractive to the Republicans' business constituency, and they would help induce the two major political parties to reverse sides on the size-of-government question. This new pattern did not fully emerge, however, until the Great Depression of 1929 gave rise to the New Deal.

3. From the New Deal through the 1970s

Budgetary balance continued to be the norm from the 1890s through the early 1930s, except for times of war or severe depression. This changed for good with the election of Franklin Roosevelt in 1932. Roosevelt campaigned on a balanced budget platform and initially attempted to reduce government spending and the deficit, but by 1934, he had reversed course, both for short-term economic stimulus and to implement a newly expansive (and expensive) vision of the role of the national government.

The New Deal completed the historical reversal under which the Democrats, rather than their Federalist/Whig/Republican opponents, became the party that supported a larger federal government. This coincided with shifts in at least the perceived distributional effects of federal government policy. On the tax side, the rise of the income tax relative to the tariff had shifted at least apparent tax burdens from consumers to the wealthy owners of large corporations. On the spending side, ambitious regulatory schemes and transfer programs with broad constituencies had emerged.

While both taxes and spending increased beginning with the New Deal, taxes increased less. Thus, chronic budget deficits replaced chronic surpluses. One reason for the shift to deficits was that once the principal federal revenue source had shifted from tariffs to income taxes, there was less political support for setting taxes high enough to pay for current spending. Whereas domestic producers, as the direct beneficiaries of tariffs, had lobbied powerfully to keep the tariffs at high levels, no one similarly benefited directly from income taxation. Thus, the pattern among private interest groups engaged in lobbying was one of near universal opposition to high levels of income taxation. Once World War II had transformed the income tax from an elite tax to a mass tax, the general public began to share this dislike for high levels of income taxation, perhaps more keenly and universally than it had ever disliked high tariffs, given that income tax liability is more overt (being paid directly to the Treasury rather than built into higher prices).

A second reason for the emergence of increasingly high deficits was the rise of Keynesianism, legitimizing the intentional use of deficits to stimulate the economy and increase employment. Keynesian theory seemed to have been verified when increased government spending in connection with World War II received the credit for at last ending the Great Depression. Keynesianism suggested rejecting the goal of budgetary balance in favor of "functional finance," or basing the appropriate level of deficit (or surplus) purely on what would stabilize the economy at full employment with only moderate inflation.

While functional finance arguably suggested wholly discarding budgetary balance as an objective, Keynesian economists were for a time more cautious than this, in part because they recognized the need for some principle that would set limits on government spending. Initially, prominent Keynesians suggested merely that the budget be balanced over the entire business cycle, rather than annually, with expansionary surpluses offsetting recessionary deficits. This proved difficult to accomplish given the economy's unpredictability and also began to attract criticism as being overly cautious.

In the early 1960s, Walter Heller, President Kennedy's chief economic adviser, suggested replacing cyclical balance with what he called full employment balance. Under this approach, budgetary balance would be sought only hypothetically, under economic projections regarding what the government's receipts and expenditures would have been at full employment. This goal made the achievement of actual budgetary balance, for any year or other period of time, unnecessary. Moreover, it suggested welcoming actual deficits, in order to stimulate the economy, whenever there was less than full employment and even if the economy was expanding.

I will defer examining Keynesianism until chapter 3. For now, it is worth noting that, even at its peak of acceptance, Keynesianism never eliminated the deep-rooted American aversion to deficits among voters or political leaders. Even President Kennedy, the politician most responsible for popularizing deficits as a tool of economic policy, retained traditional budget-balancing instincts sufficiently to alarm his Keynesian economic advisers from time to time. Their triumph in bureaucratic battles owed much to Kennedy's political advisers, who may have been swayed as much by the short-term popularity of tax reduction as by the economic arguments for fiscal stimulus. Similarly, President Nixon, who proclaimed himself a Keynesian, was motivated by the view (taught by his defeat in 1960, in the aftermath of a recession) that stimulus and increased employment even at the cost of eventual inflation were politically expedient to one for whom conditions on Election Day in 1972 mattered intensely, whereas conditions years (or perhaps even milliseconds) later mattered very little.

4. The Modern Revival of Concern about Public Debt and Deficits

The influence of Keynesianism began to decline in the 1970s, largely as a result of concern about stagflation (simultaneous unemployment and inflation), which it seemed to assert was impossible. With this decline, public sentiment returned to the norm of budgetary balance—in principle, although emphatically not in practice. Deficits continued to increase, in part because the breakdown of centralized leadership and party discipline in Congress led to a legislative free-for-all in which nearly every vote might need to be purchased by granting a particularized spending or tax benefit (Inman 1990, 81). Still, deficits were now consistently lamented and condemned.

The consensus opposing deficits, however limited its success at any point, has been enormously important in American politics since the early 1980s. It led to the tax increases of 1982, 1984, 1987, 1990, and 1993, and to various efforts to reduce (or at least constrain the rate of increase in) spending, such as the Gramm-Rudman-Hollings Act of 1985, the budget agreements of 1990 and 1993, and the budget negotiations of 1995–96. The deficit issue's prominence and salience partly reflect the public's fear of default, based on the questionable analogy between the federal government and a private borrower. In fact, however, recent deficits have not as yet created any significant default risk. Treasury bills continue to be regarded in the financial markets as the quintessential risk-free asset, and the level of federal debt is less than half as high relative to gross domestic product (GDP) as it was at the end of World War II (Krugman 1994, 158–59).

As throughout American history, however, the public's concern about deficits also has a separate symbolic content. Savage notes that the deficit now symbolizes the "inefficient and wasteful public expenditure produced by a bureaucratic and insensitive 'big government'" (1988, 195). Voters compare the federal government to a well-run business, which, even if it borrows or loses money for a time, ultimately respects the bottom line. The view that the federal government runs deficits because it is unbusinesslike has been exploited by Ross Perot, who maintained in 1992 that his business expertise would enable him to eliminate the budget deficit "without breaking a sweat" (Robinson 1992, 11).

The deficit's persistence and growth, despite years of nearly universal agreement that it ought to shrink, have greatly heightened its symbolic resonance. It both dramatizes and in fact results from the irresistible political incentives to promise benefit without cost and in practice to produce visible or apparent benefit in exchange for invisible and diffused costs or those of uncertain incidence. Many commentators, recognizing that politicians, in creating and tolerating deficits, have been the voters' servants, have come to see the deficit as connoting pathologies of the entire society, not just of the government as Other.

In an era of perceived individual powerlessness and systemic gridlock in the face of a mammoth, interest-group-dominated state, the deficit excites anxiety about profligacy, loss of discipline, and national decline. It has replaced such issues as Vietnam as a favorite testing ground for American character and resolve. Thus, Senator Warren Rudman, who, to protest ongoing deficits, retired from the Senate and founded a public interest group to organize demands for deficit reduction, insists that "[t]he country is at war. Not a traditional war, but an economic war" (Turner 1992). Senator Paul Tsongas issues a "call to economic arms" about the "crushing and unsustainable debt" that has placed us under "great economic peril" and prompted "the inexorable sale of America to foreign interests" (Tsongas 1991, 5). Perot compares us to a "person with a drinking problem [who] must admit that he is an alcoholic before he can be cured" (Robinson 1991, 10).

These anxieties help make the public susceptible to concern about deficits. Yet the issue might be less prominent if political elites did not have reason to emphasize it. To them, the deficit is an often powerful rhetorical tool in debates concerning government spending and tax policy; alarmist warnings about the size of the deficit are useful whenever one is arguing either for increasing taxes or for reducing spending. Virtually every political persuasion calls for taking at least one of these two positions occasionally, and since both positions go against the grain of promising large benefits at zero cost, the deficit argument is at least occasionally helpful to almost everyone. Those taking the other side in a tax or spending argument, calling for lower taxes or increased spending, while free to argue that deficits are irrelevant, do not need the rhetorical support as much, because they are arguing for something with greater inherent appeal. Thus, discussion of the deficit typically involves an asymmetry, whereby one side insists that it is important, and the other side, instead of answering, tries to change the subject.

The Reagan budget deficits of the early 1980s increased this asymmetry. Before those deficits were incurred, deficit reduction principally supported conservatives' argument for reduced spending rather than liberals' argument for increased taxes to pay for government programs. Indeed, the Reagan deficits may have been designed in part to create pressure for spending reductions in domestic programs. In their aftermath, however, deficit reduction through tax increases became an occasional Democratic Party theme, meaning that both political parties and both sides of the conventional divide between "small government" conservatives and "big government" liberals saw deficit reduction as a useful rhetorical tool for advancing their objectives.

Yet the reciprocally growing deficit alarm of Democrats and Republicans, liberals and conservatives, is not purely rhetorical. It reflects as well a shared and genuine experience of political frustration. As deficits increase the total public debt on which current interest must be paid—to around $5 trillion, requiring annual interest payments of more than $200 billion[4]—officeholders of all persuasions lose discretionary control over outlays. Whether they are elected by advocating lower taxes or greater social spending, they may learn once in office that their preferred programs are unaffordable. Meanwhile, they have to worry that voters will judge them on current levels of taxation and government performance, without adjusting sufficiently for the fact that interest costs reflect government services rendered in the past. This helps make the deficit genuinely distasteful to politicians, not just a convenient rhetorical outlet.

4. See Budget of the U.S. Government, fiscal year 1996, tables S–1 and S–22.

C. Summing Up the History of the Deficit Issue

Preoccupation with budget deficits has long been a unique feature of American culture, reflecting the symbolic properties of deficits as much as anything tangible. The symbolism has two main threads, of which the first, anxiety about default founded on the analogy to a private debtor, may be the less important. The second thread, distrust or fear of the national government, has been a consistent theme throughout American history.

The prospect of unconscious influence by deeply rooted historical symbolism should make us cautious and skeptical, although not dismissive, of the familiar claims that deficits are substantively important. Symbolism may mislead us, but, in the end, it neither proves nor disproves that requiring budgetary balance would reduce the size of government. Nor does it enlighten us about whether deficits are important on other grounds.

American budget history also demonstrates that propositions that we may think are cast in stone—for example, that budget deficits are endemic to democratic government because the appetite to spend exceeds the appetite to tax—actually are surprisingly time-bound. When powerful social forces opposed a strong national government, as in the early nineteenth century, or supported high tax levels, as in the later nineteenth century, regular deficit spending was anything but endemic at the national level. Moreover, we cannot necessarily recreate these earlier eras' budget practices simply by trying to make budgetary balance mandatory. Vanished political and social alignments cannot be recreated by legal mandate, and they may matter considerably more than any legal rule that attempts to dictate a particular result.

THREE

The Debate among Economists from the 1770s through the 1970s

A. Birth of the Economic Debate: Smith and Ricardo

Modern economic thought conventionally begins with Adam Smith and David Ricardo. This convention is suitable enough on the deficit issue, where Smith and Ricardo sounded nearly all the concerns that have preoccupied economists since. Yet they did not invent their ideas in a vacuum. Their precursors on the deficit issue include David Hume and the Baron de Montesquieu.

Hume's essay "Of Public Credit," published in 1764, refers to a well-developed contemporary debate concerning a form of proto-Keynesianism: the proposition that "public incumbrances are, of themselves, advantageous, independent of the necessity for contracting them; and that any State . . . could not possibly have embraced a wiser expedient for promoting commerce and riches." Hume concedes that public debt has some beneficial effects on commerce, and he commends its tendency to stimulate the development of financial markets. He nonetheless denounces it as likely to lead to injurious tax increases in the short term and possibly to default, tyranny, or even foreign conquest in the long term.

Montesquieu provides an interesting continental parallel to Hume. While evincing less extreme fear of public debt, Montesquieu likewise rejects the apparently familiar view that it "multiplie[s] riches by increasing the circulation" and maintains that it can never be advantageous to the state. His objections to public debt include its leading to the transfer of resources to foreign lenders, its requiring higher taxes to finance repayment, and its transferring revenue from industrious taxpayers to indolent bondholders (1949, 394).

Smith, writing in 1776, echoed this fiscal prudence tradition. He asserted that enormous public debts "at present oppress, and will in the long run probably ruin, all the great nations of Europe" (1976, 446). Debt financing would lead inexorably to default, whether explicit or through pretended repayment with grossly inflated and thus devalued currency. Internal debt is as dangerous as foreign debt, because both require added taxation to finance payments of principal and interest. Smith's own solution to the dangers presented by England's existing debt was to tax England's possessions, principally America—a happy theme to which he devoted more than one-third of his chapter on public debt (441–86).

In two respects, however, Smith's discussion of public debt took a modern turn not found in Hume. First, he raised the problem that we would call fiscal illusion, noting that governments often avoid raising taxes during wartime in order to conceal the real financial burden of war and that politicians cynically or shortsightedly ignore the burden of the future taxes made necessary by public debt. Second, his view of debt financing seemed strongly influenced by an issue that one could argue is analytically separate: the merits of the particular public expenditures that were being debt-financed as he wrote.

Writing at a time when debt financing had funded a century of continental and colonial war, mainly between England and France, Smith complained that without it, "[w]ars would in general be more speedily concluded, and less wantonly undertaken." As a result of debt financing, the English were "wantonly calling for [war] when there was no real or solid interest to fight for," because, "remote from the scene of action, [they] feel, many of them, scarce any inconveniency from the war; but enjoy, at their ease, the amusement of reading in the newspapers the exploits of their own fleets and armies" (462, 463, 456).

Ricardo, writing in 1817, roughly forty years later than Smith, expressed a view of deficit financing that was similar in substance but differed significantly in emphasis. While not nearly as anxious as Smith about the prospect of default, Ricardo agreed that "[t]hat which is wise in an individual is wise also in a nation" (1951, 1:247). Large national debts should be avoided when possible and repaid promptly when incurred.

Ricardo also agreed with Smith about fiscal illusion, arguing that debt financing "tends to make us less thrifty—to blind us to our real situation" (1:248). To Ricardo, however, the heedlessness resulting from fiscal illusion was felt less in public expenditure than in private expenditure by taxpayers who failed to understand the significance for their own wealth of the future taxes implied by public debt. A taxpayer whose share of the public debt had a present value of 100 pounds but was deferrable at 5 percent interest would comprehend only the interest charge of 5 pounds per year. As long as the debt remained outstanding, he would regard himself as 100 pounds wealthier than he really was and thus would spend too much and save too little relative to his actual preferences (1:247).

Ricardo also perceived an additional problem with public debt that appears today to have a distinctly modern cast. He observed that the national debt is not allocated among current taxpayers as it arises. The incidence of taxes to repay public debt remains uncertain until the taxes are actually levied. Thus, "it becomes the interest of every contributor to withdraw his shoulder from the burthen, and to shift this payment from himself to another; and the temptation to remove himself and his capital to another country, where he will be exempted from such burthens, becomes at last irresistible" (1:247–48).[1] A modern writer might use the term *rent-seeking* or *strategic behavior* to describe this incentive to shift future joint liabilities to one's fellow taxpayers.

While Ricardo therefore followed Smith in emphasizing the problems or dangers of public debt, his tone was more detached. He argued that without fiscal illusion and strategic behavior, debt financing would be no worse than tax financing. For a government no less than an individual, borrowing can be rational behavior. For example, one who owed 2,000 pounds might find that it "suited his convenience," at a 5 percent interest rate, to pay 100 pounds per annum instead of immediately settling the debt in full (1:245). No blame or adverse consequences inherently attached to such a preference.

In what may have been meant as no more than a clever postscript, Ricardo developed the logic of the view that, disregarding fiscal illusion and strategic behavior, debt financing and tax financing can be equivalent. Such equivalence is plausible enough for a farsighted taxpayer who knows that he ultimately will pay taxes with the same present value under either method of financing, but what if he knew he

1. Hume notes this problem as well and argues that proportional division of the public debt is desirable in principle but infeasible (1764, 396).

might die before the tax was finally levied, leaving it to be paid by his heirs? Ricardo explained that, assuming both accurate understanding of the future taxes made necessary by public debt and altruism toward one's heirs, the two modes of financing would remain equivalent despite the limited lifetime of a current taxpayer. Discussing a case in which one can either pay a current tax of 1,000 pounds or choose debt financing and leave this amount (plus interest) to be paid by one's heirs, Ricardo asked: "Where is the difference, whether somebody leaves to his son 20,000 pounds with the tax still [to be paid], or 19,000 pounds without it?" (4:187). He concluded there was no difference— as long as the taxpayer understood the tax burden and could not hope it would be shifted to other households.

Thus was born the "Ricardian equivalence theorem," asserting that the choice between debt and tax financing has no generational consequences because taxpayers respond to it by adjusting the bequests they leave their heirs. The theorem was named for him even though Ricardo himself, given his concerns about fiscal illusion and strategic behavior, did not believe it.

B. The Nineteenth and Early Twentieth Centuries

In criticizing debt financing as leading to default risk, or at least to imprudent public or private expenditure, Smith and Ricardo followed the conventional lay wisdom that relied on the analogy between public debt and private debt. The Ricardian equivalence theorem, by contrast, was clever, original, and counterintuitive. Perhaps it should be no surprise that as economics grew as a distinct intellectual profession run by academics with university training, a loosely Ricardian viewpoint should for a time supplant Ricardo's own viewpoint. By the mid-twentieth century, the view that debt financing was equivalent to current tax financing in its generational effects, conventional lay views notwithstanding, had become an unquestioned dogma of the economics profession.[2]

This change emerged only gradually, however. Nineteenth-century economists after Ricardo, while paying less attention to deficits as the problem receded, widely agreed that budgets generally should be

---

2. See, e.g., Pigou 1951 (a view of debt and tax financing as having different generational consequences is "everywhere acknowledged to be fallacious" [38]).

balanced and public debt held to prudently low levels. Polemically minded recent writers have therefore been able to portray the nineteenth-century writers as of a piece with Hume and Smith. A more careful examination, however, reveals significant changes in outlook over time, most obviously in tone but also extending to substance. Vehemence and fear of calamity gave way to nuance and careful qualification of the balanced budget principle.

Today, with hindsight, these changes may seem more portentous than they did at the time. Yet the nineteenth-century economists would have been surprised and, in many cases, dismayed to see themselves grouped too closely with Hume and Smith on the deficit issue. They were well aware that their predecessors' apocalyptic predictions regarding England's public debt had been proven, in the words of historian Thomas Babington Macauley, a "great fallacy . . . signally falsified by a long succession of indisputable facts" (1902, 414). England had grown steadily wealthier as its public debt increased. Given contemporary events, Macauley could conclude in sweeping terms that Hume, "one of the most profound political economists of his time," had given memorable proof of "the weakness from which the strongest minds are not exempt," while Smith "saw a little, and but a little farther" (411–12). He explained their error as follows:

> [T]he prophets of evil were under a double delusion. They erroneously imagined that there was an exact analogy between the case of an individual who is in debt to another individual and the case of a society which is in debt to a part of itself. . . . They were under an error not less serious touching the resources of the country. They made no allowance for the effect produced by the incessant progress of every experimental science, and by the incessant efforts of every man to get on in life. They saw that the debt grew; and they forgot that other things grew as well as the debt. (414)

While Ricardo already shows a change in tone, the next two prominent economists to write about deficits, Jean-Baptiste Say and Thomas Malthus, each went a step further. Say regarded debt financing as not inherently worse than tax financing. Indeed, it had the great advantage of "apportioning the burthen entailed by a sudden emergency among a great number of successive years" (1867, 479). For wars especially, it could be "a more powerful agent, than even gunpowder" (480). Well-ordered governments could and did use sinking funds to ensure the steady discharge of particular public debts (483).[3] Say objected to public borrowing simply because it permitted total government expenditure to rise. Whereas private borrowers generally invested capital productively, government diverted it to "barren consumption and expenditure" (477).[4] The public debt did not itself directly affect public wealth; it merely evidenced the allocation of property rights among different individuals. Where it existed, however, one could surmise—though presumably no more so than with tax-financed expenditure—that the entire value had been consumed and lost. Government spending was the true evil, without regard to the mode of financing.

Malthus was more tolerant still of public debt. He echoed, but less vehemently, Say's view of government expenditure as unproductive. Thus, for example, he distinguished between the productive classes who increase national material wealth and those whom they must support, such as public officials, the military, and public debt holders (Malthus 1968, 409). Yet, instead of condemning the latter as parasitical, he not only recognized that the services they rendered could be useful but also argued that their taste for consumption provided a necessary stimulus to investment and production. To achieve economic stability and growth, society needed a balance between the productive classes and unproductive consumers, and thus "it would be the height of rashness to determine, under all circumstances, that the sudden diminution of a national debt and the removal of taxation must necessarily tend to increase the national wealth, and provide employment for the labouring classes" (411). Malthus nonetheless cautioned that excessive public debt could lead to burdensome tax increases and tempt voters to embrace default.

Yet the trend toward increased tolerance of public debt went only so far. Nineteenth-century economists after Malthus, while often agreeing that large wartime debts should not be repaid too hastily, nonetheless viewed debt financing with concern, and supported balance as a general principle. John Stuart Mill, for example, criticized debt financing for adding interest payments to the government's tax financing needs, thereby increasing the burden that is "thrown upon the la-

3. Say nonetheless regarded sinking funds as pernicious, but only because they permitted public expenditure (and thus, paradoxically, public debt) to increase (485).

4. Resembling a modern public choice scholar of the James Buchanan school, Say saw an advantage to government waste, given government power. "Had not governments the happy knack of abusing resources of every kind, they would soon grow too rich and powerful" (483).

bouring classes, the least able, and who least ought, to bear it" (1926, 77–78).[5] Mill omitted to treat deferring taxes as a benefit that offset the interest charge, on the ground that there was no genuine deferral. He argued that debt-financed expenditures, no less than those that are tax-financed, are borne in full by the laboring classes. "Whatever is spent, cannot but be drawn from yearly [national] income" (77–78), which is a fixed amount assuming no use of foreign capital. Mill viewed all government expenditures as reducing the society's stock of private capital, and he argued (under the "wage fund" theory of taxation) that since these expenditures cannot be drawn from the preexisting stock of tangible physical capital, they generally must reduce the pool of capital available to be paid (and that is paid) to laborers as wages.

Mill thought this argument condemned debt financing only to a limited extent. Deficits were merely distributionally unfair, not socially catastrophic, and even the distributional effects were conditional. Mill noted that wage fund theory assumed, not wholly accurately, that England's national economy was a closed system. Where public loan capital came from foreign lenders, or replaced loans that would otherwise have been made to foreigners, it would not reduce the wage fund that was paid out to laborers. Moreover, overall societal wealth might increase rapidly enough for the wage fund to grow on balance even if debt-financed government expenditure tended to reduce it. Thus, "the effect on the labouring classes is less prejudicial, and the case against the loan system much less strong, than in the case first supposed" (78).

The next stage in economic thinking about budget deficits is well set out in C. F. Bastable's *Public Finance*, first published in 1892. This influential treatise, which synthesized contemporary literature and helped establish public finance as a separate economic discipline, once again changed the reasoning behind the era's consistent (if temperate) aversion to debt financing. Bastable started from the proposition that, barring insolvency, expenditures must equal revenues in the long run. Given this constraint, he saw "no reason why—special emergencies excepted—[they] should not do so in each financial year" (1922, 669). Heavy borrowing for a sustained period risked crippling the state financially, compelling retrenchment or the approach of insolvency. Moreover, relying on debt financing, and thereby postponing inevitable

---

5. Mill attributes this view to one Dr. Chalmers but largely accepts it over the next few pages of discussion.

tax increases, was an "easy, but dangerous course" that lay contrary to "the duty of the wise and far-seeing statesman" (669, 675).

Nonetheless, Bastable rejected, "as a sweeping and absolute rule, the proposition that the State should never at any time obtain funds through borrowing" (669). For example, he thought debt financing justified in the event of "reproductive" or "economic" outlay to purchase productive property or create increased revenue, as long as the expectation of an economic return was not too speculative. Particularly in countries with large state industries, this category of appropriately debt-financed outlay could be quite large. Even expenditure on such items as worker housing and public education could be justified in principle by the expectation of an economic return, although in practice the return was probably too speculative to support the use of debt financing (670–72).

Bastable also thought debt financing preferable to tax financing under many circumstances for large, nonrecurrent expenses. Current tax financing for such expenses should be avoided where it would (1) cause excessive disruption of the tax system as revenue needs changed from year to year, (2) inequitably overtax persons whose incomes were fortuitously high in years of high spending, (3) require taxes to be increased to the point of diminishing revenue returns and excessive distortion of behavior, or (4) cause too much public unrest (674–79).

It was only for reasons of prudence that Bastable even considered tax financing the preferred general rule and debt financing the special exception. Under ideal political conditions, requiring budgetary balance only over the long term would actually be preferable to requiring it annually, since this would permit greater stability in the tax system. The problem was that since future expenditures cannot be predicted and the public is tax-averse, such a policy would lead in practice to chronic deficits (674).

Bastable also distinguished between the systemic dangers of allowing excessive debt and the effects of public debt in any single instance. From the latter perspective, debt-financed expenditure would actually benefit society whenever the money was well spent. Moreover, even if the borrowed funds were spent poorly, at least the borrowing would tend to stimulate private saving and thereby partially reverse the apparent waste of resources (672–73). The broader systemic perspective, however, alerted one to the danger of frequent and repeated waste if debt financing were to win general acceptance.

Overall, then, Bastable viewed debt financing more tolerantly and flexibly than the eighteenth-century "prophets of evil" and even more so than his nineteenth-century precursors from Ricardo through Mill. Economists who wrote during the early twentieth century tended to be more tolerant still. Several urged that national debts from World War I not be repaid too quickly, or at least suggested that the debts were not a major concern (Kimmel 1958, 101, 120–24). By the 1930s, leading economists such as Irving Fisher and E. R. A. Seligman were arguing that increased public debt, no less than increased private debt, made possible beneficial government programs and was a natural and desirable consequence of the development of efficient modern capital markets (130–31).

C. The Rise and Fall of the New Orthodoxy

Given the American and English national governments' unmistakable solvency during the nineteenth and early twentieth centuries, along with the growth of domestic spending during this period, the shift that occurred in economic thinking concerning deficits and public debt is not surprising. Domestic spending, if there is any ground for thinking it will create future social value, encourages one to weigh benefit against cost. Several nineteenth-century continental European writers argued that debt financing, which they agreed would shift the cost of government expenditure from present to future taxpayers, was wholly appropriate if the future taxpayers would realize sufficient benefit from the expenditure. Some even thought that by virtue of the use value of money when spent, such benefit could simply be assumed (Neisser 1964, 149).

Increased domestic spending and reduced default risk do not, however, provide an obvious explanation of what happened next in economic thinking. Beginning in the 1930s, just as deficits became more frequent and important with the Great Depression and the rise of Keynesianism, a fault line appeared in economic thinking. Economists began, and through the 1950s mostly continued, to subscribe to a "new orthodoxy" (Ferguson 1964), viewing deficits not merely as acceptable within prudent limits or under various narrow circumstances but rather as totally and without qualification unproblematical.

Since the threat of default remained remote, attention focused instead on the claim by deficit opponents that public debt shifts the burden of paying for government spending to future generations, whereas the spending may mostly benefit current generations. The new orthodoxy rejected this claim and held that debt financing, relative to tax financing, inherently creates *no* increased burden on future generations and *no* transfer of the cost of government away from present generations.

The no-burden, no-transfer orthodoxy had clear roots in earlier discussion among economists. Ricardo had originally noted that the real cost of a government expenditure is the resources it uses, as distinct from the mode of financing. When the government borrows 20 million pounds to finance a year of war, "[t]he real expense is the twenty millions, and not [the debt principal as such or] the interest which must be paid on it" (Ricardo 1951, 1:244). Similarly, Mill's wage fund theory assumed that [w]hatever is spent cannot but be drawn from yearly income" (Mill 1926, 77–78) and thus ostensibly from the pockets of current laborers.

Mill's point about yearly income had clear implications for generational distribution even if one rejected his further claim that laborers are the ones whose income is reduced. He suggested that the income of *someone* now living must be reduced by government spending, no matter what the mode of financing, and thus that current citizens will bear the full cost of government expenditure whether or not they pay any tax. Using resources in a particular way requires sacrificing all alternative ways of using them. An economy, even if multinational, ultimately is a closed system and can draw only on its own resources. As Keynesian economist Abba Lerner put it, society cannot, after all, use a time machine to transport the wealth of future generations back into its own era in order to pay for current spending (1964, 17–18).

Thus, debt financing involved sacrifice even though the proceeds were provided voluntarily and in exchange for the government's promise eventually to pay the lender principal plus interest. The purchaser of a government bond, no less than a taxpayer, had to forgo consuming currently the amount paid over to the government. As economist James Buchanan later noted, viewing this as sacrifice was made more plausible by the economic theory of interest, which defended the payment of interest against traditional and religious attack by describing even voluntary saving as an act of painful abstinence.[6]

The new orthodoxy held further that there was no intergenera-

6. See Buchanan 1964a, noting Nassau Senior's development of the theory of saving as involving a pain cost of abstinence that justified the payment of interest.

tional wealth transfer even when bondholders got back their principal or received interest payments. Such payments cannot magically be transported across time. At any moment, interest payments must be from one or more living persons (such as taxpayers) to one or more living persons (such as bondholders). Therefore, for living persons in the aggregate, such payments have no aggregate wealth effect.[7]

Exponents of this view therefore denied that debt financing could burden future generations, even if the underlying expenditures failed to produce value that offset the interest cost. While bad expenditures could reduce societal wealth over time, this was wholly independent of the mode of financing. Neither the level of public debt nor the choice between tax and debt financing—as distinct from the nature and quality of government expenditure—had any relevance from a generational standpoint.

The no-burden, no-transfer view was accepted in the economics profession essentially without challenge until the late 1950s, when younger economists such as James Buchanan (1964a,b) and William Bowen (Bowen, Davis, and Kopf 1964) began arguing that it was mistaken or incomplete on three main grounds. First, debt financing did lead to intergenerational wealth transfer, although of a different sort from that which orthodox economists had shown to be impossible. While it was perfectly true that cash payments can only transfer wealth between persons who are alive at the same time, not all such persons need be defined as members of the same generation.

To illustrate, imagine a society with only two age cohorts, those born in year 0 (generation I) and those born in year 30 (generation II). In year 25, the government undertakes a new public project, which it finances, without enacting any new taxes, by selling long-term bonds to members of generation I. In year 75, when the members of generation I are retired and continue to hold all the bonds, the government repays the bonds by levying taxes on members of generation II (now age 45), in an amount sufficient to pay both principal and interest. The repaid bondholders then spend the full proceeds on consumption during their retirement.[8]

Under these stylized circumstances, it seems clear that generation

---

7. See, e.g., Lerner 1964, 17. Ricardo had anticipated these arguments, although, unlike his successors, he did not regard them as the whole story. See Ricardo 1951, 1:246, noting that canceling internal public debt would merely redistribute national wealth without changing its net amount.

8. This example is adapted from Bowen, Davis, and Kopf 1964, 69–70.

I has shifted to generation II the entire burden of paying for the public project (at least, ignoring any Ricardian claim about adjustments to bequests). To accept the occurrence of generational wealth transfer, one need not posit the magical transportation of wealth, as if by time machine, from one era to another. One need only be willing to look at the effects of government fiscal policy on lifetime consumption by "generations" in the sense of different age groups with overlapping life spans.

This illustration does not fully meet the objection that bondholders, like taxpayers, must sacrifice at the moment when they provide financing, by forgoing current consumption of the funds they contribute. Why say that a member of generation I has been burdened by the cost of the public project if she contributes $100 that we call a tax payment but not if she contributes $100 that we call the purchase of a bond? Lifetime cash flows might even be the same under the tax model as under the bond model, if members of generation I, upon their retirement, should prove so lucky as to receive sufficient transfer payments from the government, financed by taxes on members of generation II.

Here, however, younger economists made their second challenge to the no-burden, no-transfer orthodoxy. Buchanan in particular argued that bondholders, unlike taxpayers, are not engaging in sacrifice. The purchase of a bond is voluntary and thus must be viewed by the bondholder as improving the bondholder's position—presumably as a result of the potential for consumption in the future of the principal plus interest—rather than as making the bondholder worse off (Buchanan 1964b, 49–50; 1964a, 57–58). By contrast, taxpayers, if one ignores their influence as voters, pay the government involuntarily. Even if they were certain to receive transfer payments upon retirement in an amount that equaled principal plus market interest on their tax payments, their behavior would offer no proof that they regarded the notional interest as sufficient compensation for deferring their consumption. Moreover, taxpayers ordinarily have no such definite expectation as do bondholders of receiving compensation later on.

The third point made by the dissenters—again, with Buchanan taking the lead—was that debt financing leads to fiscal illusion. Voters underestimate the future tax liabilities that debt financing makes necessary. Thus, they will fail to account properly for the cost of debt-financed government programs even if they are sufficiently altruistic toward future generations to want to make full Ricardian adjustments to bequests (Buchanan 1964c, 150–63). Debt financing therefore tends to be undesirable if one assumes either that the government is liable to spend too much when politicians can conceal the costs or that better information and understanding systematically produce better decisions.

The dissenting articles openly suggested that the common man— as well as so despised a figure among intellectuals as President Eisenhower, when he criticized budget deficits for their generational effects—better understood the issue than did a generation of professional economists (Bowen, Davis, and Kopf 1964, 67; Tullock 1964a, 100–101). In the short term, this stirred up predictable outrage among orthodox economists such as Lerner, who (in Gordon Tullock's characteristically provocative words) were "proud of the difference between the professional viewpoint and that of the common man" and found "[t]he idea that the common man was more sophisticated on a rather important point than the economics profession . . . not only intellectually, but also emotionally disturbing" (Tullock 1964a, 100–101). Over time, however, a new consensus emerged, recognizing that both camps were correct in particular respects.

The orthodox school was correct regarding the notion that debt financing does not directly affect the level of existing real resources but merely leads to transfer payments between one set of living persons (taxpayers) and another (bondholders). This arguably limits the importance of the choice of financing mechanism as an issue, relative to questions that directly affect the level of real resources, such as how productively money is spent. Yet the dissenters were correct about the choice of financing mechanism possibly creating transfers between generations, defined as members of different age groups, and moreover that debt financing can lead to a host of other problems, perhaps including default risk and certainly including fiscal illusion.

One is left, however, with the ad hominem question of what made the new orthodoxy seem so much more persuasive to economists from the 1930s through the 1950s than at any time before or since. The explanation may well lie in the contemporaneous turn to deficit spending, national government expansion, and Keynesian economic theory. These developments gave economists a professional stake in dogmatic intolerance of popular aversion to public debt and budget deficits.

Like Adam Smith but in reverse, economists who supported particular expenditure programs that as a practical political matter required deficit spending let their views about the merits of these programs color their beliefs about debt financing itself. Given the lay public's fear of government debt, which it stubbornly continued to analogize to private debt, many economists felt special propagandistic urgency. As E. J. Mishan explains, "[v]isions of a nation weighed down by debt, tottering towards bankruptcy [had such a] hold . . . on the minds of influential people [that] assurances of the innocuous nature of the public debt could not be too frequently repeated" (1964, 185).

Writing in 1947, Lerner described the economics profession's vital mission of explaining to ordinary people that their fears about deficits were "imaginary" and understood to be such by "nearly all economists" (1964, 17). In the late 1950s and early 1960s, when younger economists began challenging the orthodox view, Lerner complained that the dissenters were "seriously sabotag[ing] economists in their important task in educating the public" about the innocuousness of debt financing (95). This task, he insisted, had become all the more important in the era of the Cold War:

> The false belief [that debt financing burdens future generations] may well contribute to a failure of the free nations to take the steps necessary to maintain and extend freedom in the world. There is even a clear and present danger that because of a baseless fear of impoverishing future generations by leaving them with a larger internal debt (which they will owe to themselves), we may fail to protect them from nuclear war and/or totalitarian domination; the confusion sown by [the dissenters] tends to increase that danger. (95)

The apocalyptic fears of Hume and Smith had been precisely reversed. Now balanced budgets, rather than debt financing, threatened us with ruin and foreign conquest! I should note that Lerner was perhaps the leading early post—World War II Keynesian economist in the United States, not a marginal figure or a crank.

Implicitly, whether or not consciously, Lerner was counting on fiscal illusion to expand the politically feasible scope of government. Without it, the public's ostensibly irrational fear of budget deficits would not have endangered public spending. Instead, fear of deficits would have led either to acceptance of higher taxes, if the public sufficiently valued the spending, or to an unwillingness to countenance the spending no matter what mode of financing was used. Yet, if economists in Lerner's camp realized that they were relying on fiscal illusion to trick the public into making good decisions in spite of itself, they did not say this explicitly, perhaps for the same reason that magicians try to conceal their sleight of hand.

Support for particular government programs provided only part of the motivation for professional economists to defend debt financing, however. Perhaps a greater motive was provided by the rise of Keynesian macroeconomics in response to the Great Depression, offering economists prestige and political power far beyond what their profession had ever experienced. The exercise of this power and prestige, through control of the budget by trained experts in "functional finance," was all the easier to justify if deficits raised no serious concerns beyond the technical one of reaching the proper macroeconomic target.

D. The Great Depression and John Maynard Keynes

1. Keynes's Challenge to the Classical Model

Long before the Great Depression began in 1929, classical economists had studied and sought to explain business cycles of alternating boom and bust. William Jevons blamed them on sunspots, which affected weather and therefore agricultural output (Amacher and Ulbrich 1987, 109, 159). Alfred Marshall saw a variety of causes, ranging from bad harvests to new inventions that cause temporary dislocation to the extension of loose credit, leading to panic upon the occurrence of a few business failures (Marshall 1923, 250, 258).

Classical economists tended to view business downturns as self-correcting and likely to be short-lived. While this view supported an attitude of laissez-faire, one should not exaggerate the unwillingness to countenance government action. Marshall thought the Bank of England could reduce the issuance of overly loose credit and that better education would reduce investors' susceptibility to panic (258, 262). Still, laissez-faire made sense under classical assumptions about markets. Increased unemployment, by depressing wages, would create the conditions for its own reversal. More generally, full employment seemed inevitable in the labor market, in all cases where the marginal value of production exceeded the worker's subjective disutility of providing labor. For example, if I am willing to work for anything above $3 per hour and my labor is worth $8 per hour, surely someone will seize the opportunity for mutual gain by offering me between $3 and

$8 per hour. The labor market would naturally clear, with sellers and buyers of services consummating transactions when prices they were willing to consider overlapped.

Other markets would similarly clear, with price adjustments if necessary. For example, if the supply of loanable funds exceeded demand at the prevailing interest rate, money would not long remain idle. Instead, the interest rate would be bid down until supply and demand matched. What was known as Say's law posited that supply would come to equal demand, and thus that all savings would be invested. Given Say's law, reduced consumption and added saving by society should lead to increased investment, presumably making possible increased consumption in the future.

This classical view of well-functioning markets is easily caricatured—as was fashionable from the 1930s through the 1970s—as positing an implausibly benign "invisible hand" that makes sure everything works out for the best. Yet the rise of neoclassical economics over the past twenty years testifies to the view's powerful logical core, as well as to disillusionment with the alternative of relying on government's visible hand. A view of markets as well functioning and self-correcting follows so readily from a few simple premises, such as the generally rational pursuit of self-interest by numerous disaggregated actors, that those rejecting it face a burden of more complicated explanation. For example, why should one not expect wages to decline when unemployment rises, leading to a degree of self-correction, if workers would rather earn a low wage than nothing at all?

In the 1930s, however, the classical model seemed implausible to many despite its internal logic. The Great Depression's persistence, with unemployment remaining high, output drastically depressed, and investment levels low despite reduced consumption, appeared self-evidently to refute it. These conditions also prompted intense anger—even among many who remained committed to democratic capitalism—about the model's apparent irrelevance to contemporary problems and its advocates' seeming insensitivity to widespread economic hardship. Arthur Okun, writing forty years later, captured the widespread response when he dismissed those classical economists who had accepted downturns as inevitable or even beneficial as so many "Doctor Panglosses" (Okun 1970, 32).

Demand accordingly grew for a new economic understanding that could explain why the Great Depression persisted and what could be done about it. This demand was met in 1936, when John Maynard

Keynes published his landmark work, *The General Theory of Employment, Interest, and Money,* arguing that the government could end the depression by adopting expansionary fiscal and monetary policies.

Keynes's main theme in *The General Theory* was that contrary to the classical model, markets often do not clear. Buyers and sellers whose acceptable price ranges ought to overlap nonetheless do not consummate transactions. The reasons for this failure include illusions that systematically distort rational behavior, various legal and institutional rigidities, and what we today would call externalities and collective action problems. Only the government, seen in characteristically benevolent and optimistic 1930s terms, could remedy the failures of private markets.

Keynes's advocacy of expansionary fiscal and monetary policy was far from new. Nearly two centuries earlier, David Hume had mentioned the view that public debt creation increases economic activity no matter how the money is spent. Americans in politics and government had known since colonial times that printing money or creating public debt can be stimulative but inflationary. Moreover, by the late 1920s, mainstream American economists had moved far from advocating pure laissez-faire, and President Hoover's economists had agreed that the government should respond actively to the depression, perhaps through tax cuts or increased public works spending (Stein 1969, 7–12). Keynes's main addition was a more worked-out vision of an expansive government role in managing the economy, backed by a set of arguments in the language of formal economics that purported to supplant the classical tradition. He also provided much glittering rhetoric that, by speaking to unease about the classical model's seeming assumption of an unrealistically high level of human rationality, helped make up for the lack of an alternative and comparably rigorous microfoundation at the level of individual behavior.

One should not exaggerate the extent to which Keynes saw government decision making as replacing the operations of the free market. He argued, for example, that the government should not micromanage the economy by influencing what types of investments are made. "It is in determining the volume, not the direction, of actual employment that the current system has broken down" (1964, 379). Yet Keynes also did not consider the depression a mere special case, requiring limited and temporary intervention while laissez-faire remained the rule. Rather, determining the volume of investment in order to achieve full employment was an ongoing responsibility that required "central controls [and] a large extension of the traditional functions of government" (379). He thereby paved the way for future "Keynesian" economists who—ignoring many of his own expressed views—would purport to fine-tune the economy from moment to moment, administering judicious doses of expansionary fiscal and monetary policy to prevent unemployment and contractionary policy to prevent the opposite evil of inflation.

2. *Keynes on the Problem of Persistent Unemployment*

Keynes's starting point in *The General Theory* was the depression's apparent refutation of the classical economists' assumption that business downturns involving high unemployment will be short-lived, as wages are bid down and the labor market clears. Again, suppose I can produce economic value at a rate of $8 per hour and that the disutility to me of working is $3 per hour. Even if wages in my industry were previously $9 per hour, dating from a time when consumer demand was greater, the classical view suggests that they should readjust with reasonable promptness to somewhere between $3 and $8.

The classical economists did not suggest that unemployment will always disappear instantaneously. Full employment was merely the equilibrium state, behind which we might lag—even, at times, substantially—as a result of frictional factors such as the time and effort needed to bargain, find new jobs, move to where the new jobs are located, develop new skills, adjust expectations as circumstances change, and so forth. Yet it still seemed plausible that high unemployment would be relatively transitory. The experience of the 1930s seemed to suggest, however, that it could instead become a stable equilibrium.

On this ground, Keynes dismissed the classical economists as so many

> Euclidean geometers in a non-Euclidean world who, discovering that in experience straight lines apparently parallel often meet, rebuke the lines for not keeping straight—as the only remedy for the unfortunate collisions that keep occurring. Yet, in truth, there is no remedy except to throw over the axiom of parallels and to work out a non-Euclidean geometry. (16)

He proclaimed the need for a new theoretical model of the economy that could account for the labor market's prolonged failure to clear.

Keynes would posit that one whose labor was worth $8 per hour might not be hired, even if that person's disutility of working was only $3 per hour. The worker would be "involuntarily unemployed," in the sense that failure to find a job, even after extensive searching, would reflect neither an unduly high wage demand nor a lack of productive ability. Involuntary unemployment implied social welfare loss in an amount at least equal to the excess of value over disutility—here, $5 per hour. This amount constituted a deadweight loss to society from underutilization of productive resources.

While such a result may appear odd, given the opportunities for mutual gain that it assumes workers and employers will overlook, contemporary events seemed to support it. Surely the disutility of labor could not explain the persistent unemployment during the depression. Too many people who badly wanted jobs were remaining unemployed for too long. Keynes saw no need to prove through sustained empirical analysis or logical argumentation that labor markets were failing to clear—for "who will deny it?" (16). The problem was simply to explain this failure and propose a cure.

Given the importance of eliminating involuntary unemployment, Keynes argued that even job programs that produced utterly worthless goods were better than nothing, despite the disutility of labor. Essentially *any* government program that created jobs would be desirable on balance. Wars, earthquakes, digging holes in the ground, building pyramids or cathedrals, and paying monks to sing dirges were among the events or activities that, even if wholly wasteful (or even destructive) apart from their effects on unemployment, "may serve to increase wealth, if the education of our statesmen on the principles of the classical economics stands in the way of anything better" (129, 131, 220).

Purely from the standpoint of involuntary unemployment, this would seem to make no sense. Even if the labor had zero disutility, it would also add zero valuable production. However, the rationale for such job programs lay in Keynes's account of why involuntary unemployment occurs.

In part, he blamed overly slow wage responses to changing market conditions—"sticky wages" in later Keynesian terminology. In the earlier example, if hourly wages were previously at $9, they might not decline fast enough as the labor's value dropped. More fundamentally, however, Keynes blamed inadequate consumer demand. In effect, the unemployed worker could not be hired for $8 per hour (or perhaps any positive wage), even though the worker's labor was in some sense worth that much, because no employer would be able to sell the product of that labor for that amount (or perhaps at any positive price).

Put crudely, this is a theory of inherent, as distinct from market, value. Put sophisticatedly, Keynes recognized the contingent and changeable nature of market prices and their capacity to stabilize at more than one level, with very different social welfare effects in the aggregate. An item that could not be sold at all might "really" be worth $8 all the same, if people *would* be willing to buy it for that price if their circumstances, or at least their expectations regarding their future circumstances, were to change.

For this reason, even absurdly wasteful public works projects could enhance social welfare. Digging holes in the ground, while useless for its own sake, would stimulate worthwhile economic production elsewhere by increasing consumer demand. The workers hired to dig the holes would buy increased quantities of genuinely useful products, thus causing others to be hired—although no more so, presumably, than if they had simply been given welfare payments. Because of the "multiplier effect" of government expenditure, the social welfare gain from creating a new job would vastly exceed that derived from that sole transaction. The multiplier effect is a claimed positive externality of job creation, in which paying me to work can be seen to benefit society even if my output is worth zero, and I thus am not among the involuntarily unemployed. To fully understand this claim, however, we must turn to Keynes's theory of demand, which he thought depended in large part on people's choices between current consumption and saving.

3. The Effects of Consumption and Attempted Saving on Economic Growth

Again, Keynes blamed unacceptably high unemployment mainly on inadequate demand. Without governmental stimulus, people would buy too few goods to support sufficient output. One might ask: why boost output if, in the absence of stimulus, people do not sufficiently want the additional consumer goods to pay a market price for them that reflects the costs of production? Even if we dislike unemployment because of its distributional effects, we can simply give the poor transfer payments, without requiring them to do work that the market evidently judges not worth its production cost. While extra production raises gross domestic product (GDP),[9] it does not necessarily raise aggregate social welfare, given that it requires the use of additional resources such as unpleasant labor.

Keynes rejected such arguments, however, and up to a point favored increased production at all costs. He viewed high GDP and low GDP as alternative equilibria, of which the former was better yet often unreachable by the sum of private decisions. He based his argument on a radically different view of people's attempted saving than that held by most pre- or non-Keynesian economists.

Under a conventional life-cycle view of behavior, saving is a vehicle that people use to help them maximize the value of their lifetime consumption, subject to bequest motives. People save, or forgo current consumption, in order to preserve or enhance future consumption opportunities. Even if saving offered no positive return, people would engage in it anyway, given the need to smooth out the path of their lifetime consumption. Having two dinners today is not as good as having one today plus one in the future. Still, because people are to some extent impatient and eager to consume, prospective borrowers must offer prospective savers a positive interest rate (even above compensating for inflation and risk). In a world where risk-adjusted real interest rates are positive, reflecting not only borrowers' impatience to consume but also the availability of productive and profitable investment opportunities, both individuals and society are thought by most non-Keynesians to choose, at the margin, between consumption today and more consumption in the future.

Under this view, when current consumption declines, there is no reason to be alarmed. Reduced current consumption should not even reduce GDP or affect employment levels. Valuable resources that are not being currently consumed will be productively invested, since surely their owners will not waste their current value by keeping them idle and since surely there are profitable opportunities to provide for future consumption.

Keynes rejected this view of the decision to save as merely deferring consumption:

9. For convenience, I will always refer to GDP (gross domestic product) rather than GNP (gross national product), even where the latter is more strictly correct (for example, as a matter of historical usage). The two differ in that GDP includes wages, interest, dividends, and profits earned in the United States by foreign residents, in lieu of those earned abroad by Americans, a difference that is not critical to this discussion.

An act of individual saving means—so to speak—a decision not to have dinner today. But it does *not* necessitate a decision to have dinner or to buy a pair of boots a week hence or a year hence or to consume any specified thing at any specified date. Thus it depresses the business of preparing today's dinner without stimulating the business of making ready for some future act of consumption. It is not a substitution of future consumption-demand for present consumption-demand—it is a net diminution of such demand. (210)

Keynes speculated that some people save merely to "enjoy a sense of independence and the power to do things, though without a clear idea or definite intention of specific action" (108). Others might have a bequest motive that their heirs would replicate indefinitely. Still others might be satisfying "pure miserliness, i.e., unreasonable but insistent inhibitions against acts of expenditure as such" (108). In a depression setting, with people insecure about their future economic prospects, many would attempt indefinitely to minimize their consumption spending out of fear that they could not afford it.

To Keynes, the proof that he was correct lay in how businesses typically respond to reduced current consumption. Suppose that shoe sales decline. Are shoe manufacturers likely to respond by feverishly building new factories in anticipation of heightened future demand for shoes? Or will they more likely close factories and reduce their planned investments in new ones? Surely the latter, Keynes thought, thus showing that when current consumption declines, so does investment to provide for future consumption.

A classical economist could concede this point without accepting Keynes's broader claim that reduced consumption reduces investment as well. The shoe example might simply reflect a change in taste. At the prior level of shoe output, people no longer value shoes enough to pay a price reflecting the marginal costs of production (which should be all the manufacturer considers if the factory is a sunk cost). Society's resources must perpetually be reallocated to meet people's changing tastes, but it is silly to complain about the resulting inconvenience to existing businesses.

What if we observe that businesses of all kinds are closing and overall economic production is down? To the classical economist, the same point holds. At the prior level of total output, people evidently do not sufficiently value any of the current consumption opportunities that businesses offer them. Yet one would still expect them to be planning greater future consumption, if only because consumption is what one does in economic life and because less resources, such as shoe leather, are currently being consumed.

Another example may help to clarify the classical/Keynesian dispute. Keynesian economist William Vickrey posits: suppose that I must choose between saving $10 or consuming it by paying for a haircut. If I decide not to take the haircut, I will merely reduce consumption over time, not reallocate it to the future. After all, while I will be $10 poorer if I take the haircut, the barber will be $10 richer. Either way, the amount the two of us collectively have in our bank accounts will be the same. The level of real resources will also be about the same since depreciation of the scissors should be trivial. Thus, my decision to save has no positive effect on society's future consumption opportunities, seemingly supporting the Keynesian claim that reducing current consumption does not lead to increased future consumption.[10]

The classical economist could respond that Vickrey has erred in assuming that my decision to save would reduce current consumption. In truth, while it would reduce *my* consumption, it would increase the barber's. Not giving me the haircut leaves him with increased leisure, or time to engage in other work. If I do not buy a haircut for the $10 cost of his time and effort, then apparently his time was worth more to him than it was to me. Otherwise, we would have agreed to a transaction. Vickrey has defined consumption too narrowly. Market consumption, purchased in arm's-length transactions, is all that GDP counts, but it is not all that matters. GDP fails to include nonmarket goods such as leisure and household production.

One need not share the classical view in order to recognize that these omissions from GDP, however unavoidable computationally, are incorrect in principle. With regard to household services, economist Arthur Pigou once pretended to complain about men who marry their housekeepers or cooks, thus causing measured national income to diminish. His point holds as much for leisure as for explicit household production. Healthy, sentient individuals (the only ones capable of working) are always involved in doing and experiencing something, even if, in common parlance, they are doing nothing. Leisure, or the

10. See Vickrey 1993, 6; see also Eisner 1993, 35. Vickrey is less well known as a Keynesian than for his long and distinguished career in microeconomics, far from the macroeconomic fray.

opportunity to use one's time as one pleases, is itself a product with value. That people value it is proved not only by intuition but also by their demanding a positive wage in order to work.

Yet Vickrey and the Keynesians have an answer, going at last to the heart of their dispute with classical economics. It flows from their recognition that consumers make decisions at two margins. One is between present and future market consumption. The other is between greater and lesser market consumption, where the alternative is non-market consumption—as from cooking one's own food rather than going to a restaurant, or letting one's hair grow (or cutting it at home) rather than paying a barber to cut it.

In evaluating this second margin, the Keynesian and classical viewpoints inhabit different universes. Under the classical view, it is perfectly plausible that people's taste will shift away from all market consumption, with the consequence that fewer resources will be used in production. The observation seems to have no consequences for policy, however. If people begin to choose reduced market consumption, the classical economist concludes that they must know best what is good for them. The resources have no production value and thus are not being "wasted" even if idle, if consumers do not value the output sufficiently to pay the marginal operating costs.

This view, which continues to inform modern neoclassical microeconomics, has an element of deliberate tautology. Given the impossibility of observing psychic states directly, economists often conclude that one must accept as definitive the preferences people reveal through their behavior. Moreover, with revealed preferences providing the only reliable lens, one cannot meaningfully analyze whether one set of preferences, for an individual or a society, would lead to greater happiness or satisfaction than another set. Taking preferences as given and resolutely ignoring questions of conceded importance regarding how they arise, whether they can be changed, and whether some sets of preferences lead to better overall outcomes than others are considered necessary preconditions of coherent and testable inquiry.

The Keynesian economist, unlike the neoclassical one, is willing to look behind revealed preferences. The Keynesian asks, for example, why market consumption declined so sharply during the Great Depression. Surely people did not become less materialistic—say, because of a spiritual revival. Instead, what happened is best understood by returning to the barber example. Suppose that I would want the haircut if only I were confident enough that I could afford it, but that this depended on the expected profitability of my restaurant. Suppose as well that the barber would eat regularly in my restaurant if only he were confident enough about his future earnings. Perhaps a third individual, a lawyer, would regularly get his hair cut by the barber and eat in my restaurant if only he were confident enough that we would use his services, but that this, again, would depend on the barber's and my confidence about our earnings prospects. Multiply this problem by the millions of people who continually decide how much to spend on market consumption in a variety of settings, and one can begin to understand the dilemma that can make a socially irrational outcome (such as a recession) the outcome of everyone's individually rational decisions.

To put Keynes's argument in modern terminology, the decisions about whether to consume or to save and whether to maintain production or lay off workers involve a collective action problem and an externality problem. The collective action problem is that once a recession is under way, any number of consumers might be willing to spend money, and businesses would be willing to hire workers and expand output, if only enough others would do the same. Only if enough businesses, responding to enough demand, employ enough workers, who then have enough income that they can and do spend, is a high level of output sustainable. Yet individual consumers and businesses may be afraid to act alone in this regard, absent grounds for expecting others to follow suit. The universally desired high level of consumption depends on a treacherous interpersonal confidence game.

The externality problem is that any one person's decision to save, or to lay off workers, adversely affects other people, both directly and indirectly. Directly, saving reduces consumer demand, as does laying off workers who then will start spending less, in each case with a multiplier effect as reduced consumption yields further layoffs. Indirectly, Keynes thought that people's herd instincts would tend to magnify the negative effect. Lacking adequate information about what to expect from the future, people all too readily assume, when they observe someone else's decision to save or close a factory, that the other person knows something they do not and is not merely acting on whim or irrational fear.

The result in the depression, according to Keynes, was a wholesale collapse of both consumption and investment demand. Resources remained idle, and potentially productive workers were unemployed. Even short of a severe recession, however, Keynes thought this picture held to some extent whenever the economy was short of full employment. Attempts to save, because they reduced present consumption demand and future investment demand, led in part to social waste. Under what came to be known as the paradox of thrift, the more people tried to save, the less they would collectively succeed in saving. Their attempt to save more, by reducing national income, would reduce saving and future consumption, not just current consumption.

Given the stable low-GDP equilibrium that this produced, market forces could not do anything about it. Hence the need for government action, both directly to increase demand and indirectly to create the "animal spirits" and "spontaneous optimism" that private parties could not sustain (Keynes 1964, 162). The next question is on what grounds Keynes concluded that expansionary fiscal and monetary policy would correct the situation.

4. Keynes on the Grounds for Expecting Fiscal Stimulus to Work

Again, Keynes proposed fiscal and monetary stimulus to cure economic recession. As he wrote in perhaps his most famous passage on the subject:

> If the Treasury were to fill old bottles with bank-notes, bury them at suitable depths in disused coal mines which are then filled up to the surface with town rubbish, and leave it to private enterprise on well-tried principles of laissez-faire to dig the notes up again . . . there need be no more unemployment and, with the help of the repercussions, the real income of the community, and its capital wealth also, would probably become a good deal greater than it actually is. It would indeed be more sensible to build houses and the like; but if there are political and practical difficulties in the way of this, the above would be better than nothing. (129)

The buried-banknotes suggestion was an example of monetary policy—expanding the money supply—accomplished by absurdly inefficient means that wasted real resources, to provide rhetorical emphasis for the point that such waste would nonetheless be less than that resulting from involuntary unemployment. Building houses—assuming this was debt-financed, not paid for by tax increases or spending reductions elsewhere—was an example of fiscal policy, or altering the budgetary balance between tax revenues and current expenditure. Keynes argued that both an expansionary monetary policy and a fiscal policy of running large deficits could increase economic production and eliminate involuntary unemployment. Thus, both were desirable under depression circumstances even if, their stimulative effects aside, they were wasteful and inefficient.

The point of government spending, especially if not paid for by current taxes, was twofold. First, it would give people more cash in hand and induce them to feel wealthier, thus leading them to spend more on current consumption. (They were assumed not to discount commensurately for any expected future taxes that the spending might be thought to imply.) Second, because attempted saving led to social waste, the increased current consumption would represent an increase in total consumption over time, not merely a reallocation of consumption from the future to the present.

The distinctness of these two claims should be kept clearly in mind. Abandon the first, and deficit spending fails to increase current consumption. Yet one need not be a Keynesian to accept it. One need only believe that people tend not to discount for the future taxes arguably implied by deficit spending, or that the spending at issue redistributes wealth to people with relatively high propensities to consume (such as the poor or elderly).

Abandon the second claim, however, and, while the Keynesian prediction of increased current market consumption as a result of deficit spending may continue to hold, it is no longer clearly desirable. If the paradox of thrift does not hold, and increased attempted saving therefore does not lead to waste (and reduced investment)—or, alternatively, if permanently increasing market consumption involves a mere change in taste, with no implication of greater well-being—then stimulus has no particular benefit, and may even be bad on balance if (as in the hole-digging example) it involves otherwise wasteful policy.

5. Keynes in Retrospect

a. The Rise, Fall, and Partial Rise of Keynesianism
In the years since Keynes published *The General Theory*, perhaps no stock traded in the public markets has proven as volatile as his own intellectual stock. In the years after World War II, a "Keynesian revolution," initially almost unopposed, swept first the economics profession

and then public policy. By the 1950s, even President Eisenhower, although an advocate of budgetary restraint who condemned deficits as irresponsibly burdening future generations, was Keynesian enough to eschew attempting to reduce the countercyclical budget deficits that occurred automatically during recessions.

In the 1960s, Keynesianism reached its high-water mark. President Kennedy entrusted his economic policy to advisers, such as Walter Heller and Arthur Okun, who had learned it as gospel in school and were now making newly aggressive claims for it, including some that Keynes would have found preposterous. No longer, Heller and Okun proclaimed, should Keynesian policy be merely countercyclical, using budget deficits in response to recession and surpluses in response to the opposite evil of inflation. Instead, they counseled running stimulative deficits all the time, pending achievement of the elusive state of full employment. Budget deficits should be limited only by the principle of full employment balance, requiring only that, hypothetically, the budget would have been balanced under the counterfactual circumstance of full employment.

By the mid–1960s, Heller and Okun were claiming to have permanently abolished the evils of the business cycle (Heller 1966, vii, 1, 83). Perennial prosperity and economic expansion required only that government economists perform the "delicate" and "comparatively unemotional—if technically intricate" job of determining the exact timing and size of the tax cuts needed to offset the increased revenues that resulted from economic growth (62, 65–66). Moreover, under the Phillips curve, which ostensibly expressed the inverse relationship between the twin evils of unemployment and inflation, economists could guide ongoing discretionary tradeoffs between the two evils, thus keeping either one from getting out of hand. The economy could be fine-tuned from moment to moment and current economic data analyzed to provide determinate scientific answers to such questions as whether, in 1963, a $3 billion tax increase was needed to pay for the Berlin defense buildup (32).[11]

These fantasies of omnipotence ran into harsh reality soon enough. By the late 1960s, the rise of inflation was beginning to erode Keynesianism's prestige—although Keynesians blamed it on President

---

11. Keynes, by contrast, had argued that "human decisions affecting the future, whether personal or political or economic, cannot depend on strict mathematical expectation, since the basis for making such calculations does not exist" (1964, 162–63).

Johnson, for not listening to their advice that he seek tax increases to pay for the Vietnam War. The real damage occurred in the 1970s, when stagflation, or combined high inflation and high unemployment, seemed to rebut the Phillips curve, eliminating the relatively benign tradeoff between the two that had once seemed possible and discrediting fine-tuning.

Adding to the theoretical damage done by stagflation itself was that Milton Friedman, long the leading academic opponent of Keynesianism, had predicted it in advance. Friedman argued as early as 1969 that any observed inverse relationship between unemployment and inflation, susceptible to manipulation by Keynesian fine-tuners, was merely a short-term consequence of expansionary policy that the public underestimated. For example, a 5 percent expansion in the money supply might lead initially to only, say, 2 percent inflation, if firms and workers initially failed to anticipate fully the extent to which their own costs would rise. It would, therefore, by fueling new demand in excess of price increases, lead in part to increased output that would reduce unemployment. The problem, however, was that eventually people would catch on to the real level of monetary expansion, at which point the increase in output that resulted from their being fooled would dissipate. Five percent inflation would now be built into people's expectations. The next time the government wanted to increase output, it would need to fool people again, by choosing, say, 10 or 20 percent expansion. Over time, then, inflation would accelerate, and the expansionary effects of Keynesian policy would grow ever weaker. Friedman's argument seemed to fit the events of the late 1960s and early 1970s.

Without a stable Phillips curve, 1960s-style Keynesianism not only had been disconfirmed in an important respect, but it seemed to have little to offer public policy. Its central claim had been that it could manage the tradeoff between unemployment and inflation. Such a theory could not as helpfully inform policy in a world where not only was inflation rampant but unemployment remained high despite substantial and increasing budget deficits.

These difficulties helped to prompt a harsh critique of Keynesianism by rational expectations economists, who began in the 1970s— building on the logic behind Friedman's challenge to the Phillips curve—to examine the significance of private behavior that responds to and anticipates the future effects of government policy. The most rigorous and thoroughgoing rational expectationists argued that systematic fiscal and monetary policies inherently have no effect, in large part because economic actors anticipate and respond to them—if not always accurately, then at least without systematic error. Only random and hence unpredictable fiscal and monetary policies could alter macroeconomic aggregates such as output and employment, but such policies by definition would not be following plausible norms such as stabilizing the economy or promoting full employment.[12]

By the mid–1970s, many economists thought that rational expectations had dealt Keynesianism a decisive coup de grâce. The 1980s and 1990s have seen a considerable Keynesian revival, however. In part, this has resulted from what many see as the rational expectationists' failure to provide a convincing explanation for the business cycle. Can long-lasting recessions really be explained, as they have suggested, in terms of workers' decisions to take prolonged vacations from market production (Krugman 1994, 202–5)?

In addition, Keynesians have developed more sophisticated explanations for various of their claims. Today, a host of "new Keynesians" posit multiple stable equilibria for the economy that call for regular government monitoring and intervention. They differ from their 1960s precursors in such respects as avoiding absurd claims to scientific precision; placing more emphasis on wage and price rigidities and less on overall demand; promising limited countercyclical benefits rather than perennial prosperity and expansion; and recognizing that rising inflationary expectations can radically shift the Phillips curve. Their views are sufficiently widely accepted that while rational expectations retains an academic following, it is largely ignored in Washington. The Federal Reserve Board takes a loosely Keynesian, countercyclical approach to monetary policy whether economists appointed by liberal or conservative presidents are at the helm.

In several respects, however, Keynes's views—and not just those of his overenthusiastic 1960s successors—continue to seem problematical, at least as a guide to current policy.

b. Changing Views of Whether Attempted Saving Is Too High

Keynes's explanation of how attempted saving can reduce both consumption and the level of saving that is actually achieved remains controversial, even as an explanation of the Great Depression. Milton

---

12. See Lucas and Sargent 1981a,b; Lucas 1972; Sargent and Wallace 1975. For an accessible discussion and explanation of the rational expectationists' main work, see Maddock and Carter 1982.

Friedman argues that the depression's length and severity resulted simply from a one-third contraction in the money supply, largely a result of bank failures, which the national government did not recognize or counteract (1969, 79–80). The problem, under this view, was a lesser case of what would happen if money ceased to exist or if the government continually changed the currency and made the prior one worthless. Thus, Friedman argues, the only market failure established by the Great Depression was an easily corrected breakdown in capital markets, which could not function well absent stable and reliable mechanisms for transferring financial resources from lenders to borrowers.

Even if one accepts Keynes's rather than Friedman's version of depression history, one is left with the question of its relevance to present-day economic concerns. Support among economists for stimulating current market demand during periods of reduced economic activity that reflect low confidence is widespread. It underlies decisions by the Federal Reserve Board to slow down or heat up the economy by raising or lowering interest rates. Yet few agree that Americans today are attempting to save, rather than consume, too much or that the paradox of thrift remains operative. To the contrary, we hear instead the perennial refrain that our national rate of saving is too low and that this results from a propensity to consume too much and save too little, rather than the reverse as in the 1930s.

Consider the 1980s, an era of low saving rates and relatively low national economic growth. Can one really argue against the weight of cultural evidence about the decade's emphasis on consumption, backed by such data as its burgeoning level of consumer debt—not to mention the decade's ongoing Keynesian stimulus via massive budget deficits—that the low rate of saving resulted from people's attempting to save *more* than previously, rather than less? The contemporary domestic evidence seems particularly compelling when one considers the high rates of both saving and economic growth in Asian countries such as Japan, Taiwan, South Korea, and Singapore. Scholars who have studied those countries generally agree that their residents tend to regard saving as a higher priority than do people in the United States, either for cultural reasons or in response to their governments' anticonsumer policies. Yet if this is true and the paradox of thrift currently held, one would expect (all else equal) *lower* rates of saving, investing, and economic growth in those countries than here, rather than the higher rates we mostly observe.

The view that consumption rather than attempted saving is too high makes much of what Keynes says, even if correct about the 1930s, seem less applicable today. Indeed, his theory remains important mainly because of concern about unemployment, rather than about attempted saving's effect on long-term economic growth. In the area of unemployment as well, however, much has changed since Keynes asked who could deny that labor markets were systematically failing to clear.

c. Alternative Explanations of High Unemployment Levels

In at least three main respects, Keynes's account of unemployment has stood the test of time well. First, as he argued, high unemployment levels can be surprisingly durable and indeed a stable equilibrium, rather than merely reflecting transitory friction. The labor market often fails to clear promptly (or at all) through wage reductions—unlike, say, the markets for wheat and oranges, which are more price-flexible and thus clear more readily.

Second, involuntary unemployment, defined as the case in which one cannot find a job even though the value of one's labor exceeds one's disutility-based demand wage, appears to many to be a genuine phenomenon. Both of Keynes's main explanations for it—"sticky wages" that fail to change promptly with market conditions, and alternative equilibria based on different levels of demand—retain some force, although other explanations may hold as well (e.g., Solow 1986).

Third, high unemployment levels are undesirable and should be addressed by government policy if sufficiently practicable. Lost output from involuntary unemployment provides one basis for this conclusion. Others include the effects of unemployment on societal wealth distribution if welfare payments will be inadequate or have efficiency costs of their own, and what an economist would call human capital formation. People decide from early childhood, and often on an ongoing basis, what tastes and skills to cultivate. The extent to which they apply themselves in school and subsequently develop and maintain marketable skills and reliable work habits varies with the perceived payoff from future employment. This perception, in turn, is affected by the actual level of job opportunities. Even assuming a generous welfare system, a society with high unemployment levels is likely to have more crime, unrest, and self-destructive behavior than one in which any productive worker can get a job.

One might therefore be inclined to embrace Keynes's proposal of stimulative fiscal policy—even if it paid for wasteful ditch-digging and the like—if it seemed likely to be sufficiently effective. The problem, however, is that more recent explanations of unemployment reduce the applicability of his cure. While Keynes addresses cyclical unemployment, emerging when the economy is in recession, economists increasingly agree that the economy has, at any time, a surprisingly high "natural" rate of equilibrium unemployment, the level of which depends on a host of cost, demand, demographic, technological, and regulatory factors. Or, to use a less politically charged and complacent-sounding terminology, there is a "nonaccelerating inflation rate of unemployment," or NAIRU. This name expresses the underlying view that while, in principle, the government could always eliminate unemployment by offering everyone a job, this would lead over time to accelerating inflation. Absent a government effort to push the unemployment rate below the NAIRU, the actual rate continually approaches the equilibrium rate as people's expectations adjust, although the equilibrium rate itself changes constantly.

To the extent of the NAIRU, unemployment is "structural." Yet the existence of a NAIRU does not mean that nothing can be done about it. In particular, changes in the legal regime such as reducing the work disincentives that often result from taxes, regulations, and social welfare programs can have significant effects. The structural nature of unemployment does, however, mean that the conventional Keynesian tools of fiscal and monetary policy cannot affect it beyond a certain point without sending inflation through the roof. Thus, while countercyclical Keynesian policy may help to ease recessions, the 1960s Keynesian nostrum of perennial demand stimulus until full employment is reached remains discredited.

Exponents of the NAIRU argue that it results, in the main, from rational behavior by employers who must respond to the fact that the human beings who work for them are more complicated and less controllable, and thus have more variable output, than inanimate productive inputs such as commodities and machines. It is expensive to hire and fire workers, given search and training costs, but workers are free to quit and often cannot commit credibly or enforceably against doing so. Moreover, workers can shirk or provide less than their best efforts, but whether they are doing so is hard to observe. Getting workers to contribute their best efforts requires providing incentives that make them more reluctant to risk losing their jobs through poor performance (Akerlof and Yellen 1985, 4–7; Shapiro and Stiglitz 1986,

45–55). It also depends on retaining their goodwill, which in turn depends in part on their perception that the employer is paying them a "fair" wage (Thaler 1991, 216; Akerlof 1984, 145–72; Solow 1986, 42).

These considerations lead employers to pay what are called efficiency wages. In various settings, employers offer a wage that is high enough not just to fill the position but also to attract and retain a satisfied quality applicant, to whom job loss would be a real sanction. Competing employers bid up wages, with consequently reduced employment levels, until there is sufficient job queuing to create the optimal level of sanction (Phelps 1994a, 12–13). Thus, efficiency wages lead to involuntary unemployment among those who, having lost what may in effect be a game of musical chairs for the available jobs, cannot credibly commit to work hard and stay on the job for less than the efficiency wage.

Keynesian fiscal and monetary policy does not respond effectively to involuntary unemployment of this kind. Better responses may include, again, modifying tax and regulatory rules that deter employment or providing wage subsidies on behalf of marginal workers. In particular, some job expansion might result, at no net budgetary cost, from enacting wage subsidies in lieu of social welfare and social insurance benefits that, by making job loss less painful, tend to raise the needed efficiency wage (Phelps 1994b). This would, however, reduce the benefit to the neediest individuals in the society (such as those who would not get jobs in any event) from redistributive government spending.

d. The Role of the Government in Boosting Consumption through Stimulative Fiscal Policy

Keynes wrote at a time of relatively great trust in government—a trust he shared, perhaps unsurprisingly given the extent of his contacts in the British and American governments. He evidently thought it reasonable to assume that as long as the government is capable of doing some good, we should urge it to expand its role. With sixty years' experience, however, we can see, as he did not, the problems with Keynesian fiscal policy in an imperfect political environment.

In practice, countercyclical fiscal policy has functioned as a one-way ratchet, increasing government spending and reducing taxes. As a political matter, enacting stimulative tax cuts and spending increases tends to be easy, whether for good-faith Keynesian reasons or because both these measures are politically appealing in any event. Enacting offsetting tax increases or spending cuts, whether to ward off inflation or simply because the need for stimulus has passed, is quite a different matter. In practice, therefore, an ostensibly Keynesian policy seems to yield chronic budget deficits and a host of inefficient but politically entrenched tax concessions and pork-barrel spending programs.

A second problem with responding to recessions through fiscal policy—conceded by Arthur Okun as early as 1970—is implementation lag (1970, 65). Before any fiscal response can be devised, an impending recession must first be observed by economists sifting through imprecise and already time-lagged economic indicators. Then someone, typically the president, must make a legislative proposal to stimulate the economy through tax cuts or spending increases. Inevitably, given Congress's committee structure and the need for extensive negotiations in a Madisonian political system, enactment takes time.

The lag does not come to an end even once a stimulus program has been enacted. Government contracts may need to be bid out, or market mechanisms developed for disseminating the use of new tax incentives, or tax filing season awaited. If implementation lag is great enough, Keynesian fiscal policy may end up heightening, rather than moderating, the business cycle. Milton Friedman used the metaphor of a thermostat that, reacting slowly to cold temperatures in December, at last turns the heat on in July.

Worse still, perhaps, are the consequences of the 1960s Keynesian claim that the season for stimulus never passes and that, short of full employment, government spending is effectively free—merely employing resources that would otherwise lie idle rather than crowding out private production. This view can become a pretext for treating all questions of allocating resources efficiently, or using them effectively, as distinctly secondary. Whoever most forcefully demands government-financed consumption can be satisfied with no questions asked and no concern about tradeoffs. Politics seems to provide a limitless number of free lunches and fiscal policy a perpetual motion machine.

E. Summing Up the First Two Centuries of the Deficit Debate among Economists

The deficit debate among economists from the 1770s through the 1970s has a surprisingly consistent theme. Economists generally agreed that, default risk aside, deficits matter because they cause consumers to feel (and perhaps to be) wealthier than under a regime of full current tax financing. Economists disagreed, however, about whether this perception was accurate or instead merely reflected fiscal illusion.

Adam Smith viewed the reduced-cost perception as illusion and argued that it promoted bad public policies, such as being too ready to go to war. David Ricardo agreed that it was illusion but emphasized a tendency to yield heedless private expenditure. Debt financing would induce people who failed to understand the future tax charges on their households to spend too much today relative to their own long-term preferences. Over the next century, economists generally shared Smith's and Ricardo's views, although with decreasing vehemence. By the time of C. F. Bastable, they had evolved a prudential belief in annual budgetary balance as a useful though arbitrary norm, worth following most of the time in order to restrain the inclination to debt-finance unduly.

Keynesianism, however, created a violent rupture in economists' views of budget deficits. The "new orthodoxy" of the 1930s through the 1950s suggested that current taxpayers bore the full cost of government spending no matter how it was financed. The illusion of reduced cost from debt financing was now desirable, however. Abba Lerner argued that without it, vital government spending programs would be allowed to wither. Moreover, from a Keynesian macroeconomic perspective, the illusion of greater taxpayer wealth from debt-financed spending played a crucial role in encouraging greater consumer spending during recessions. Indeed, with this response, the illusion would become reality. People really would be better off when consumer spending increased. Moreover, short of full employment, the debt-financed government expenditure would in effect be free, since it would replace lost output rather than crowd out private expenditure.

The decline of Keynesianism moved economic thinking back toward the earlier perspective. Yet Keynesianism survived sufficiently to add an enduring new element to the mix. It continued to suggest persuasively that, at least during recessions, budget deficits could be desirable, even if they ought to emerge only automatically (as an economic slowdown causes income tax receipts to decline and welfare or social insurance payments to increase) rather than through the enactment of policy changes.

From the standpoint of economists, the 1970s witnessed a striking new development. Just as economists had mostly ceased to subscribe to the 1960s Keynesian belief in perpetual stimulative deficits, historically unprecedented peacetime deficits became a regular phenomenon. This helped to enliven and transform the deficit debate. Old and forgotten perspectives on deficits were revived and new ones developed.

FOUR

The Modern Deficit Debate

In all likelihood, vastly more words have been published about budget deficits in the last twenty-odd years than during the entire previous history of humanity. The size and prominence of modern budget deficits, along with the general explosion of both popular and academic publishing, help to ensure the current era's preeminence in quantity. Does this preeminence extend to quality as well? In a sense it does, even though few modern contributions are fundamentally new and most modern writers lack the balanced judgment of a Ricardo or a Bastable.

Analysis of budget deficits has benefited from the fact that, in the words of the old Chinese curse, we live in interesting times. Recent years have brought unprecedented peacetime deficits, at a time when the national government's operations are far greater and more complex than ever before. Alexander Hamilton's call for a national government large and powerful enough to manage the economy and build extensive public works has long since been left behind. Today's national government does these things on a far larger scale than Hamilton could have imagined, plus vastly more. It directly employs millions of Americans, through a huge permanent bureaucracy and defense establishment. It operates large-scale transfer programs such as Medicare and Social Security. It regulates or intervenes in every sector of the economy, from farming to communications to education to health care to home ownership. All of these interventions raise interesting and difficult questions, going not only to familiar deficit issues such as macroeconomic policy but also to an underlying problem, previously taken for granted, of how budget deficits should be defined.

Yet even as the debate has grown more interesting and varied, it has lost coherence. Economists not only disagree, but they often obliviously engage in wholly separate conversations. Karen Vaughn and Richard Wagner have called the post—World War II literature a "three-ring circus," featuring "players" who "proceed as if the other ring[s] did not exist" (1992, 37). The rings they identify—as redefined by me to focus more narrowly on the 1970s through the present—involve, respectively, James Buchanan and his colleagues in the "Virginia school" of public choice theory, the Keynesian Robert Eisner, and the rational expectationist Robert Barro.[1] One could also add a fourth ring, involving Laurence Kotlikoff's work on generational accounting, and note that work by Martin Feldstein, if not quite a fifth ring since it concerns Social Security rather than budget deficits, has contributed importantly to the debate.

Vaughn and Wagner argue that the rings they identify are mutually incomplete rather than antagonistic. "All sides to this controversy represent incomplete descriptions of the same analytical elephant, so to speak" (38). Whether or not this is correct—especially under my even more discordant rendering of the circus—Vaughn and Wagner *are* right about the need to start with disaggregation. Accordingly, this chapter examines in turn each of the five main contributions to the deficit debate since the early 1970s, as a prelude to reaching broad conclusions later.

A. Robert Barro's Revival of the Ricardian Equivalence Theorem

1. The "Ricardian" Claim That Debt Financing and Current Tax Financing Are Equivalent

Again, during the 1970s, the theory of rational expectations gained great prominence in economics. Its core notion was to apply more explicitly to the question of how people use information about the future to guide their current behavior the standard rational actor model that underlies classical microeconomics. Rational expectationists believed that the forecasting that drives behavior in marketplace settings

---

1. Vaughn and Wagner anoint Abba Lerner as the Keynesian "ringmaster" and assign a "ring" to Buchanan for his challenge in the 1950s to the no-burden, no-transfer orthodoxy, rather than for the 1970s work that I discuss in this section.

tends to be fairly sophisticated, or at least not predictably and systematically erroneous. Thus, capital markets are relatively efficient and respond swiftly to new information. Even if only a few market actors have good information, they ostensibly can produce systemwide effects—for example, by bidding up the price of any stock that appears undervalued.

Rational expectations theory was inherently in tension with Keynesian macroeconomics. This tension centered on the word *rational*, not *expectations*. While Keynes likewise attached great importance to people's long-term expectations, he thought them driven by "irrational psychology" (1964, 162). In addition, his belief in labor and capital market rigidities, such as "sticky" wages and prices, conflicted with the rational expectationists' view of markets as adjusting swiftly to changed circumstances.

During the 1970s, as Keynesianism seemed to be refuted by stagflation, Robert Lucas and Thomas Sargent brought rational expectations to bear on Keynes's starting point: business cycles and the labor market. Viewing labor markets as driven by rational behavior and as clearing rapidly in accordance with the classical model, Lucas and Sargent argued that unemployment cannot be altered through fiscal and monetary policy unless the government somehow "tricks" employers and workers into misjudging the economic environment in which they are operating. To Lucas and Sargent, even more than to Milton Friedman in his attack on the Phillips curve, this was a hopeless task beyond the very short term (Lucas and Sargent 1981b; Sargent and Wallace 1976). Much of their analysis depended, however, not just on assuming well-informed rational behavior but also on controversial premises about such matters as the structure of the labor market and the role of money in the economy. Lucas and Sargent also focused more explicitly on monetary than fiscal policy, although their approach's implications for the latter were not hard to guess.

It remained for Robert Barro to drive home the implications of rational expectations for Keynes's claim that budget deficits are expansionary. Again, Keynes had argued that if the government increases its outlays or reduces taxes, people will have more money on hand, feel wealthier, and therefore begin to spend more on consumption, leading swiftly to increased output and employment. To Barro, however, this seemed to assume an unrealistic level of public myopia. Since deficits imply higher taxes in the future, taxpayers should not feel better off by reason of an increased budget deficit; they will have to pay later for the increased transfers that they are receiving now. Thus, if they are rational actors and neither myopic nor highly cash-constrained, they would seem unlikely to change their spending decisions because of current largesse.

Perhaps the most obvious response to Barro is that current taxpayers are *not* certain to pay higher taxes later on, since their lives are finite. The future taxes to repay current debt may not be levied until future generations are paying taxes. Even if current taxpayers care somewhat about their descendants' well-being, one might think that anything short of total altruism, extending indefinitely into the future, would lead them to prefer debt financing to current tax financing, and indeed to view it as enriching them.

Barro argues, however, that current taxpayers need not be complete altruists in order to be indifferent about deficits versus current tax financing. Instead, indifference requires only that they plan to leave some positive bequest when they die:

> [I]f, prior to the government bond issue, a member of the old generation had already selected a positive bequest, it is clear that this individual already had the option of shifting resources from his descendant to himself, but he had determined that such shifting, at the margin, was nonoptimal. *Since the change in [bond issuance] does not alter the relevant opportunity set* in this sense, it follows that—through the appropriate adjustment of the bequest—the values of current and future consumption and attained utility will be unaffected. (1974, 1103; emphasis added)

The italicized words above are the critical ones. Barro, as a rational expectationist, thinks that people choose and pursue consistent goals without being affected by how choices are framed or presented to them, or by information costs. Thus, keeping the "opportunity set" constant, so that preexisting goals can still be achieved, ensures that outcomes will not change.

In Ricardo's terms—although Ricardo rejected the argument because of his belief in fiscal illusion—if I want to leave my children $20,000 assuming no deferred taxes, and the government runs a budget deficit implying future taxes on my household with a $1,000 present value, then I will save a little extra and leave my children $21,000. In effect, the deferred taxes will simply end up in a dedicated bank account, permitting them to be paid whenever the government gets around to levying them. Apart from that adjustment to my saving, I will act no differently from and regard myself as no wealthier than if the government had taxed me $1,000 today and thus eliminated the deficit.

Barro's claim does not require that taxpayers actually estimate correctly the expected future taxes implied by budget deficits. He argues only that their estimating errors are not systematic and thus lack a consistent or predictable direction. In the above example, if $1,000 is the correct estimate, Barro claims that in principle I am no more likely to err on the high side than on the low side and thus that on average I will guess $1,000, even if I never hit the nail precisely on the head. (Ricardo, by contrast, argued that people would systematically underestimate future taxes.)

Even if one otherwise believes in rational expectations, one could object that the great majority of households do not leave cash bequests (Lord and Rangazas 1993). Barro argues, however, that bequests are unnecessary for his claim to hold. Rather, it is sufficient that parents during their lives make *any* net transfers to their children, such as for upbringing and education, since such transfers can always be adjusted up or down.

As for people without children, who presumably benefit from deferring taxation until their households have vanished, Barro has two responses. First, they are but a small part of the overall picture. Second, their preference for deficits is offset by the preference for current tax financing that Barro attributes to people with large numbers of children (whose current households' share of the tax burden seems likely to increase over time, as each child becomes a separate earner and taxpayer) (1989, 41).

Barro concludes that budget deficits have no effect on the business cycle, the intergenerational distribution of wealth or consumption, or the amount and incidence of saving. Similarly, express generational transfers, as through Social Security payments to retirees that exceed the value of their contributions, have no net impact, given offsetting adjustments to discretionary transfers between generations (1974, 1107).

Since the timing of taxation relative to spending is otherwise irrelevant, Barro endorses a fiscal policy of "tax smoothing," under which tax rates generally remain constant, even as spending fluctuates, in order to minimize tax-induced distortion in the timing of economic behavior. Contrary to the norm of annual balance, changes in spending do not imply changes in taxation. Instead, the spending and revenue sides of the budget should be completely divorced from each other, apart from adjusting tax levels periodically to accommodate long-term changes in spending levels.

One might argue that tax smoothing is a device, not only for stabilizing the tax system but also for concealing from taxpayers the real cost of new government spending. This is what Adam Smith argued about the English government's handling of the costs of war. From Barro's perspective, however, such a device would be futile, because taxpayers understand real costs without regard to the mode of financing.

Barro likewise does not believe (as did Bastable) that seeking a match between revenues and expenditures only over the long term, rather than annually, leads in practice to chronic deficits. No critic noticed that Bastable had anticipated Barro on tax smoothing, just as Ricardo had on debt equivalence. Again, Bastable had in substance recommended tax smoothing for large, nonrecurrent expenditures and declined to endorse it more generally solely because of his concern that it would lead in practice to chronic deficits (1922, 674–79). The main difference between Barro and Bastable, as between Barro and Ricardo, was that the earlier writer saw the issue as more complex given fiscal illusion and the consequent potential for systematic underestimation of future tax burdens.

In recent writing, Barro has moderated his "Ricardian" position. He now clarifies that, as a result of Ricardian offsets, the timing of taxation and the current budget deficit have no "first-order effect" on the economy. He concedes that a number of significant "second-order" effects are possible, because of such factors as the distorting effects of tax changes, imperfections in capital markets, and possible effects of uncertainty concerning future earnings and tax burdens. He nonetheless claims that Ricardianism has gained stature in the last decade— as shown by the fact that "[m]ost macroeconomists now feel obligated to state the Ricardian position, even if they then go on to argue that it is either theoretically or empirically in error." Widespread criticism, far from chastening him, instead emboldens him to "predict that this trend will continue and that the Ricardian approach will become the benchmark model for assessing fiscal policy" (1989, 52). One almost envies Barro's ability to deduce approaching victory from swelling criticism.

2. *Problems with the Claim of Ricardian Equivalence*

Barro's claim of Ricardian equivalence is highly controversial. He is right to observe that it is more cited, admired, and studied than accepted.[2] The core problem is that his claims concerning how people perceive and respond to debt financing, as well as to unfunded Social Security benefits, cannot be plausible to anyone who is even remotely familiar with twentieth-century politics. For example, does Barro regard it as pure coincidence that Social Security benefits were initially granted in the 1930s to retirees who had not contributed to the system, and then repeatedly expanded on an unfunded long-term basis (Nash, Pugach, and Tomasson 1988, 313–21)? Does he think it equally coincidental that budget deficits have been endemic since the 1930s (when government spending increased and the main revenue source shifted from tariffs to the income tax)? Why should not deficit and surplus be equally common if taxpayers respond with indifference to the tradeoff between current and future taxes?

Does Barro claim to understand politics better than not only Adam Smith but also President Johnson, who feared that a tax increase to pay for the Vietnam War would be politically unpopular and make the war more controversial? Is he unfamiliar with powerful lobbying groups on behalf of the elderly, such as the American Association of Retired Persons (AARP), which fight to protect and expand benefits for their clientele notwithstanding multigenerational households? Would he predict, as Ricardianism implies, that a balanced budget amendment would yield no spending cuts, given the presumed lack of any opposition to accelerating the taxes needed to pay for current spending? Avoiding casual empiricism—a charge Barro flung at early critics who made arguments of this sort (Buchanan 1976, 341; Barro 1976, 348)—is one thing, but ignoring all factors that cannot be deduced from an abstract model or proven algebraically is something else entirely.

Barro's rejection of fiscal illusion looks even less plausible when one examines politicians' behavior in more specific detail. Consider

2. See, e.g., Musgrave and Musgrave 1989, 521; Vaughn and Wagner 1992; Stein 1989b, 53–56; Eisner 1986, 69–71. While largely rejected in the public deficit debate, Barro's assertion that families behave as if they were single infinite-lived individuals has become a "standard research tool" for much of public finance and macroeconomics (Bernheim and Bagwell 1988, 309).

the changes to the Social Security system, to prevent immediate system insolvency, that were debated in 1982 (an election year) and passed through bipartisan consensus in 1983. In 1982, although the system's impending insolvency was well known in Washington,[3] the Democrats based their congressional campaign on attacking the Republicans' purported plan to slash Social Security benefits. The Republicans responded with "a television commercial featuring a winsome postman delivering Social Security checks. 'This year's 7.4 percent cost-of-living increase [in benefits],' said the mail carrier, 'was promised and delivered by the President' " (Achenbaum 1986, 83). (In fact, the benefit increase resulted automatically from legislation enacted before Reagan's presidency.) Once the 1982 elections were over—with concern over Social Security underlying Democratic success and two-thirds of those elected in 1982 pledged to oppose both tax increases and benefit reductions in Social Security (Achenbaum 1986, 83)—the serious work of avoiding system insolvency, by following the recommendations of a bipartisan panel so that neither party would have to take the lead, could begin. Even now, however, Congress showed a strong preference for indirection, relying in large part on such devices as postponing cost-of-living benefit increases and raising retirement ages but only in the distant future. Such choices by Congress, relative to alternative ways of reducing benefits, are hard to explain other than as means of providing as much cover as possible for changes that both parties agreed were necessary but politically risky (Achenbaum 1986, 86–87; Kotlikoff 1992, 24–25).

Is this the behavior one would expect in a world where voters possess good information, untainted by systematic fiscal illusion, and are pursuing unlimited time horizons? Yet the example is hardly unique. Those who recall more recent budget standoffs, as in 1990, 1993, and 1995, can easily think of similar examples.

These considerations suggest that Ricardian equivalence cannot possibly hold. Voters evidently regard themselves as better off when taxes are deferred relative to spending, or unfunded benefits are provided, even if they otherwise are making net transfers to members of future generations. Yet they would not regard themselves as better off if they were adjusting in full for expected future taxes, the present value of which they were estimating without systematic error. While I

---

3. A Social Security Trustees' report issued in 1982 indicated that by July 1983, funds on hand would be inadequate to pay old-age benefits. See Achenbaum 1986, 81.

will wait until chapter 6 to discuss detailed empirical evidence, I next consider *why* Ricardian equivalence fails to hold.

Perhaps the main reason is that society consists of multiple households, among whom the burden of future taxes remains unallocated. Barro's view might be correct in a society that consisted of a single household, given that people generally do not view themselves as enriched by, say, mortgaging their homes to the hilt. He also might be correct if the national debt were explicitly divided among all households in the country, such that each household owed bondholders its separate share as a legally binding debt and had to pay interest on that share at a rate that reflected default risk.

The existence of multiple households promotes what economists call rational ignorance. Say that in a society with one hundred households, a proposed spending program for the benefit of five households would be financed through a tax borne exclusively by ten households. If the ten unlucky households were selected up front, they might organize and fight the program, even if the taxes were not due until later. Yet if not only the levy but determination of its incidence is deferred, then organizing to fight the program (or even taking time to learn about it) may not be worthwhile to any of the ninety-five nonbenefiting households.

Barro could argue that the resulting transfer is intra- rather than intergenerational. Similarly, when members of AARP seek additional unfunded spending on Medicare and Social Security, they may be seeking transfers from unspecified households that include members of their own generation, rather than from younger generations. Yet recognizing the murkiness of what type of distributional struggle is actually going on does not eliminate the difference between debt and tax financing.

The existence of multiple households also matters because particular households may die out (or expect to die out) before the future taxes are ever levied. In modern industrialized countries, about 2 percent of households disappear each year. Awareness of this process may encourage feelings of disconnectedness from future generations and cause households to act on short time horizons (Evans 1993, 535, 541). In addition, about one-fifth of households are permanently childless (Seater 1993, 158). While Barro is correct that, in principle, such households' preference for debt financing could be offset by a preference for current tax financing in households with above-average numbers of children, one searches in vain for evidence that the latter preference actually exists in practice. Politicians who claim to be pro-family typically propose reducing, not increasing, current taxes. Indeed, the view that demanding current tax increases could be a plausible political strategy for donning the pro-family mantle can only be described as absurd. Once again, therefore, Barro's account of people's expressed preferences is politically counterfactual.

Even to the extent that households rationally weigh the differences between their current and expected future shares of the overall national tax burden, it would appear that those likely to owe *less* in the future than today are more powerful politically than those likely to owe more. For example, elderly retirees are far more politically potent as a group than young parents who are raising children. Retirees have more time to devote to political activity and also tend to have simpler and more unified economic interests. Thus, for all the political talk one hears about helping families, there is no young parents' analogue to the AARP.

A separate set of reasons explaining why Ricardian equivalence does not hold goes to the nature of altruism within the household. Even though parents spend resources on their children, it need not follow that the parents are indifferent or averse to benefiting at their children's expense through government fiscal policy. Parents may exhibit a form of limited altruism, where context strongly affects how distributional goals shape behavior.

The importance for Ricardianism of limited altruism was first noted by B. Douglas Bernheim and Kyle Bagwell, who criticized Barro's model of the family as too linear and dynastic. In each household in his model, parents are succeeded by children, who are succeeded by the children's children, and there are no outside affiliations to other households. Bernheim and Bagwell argued instead that family networks are complex and overlapping, because marriages link previously unrelated family groups, and other linkings emerge over time. Hence, individuals tend to belong to multiple altruistically linked groupings, and ultimately the entire population is altruistically linked.

Initially, this seems to make the Ricardian line of analysis even more powerful than Barro recognizes. Given the universality of linkages and interrelatedness, virtually *all* wealth redistributions by the government (not just those between generations) may seem likely to be reversed by private transfers such as gifts and bequests, designed to achieve the distributions that people prefer. Bernheim and Bagwell (1988) argue, however, that this is implausible, and therefore that

Barro's underlying assumption—that transfers such as gifts and bequests reflect donors' preferred distributional end results—must be incorrect. Instead, the distribution prior to private decisions about gifts and bequests must matter, and making a gift or bequest of a given size must be an end in itself.

A view of gifts and bequests as ends in themselves, rather than as means to distributional end results, would challenge Barro's model even if one accepted his dynastic model of the family. In Ricardian terms, the view suggests that even if there is no distributional difference between leaving, say, a $20,000 estate with no deferred taxes and a $25,000 estate with $5,000 of deferred taxes, a rational parent may nonetheless plan to leave $20,000 *whether or not* there are deferred taxes.

For example, the parent may enjoy thinking of himself or herself as someone who leaves $20,000 (ignoring any deferred tax bill as the product of collective political decisions rather than individual will). James Andreoni calls this "impure altruism," motivated by the "warm glow" one gets from giving rather than by altruistic concern for the aggregate well-being of future generations, and notes that it would defeat Ricardian equivalence (1989, 1447). Alternatively, the parent may be strategically motivated, using the promise of a $20,000 estate to maintain leverage over the children and unable to "trade" with them his or her contribution to the collective political decision. In such a case, a bequest is part of an implicit parent-child exchange of wealth for services, and private behavior therefore would not reverse the redistribution accomplished through government fiscal policy.

Barro, while presumably regarding "warm glow" altruism as too irrational to fit in with his model, has responded to the claim of deliberate strategic behavior by parents. He discounts the importance of parental strategic behavior on the ground that the threat to disinherit or to dissipate one's estate often would not be credible. In addition, he argues that if parents and children were exchanging money for services, one would expect them to agree to explicit wages. This claim seems even more obtuse about family relations than Barro has elsewhere shown himself to be about politics. In some cases, the very good that is being bought—expressions of love and concern, as distinct from more tangible services—may require avoiding an explicit market exchange, even if one is taking place implicitly.

While the question of the relative importance of different bequest motivations remains empirically open (see Seater 1993, 157), some evidence appears to support the significance of impure altruism and implicit exchange. For example, bequests tend to be split evenly among children even if they differ significantly in earnings capacity and thus presumably in need (Menchik 1980; Lord and Rangazas 1993). On average, children provide more services, such as visits and telephone calls, both when the parental estate is greater and in multiple-child families, where there is more competition for the bequest (Bernheim, Shleifer, and Summers 1976).[4] Moreover, parents tend to make larger lifetime gifts to those of their children whose income is greater and who thus presumably demand a higher implicit compensation rate for their time and services (Cox 1987).

To be sure, the strategic claim may seem inconsistent with the altruism and sacrifice that all concerned and involved parents come to know in the course of raising children. John Seater argues:

> Feeding, clothing, housing, educating, and chauffeuring children absorb an enormous amount of resources but confer no direct utility, in the selfish sense of classical consumer theory, on the providers. Moreover, the return in increased future direct utility, in terms of provision for old age and so on, generally seems miniscule compared to the current cost. The investment seems a poor one in that sense, yet it is routinely undertaken by most married couples. One-sided altruism seems an accurate description of reality. (1993, 150)

Yet Seater fails to rebut the claim that raising children mainly involves consumption and impure altruism—even if not narrowly strategic behavior. Parents may enjoy or care about all of the following—raising their children, forming their characters, spending time with them, winning their love and gratitude, and being remembered by them after they die—without caring so much about the children's later consumption levels. Moreover, the fact that children are unlikely to blame their parents personally for a collective political decision by members of the parents' generation to burden them with outstanding public debt may liberate parents emotionally to assent to policies that benefit their age cohort in the aggregate.

---

4. While Seater (1993, 158) notes that this evidence concerns the behavior of children rather than of the parents who leave the bequests, it is plausible to infer that the children may know what they are doing.

In addition, the value of the goods and services "transferred" to children in the course of raising them to adulthood may be vastly less sensitive to Ricardian adjustment than are bequests. Evolution and culture have equipped parents with child-raising norms that may guide their behavior relatively inelastically. Those not so equipped, no matter how rationally they optimize during their lives, presumably leave fewer descendants.

To express the underlying norm in rational expectations terms, suppose that parents are pure but limited altruists who view child rearing as more crucial to their children's well-being than financing additional consumption by the children once they have grown up. Perhaps I am just altruistic enough to place equal value, at the margin, on x units of my own consumption and $5x$ units of my children's consumption. I may estimate that giving them adequate parental care conveys benefits to them far greater than the cost of such services to me. By contrast, I may regard leaving a large bequest, or even paying sufficient current taxes to avoid creating future burden, as increasing their lifetime consumption by too little, since their consumption opportunities would exceed mine only to the extent of accrual at the market rate of interest. Thus, there is no contradiction in my making a fixed level of child-raising investment and at the same time favoring tax lag that benefits me at my children's expense (and not adjusting my child-raising investment for the amount of such lag).

A final ground for doubting Ricardian equivalence goes to the time horizon over which people make spending and saving decisions. The lifetime or permanent income hypothesis, which holds that consumption decisions reflect expected future income as well as current income, predicts that such adjustments often will take place over long periods of time. For example, if I win $50,000 in the lottery, I ostensibly will spread the newly presented consumption opportunities over my remaining life span. Ricardianism takes the lifetime income hypothesis a step further, by eliminating one's own life span as a boundary on the adjustment period.

To many readers, assuming this degree of farsightedness may seem implausible. Their skepticism is supported by recent empirical studies that suggest that people tend to smooth out their consumption over a time horizon of only a few years and let current consumption spending vary more with current income than one might expect from the lifetime (much less the Ricardian) perspective (see Carroll and Summers 1991). Use of the longer perspectives may be discouraged by the future's inherent unpredictability, the cost of attempting to engage in sophisticated long-term planning, and the general lack of capital markets permitting one to borrow against future labor income, leading to liquidity constraints. One recent study suggests that 16 percent of aggregate consumption in the United States is by liquidity-constrained households (Mariger 1987), while another suggests that liquidity constraints reduce average consumption by close to 3 percent (Hayashi 1985). All this implies that at least to a significant degree, people will not make Ricardian adjustments to the future taxes implied by present budget deficits, unless they expect those taxes to be levied quite soon. Instead, they may systematically underadjust for long-term considerations of this kind.

For all these reasons, Barro's work is more an elegant intellectual exercise than a plausible description of reality. Still, he has contributed to the deficit debate. Just as Abba Lerner's no-burden, no-transfer position overstated an important truth—that the mode of financing does not directly affect the real level of resources—so Barro supplies an important corrective to the deficit debate. Government policy cannot as easily change distribution within households as between households. In evaluating the effects of budget deficits, we must consider the possible effects on behavior within the household. Moreover, even if Barro is too simplistic in treating expectations as invariably well informed (or at least not subject to systematic error), he is right to focus on their importance.

B. Martin Feldstein and the Relevance of Government Commitments (Not Formally Constituting Debt) to Make Future Expenditures

One important insight of Barro's—that using debt financing to pay for current government spending is economically similar to providing retirees with Social Security benefits in excess of the value of their contributions—was also developed independently, and explored more systematically, by Martin Feldstein. According to Feldstein's still-controversial 1970s research, Social Security reduced the rate of private saving by at least 50 percent and thus, over time, greatly lowered our rate of economic growth (see Feldstein 1974). Feldstein's work on

Social Security is worth examining with regard to both the broad underlying point, concerning the similarity between debt financing and the operations of Social Security, and the narrower claim about its effects on private saving.

1. Social Security as a Vehicle (Like Debt Financing) for Intergenerational Wealth Transfer

If Social Security were merely a forced saving program, whereby people were required to fund annuities for their own retirement, it would raise few, if any, deficit-related issues. The program would neither transfer wealth between members of different age cohorts nor raise long-term financing difficulties. In fact, however, Social Security is *not* a true annuity program, except in small part. While its complex benefit formulas create positive correlation between how much one contributes and how much one gets back, the correlation is extremely rough.

This lack of correlation between contributions and benefits is deliberate and dates from the system's enactment in 1935. The system's drafters consciously wanted to provide social insurance and progressive income redistribution, while using the annuity element for political cover. The deliberately confusing combination that they hit upon between redistributive and annuity functions was a brilliant political success, which ever since has encouraged Congress to provide the elderly (rich and poor alike) with benefits that they have not paid for yet are portrayed as something that they have earned and that cost no one else anything.

Despite the progressive intent, Social Security has mainly redistributed wealth not from rich to poor but from younger to older Americans. From the start, retirees received benefits far in excess of the value of their collective contributions. The first benefit payments began only three years after the program's inception, providing initial retirees with windfalls that were financed by current workers. While this gave needed aid to the poorer elderly, it was not limited to them, and it served obvious political purposes by so visibly benefiting early retirees at a diffused, deferred, and uncertain cost. Indeed, the program could not possibly have been enacted had it provided only the measly benefits that the first retirees could collectively self-finance in three years, or if instead it had provided no benefits for the lengthy period necessary for the first group of eligible beneficiaries to provide significant self-financing.

This initial pattern of giving retirees—invariably a well-organized bloc of current voters—benefits far greater than the value of their contributions became standard in Social Security. Benefits were repeatedly increased during the 1950s and 1960s, such as by expanding eligibility, compensating earlier retirement, and adding social welfare programs such as Medicare and Medicaid. Robust economic growth, along with the large size of generational cohorts in the workforce compared to those living in their retirement years, made all this affordable.

The policy of providing ever larger windfalls to current voters proved enormously politically seductive. For decades, almost everyone supported Social Security—Democrats and Republicans, business and labor, large business and small (see Achenbaum 1986, 44–47)—reflecting the perception that it had winners but no losers. The few who expressed any opposition—such as Barry Goldwater during his 1964 presidential campaign, when he criticized mandatory participation—were dismissed as extremist cranks. In 1972, when President Nixon and Ways and Means chairman Wilbur Mills, both mindful of the upcoming presidential election, proposed a 20 percent increase in Social Security pension benefits along with increased welfare-type benefits and automatic cost-of-living adjustments to follow shortly—all without added funding—the House of Representatives approved by 302 to 33, with the Senate voting 82 to 4 (Achenbaum 1986, 58). Media commentators generally applauded—noting, for example, that Social Security was "not a bad deal [because] it is highly likely that current workers will get back from Social Security more than they paid in if they live only a few years past their retirement age, and a great deal more if they live a long life."[5] The question of how a program that merely shifted money around could make *everyone* better off provoked little perplexity.

Even though, under Social Security, retirees received net transfers from current workers, rather than paying in full for their age group's benefits, the program was meant to be financially self-supporting. This commitment was consistent with two extremes of funding method, or anything in between. One extreme would have been to run the system on a pure cash-flow, pay-as-you-go basis. Under this method, the amount collected each year through Social Security taxes would have

5. Achenbaum 1986, 61, quoting Dale 1973.

been fully paid out that year in program benefits, leaving nothing in reserve to fund expected future benefits. Under the opposite extreme, the system would have been fully funded on a long-term economic accrual basis. That is, taxes and benefits would have been set at levels such that, as best one could tell, the one would precisely pay for the other over time.

In practice, the funding method has oscillated within the range between the two extremes. It has resembled pay-as-you-go in that surpluses, while allowed, have tended to prompt benefit expansion. The funding method has also partaken of economic accrual, however, in that there has always been long-term actuarial forecasting, leading to the buildup of notional cash reserves that remain undissipated.

For purposes of measuring the budget deficit, Social Security is mainly ignored. Of the three most widely used deficit measures—unified budget deficit, Gramm-Rudman-Hollings deficit, and National Income and Products Account (NIPA) deficit—only the last includes Social Security (see Kotlikoff 1992, 11–12, 83). Social Security is currently running large cash-flow surpluses. Thus, its inclusion reduces the NIPA deficit substantially—in 1994 by $58 billion. Yet Social Security is projected to be insolvent over the long run. According to the most recent projections, assuming no legislative change and applying "intermediate assumptions," current year outlays will begin exceeding receipts by 2020, and the system will exhaust its accumulated reserves in 2030. The long-term revenue shortfall under these projections has a present value that already equals several trillion dollars, and that is increasing by dozens of billions of dollars per year.[6]

This distinction between current cash-flow surplus and long-term deficiency helps to show the danger of relying on a cash-flow measure, such as all three budget deficits for the items they include. Suppose that we care about budget deficits out of fear that the federal government will default on its debts—or, at least, that present policies will become impossible to sustain. Social Security, despite its current cash-flow surplus, raises dangers of policy unsustainability, and perhaps even default, if over time its taxes are inadequate to finance its benefits, thus requiring either program curtailment or reliance, for the first time, on financing from outside the system.

6. See *1995 Annual Report of the Board of Trustees of the Federal Old-Age and Survivors Insurance and Disability Insurance Trust Funds* (April 3, 1995), pp. 6, 7, 23, 129. All figures include both Old Age and Survivors Insurance (OASI) and Disability Insurance (DI).

To be sure, for the government to forgo providing current workers, upon retirement, with the Social Security benefits specified by present law would be neither practically nor morally equivalent to defaulting on the national debt. Current workers have received no such definite promise of future payment as have federal bondholders. Moreover, whereas bondholders simply get back the time-adjusted value of their contributions, Social Security, under present policy, offers retirees and older workers benefits far in excess of the value of their contributions.

Yet the two cases are not entirely different, either. They create comparable fiscal pressure to raise taxes or reduce spending, even if the option of reneging on current commitments seems less harmful and unfair in one case than in the other. Moreover, reneging in either case would involve disappointing expectations that some people actually had, were encouraged to have, and relied upon, with likely effects on people's willingness to rely on similar types of government promises in the future.

The fact that the NIPA deficit's treatment of Social Security presents so misleading a long-term picture also helps to illustrate a broader point. Pay-as-you-go, resulting in annual balanced budgets, is the ideal toward which a cash-flow measure seems to point. Yet pay-as-you-go may conceal not only long-term sustainability problems if large future commitments are approaching but also present fiscal policy's actual distributional effects. Pay-as-you-go may seem to imply that as "we" receive benefits, "we" pay for them, thus suggesting an absence of large-scale transfers between taxpayers. Yet the two "we's" who pay and receive benefits need not be the same. Under Social Security, taxing today's workers to pay today's retirees, in the expectation that tomorrow's workers will finance today's workers' retirement, has massive distributional effects. For example, large age cohorts can support small ones at a far more comfortable level than small age cohorts can support large ones.

As Laurence Kotlikoff has aptly noted (1992, 97), the classic example of pay-as-you-go financing is a Ponzi scheme such as a chain letter. It is well known that while in principle Ponzi schemes need not break down, in practice they nearly always do. Indeed, Social Security has faced this danger before. During its enactment, President Roosevelt suppressed information suggesting that it would face serious revenue shortfalls within thirty years (see Achenbaum 1986, 20, 28, 32). This prospect was then long staved off, despite the immense unfunded benefit enhancements of the post—World War II years, as a result of that period's unexpectedly high rate of economic growth. Social Security faces renewed fiscal crisis today because since the early 1970s, economic growth has slowed, larger age cohorts have neared retirement age, and improved medical care has increased life spans.[7]

Problems of this sort were almost certain to arise eventually, given the decades of thoughtless and irresponsible unfunded benefit enhancement. While system default could be staved off once again if economic growth unexpectedly increases, one cannot count indefinitely on Social Security's being fortuitously rescued each time Congress follows its inclination to shower new benefits on current voters or ever-shifting economic, demographic, or medical trends turn out to have adverse fiscal consequences.

The very fact that the government now runs large-scale, long-term, ostensibly stand-alone entitlement programs such as Social Security and Medicare (which faces similar, yet even harsher, fiscal pressures) has caused the budget deficit—and even the national debt, which counts only outright current commitments—to lose much usefulness and accuracy. A cash-flow system of accounting did not misrepresent the national government's operations nearly so badly in, say, 1872 as in 1972.

Yet even apart from Social Security's direct effects on the accuracy of a cash-flow measure, the difficulty of accounting for it properly illustrates a broader point. Suppose that rapid political or technological changes made likely greatly changed levels of military spending in the near future (as with the hoped-for "peace dividend" of several years back). The national government's long-term fiscal picture would change at once, with immediate policy implications resembling those of an unexpected current budget deficit or surplus. Yet no cash-flow measure would capture the long-term implications.

Awareness of a cash-flow measure's limitations became inevitable once awareness of Social Security's long-term fiscal problems emerged in the early 1980s and once deficit politics had made multiyear budget forecasts a focus of intense partisan debate. As we will see next, however, Martin Feldstein, as early as 1974, took the first vital step in promoting awareness of the overlap between the issues raised by budget deficits and those raised by funding Social Security.

---

7. Since the late 1960s, death rates for persons sixty-five and older have been reduced by 20 percent (Espenshade and Goodis 1987, 17–18).

2. Did Social Security, When It Provided Benefits in Excess of the Value of Contributions, Reduce Saving and Economic Growth?

As we saw earlier, by the early 1970s, Keynesian fiscal policy had lost much prestige. Stagflation during an era of unprecedented peacetime, nonrecessionary budget deficits seemed to refute both the stability of the claimed tradeoff between unemployment and inflation, and the efficacy of deficits in reducing unemployment. Moreover, concern was rising about low levels of national saving and economic growth, and economists were increasingly rejecting the current applicability of the Keynesian view that these problems reflected inadequate stimulus and the paradox of thrift. Rather, many now thought, saving and investment were too low for the standard, nonparadoxical, non-Keynesian reason that the propensity to save and invest were too low.

One widespread response was to blame the budget deficit for low saving and growth rates—based on rejecting the paradox of thrift but continuing to accept the Keynesian claim that deficits induce people to feel wealthier and therefore spend more on current consumption. However accurate this view may have been, it did not involve intellectual innovation. Against this background, while Barro showed one possible direction of innovation—rejecting even the remaining Keynesian claim on rational expectations grounds—Feldstein showed another. He agreed that budget deficits promote current consumption and that this was deplorable, but he argued that they were only one element in a more broadly proconsumption, antigrowth fiscal policy. Social Security, he claimed, had even greater ill effects.

While Feldstein based his claim that Social Security reduced saving and economic growth on econometric analysis of historical data, its intuitive basis was as follows. By promising current workers retirement benefits far in excess of the value of their contributions, Social Security encouraged them to save far less than they would have otherwise—even counting their forced Social Security contributions as saving. Workers did not feel the need to save very much, since they knew that others would pay to support them when they were old. Similarly, I might be likely to save less during my working years if I had won a lottery jackpot that would begin paying me a large annuity immediately upon retirement. This discouragement of retirement saving by the prospect of being supported by others became known in the literature as the "asset substitution effect" (Feldstein 1974, 908; Leimer and Lesmoy 1982, 607).

Feldstein conceded, however, that Social Security also tended, in one respect, to increase saving. It offered annual benefits that one could not receive until one retired and that were not increased if one delayed retirement. Thus, it gave older workers a large financial inducement to retire as soon as they were eligible for Social Security benefits. A longer period of retirement implied that one needed to accumulate more assets than otherwise and thus to save *more* during one's working years—an inducement that became known in the literature as the "retirement effect" (1974, 908). Feldstein agreed that the relative magnitude of the asset substitution and retirement effects, and thus Social Security's overall effect on saving, was theoretically indeterminate. Hence the need for empirical testing through econometric research (908).

The underlying theoretical analysis arguably was incomplete in that it ignored the effects of Congress's predilection constantly to increase Social Security and related benefits. Yet this predilection probably tended to reduce saving further. To the extent that workers failed to anticipate it, it would have no advance behavioral effect but would simply give retirees a windfall. For life-cycle reasons, however, older individuals tend to consume more at the margin than younger individuals (Kotlikoff 1992, 191). Thus, an unanticipated transfer would likely reduce saving.

A final underlying point is that the retirement effect, while perhaps tending to increase saving, was bad social policy in other respects. When productive workers retire early in order to increase the value of their lifetime Social Security benefits, society loses the value of their production at a point when it still presumably exceeds the value they place on increased leisure. Economically speaking, the loss of benefits (even unearned windfall benefits) functions as a tax on continuing to work. Since younger workers do not incur this tax, it distorts the composition of the workforce in the same manner as a penalty tax on goods produced by older people or a subsidy for goods produced by younger people. The distortion is likely to be great if, as seems likely, older workers' decisions about whether to continue working are relatively elastic.

Recent developments in medical treatment have made the retirement effect ever more destructive. During the twentieth century, life expectancy at birth in the United States has increased by an astonishing 60 percent—from forty-seven years in 1900 to seventy-five years by 1984. Much of this increase has resulted from declining death rates among the elderly, particularly since adoption of Social Security. Since the late 1960s, death rates among the elderly have dropped by 20 percent. This trend is expected to continue (Espenshade and Goodis 1987, 17–18). Thus, ever greater productive potential among the elderly is being wasted if the retirement age is not commensurately increased. The trend also implies ever greater consumption by the elderly—particularly on expensive new medical technology that prolongs lives—not necessarily increasing pre-retirement saving if the increased life spans and medical costs are unanticipated or if people expect not to pay for their end-of-life medical care (or mistakenly expect not to want or receive it). Thus, even if the retirement effect is great, and even if one welcomes its effect on saving, the view that Social Security has substantial ill effects on societal well-being may not be weakened.

Feldstein focused, however, on attempting to prove econometrically that the asset substitution effect greatly outweighed the retirement effect and thus that Social Security greatly reduced saving and economic growth. This claim remains hotly contested.[8] Both sides insist that they have marshaled decisive proof—as often happens in econometrics. (We will discuss the reasons for this further in chapter 6.)

However one resolves this dispute—which is not vital to us here—Feldstein's claim probably no longer holds even if it was true when he made it. Under present policy, most current workers should anticipate receiving *less* than the value of their contributions when they retire. It appears, moreover, that workers in recent years have often anticipated receiving even less from Social Security than prevailing policy appeared to offer them. Consider the changes to the system that were enacted in 1983, which, according to Kotlikoff, reduced the present value of benefits due people in the "baby boom" age cohorts by more than $1 trillion current dollars (1992, 3). Even given the bipartisan effort to conceal these changes as fully as possible, one suspects, given

8. Compare Gultekin and Logue 1979 ("The Social Security system adversely affects personal saving. It is not clear whether the primary cause of the adverse effect is due to the prospect of receiving benefits which have a much higher present value than future taxes or because of the contemporaneous social security tax burden" [126–28]) with Eisner 1986 ("The data, after correction of computational errors in Feldstein's original work, do not generally support his argument with regard to social security wealth" [68]).

the lack of public outcry, that the affected individuals had already discounted substantially for the inevitability of policy change. Over time, therefore, and at the cost of arguable distributional unfairness, Social Security—through the refutation of the absurd pretense that it could pay everyone, forever, more than the value of their contributions—has ceased to affect the level of saving as Feldstein claims it long did.

The broader value of Feldstein's contribution lies on separate grounds, however. He showed that Social Security—and any other long-term, ostensibly self-financing spending program—can have the same types of distributional and macroeconomic effects as a budget deficit, even if the program is accumulating current cash-flow surpluses. Thus, no matter why one cares about budget deficits—whether out of concern about default, policy sustainability, the level of saving, Keynesian stimulus, or generational distribution—one should likewise care about such programs' long-term effects. The budget deficit and Social Security debates are not merely similar; they are two parts of the same broader debate.

C. James Buchanan's Political-Institutional Attack on Keynesianism

1. Public Choice Theory and the Virginia School

Through the mid–1970s, the modern deficit debate had focused almost exclusively on macroeconomic and, to a lesser extent, generational issues. The debate widened in the late 1970s to include issues of history and political science, concerning why deficits have become endemic and how they affect the size and character of the national government. These questions were pursued most vigorously by James Buchanan, broadening the attack on public debt that he had prosecuted since the 1950s, along with economists such as Geoffrey Brennan, Robert Tollison, and Robert Wagner. These individuals were often grouped together as members of the "Virginia school" in public choice theory—"Virginia" because they for a time resided at one of that state's universities, and "school" because their often collaborative work expressed and explored a common set of premises.

Public choice theory, along with its cousins rational choice and positive political theory, can be defined as the economic study of public or political decision making. Like microeconomics generally, it attempts to develop strong empirical predictions from parsimonious premises, such as the rational self-interest model of human behavior. It does not require assuming that people have any particular set of preferences, such as for monetary wealth over other goods. Indeed, sometimes alternative motivations, such as ideological altruism, are assumed. While public choice theory does generally require assuming rational utility maximization given whatever preferences people have, even this is but a simplifying assumption that need not be wholly true.

Public choice theory has numerous loosely related branches. One branch studies the difficulties of aggregating preferences appropriately through voting (e.g., Arrow 1963) and the systematic relationships between voting structure and substantive outcomes (e.g., Buchanan and Tullock 1962). Others analyze the consequences of politicians' re-election incentives (e.g., Mayhew 1974) and voters' efforts either to reward ideological proximity to their own views (e.g., Downs 1957) or to maximize transfers received relative to taxes paid (e.g., Tullock 1959). The theory of interest groups examines why government policy often conveys highly concentrated benefits to small, well-organized groups while imposing widely distributed costs on society as a whole (e.g., Olson 1965). The explanation focuses on collective action problems and rational ignorance, which disproportionately affect large groups and those whose members' individual stakes in an issue are small. The economic theory of regulation, an extreme and unnuanced form of interest group theory, treats legislation as a cash commodity that legislators sell at auction to the highest bidders (e.g., McChesney 1987; Doernberg and McChesney 1987; and the critique in Shaviro 1990).

Sometimes, especially in the hands of economists, public choice theory has a theme of exposing collective decision making as generally worse than private market decision making, on two main grounds. First, market actors can implement their own decisions and thus are highly motivated to find out what decision is best. Voters, by contrast, know that their single votes are highly unlikely to be decisive. This induces them to shirk contributing to well-informed decision making, even where the decision is important to them. Second, market actors often internalize most of their decisions' effects, whereas government decisions often have societywide effects. This gives rise to fertile "rent-seeking" opportunities for some to gain wealth transfers from others through the political process (see, e.g., Buchanan 1986a, 229–36). To the claim that collective decision making has the offsetting advantage of inspiring altruistic behavior, these writers respond that people generally are not divided into Dr. Jekyll and Mr. Hyde and thus will act the same in the private and public sectors (McCormick and Tollison 1981, 5), and that altruism is unsustainable because it invites systematic exploitation by other voters (Tullock 1959; 1989).

A view of collective decision making as inherently flawed might suffice to support imposing strict limits on government behavior—perhaps in the area of fiscal policy and perhaps by restricting budget deficits. Yet Buchanan and the other Virginia theorists go considerably further. They argue that government should be viewed as a monolithic "Leviathan" that attempts, with the singlemindedness of a ruthless monopolist, to maximize its revenues. Thus, for example, it seeks every dollar of private wealth that it can reach through taxation or otherwise, and it manipulates the monetary system to devalue its debts by causing unexpected inflation (see Brennan and Buchanan 1977; 1980, 15–16, 28–30). Leviathan is too powerful to be resisted effectively during the course of ordinary politics.

Rather than despair, however, the Virginia theorists draw a distinction between ordinary and "constitutional" politics. In the latter setting, when society is deciding on general operating rules for the political system, both the power of Leviathan and the broader defects of collective decision making are greatly mitigated. Voters recognize that whatever rules are adopted will apply for a long time and in a wide range of circumstances, few of which can be foreseen. Thus, they are not only unusually motivated to participate but are also subject to an almost Rawlsian veil of ignorance, dramatically narrowing the gap between individual and collective well-being.

For a commonplace illustration of the distinction, consider the First Amendment to the Constitution. During ordinary politics, I might favor making my faith the state religion, oppressing rival religions, and suppressing my opponents' speech. In the constitutional setting, however, I must consider the possibility that at some point my opponents will control the government and do these things to me. Since the harm from being oppressed exceeds the benefit of oppressing, and since I cannot predict who will predominate over the long run, I therefore may favor a rule like the First Amendment, reducing everyone's future political discretion. The goal I share with other constitution makers, including those with whom I am in conflict during ordinary politics, is to tie ourselves to the mast so firmly that none can ever hope to escape.

In principle, limiting the government's powers is not the only conceivable constitutional goal. Voters might also, in some settings, want to increase its powers, thus permitting *more* to be accomplished through ordinary politics. Recall, for example, that the main motivation for replacing the Articles of Confederation with the Constitution was to increase the national government's powers, such as by authorizing it to levy taxes. The Virginia theorists argue, however, that voters' main constitutional concern is and should be constraining Leviathan's tendency, irresistible during ordinary politics, to expand far beyond its needed size and thereby to enrich itself at their expense.

2. The Virginia School on Budget Deficits and Related Issues

Perhaps the Virginia school's most prominent broadside regarding the issues raised by budget deficits was the publication in 1977 of James Buchanan and Robert Wagner's *Democracy in Deficit: The Political Legacy of Lord Keynes*. In this book, Buchanan and Wagner argue that Keynes's most serious, though not his only, error was ignoring the effect of democratic political institutions on operationalizing his proposed fiscal policy. In particular, they argue, fiscal illusion and disregard for the welfare of future generations give democracies a bias in favor of debt financing over current tax financing. Once permitted, debt financing reduces the perceived cost of government programs, causing taxpayers to tolerate programs that they would oppose if the costs were more visible. The result is undesirable government expansion.

Buchanan and Wagner argue that debt financing also worsens inflation, which democracies tend to produce in any event through expansionary monetary policy. Voters fail to understand that inflation is a kind of tax. Moreover, many of them benefit in the short run from devaluing existing debt and thus support "easy money" without understanding the feedback effect on interest rates as lenders adjust their inflationary expectations. Buchanan and Wagner assert that the high inflation of the late 1970s reflected fundamental defects in democratic political institutions and should be expected to continue indefinitely barring dramatic institutional reform.

Under this view, one might expect—as it happens, counterfactually—to find both deficits and inflation at high levels throughout American history. Buchanan and Wagner argue, however, that from the American Revolution through the 1930s, a norm of fiscal responsibility and annual budgetary balance—relaxed only in the extraordinary circumstances of war and depression—consistently dominated national politics. The basis for this constraint, which they describe as an unwritten constitutional rule, remains mysterious and unexplained, although they note that economists before Keynes generally endorsed it. Beginning in the 1930s, however, as Keynesianism conquered first the academy and then Washington and taught that budget deficits were not only permissible but good policy, the norm of budgetary balance was gradually (and by the late 1960s completely) relaxed. The inevitable result was annual budget deficits of ever increasing size, leading to a larger federal government and high rates of inflation. They assert that even with the collapse of the Keynesian consensus, the damage had been done and the old unwritten norm of budgetary balance irrevocably destroyed.

Buchanan and Wagner describe Keynesianism's success as proof that ideas have consequences. Even keeping in place all social and political forces that influenced events from the 1930s on, they maintain that both deficits and inflation would be lower today if not for Keynes's "towering . . . presence." Keynesianism was an avoidable "intellectual error of monumental proportion" that had "changed the fiscal constitution in political democracy, and with destructive consequences" (Buchanan and Wagner 1977, 4, 105, 24). Buchanan and Wagner conclude—criticizing yet in a sense flattering their profession—that economists' mistakes, made at least consciously in good faith, had been a crucial event in American political and economic history.

Absent grounds for confidently predicting the imminent revival of the pre-Keynesian norm of budget balance, Buchanan and Wagner advocate changing the legal rules that govern our political institutions, in order to rein in democracy's biases toward deficit and inflation. One model for legal change that one could imagine trying to extend to the budgetary context is that currently used for monetary policy. The Federal Reserve Board, or "Fed," which is empowered to manage the money supply, has independent powers, backed by term appointments of its governors (fourteen years for all but the chairman, who serves for four years). Buchanan and Wagner argue, however, that the Fed's independence is inadequate. As "an established bureaucracy, whose members seek to remain secure in their expected perquisites of office" (123), it can be expected to do the inflationary bidding of elected officials. If the Fed tried to do anything different, its nominal independence would likely be curtailed—as politicians have often threatened.

Therefore, Buchanan and Wagner urge that the requirement of annual fiscal balance take written and legally enforceable form. They advocate a balanced budget amendment to the Constitution, requiring the president to propose and Congress to enact annual budgets that are projected to be in balance. Under the amendment, if budgetary projections proved in error, federal outlays would be automatically reduced as necessary to restore projected balance within three months. Budget surpluses would be used to retire the national debt. A second constitutional amendment would require the Fed to increase the monetary base at the same rate as the national economy's growth in real output, thus providing approximate price stability.

Other works by the Virginia theorists press a similar analysis and agenda. Buchanan and H. Geoffrey Brennan's *Monopoly in Money and Inflation* discusses Leviathan's tendency to use inflation, which devalues existing money and public debt, to maximize its revenues from the monopoly power of money creation. They propose responding with any of several possible constitutional amendments, such as mandating a particular rate of monetary growth, eliminating the government's monopoly over money issuance, or even eliminating its power to issue and regulate money (Brennan and Buchanan 1981, 58–62).

Brennan and Buchanan's "Towards a Tax Constitution for Leviathan" and their book *The Power to Tax* challenge the standard tax policy norm that under certain circumstances the tax base should be as comprehensive as possible. The standard view aims to forestall tax avoidance behavior, such as exploiting loopholes in the tax base, on the ground that such behavior leads to deadweight social loss. Successful tax avoiders reduce their own well-being (since they would have acted differently, taxes aside) without benefiting anyone else. Tax payments, by contrast, merely transfer resources from the individual to the collectivity, rather than reducing them. Tax policy's goal, under the standard approach, is to minimize the "excess burden" of taxation—that is, the excess of the burden imposed on taxpayers over the value that they transfer to the government.

To Brennan and Buchanan, this norm is "institutionally vacuous" (1977, 256) because it ignores government's Leviathan tendency. Thus, they advocate "constitutional" rules that preserve loopholes, thereby keeping open opportunities to engage in tax-avoidance behavior. They regard the standard economic definition of an ideal tax as precisely backward. Once government's relatively minimal legitimate financing needs have been met, the better (if not ideal) tax is one that maximizes excess burden relative to taxes paid, rather than the reverse. Only thus can one limit the growth of Leviathan.

The main example of a base limitation that they analyze is confining the income tax base to money income, thus permitting tax avoidance through nonmarket production (such as by using self-rendered services or substituting leisure for paid work) (256). The argument could equally support replacing the federal income tax with a protectionist tariff on foreign goods. Such a tax would be even more avoidable than the income tax, since most taxpayers can more easily purchase exclusively domestic goods than avoid generating money income through the labor they must engage in to support themselves.

Similarly, Brennan and Buchanan (1980) challenge the "optimal taxation" literature in economics, which seeks to advance the standard goal—minimizing excess burden—by varying, rather than making uniform, the tax treatment of different items. Suppose that the demand for oranges is more price-elastic than that for apples—meaning that if the prices of both increased by the same percentage, orange sales would decline more than apple sales. An optimal tax theorist might propose applying a lower sales tax rate to oranges than to apples, hoping to minimize changes in consumption. Brennan and Buchanan argue, however, that the correct analysis is opposite. They would mandate uniform rates of tax on oranges and apples, in the hope of constraining Leviathan's revenue capacity—much as one might try to constrain a private monopolist by barring price discrimination. Their point follows almost without demonstration once one recognizes that they have simply reversed the standard analysis, making excess burden rather than tax payment the preferred effect of a tax.

3. Problems with the Virginia School Analysis

The work of the Virginia school presents a powerful, cohesive set of arguments, proceeding logically from a clear analytic framework and adding important historical and political science dimensions to the deficit debate. It shows that macroeconomics and generational distribution are not the only relevant issues presented by fiscal policy. Effects on the size and character of government must be considered as well. *Democracy in Deficit* in particular, while written for a popular audience, is a brilliant polemic, filled with shrewd observations and focused on a serious problem—the growth of government resulting from fiscal illusion—to which Buchanan and Wagner propose a solution, the balanced budget amendment, that has ever since attracted serious and widespread attention.

Yet being polemical is a weakness as well as a strength. Viewed favorably, the Virginia theorists make important contributions but have significant limitations. Viewed more harshly, they move from oversimplified diagnosis to obtuse prescriptions. The following are the main shortcomings, which lie, in keeping with their laudably interdisciplinary approach, in the areas of history, political science, and economics.

a. History

An initial problem posed by the Virginia theorists' analysis of budget deficits concerns its accuracy as history. Their account is puzzling on its face. What restrained deficit spending before the Great Depression? The Virginia theorists display no sense of the political and social context in which institutions operate—for example, the Jeffersonian aversion to locating power at the national government level or the political popularity of raising revenues through tariffs in the later nineteenth century.

As for the 1930s, more careful and thorough historical studies of American fiscal policy, such as Herbert Stein's classic *The Fiscal Revolution in America* (published eight years before *Democracy in Deficit*), reveal that Keynes's influence on the Roosevelt administration's gradual and hesitant decision to respond to the depression through regular deficit spending was "at most uncertain and probably marginal" (Stein 1969, 133). The depression created not only automatic budget deficits as income tax revenues fell but also immense political pressures to provide expanded transfer payments in excess of current taxes. It also helped prompt a general ideological shift to the view that capitalism and capitalists needed to be restrained by a much larger and more active national government. Keynesianism reflected this shift but may have been a mere bit player in the overall political and intellectual landscape. Institutional developments, such as irreversible government growth in response to World War II and the shift to income taxation, also surely had greater historical impact on fiscal policy than did Keynesianism.

As for the 1970s, one wonders why deficits increased just as Keynesian fiscal policy lost influence. Some recent scholars have argued that the main cause of increased deficits was the decentralization of political power, as party organizations lost clout when voting patterns changed and the congressional leadership lost clout when institutional "reforms" shifted power to subcommittees (see, e.g., Fitts and Inman 1992). This ostensibly produced greater, more disaggregated logrolling to assemble winning legislative coalitions. Institutional structure therefore mattered more than economic doctrine.

Finally, consider history since the 1970s, and in particular the decline of inflation, which the Virginia theorists argue is endemic in democracies. Evidently, the politically convenient "hidden tax" of inflation ceased to be such. Moreover, the Virginia theorists' view of the Fed soon began to look time-bound. When *Democracy in Deficit* appeared, not only had it failed as yet to respond effectively to inflation but a recent controversy seemed to show that it was merely the tool of elected officials. In 1972, while Arthur Burns was chairman, the Fed had dramatically expanded the money supply, precisely as President Nixon, in his meetings with Burns, was vociferously demanding. The result, to Nixon's delight, was short-term economic expansion that helped his reelection, at the cost of increased inflation shortly thereafter. Burns denied that politics had dictated monetary policy, but he had difficulty explaining the reason for the Fed's actions.

In 1979, Paul Volcker was appointed Fed chairman and began using tight monetary policy to suppress inflation, at the cost of recession. Volcker evidently was indifferent to the short-term political cost to incumbents in both parties—President Carter and congressional Democrats in 1980, and President Reagan's congressional Republican colleagues in 1982. Once the recession had ended while inflation remained low, Volcker became a "folk hero,"[9] and the Fed benefited institutionally. It overcame the stench left by Burns's 1972 policy and by subsequent failures to control inflation, thus decisively putting to rest challenges to its autonomy that had been building in the late 1970s (Krugman 1990, 81–83). Evidently, then, even if the Fed was as politically motivated and accountable as the Virginia theorists claimed, the incentive effects could be anti- as well as pro-inflationary.

Perhaps one should be lenient toward Buchanan and Wagner's natural tendency, as economists, to exaggerate the importance of academic debates within their discipline. Yet the problems with their his-

9. For examples of newspaper articles describing Volcker as a folk hero, see Neikirk 1987; Redburn 1987, 1989; Foell 1986.

torical account raise questions. Can a wrong diagnosis lead to a proper cure? What critical factors have they ignored, with what consequences?

b. Political Science

As political science, the Virginia theorists' work is flawed in its account of both ends and means. The ends problem is that the Leviathan model is implausible—although this matters less than one might expect, since a more conventional public choice perspective similarly supports limiting the size of government. The means problem is more serious. The Virginia theorists ignore the importance of how political institutions are structured—a surprising omission, given Buchanan's own seminal contributions to institutional public choice theory (see, e.g., Buchanan and Tullock 1962). They thereby fail to show that their proposals would work or even go in the direction of limiting government.

Starting with ends, the Leviathan model lacks a clear theoretical basis. Brennan and Buchanan argue that it follows simply from assuming self-interested behavior by government officials, and they compare their approach to studying monopoly under the assumption that monopolists are selfish profit maximizers (1980, 16; 1981, 15–16). They overlook the significance of the government's being run by a multiplicity of individuals, holding office only temporarily and lacking the power to bequeath their positions (like corporate stock) to heirs. A conventional public choice perspective suggests that this gives rise to severe agency costs. Officeholders seem likely to focus on their own private agendas and to "shirk" pursuing the government's revenue interest. Consider a politician who gains reelection by declining to seek unpopular tax increases, leading over time to lower government spending if there is an upper bound on permissible budget deficits.

While conceding that agency costs present a problem for the Leviathan model, Brennan and Buchanan suggest that perhaps revenue maximization "emerges from the interaction of the whole set of governmental decision makers even if no person explicitly sets maximum revenue as the goal of his own action" (1980, 29). They note William Niskanen's theory of bureaucracy, which treats budget maximization as a plausible utility function for bureaucrats and argues that even "a bureaucrat who may not be personally motivated to maximize the budget of his bureau is usually driven by conditions both internal and external to the bureau to do just that" (Niskanen 1971, 39). Brennan and Buchanan fail to recognize, however, that even if federal agencies generally attempt to maximize their budgets, the federal government as a whole may not act from such a standpoint.

Niskanen discusses the techniques available to bureaucracies to increase their funding, such as playing off Congress against the president or catering to congressional committees. He also notes Congress's frequent tendency to demand that agencies expand popular programs. In his model, however, Congress and executive officials perform an active review function regarding bureaucracies' demands for more resources and agree to these demands only when they regard the expected added output as worth the extra cost (36–42). Given the political authorities' control over taxes and spending, one cannot make the leap from bureaucrats' revenue maximization to an overall tendency of government. Bureaucracies, to a large extent, are engaged in a zero-sum game among themselves.

More recent studies of administrative agencies have tended, if anything, to go beyond Niskanen in emphasizing Congress's exercise of ultimate control. Political scientists such as Matthew McCubbins, Roger Noll, and Barry Weingast have shown how Congress overcomes its limited oversight capacity by designing agencies' administrative procedures with an eye to the outcomes it prefers (e.g., Weingast and Moran 1983; McCubbins, Noll, and Weingast 1989). A credible Leviathan theory would have to explain congressional and presidential, more than bureaucratic, behavior.

All plausible models of politicians' behavior emphasize goals, such as reelection, that do not consistently correlate with revenue maximization (see, e.g., Mayhew 1974; Fenno 1973). Consider Congress's tradition of underfunding the Internal Revenue Service even when added funds would likely more than pay for themselves through added tax revenues. Or consider that since the federal income tax became a mass tax with the onset of World War II, legislative changes to the Internal Revenue Code have usually lowered taxes (Witte 1985, 249–51). To increase revenues, Congress likes to rely on automatic methods that leave few fingerprints. An example is bracket creep, which results when tax brackets are not indexed for inflation and therefore taxpayers whose nominal, but not real, income has increased enter higher rate brackets. While the Virginia theorists would not be discomfited by this example of fiscal illusion—which Buchanan in particular has long emphasized—they cannot explain why rate brackets have been indexed for inflation since 1981, thus putting an end to bracket creep. The adoption and retention of indexing show Congress "shirking," from the standpoint of revenue maximization, at the expense of the future Congresses that would benefit most from automatic rate increases.

The Leviathan model therefore seems implausible as a basis for setting the goals of constitutional politics. Nonetheless, one could argue more modestly, and on more conventional public choice grounds, for limiting the government's size. Again, interest group theory predicts that collective action problems will lead, through the mechanism of government policy, to pervasive, societally costly transfers to small, well-organized groups. Reducing the size of government might reduce the harm caused by such transfers. While collective action problems can also yield too little government—since no one may have sufficient incentive to demand general public goods—one can certainly argue that, at the margin, reducing the size of government would do more good than harm. (We will examine these issues further in chapter 7.)

Accordingly, the Virginia theorists' goal of reducing the size of government is plausible, although their argument for it is not. This brings us, however, to the problem of means. Is reducing Congress's discretion to incur budget deficits and the Fed's discretion to direct monetary policy likely to prove effective? Constitutional requirements are not meaningful unless enforced—presumably by the courts. Yet the Virginia theorists fail to explain why the courts, unlike the Federal Reserve Board, will resist contemporary political pressure. Moreover, if one asserts that the courts can and will resist such pressure—noting, for example, that they generally uphold the First Amendment—then one has acknowledged the importance of *institutional design* (since otherwise the courts would act no differently from Congress). This crucial element is one that the Virginia theorists' work on budget deficits and monetary policy generally ignores.

Consider the structure of the Federal Reserve Board. Why has it been granted nominal independence to begin with? The answer, perhaps—public-spiritedness aside—is that elected politicians actually benefit from being able credibly to deny that they are controlling monetary policy. The Reagan White House, while frequently criticizing Chairman Volcker's contractionary policy and trying to make him (or President Carter) bear the blame for the 1982 recession, made no real effort to stop him (Krugman 1990, 58). Conceivably, the White House was glad to have an independent Fed pursue a policy that it could not itself pursue at an affordable political cost. In the public choice literature, it is well known that politicians often shun, rather than seek, responsibility for controversial decisions. They understand that responsibility can bring blame.

Why, however, should the Fed act any differently from how Congress would act if it directly controlled monetary policy? Here again, a closer institutional analysis provides the answer. To begin with, Fed officials other than the chairman serve longer terms than any national elected official. Even the Fed chairman, with his four-year term, often expects to return to a business or academic career rather than serve as a lifelong government officeholder. Fed officials therefore may have longer time horizons than politicians and may cater to a constituency that places special weight on quelling inflation or simply (for reasons of prestige) on showing a firm and effective hand.

Differences in internal design may be even more important than those in motivation. The Fed is run by a small group of governors, making it far more centralized than the bicameral, committee-run, 535-member Congress. In general, centralized decision makers can more readily pursue coherent policies, and resist concessions to interest groups, than decentralized ones, which need extensive logrolling to assemble a voting majority. Suppose that Congress had controlled monetary policy in the early 1980s but that—to mirror its conduct of fiscal policy—in practice it decided case by case how much money to lend, at what rates of interest, to each prospective borrower. Can anyone doubt that it would have sharply expanded the money supply, notwithstanding the public demand for an end to high rates of inflation?

The Virginia theorists' failure to address institutional design in their work on budget deficits and monetary policy is all the more disappointing given the work of an earlier political theorist from Virginia—James Madison—that is central to our political and constitutional tradition. Madison's main claim, made eloquently in the *Federalist Papers*[10] and reflected at numerous points in the Constitution—as in the separation of powers among the executive, legislative, and judicial branches and the creation of a bicameral legislature—was that disaggregating decision-making powers among rival institutions was crucial to preventing majoritarian tyranny. This claim is the opposite of the modern political science tradition favoring centralization. A

10. Hamilton, Madison, and Jay 1961. See especially papers 10 and 51 (Madison).

centralized authority's power to pursue coherent policies and override particular groups' objections inevitably risks promoting policy instability and the imposition of extreme or tyrannical policies.

Today, many political scientists disagree with Madison on the centralization tradeoff, for two main reasons. First, reflecting the differences between our political environment and that of the 1780s, they are less concerned about tyranny or instability and more about policy incoherence. Second, Madison thought a disaggregated government would do less, given the difficulties of assembling majority coalitions. Today, disaggregation seems to lead to *more* laws and *more* particularized benefits, because now each interest group can demand something, and each politician can fruitfully pursue his or her own set of legislative initiatives. Whatever side one takes in this debate about centralization, it is far more important than the Virginia theorists recognize. Without greater centralization in the exercise of legislative authority, the constitutional changes that they advocate might be ineffective. With it, the changes might be unnecessary.

c. Economics

The most serious problem with the Virginia theorists' work on budget deficits is economic. In advocating a balanced budget rule to constrain Leviathan (or, if one prefers, interest group transfers), they confuse labels with underlying economic substance. Neither eliminating the budget deficit nor reducing government spending (by increasing its perceived cost through the elimination of debt financing) has the straightforward implications that the Virginia theorists assume.

We have already seen one of the deficit's failings as an economic measure: it does not accrue future spending obligations under programs such as Social Security and Medicare. These programs, no less than current deficit spending, may induce fiscal illusion, transfer wealth from future to present voters, and affect resource allocation. As we will see below, the deficit's lack of accrual accounting barely scratches the surface of its flaws as an economic measure. Because of these flaws, a host of devices—such as slightly changing the timing of taxes or spending, selling government assets, or relabeling taxes and transfers as "loans" and "repayments"—can be used to manipulate the deficit without actually reducing spending over the long run.

Suppose that we could somehow be certain that adherence to this manipulable measure would lead to some actual reductions in government spending, not just to smoke-and-mirrors changes. Now the measurement problem would shift to the issue of whether Leviathan, or the magnitude of interest group transfers, had actually been affected. "Government spending" is itself an arbitrary label, correlating only crudely, at best, with the actual size of government or the scope of government activity.

An initial problem with equating spending levels and the size of government arises from the arbitrariness of the distinction between "taxes" and "spending." Stanley Surrey (1973) first made the point that certain income tax rules—say, the statutory exclusion for interest on municipal bonds—could accurately be termed "tax expenditures," because their effect and intent closely resembled that of following the "normal" income tax rule (here, taxing interest income) and giving cash subsidies to municipal bondholders. While tax expenditure analysis has always been controversial—mainly because Surrey linked it to a separate debate about the ideal tax base (see, e.g., Bittker 1969; Thuronyi 1988; Griffith 1989; Kahn and Lehman 1992)—the underlying claim about the interchangeability of tax and spending rules is clearly correct. David Bradford makes the point by describing the following tongue-in-cheek "secret plan" to eliminate the budget deficit by cutting "spending" rather than raising taxes:

> Step 1 of the Bradford Plan is to cut the weapons procurement appropriation to zero. Taken by itself, step 1 would harm the defense effort. Step 2, designed to offset this unfortunate effect, calls for the enactment of a new "weapons supply tax credit" (WSTC). To qualify for the WSTC, manufacturers . . . deliver to the appropriate depots [the] weapons . . . previously specified under procurements contracts. . . . Step 2 is, of course, a tax cut.
>
> Taken by themselves, steps 1 and 2 result in equal cuts in spending and taxes. But a time of budget deficits is a time to be cutting spending, not taxes. Step 3 of the Bradford Plan, then, rounds out the tax program into a "revenue neutral" reform by [raising income taxes in the amount of the WSTC "tax cut"]. (1988, 10–11)

In the end under the "Bradford Plan," the only *real* change would be the Step 3 tax increase. For formal measurement purposes, however, "taxes" would have remained constant overall, and "spending" would have decreased. While the example may seem preposterous, Bradford notes that its "basic logic is very close to what one sees in actual budget politics." Thus, various proposed tax cuts from the 1995–96 budget debate would affect resource allocation and wealth distribution in much the same way as explicit spending and likely took the form they did purely for formalistic or perceptual reasons.

A second problem with equating spending levels to the size of government arises from the close similarity between spending on the one hand and regulatory mandates on the other. For purposes of affecting private behavior, or imposing costs and benefits through government policy, it does not matter whether the government's directives are executed by its own paid employees (the spending route) or by private individuals acting under threat of regulatory sanction. Indeed, the choice between explicit government spending and reliance on regulatory mandates often depends purely on considerations of political and administrative convenience. Consider the Americans with Disabilities Act of 1992, mandating many billions of dollars of private expenditures to provide adequate building access and job opportunities to the disabled. Whatever its merits, the ADA expanded the federal government's reach in a manner not reflected in direct government expenditures. Or consider the minimum wage—in substance, a wage subsidy for low-wage employees, financed by a tax on their employers—or the Clinton administration's ambitious 1994 health-care reform plan, which used employer mandates in lieu of explicit taxes and spending to give employees specified health insurance packages.

A third problem with equating spending levels to the size of government arises from the radical differences, in meaningful size-of-government terms, between same-dollar spending programs. Suppose that Social Security were a pure annuity program, simply providing people with the interest-adjusted value of their contributions. Its effects on distribution and behavior would become far smaller than at present, even if the dollar amounts involved remained the same. Suppose instead that one revised the present Social Security system to offer beneficiaries specified in-kind benefits, such as government-furnished food and housing, rather than cash. Now the system's imprint on the economy and people's lives might grow considerably larger.

The same point holds for same-dollar tax provisions. Suppose that Congress decided to slash tax revenues by $20 billion per year but had not decided whether this should involve providing special tax benefits to farmers or enacting across-the-board rate reductions. Plainly, the former option would increase the tax system's effect on wealth distribution and resource allocation, while the latter would reduce it.

As all these problems show, what one would need to make the analysis meaningful is an underlying norm for measuring the size of government. This suggests focusing on the actual effects that government policy has—perhaps with reference to one's particular reasons for concern about the size of government. A libertarian might want to focus on effects on individual freedom. A devotee of economic efficiency might want to focus on effects on resource allocation. An opponent of government-sponsored wealth redistribution might want to focus on the distributional effects of government policy.[11]

The Virginia theorists fail to do any of this, however, or even to recognize that it is necessary. Indeed, they show their misunderstanding when they treat the imposition of excess burden through taxation as an *alternative* to feeding Leviathan rather than as an example of Leviathan at work. The example of tariffs on foreign goods, set at such punitive levels that no goods are imported and thus no revenue raised, helps to make their error clear. Is a government that in effect bars imports through punitive tariffs—or, for that matter, that simply bars them outright—really the kind of small government, having only minimal effects on liberty, efficiency, or wealth distribution, that opponents of Leviathan should want? Plainly not. Excess burden is a kind of tax burden. Excess government is merely a variety (and a cause) of resource waste.

In the end, therefore, the Virginia theorists have made an important but limited contribution to the deficit debate. They deserve much credit for reintroducing long-ignored size-of-government concerns and for reviving the plausible claim that budget deficits increase government spending by reducing its perceived cost. Yet the Virginia theorists fail to show that requiring annual budgetary balance, and thus making but one of the government's many tools politically costlier to exercise, would actually lead to a smaller government rather than simply to changes in the relative usage of alternative tools. Their analysis ends where it ought to begin.

11. In each of these cases, the analysis would involve a "baseline" problem. Since one cannot tell what society would look like if the government did not exist, one would need to specify an assumed starting point from which to measure departures.

D. Robert Eisner and the Problems of Accurately Measuring the Deficit and Public Debt

1. Beyond the Cash-Flow Budget Deficit

By the late 1970s, both Barro and Feldstein had pointed the way to questioning the budget deficit's adequacy as an economic measure. They had noted that giving retirees benefits in excess of the value of their contributions under Social Security (even if it runs a current cash-flow surplus and is solvent over the long run) may affect generational distribution in the same way as giving current taxpayers benefits in excess of their taxes through debt-financed government spending.

Broader insights about the budget deficit's adequacy as a fiscal policy measure did not emerge immediately. Only in the early 1980s did economists begin extensively and directly addressing its limitations. Michael Boskin (1982), for example, noted that it fails to account either for changes in the value of the government's real and financial assets or for various off-budget commitments such as loan guarantees. Various other writers addressed smaller pieces of the problem, such as the difference between the nominal value of outstanding public debt and its market value. Increased interest rates can cause old debt's market value to be less than its nominal value, and inflation can cause such debt to lose real value even if its nominal value remains unchanged (see, e.g., Seater 1981; Cox and Hirschhorn 1983).

Once economists had begun to critique in detail how the deficit is computed, a number of problems jumped out. Recall the problem of long-term Social Security solvency, as distinct from benefiting present program participants at the expense of future ones. The budget deficit ignores the increasing present value of an approaching shortfall. If I kept my own accounts this way and someone paid me $50,000 today in exchange for a promise to pay him $1 million next year, my current-year "deficit" would seem to have declined by $50,000, although in fact my fiscal position would have grown far worse. At least, this would be the effect if I chose not to label the transaction a loan. If I chose the "loan" label, then my current-year computations would ignore the transaction altogether and thus show no change—achieving only slightly greater accuracy. The problems therefore were twofold: the "loan" label could be applied or withheld arbitrarily, leading to different current-year measurements; and either way, I could misrepresent the year's changes to my long-term financial condition.

Or suppose that I sold a million-dollar house for only $50,000. Under most versions of the measure, my deficit would again decline by $50,000 despite the foolishness of the transaction. By contrast, if I managed to acquire a million-dollar house for only $50,000, then my deficit would *increase* by that amount despite the transaction's benefits.

These problems were no mere idle hypotheticals. During the 1980s, Congress's use of smoke-and-mirrors games to accomplish nominal deficit reduction made them seem increasingly pertinent. Other smoke-and-mirrors games involved trivially changing cash flows to reduce current deficits—for example, postponing military paydays for a day to place them in the next fiscal year, or adopting tax rules that would slightly increase current revenues at a substantial long-term cost. Equivalent transactions for a business might involve offering ridiculously large prepayment discounts to customers and deferral premiums to creditors, all ostensibly in the interest of financial responsibility.

Many of the same problems that afflicted the deficit's adequacy as a measure applied as well to the national debt. That measure includes only explicit debt obligations, evidenced by government bonds and the like. One could argue, however, that future spending commitments under a program such as Social Security—which the national debt ignores—are not entirely different, even if the expectation of repayment is less definite.

With regard to the budget deficit, there also was the problem of its serving multiple purposes. Perhaps one measure was appropriate for purposes of measuring Keynesian stimulus; a second for imposing Virginia school—type constraints on government spending; a third for estimating fiscal policy's impact on generational wealth distribution; and a fourth for evaluating whether present fiscal policy, without tax increases or spending cuts, was likely to prove sustainable.

For any of these purposes, perhaps in varying degree, the right answer might involve shifting from a cash-flow measure to one that employed economic accrual, in the sense of including future expected revenues or outlays at their interest-adjusted present value. Or the right answer might involve examining people's subjective perceptions of the taxes and transfers that they could expect to bear and receive over time, as opposed to estimating fiscal policy's objective character under present law and policy. The subjective and objective measures might differ as a result of people's myopia and fiscal illusion on the one hand or their farsighted anticipation of policy changes on the other.

These issues left a need and an opportunity for substantial intellectual innovation. In the mid–1980s, Robert Eisner became the first economist to suggest a comprehensive response. He began advocating a revised deficit measure with elements of both cash-flow and economic accrual, and reflecting explicit surmises about fiscal policy's effect on people's perceptions. Eisner's work is very much a product of his own intellectual starting point and of the purposes he saw the deficit measure as serving.

Eisner is a relatively traditional Keynesian. Dismayed by Keynesianism's loss of public and academic acceptance in the 1970s, he believes that the crucial blow was the occurrence of recession with high unemployment during periods when the budget deficit, as conventionally measured, was unprecedentedly high. He seeks, therefore, to show that deficits, as correctly measured, actually do have the stimulative and employment-promoting effects that Keynesianism predicts.

Unlike some Keynesians, he rejects money illusion and "sticky wages" as explanations for sustained unemployment. Instead, he focuses exclusively on inadequate demand for market consumption, resulting from people's fear-based efforts to save too much. He proposes to sketch "a new 'Keynesian-neoclassical synthesis'" (Eisner 1986, 5) by "infus[ing the Keynesian model] with the traditional neoclassical emphasis on the role of real wealth and abhorrence of money illusion" (xiii). The model remains purely Keynesian, however, in its view not only of saving but also of people's disregarding the wealth effects of the future taxes that deficit spending arguably implies.

To Eisner, "true" deficits remain the way to make people feel wealthier and spend more, thus eliminating Keynesian involuntary unemployment. He believes, moreover, that such unemployment is enormously important, relative both to noncyclical or "structural" unemployment that calls for quite different policy responses (such as reducing regulatory and tax burdens on the employment relationship) and to the risk of inflation. Involuntary unemployment represents pure waste from a societal standpoint, not just a problem of wealth distribution or social peace and morale.

Eisner considers debt-financed government programs wealth-enhancing for both spending and financing reasons. On the spending side, he views government investment expenditure, such as constructing roads and airports, improving health and education, and paying for research and development, as the main source of societal capital formation (154). Indeed, he argues that GDP tends to understate the value of government spending, since it counts only market inputs, such as the salaries paid to schoolteachers, whereas if the government sold the end products (such as education) in arm's-length transactions, GDP would also include the government's return to capital and creation of value above the cost of its market inputs. The opposite argument—that GDP overstates the value of government spending, since absent revealed preferences from market transactions, we cannot be certain that the goods produced are worth their production cost—he rejects as a mere "value judgment" that national income measures should avoid (Eisner 1994, 25–26).

Yet Eisner does not believe that government programs need to be more productive than private investment in order to be worthwhile. Under his Keynesian view, society is simply wasting substantial resources as long as the economy is short of full employment. Thus, government spending increases societal wealth if it yields *any* positive value. Suppose that the government is considering building a road that will cost $100 million in real resources (such as labor, trucks, and concrete). A neoclassical economist might ask whether this use of the resources is better than the uses (including leisure) that would result if they remained in private hands. To Eisner, however, the spending is worthwhile (whether or not the best available choice) even if the road is worth only $1 million upon completion, and even disregarding Keynesian stimulative effects. Wasting 99 percent of the resources' value is better than losing them all.

All this goes only to the virtues of government spending, without regard to how it is financed. Yet Eisner also values debt financing without regard to how the money is spent. Its main benefit is the Keynesian one of increasing perceived wealth and consumer spending, thus permitting the attainment of a universally preferred higher-consumption equilibrium. He argues that debt financing also has collateral benefits. For example, it involves lower transaction costs and default risk than the private borrowing that would replace some of it if people had to pay more current taxes. Moreover, it avoids the excess burden that current taxes would generate by motivating people to engage in tax-avoidance transactions (50–53). Debt financing does not induce people to assume greater future taxes that they eventually will want to avoid, because public debt can be sustained indefinitely.

Thus, in Eisner's view, the positive effect of debt financing on perceived wealth is no mere fiscal illusion. Government decisions to borrow rather than tax actually make people wealthier. He sees only two upward limits on the amount of public borrowing that is desirable. First, as the economy approaches full employment, deficits may prove unduly inflationary rather than stimulative. Second, if there were so much public debt that the average American family felt too wealthy to need to work, then labor production in the society would collapse (Eisner 1986, 54–56). He notes that we are far from this point, however. Eisner treats debt financing's wealth effect on the choice between leisure and work as an all-or-nothing proposition and fails to explain why the wealth effect ordinarily influences only the choice between consumption and attempted saving.

Again, Eisner's Keynesianism may seem to beg the question of why we have recently experienced recessions and high unemployment levels during years of high deficits. Here, however, he finally turns from pure Keynesianism to the promised neoclassical synthesis and draws on his acceptance of the rational expectations claim that illusion does not systematically shape economic behavior. He understands that the conventional debt and deficit are merely nominal measures, based on cash flow rather than on real economic values, and thus that they may differ from the measures that rational actors would take into account. He argues that we therefore need to develop measures that are more economically meaningful and perceptually realistic.

Unfortunately, he seems to have undertaken this process of measuring the real debt and deficit with a preconceived bias. Given his commitment to traditional Keynesian certitudes about unemployment, saving, and demand, Eisner thinks it simply must be the case that we have not had large deficits and growing national debt over the last twenty years. Otherwise, the economic results would be inexplicable. His conviction that we are failing to enact worthwhile government programs out of misguided fear about their affordability pushes him in the same direction. Thus, he tends to accept plausible downward adjustments to the deficit and national debt while rejecting plausible upward adjustments, even when the arguments for the two are similar.

2. Eisner on the Propriety of Various Adjustments to Our Measure of the Deficit and National Debt

This brings us to the most important and original part of Eisner's work: his proposed changes to the budget deficit. He makes two very different kinds of points, relating to his advocacy of debt financing, no matter how spent, and government spending, no matter how financed. He thus essentially proposes two distinct measures.

a. Correcting the Deficit Measure for Purposes of Measuring Keynesian Fiscal Stimulus

For purposes of Keynesian fiscal stimulus, Eisner proposes two main adjustments to the budget deficit, one substantive and one merely computational.

i. Inflation adjustment. The substantive change is a downward adjustment to take account of inflation's effect on the value of outstanding government debt. Suppose that at a time of zero inflation, both current and expected, I lend the government $100 for ten years at 3 percent interest. Suddenly, all prices go up by 10 percent, and expectations change to reflect the view that 10 percent annual inflation will now prevail indefinitely. Now, even if I had $100 cash, its purchasing power would equal only $90 in pre-inflation terms. What is worse, however, I do not have the cash. Instead, I must wait ten years for it, during which time my money will be "earning" at a real interest rate of minus 7 percent. My 3 percent bond—unlike new bonds, which, all else being equal, might now have to offer 13 percent interest—is worth only about $43 in pre-inflation terms.

Eisner expects government bondholders to understand inflation rather than suffering from money illusion. Thus, if the government has a $40 billion budget deficit, which it finances by selling new bonds, but inflation reduces the value of old bonds by $35 billion, then bondholders in the aggregate will understand that the value of their holdings has increased by only $5 billion. Thus, $5 billion, not $40 billion, is the true stimulative budget deficit.

The inflation adjustment can have huge arithmetic effects. Between 1977 and 1980, Eisner notes, inflation caused federal bondholders to suffer a $53 billion loss in the market value of their debt instruments (14). This amount offset nearly 30 percent of the federal budget deficit that was reported for the period. Eisner therefore concludes that fiscal policy during this period was not nearly as stimulative as most people, responding to what were then unprecedentedly large nominal deficits, had supposed.

This proposed change seems clearly appropriate for purposes of measuring the stimulative budget deficit. Bondholders have ample motive and opportunity to avoid persistent money illusion. What about for other purposes that the deficit measure may serve? The change appears equally relevant to gauging the generational impact and long-term sustainability of government fiscal policy. To the extent of inflation, the value of repayment to bondholders declines, along with its real cost to the government. For purposes of constraining the size of government, however, the adjustment may be inappropriate. Inflation is a tax that can make government spending seem cheaper than it really is.

ii. Basing computations on the high-employment deficit. The second adjustment to the stimulative deficit that Eisner proposes is merely computational. It relates to his purpose of trying to establish empirical correlations between the inflation-adjusted budget deficit on the one hand and observed levels of unemployment and economic growth on the other. Eisner argues that we must avoid confusing what really interests us, the deficit's effect on the economy, with the economy's effect on the deficit. The latter is a problem because economic slowdowns, no matter what their cause, tend to increase the deficit, as by reducing income tax revenues and increasing social insurance payouts. These effects cause deficits to be associated statistically with recession even if they counter it—just as police may be found primarily in high crime areas even if they deter, rather than encourage, crime.

Accordingly, following familiar econometric procedure, Eisner seeks to corroborate the stimulative effect of deficits by analyzing not the actual inflation-adjusted deficit but a counterfactual and hypothetical number: the high employment deficit, equaling what the actual inflation-adjusted deficit might have been had unemployment been only, say, 4, 5, or 6 percent. On this basis, he claims to show that deficits (as adjusted) really *were* larger during the 1960s, with their relatively high growth and low unemployment, than during the 1970s, with their worse performance in both respects. He has more trouble explaining why the 1980s, which had higher deficits than either of the two preceding decades even on an inflation-adjusted, high-employment basis, should have featured higher unemployment and slower growth than the 1960s.

Eisner is correct that without this adjustment, data showing that deficits correlate with recession, rather than with expansion and increased job levels, would be misleading. Yet the adjustment may nonetheless be problematical. He attempts to deduce people's perceived wealth from a counterfactual state of affairs, relating to the taxes they would pay and the transfer payments they would receive if only things were different. Not all problems in meaningful statistical measurement have good solutions.

In any event, his empirical claim that deficits over the last few decades have actually fit the Keynesian pattern is widely regarded as unconvincing. Even concerning the 1960s and 1970s, his use of the data has been criticized as technically crude and simplistic. He does not control for certain factors, such as policy changes in response to recession, that could lead to spurious correlations based simply on the boom-and-bust business cycle. As B. Douglas Bernheim puts it, "those who are sympathetic with his evidence will also agree that policy makers should endeavor to reduce national income, in that national income is negatively correlated with future growth of national income" (1989, 70).

iii. Adjustments to the stimulative budget deficit that Eisner rejects.

Thus far, we have examined only the adjustments (both downward) to the stimulative deficit that Eisner accepts. Equally important, however, are the upward adjustments that he rejects, as he must in order to explain why recent large nominal deficits have not proved more stimulative. The main such adjustment relates to unfunded future Social Security benefits—the annual increase in value of which might be included in an economic accrual version of the budget deficit. One might think that the expectation of receiving future Social Security benefits, like the expectation that one's government bonds will be repaid, would increase perceived wealth and thus current consumer spending.

Eisner rejects this adjustment on the ground that the commitment to make the future payments promised under present Social Security law is more contingent than the commitment to repay explicit public debt. Yet while it surely makes sense to assume that prospective retirees would discount for the risk of a change in policy leading to nonpayment, how can a 100 percent discount be justified? Eisner has only this to say:

> [C]onstruction of measures of government commitments that go beyond net current liabilities would take us into uncharted and unfathomable waters. The task would face huge uncertainty regarding the anticipated tax receipts to meet the commitments. One not implausible assumption . . . is that we can

expect taxes generally to be adjusted so that the net actuarial value of government obligations and the taxes to pay for them will approximate zero. They would then contribute nothing to an enlarged measure of the deficit, or to the public's perception of its net wealth. (1986, 38; emphasis omitted)

Whatever happened to Eisner's usual assumption that people ignore the prospect of future tax increases? Why not assume, in keeping with his general methodology, that unfunded Social Security benefits can and will be debt-financed, even though Social Security law presently mandates that the system break even? Once we decide to assume future tax increases (or benefit cuts), why continue assuming that other government programs will be indefinitely debt-financed and thus that taxes need not and probably will not go up (or that other expected benefits will be reduced)? Moreover, while one can understand Eisner's concern about "uncharted and unfathomable waters" once we start accounting for contingencies, he does not adequately address the concern that ignoring contingencies makes his measure of the stimulative deficit unacceptably inaccurate.

As an empirical matter, Eisner has some support, at least for the early 1980s, for his claim that people ignore the value of the unfunded Social Security benefits that they would receive under current policy. As he notes, changes to the system in 1983 that enormously reduced the value of projected benefits—according to Laurence Kotlikoff, costing "baby boomers" more than $1 trillion current dollars (Kotlikoff 1992, 3)—were largely ignored by voters and consumers, perhaps because they had already wholly discounted the benefits on the ground that current policy was unsustainable (Eisner 1994, 129). Considered more broadly, however, this example hurts, rather than helps, Eisner's contention that as a general matter, no substantive adjustment other than for inflation is necessary.

Again, recall that in 1983, the Democratic and Republican parties carefully colluded to ensure that neither could blame the other for reducing Social Security benefits. This suggests that people could have been led to believe that the changes reduced their well-being, unless no one prominent made the argument. Moreover, consider the Nixon-Mills initiative in 1972 vastly to increase unfunded Social Security benefits on the eve of a presidential election that both of them hoped to win. This change was widely regarded by commentators as making people better off, and essentially no one complained that it would prove unsustainable without tax increases.

Perhaps, then, in 1972 though not 1983, unfunded Social Security benefits were a part of people's current perceived wealth. The eleven-year gap saw a gradual loss of faith in the stability of Social Security policy. More generally, in measuring fiscal policy's affect on perceived wealth, one cannot uniformly exclude—or, for that matter, include—unfunded future benefits that present policy seems to promise. Perceptions are too variable for any one methodology or set of assumptions to be correct all the time.

b. Correcting the Deficit and Debt Measures for Purposes of Assessing Changes in the Government's Long-Run Solvency under Present Policies

Thus far, I have discussed only the adjustments to the deficit that Eisner considers for purposes of measuring Keynesian fiscal stimulus. This part of his work aims to be scientific and precise, in the sense of asserting specific correlations between government fiscal policy and national economic performance. A second part of his work concerning deficits is more general and hortatory. It aims to reassure people who are concerned—however misguidedly, under Eisner's broader assumptions—about the affordability of desirable government spending.

To people with such concerns, Eisner in effect says: "Suppose that you reject my claims that vastly increasing both public debt and government spending are good in themselves and believe instead that government spending programs, even if otherwise desirable, cannot prudently be contemplated if they leave too large a tax bill for the future. Even under this too-cautious view, you should agree with me that we can afford substantial new spending that is debt-financed. Realistic economic measures of the deficit and national debt, as distinct from the nominal measures that have received so much attention, suggest that the government is well within the limits that would be prudent even for a private business that lacked the power to raise taxes or print money."

To this end, Eisner proposes a set of additional adjustments to the deficit measure that, while not affecting perceived wealth, help to indicate the long-term sustainability of current fiscal policy. One could describe these adjustments as yielding a "sustainability deficit," as distinct from the Keynesian stimulative deficit. Since the sustainability deficit serves merely rhetorical purposes, Eisner does not attempt to measure or even define it precisely. He is satisfied if he can support the broad claim that the government's fiscal obligations have not been growing appreciably in recent years relative to available resources.

i. Appreciation of government assets. Eisner argues that for the government no less than a private business, a meaningful fiscal evaluation must take account of both sides of the balance sheet. Increases in the market value of publicly owned assets improve the government's fiscal position no less than reductions in the market value of its liabilities. Thus, for any year, such appreciation should be counted as reducing the sustainability deficit.

This adjustment's effects can be enormous, particularly during periods of high inflation. During the 1970s, for example, when federal deficits, as conventionally measured, totaled about $314 billion (see Savage 1988, 12), federally owned structures, equipment, inventory, and land alone increased in value by more than $500 billion (see Eisner 1986, 28–29). Thus, in effect, the federal government ran a large surplus for the decade and substantially improved its fiscal position, even if one disregards its other assets such as gold.

In keeping with this focus on the value of federally held assets, Eisner cogently criticizes treating federal asset sales—for example, of mineral rights or loan portfolios—as deficit-reducing. This practice reminds Eisner "of the story of my late father-in-law, who unwisely tried to open a law practice in the gloom of 1932. 'Had a good day in the office,' he quipped as he came home one night. 'Sold my desk!' " (34).

The adjustment plainly makes some sense, especially for purposes of measuring present fiscal policy's sustainability. In some cases, however, government asset appreciation may tell us little about the likelihood of future tax increases or spending cuts. Consider assets that have symbolic significance, such as the Lincoln Memorial, or that are necessary to government functioning, such as federal office buildings and strategic oil reserves. They seem unlikely to be sold in order to raise needed cash. Thus, their appreciation might have little practical effect on the future course of fiscal policy.

ii. Capital accounting. Private businesses generally use capital accounting, which distinguishes between expenditures whose value is consumed in the current year and those that create more lasting value. The former are expensed, or currently deducted in full, while the latter are depreciated or amortized over the useful lives of the assets (whether tangible or intangible) that have been created. For the purchase of an asset such as land that is not expected to depreciate at all, one generally does not deduct anything as long as one continues to hold the asset.

Rational individuals who are assessing their financial positions do much the same thing as a business, even if less formally. They commonly recognize, for example, that losing $500,000 at the racetrack is quite different from spending it to buy a home; and that higher education may bring future wages that exceed its current-year cost in tuition and forgone wages.

The government follows no such method in computing the federal deficit. For deficit purposes, all outlays (other than repaying debt principal) are expensed or treated in full as current-year costs. Thus, an expenditure of $10 billion to build a federal office building that will last for fifty years receives the same treatment as spending that amount on Fourth of July fireworks. Costs of educating children to make them more productive workers through the middle of the next century are treated no differently from paying pensions to elderly war veterans.

Adjusting the deficit measure to make use of capital accounting would have large computational effects. Eisner notes that during the mid-1980s, the federal budget deficit was roughly equal to the amount that the Office of Management and Budget classified as "investment-type outlays" that "yield long-term benefits." He argues, therefore, that "all of the federal budget deficit, and more, is accounted for by investment" (32).

In one important respect, this claim is inaccurate. Capital accounting involves deducting the amortizable portion not only of current-year expenditures but also of past years' expenditures that continue to lose value as their useful lives move toward completion. All else being equal, capital accounting reduces net current-year deductions only to the extent that the amount being spent annually has increased. For example, suppose that every year I incur a $100 cost to buy equipment with a useful life of two years. From year 2 onward, I will be deducting $100 per year regardless of whether I am expensing, or amortizing over two years, each year's cost.

Since federal expenditures generally increase each year—even adjusting for inflation and even in times of supposed retrenchment—Eisner probably remains correct that the use of capital accounting on a historically consistent basis would reduce the size of the reported deficit. However, a multiyear perspective would greatly lessen the effect of shifting to capital accounting and prevent him from claiming that the entire deficit is accounted for by the creation of long-term value.

A more fundamental problem with Eisner's proposal to use capital accounting involves measurement reliability. Even in the case of the federal office building, one might have one's doubts about the value created, given the lack of a profit constraint to influence, or an explicit bottom line to assess, government officials' behavior. Were there sizable cost overruns, reflecting failure to exercise adequate oversight? What is the true value of the functions that will be performed in the office building? Much of the government spending that Eisner, following the Office of Management and Budget, terms "investment-type outlays" consists of items emerging from the deliberations of the House Appropriations Committee—a notorious source of localized pork-barrel spending that may reflect logrolling deals and the exercise of political influence to win approval of wasteful spending. Yet the measurement problem only grows worse with regard to claims of broader social benefit from government spending. Intangible benefits to society are inherently hard to measure, or even to agree upon in principle. Some dispute, for example, that spending levels on education have been well correlated with results.

Even if in principle one could devise accurate capital accounting for government expenditures, one would have to worry about abuses in practice. Political shenanigans, such as the bookkeeping tricks that postponed acknowledgment of New York City's approaching insolvency in the late 1960s and early 1970s, would be all too likely. At a minimum, one might have to assign the accounting function to an independent agency. Even so, one could not easily replicate the incentive structure that helps to preserve the integrity of private-sector financial accounting. While accountants can be pressured by managers to overstate income—with the threat of losing business to another accountant—they at least face the risk of legal liability if they succumb to this pressure.

One can see the importance of such incentives by comparing financial accounting to tax accounting. For tax accounting purposes, the client's bias (here, to understate income) generally is even stronger, since it directly and immediately affects one's tax liability. Moreover, the countervailing pressure on accountants is absent, short of conduct extreme enough to trigger civil or criminal sanctions. Largely for this reason, tax accounting is far more rigid and less judgmental than financial accounting and generally does not aim to be as accurate. For example, it does not permit discretionary present deductions for expected future liabilities or lines of business that have lost substantial value.

iii. Social Security cash-flow surpluses. Social Security's current cash-flow surpluses are excluded from the unified and Gramm-Rudman-Hollings budget deficits, in deference to the expected long-term funding shortfalls, as well as Social Security's notional separateness as a self-funding system. Eisner argues, however, that the National Income and Products Account (NIPA) deficit rightly treats current Social Security surpluses as deficit-reducing. Separating these revenues from others "makes little economic sense. . . . My mother used to assure me that all the food I ate 'went into the same stomach' " (1994, 133).

Eisner offers no good explanation of why, for sustainability purposes, it makes sense to count current surpluses and ignore long-term shortfalls. His earlier-discussed claim that people discount the unfunded future liabilities by 100 percent, and thus do not regard them as wealth, relates only to the issue of Keynesian stimulus. Yet the exclusion is crucial to his conclusion that the "real" deficit, for sustainability purposes, is smaller than the official one.

In 1986, the accounting firm Arthur Andersen and Company estimated that if the generally accepted accounting principles (GAAP) used by most private businesses had been used to measure the 1984 budget deficit, its amount would have increased from about $185 billion to about $333 billion. This increase resulted from an excess of upward adjustments for future liabilities that a business would be required to accrue currently at present value under GAAP, over downward adjustments to reflect capital accounting for investments in fixed assets (although apparently not for items such as education) (see Egol 1986). The conditions that gave rise to this estimate, such as Social Security's and Medicare's expected long-term insolvency, remain in place and indeed have grown more pressing.

iv. Additional downward adjustments. In a more tentative vein, designed more to show the lack of a sustainability problem than to establish precise computational rules, Eisner suggests shifting to a measure, known as a "primary" budget, that excludes interest payments on the

national debt. The rationale is that if the primary budget were in balance and only interest payments created an ongoing deficit, then the
national debt would be growing only by the interest rate, which might
equal, over the long term, the real rate of economic growth in the economy. The national debt, therefore, while nominally growing, would remain constant as a proportion of gross national product. For 1984, he
notes that shifting to a primary budget that excluded interest payments
would have reduced the reported federal budget by nearly two-thirds,
from about $185 billion to $59 billion (Eisner 1986, 39–40).

In addition, Eisner notes that since only money that people place
in use (or offer for use) affects prices, increases in the amount of cash
that the public wishes to hold or hoard enable the government to
finance its spending by printing additional money, without thereby
causing inflation. He therefore suggests that any such increase should
be excluded from the deficit, since the newly issued money provides
financing without any need for future taxes (40). For convenience, one
might term this a downward adjustment to the sustainability deficit to
reflect the increase in people's "hoarding capacity."

Both of these adjustments make some sense for "sustainability"
purposes. They may, however, be inappropriate for other purposes,
such as attempting to constrain the size of government. Even if spending is affordable, or in a sense free because of cash hoarding, it represents resource commitments that people might dislike if they understood the opportunity costs.

In the end, Eisner's work is fruitful yet unsatisfying. His two great
contributions are moving toward the design of a meaningful economic
measure that reflects accrual principles or aspects of perceived wealth,
and showing that different measures may be appropriate for different
purposes. Moreover, some of his particular proposed adjustments,
such as for inflation, the value of government assets, and capital accounting, have merit, at least for some of the purposes that a revised
deficit measure might serve.

Yet some of his conclusions, such as that long-term Social Security
shortfalls are irrelevant for both stimulative and sustainability purposes, are both implausible and inconsistent with his general premises. Moreover, as I argued in chapter 3, while a countercyclical fiscal
policy (at least through automatic deficit changes) makes sense as a
tool to combat recession, one should not accept Eisner's 1960s Keynesian belief that perpetual deficit spending is the magic elixir that will

permit us to achieve full employment and bountiful economic growth at almost no real cost. Overall, then, while he helps to show the direction in which future analysis should go, he does not get us there.

E. Laurence Kotlikoff and Generational Accounting

In work appearing since the early 1990s, Laurence Kotlikoff, while building on insights similar to Eisner's, has attempted to reshape the deficit debate far more dramatically. His work has both a destructive and a constructive side. The former involves attacking the budget deficit as an "outdated, misleading, and fundamentally noneconomic measure of fiscal policy" that should be discarded (1992, 217). On the constructive side, he proposes replacing it with a new fiscal policy measure that he developed in collaboration with Alan Auerbach and Jagadeesh Gokhale,[12] called "generational accounting—the direct description of the government's treatment of current and prospective generations over their lifetimes" (217). Both sides of his analysis merit attention.

1. Rejecting the Budget Deficit

In rejecting the budget deficit as a measure, Kotlikoff expresses neither hesitation, qualification, nor nuance. He considers it not merely incomplete or potentially misleading but entirely meaningless. Thus, for example, while criticizing Eisner's refusal to apply accrual principles to Social Security, his main criticism is more fundamental: "[W]ithout doubt, Eisner's deficit has as much claim as any other to being a true calibration of our fiscal posture, but this is really no claim at all. . . . *There is no right way* [to measure the deficit]" (Kotlikoff 1993, 104). It is "a number in search of a concept" (Kotlikoff 1992, 18). Using it to guide economic policy is "akin to driving in Los Angeles with a map of New York" (in Pellecchia 1992).

As a guide to policy, Kotlikoff argues, the deficit encourages not only cynical smoke-and-mirrors games but good faith confusion. He makes much of examples such as the 1990 budget agreement, with its controversial, painfully agreed-to deficit reduction that was casually

---

12. For convenience, in the discussion that follows, I will refer solely to Kotlikoff even when Auerbach and Gokhale deserve equal credit.

and obliviously offset by the conferees' agreeing that future Social Security benefit increases would be appropriate on a pay-as-you-go basis
(1992, 140–41). Other examples abound. Recall President Eisenhower,
who warned in his last State of the Union message against the generational effects of budget deficits but evidently missed the generational
significance of his era's massive unfunded expansion of Social Security.

Kotlikoff views a focus on the budget deficit as misleading economists no less than politicians. Econometric analysis of the deficit's effects on the economy "is not worth the paper it's written on."[13] A noneconomic measure cannot be expected to correlate with any of the ills
for which it is commonly blamed, such as inflation, trade deficits, and
reduced national saving (46–47, 72). While Kotlikoff argues that the
data in fact show no historical correlation, he supports this conclusion
mainly on theoretical grounds. He makes much of the sheer number
of commonly cited measures—such as the unified, Gramm-Rudman-
Hollings, NIPA, and full-employment deficits, along with Eisner's variants—any of which economists in search of correlation can use. In the
end, however, he relies mainly on what he considers the deficit's two
fatal design flaws under all variants.

The first of these is its reliance on cash flow rather than economic
accrual. This, he thinks, leads all versions of the deficit to misrepresent
not only the generational impact and long-term sustainability of our
fiscal policy but also its effects on current behavior. For a mere cash-
flow measure to influence perceived wealth and therefore consumer
spending as Keynesians posit, people would have to be either myopic
or cash-constrained. Kotlikoff argues, however, that they are neither.
He is a rational expectationist until death's door—although not, like
the Ricardians, beyond it—and thus expects people to rely on long-
term estimates of their own future taxes and transfers that, even if
imprecise, are not systematically erroneous. He also cites evidence
that cash-constrained individuals account for only a tiny percentage
of overall consumption in the United States (154–56). Finally, he argues that the U.S. government's borrowing levels, which reflect the current balance between its inflows and outflows of cash, do not affect
interest rates. Supply and demand on world capital markets are too
vast for even so large-scale a borrower as our government to bid up
interest rates discernibly (80–82).

The deficit's second fatal flaw, in Kotlikoff's view, is its reliance

13. Letter from Laurence Kotlikoff to the author, 25 October 1995.

on mere labels, by treating cash flows called "taxes" and "transfers" differently from those called "loans" and "repayments" (31, 152–54). Cash flows called "taxes" and "transfers" generally are included in full when received or paid; if they are called "loans" and "repayments," "interest" is deemed to accrue, but flows of "loan principal" are ignored. Kotlikoff notes that had Social Security contributions been called "loans" rather than "taxes" and benefits called "repayments" rather than "transfers," the identical set of cash flows over the last fifty years would have yielded a different sequence of deficits, and the current level of officially recognized government debt would be roughly $8 trillion higher. Hence, "the deficit is inherently arbitrary— ... reflect[ing] how one labels the government's receipts and payments, rather than some fundamental facet of its fiscal policy" (1993, 104). A measure that depends so heavily on mere terminology cannot be economically significant.

In response, one could argue that the government's description of Social Security as involving "taxes" and "transfers" rather than "loans" is not wholly arbitrary. The choice of labels reflects two of the system's key features: involuntary participation and the fact that benefits generally do not equal the value of one's contributions plus interest. Kotlikoff argues, however, that the first of these features is irrelevant from a budgetary standpoint. As for the second, he notes that one could adjust for it by treating Social Security benefits as loan repayments with market interest plus an extra "benefit" or minus an extra "tax" at the time of payment. This mere terminology change would suffice to alter greatly the reported sequence of budget deficits, even though it would change nothing of substance (see Kotlikoff 1995).

One might think the deficit's two main flaws could be cured by converting it into an economic accrual measure, in which expected future cash flows were counted at their present value and capital accounting was used for investment expenditures. This would solve the labeling as well as the economic accrual problem, since loans at market interest would net out to zero in present value terms, while other transactions would give rise to accrual adjustments no matter what they were called. Kotlikoff does not propose this, however, and for a good reason.

Suppose that Congress in 1998 enacted a lump-sum tax of $50,000 per adult American per year (in 1998 dollars), to take effect in 2030 and remain in place as long as needed to eliminate the national debt as well as long-term funding shortfalls in Social Security and Medicare. Such an enactment might not alter one's views of our current fiscal policy, even if one disregarded the possibility that the tax would never take effect. What really matters in fiscal policy is *who* pays taxes and receives transfers. As long as we reject the Ricardian claim that people wholly offset the generational effects of fiscal policy by adjusting private transfers, taxing our children in the future is very different from taxing us today, even if the two taxes have the same present value.

For a more realistic example, consider two alternative responses to the projected exhaustion of the Social Security Trust Fund in 2030. One would be to terminate the program "cold turkey" at that time, leaving millions of younger Americans to receive nothing from a program to which they had contributed extensively. The second would be to begin in 1998 phasing in gradual adjustments to Social Security taxes and benefits, under a plan that was projected precisely to restore the fund's long-term balance. While these two courses would have identical effects on an economic accrual measure of the budget deficit or the national debt, they would have radically different distributional and, one imagines, behavioral effects in practice.

Hence the shift Kotlikoff proposes to generational accounting, which attempts to measure *who*, as between members of different age groups, pays taxes and gets benefits. By providing generation-specific breakdowns, generational accounting offers information that even an economic accrual measure of the budget deficit, with its statement merely of an aggregate number, cannot. For multiple purposes, therefore, generational accounting has the potential to be a major step forward. It provides data bearing directly on fiscal policy's impact on both generational distribution and current consumers' perceived wealth (assuming rational expectations on a lifetime basis). In addition, it helps in evaluating whether current fiscal policy is likely to be sustainable over the long term. Even on size-of-government issues, which Kotlikoff generally ignores, one could argue that shifting tax burdens from present to future generations is the real phenomenon that the Virginia theorists have misattributed to cash-flow budget deficits.

2. Description of Generational Accounting

Generational accounting begins by dividing people into age cohorts, typically at five-year intervals and with separate groups for men and women. Unborn members of future generations are grouped together without regard to future years of birth. The system then involves estimating, for the average member of each group, the net balance in present value terms (either on a lifetime basis or from the present moment forward) between expected cash payments to and receipts from all levels of government. This, in turn, requires analyzing a wealth of government-published data and making assumptions about such matters as future interest rates, economic growth, demographic trends, and discretionary spending levels. Overall, payments to the government greatly exceed receipts therefrom, because much government output takes the form of goods and services that cannot readily be valued or attributed to particular age groups.

The amount thereby computed is called the *net tax payment* ("lifetime net tax payment" in the case of a lifetime, rather than going-forward, computation). Suppose, for example, that the average man born in 1990 were estimated to pay lifetime taxes with a present value at birth of $2 million and to receive lifetime benefits with a present value of $500,000. His lifetime net tax payment would be $1.5 million.

Generational accounting also involves estimating *lifetime net tax rates*, which equal lifetime net tax payments divided by the present value at birth of estimated lifetime income. Thus, if the average man born in 1990 had lifetime income of $3 million, his lifetime net tax rate, given the above lifetime net tax payment, would be 50 percent. For this purpose, lifetime income includes labor earnings, inherited wealth, and capital gains in excess of the normal return to saving. (It sometimes is restricted to labor earnings, because of the difficulty of estimating the other components.) Lifetime income does not, however, include the normal return to saving, defined as the assumed interest or discount rate. Such inclusion would lead to double-counting in a present value measure (which treats, for example, $100 in year 1 as inherently equal to $106 in year 2 if the annual discount rate is 6 percent).[14]

While, for the most part, generational accounting looks only at actual cash flows (such as tax and transfer payments), as distinct from burdens and benefits more generally, in principle it can be adjusted to reflect anything else that is susceptible to estimation and attribution. Kotlikoff himself goes beyond direct cash flow in circumstances where he thinks this can be done with sufficient confidence. For example,

14. See Office of the President, *Budget Baselines, Historical Data, and Alternatives for the Future* (January 1993), 537.

he treats changes in capital income taxation that change the value of existing, relative to new, assets as a one-time tax on or transfer payment to owners of existing assets (1995, 67–69). And he allocates corporate income tax to owners, rather than, say, consumers or workers, following a widespread incidence view among economists.

In general, the system's long-term computations are done under the assumption that current policy will continue indefinitely. "Current policy" refers both to existing legal rules for multiyear systems such as income taxation and Social Security and to reasonably expected levels of discretionary outlay for items, such as national defense, that are funded separately each year. To measure current discretionary outlays, Kotlikoff imputes rent to durable government assets, rather than counting in full current expenditures (or ignoring past expenditures) to create such assets. He thus avoids treating current consumption and long-term investment as equivalent.

Over time, Kotlikoff generally assumes, discretionary outlays will remain constant relative to GDP. Thus, higher economic growth has little systematic effect on the long-term adequacy of existing taxes to pay for projected spending. Instead, it comparably increases both sides of the ledger. If one assumed instead that discretionary spending would remain more constant in real terms, increasing to keep pace only with inflation and perhaps population growth, while tax revenues grew automatically with the economy, productivity-fueled economic growth would greatly increase the long-term adequacy of existing taxes to pay for projected spending under current policy.

The general assumption that "current policy" will continue indefinitely is subject to one important exception, Kotlikoff notes. Generational accounting applies an "intertemporal budget constraint," under which "the sum of generational accounts of all current and future generations plus existing government net wealth [must] be sufficient to finance the present value of current and future government consumption" (56). In short, government net wealth aside, total revenue must ultimately equal total expenditure in present value terms. Any long-term shortfall under current policy is assumed to require additional tax payments—if only to pay interest indefinitely—that will come exclusively from future generations. The deficit and national debt must ultimately be reduced to zero, but our unborn descendants, not we, will pay for this in full to the extent that current policy fails to accomplish it.

Table 1 Generational Accounts Showing Present Values of Net Receipts and Payments from Today Forward (in thousands of dollars)

Generation's Age in 1991	Average Net Payment (receipt)	
	For Men	For Women
0	78.9	39.5
5	99.7	48.7
10	125.0	59.4
15	157.2	72.4
20	187.1	84.0
25	204.0	86.4
30	205.5	81.1
35	198.8	71.9
40	180.1	55.3
45	145.1	29.5
50	97.2	(2.2)
55	38.9	(39.5)
60	(23.0)	(80.8)
65	(74.0)	(112.5)
70	(80.7)	(110.6)
75	(75.5)	(100.6)
80	(61.1)	(83.3)
85	(47.2)	(65.6)
90	(3.5)	(9.8)
Future generations	166.5	83.4

Source: Auerbach, Gokhalle, and Kotlikoff 1994, 80–81.

Generational accounting's results are quite striking. In table 1, I present Kotlikoff's estimates for expected future (rather than lifetime) net tax payments, as of 1991. The table shows that younger men and women owe huge net taxes, peaking, in present value terms, at around age twenty to thirty, where for men it exceeds $200,000. Older men and women, by contrast, are projected to receive huge net payments from the federal government, with present values for some age cohorts in excess of $100,000.

As Kotlikoff recognizes, these raw numbers are incomplete and potentially misleading (1992, 122–25). For example, the gender gap in the numbers, apparently favoring women, results from the fact that women on average earn less and live longer than men, and thus reflects redistributive and social insurance policies that are not gender-specific

(122). The life-cycle effect, whereby aggregate burdens first increase until early adulthood and then decline steadily, reflects not only redistributive and social insurance policies but also the practice of taxing people most heavily during their prime income-earning years, when the payment of tax may be most convenient.

While table 1 portrays all groups older than sixty as net recipients of government largesse, it ignores the net tax payments that they may have made earlier in their lives. Thus, it cannot tell us what, if any, generational transfers are taking place on a lifetime basis, and it has no direct normative implications for policy.

This style of information does, however, provide a snapshot of current fiscal policy, facilitating comparison to other snapshots computed at different times or under different assumed policies. These comparisons can be used to estimate the distributional, or predict the macroeconomic, effects of actual or proposed policy changes. By comparing snapshots that apply different eras' policies to the present, Kotlikoff shows that the dominant trend of generational policy since at least the 1950s has been to transfer substantial wealth from younger and unborn Americans to older Americans (172, 175, 177, 184). He argues that these transfers are largely responsible for Americans' low rates of saving in recent years, since the elderly tend to save less (Gokhale, Kotlikoff, and Sabelhaus 1995). More narrowly, he estimates that Social Security legislation enacted in 1983 cost baby boomers more than $1 trillion current dollars (Kotlikoff 1992, 3). He also detects such often overlooked generational implications of various policy proposals as the following:

- Shifting from labor income taxes to sales or consumption taxes would redistribute wealth to younger Americans, since the elderly engage in proportionately more consumption and, even if still in the workforce at high wages, have expected remaining lifetime wages with a relatively low present value (177).
- Tax incentives for new investment, such as accelerated depreciation or investment tax credits, redistribute wealth away from older Americans by reducing the value of existing investments (which they disproportionately own) (177–80). For the same reason, repealing tax incentives for new investment redistributes wealth toward the elderly. The effects can be huge. Kotlikoff estimates that the Tax Reform Act of 1986 handed the predomi-

Table 2 Estimated Lifetime Net Tax Rates as of 1991 (average for males and females)

Generation's Year of Birth	Lifetime Net Tax Rate (percentage)
1900	23.6
1910	27.0
1920	29.1
1930	30.4
1940	31.4
1950	32.6
1960	33.5
1970	34.1
1980	34.2
1990	34.2
Future generations	84.4

Source: Kotlikoff 1995, 9.

nantly older holders of existing capital a gain of $747 billion (179).

- Tax preferences for capital gains, in contrast to incentives for new investment, redistribute wealth to older Americans by benefiting holders of existing capital.

In sum, the style of information in table 1 is valuable empirically but tells us little about generational policy. To assess that, one needs computations on a lifetime, not a going-forward, basis. In addition, if one considers lifetime income relevant to the proper allocation of lifetime net tax burdens, then one should examine lifetime net tax *rates*. Hence the need for data as in table 2, which provides such rates for groups born in 1900 or later. These results are no less striking than those in table 1.

As table 2 shows, lifetime net tax rates have risen fairly steadily throughout the twentieth century. For future generations, the computed rate is staggering, and surely well beyond the maximum that could realistically be levied. Accordingly, table 2 suggests that deficit alarmists—however misguided in their reliance on an outmoded measure—are right to be concerned about the generational impact and long-term sustainability of our current fiscal policy.

From such data, Kotlikoff concludes that our current generational policy both will have to change soon and—relying on a normative view that we will examine in chapter 5—is grossly unfair. He believes, moreover, that few voters would support current policy, despite their self-interest in transferring tax burdens to future generations, if they correctly understood it (see, e.g., 1992, 188–90, 196). This assumption of political myopia is in some tension with his rational expectationist view of people's private decision making. Given his assumption of political myopia, however, Kotlikoff believes that generational accounting has enormous potential to transform public policy.

Before getting to such claims, however, we must more fully assess the system, both in its current form and in principle. Table 2's results reflect underlying methodological and empirical assumptions that need to be examined more carefully. Both the system and its conclusions depend on what assumptions one deems are most appropriate to adopt.

3. Assessing Generational Accounting as a Replacement for the Budget Deficit

Generational accounting represents an ambitious conceptual and technical effort. Through its long-term focus, its use of economic accrual, and its analysis of *who* pays taxes and receives benefits, it goes considerably beyond *any* possible version of the budget deficit. To the extent that one disagrees with any of Kotlikoff's methodological and empirical assumptions, one can simply modify them and produce one's own version of generational accounting.

Suppose, for example, that one thinks Medicare spending is likely to decline in real terms because of comprehensive health reform. One could revise Kotlikoff's figures accordingly, creating a less alarming picture. Or suppose one thinks that consumers either look no more than ten years ahead or else are presently assuming that Social Security will gradually be modified to eliminate the projected funding shortfall. Either way, one could prepare a set of estimates for macroeconomic purposes that reflected the changed assumptions.

For academic and intellectual purposes, therefore, Kotlikoff has not exaggerated the importance of his innovations. Yet he has only begun the debate, not ended it. Pride of authorship does not make his version canonical. Moreover, we must consider whether the budget deficit is as meaningless as he claims and, if not, whether it may retain value for public political purposes, given its familiarity and symbolic appeal.

a. Evaluating Kotlikoff's Main Assumptions

This is not the place to critique the fine points of Kotlikoff's methodology[15]—concerning, for example, how he treats the "seigniorage" accruing to the government when people hold cash (and thus, in a sense, act as zero-interest lenders). Most such narrow items would not greatly change the big picture he presents in any event. Moreover, while his empirical assumptions about such matters as productivity trends and population growth have important bottom-line implications, he derives them from respected official sources such as the Congressional Budget Office and the Social Security Administration.

Several of Kotlikoff's main assumptions require closer examination, however, as they raise questions about generational accounting's suitability for various purposes, or about its portrayal (in his hands) of current fiscal policy as dramatically unsustainable.

Assumption of policy continuity until the unspecified moment when tax increases or benefit cuts become necessary. Kotlikoff's stylized treatment of future policy, which he assumes will retain its present form indefinitely until future generations are forced to bear tax increases or benefit cuts, has aroused criticism. In the real world, policy is in constant flux. At times, the likely direction of change can even be predicted—as with Social Security and Medicare, which are widely expected to draw spending cuts or tax increases while present generations are still alive. In any event, surely future generations cannot and will not pay, as table 2 suggests, an 84 percent lifetime net tax rate.

Kotlikoff recognizes, however, that policy frequently changes, and indeed this is part of his central analytical purpose. He defends the assumption of policy continuity as providing useful "as if" information, by showing in objective terms where we are currently headed and how policy is likely to have to change (see, e.g., Auerbach, Gokhale, and Kotlikoff 1994, 88).

To the extent that generational accounting provides an objective measure—illuminating, for example, current policy's generational effects and likely sustainability—this defense is well taken. However, to the extent that one wants an across-the-board replacement for the budget deficit, the problem of policy flux is more troubling. Economists

15. For some such evaluations, see, e.g., Cutler 1993; Goode and Steuerle 1994; and Congressional Budget Office 1995.

since Keynes have thought that budget deficits affect macroeconomic trends and can guide countercyclical fiscal policy, mainly through the mechanism of perceived wealth. Yet such wealth is a subjective, not objective, phenomenon.

Thus, for generational accounting to provide an appropriate measure for macroeconomic forecasting, it must be modified for this purpose to reflect the future policies that people actually expect. Otherwise, it will prove significantly inaccurate. Recall Kotlikoff's estimate that the Social Security legislation enacted in 1983 cost baby boomers more than $1 trillion current dollars (1992, 3)—a change that never had the radically contractionary effects one might have predicted, presumably because people had already, over the preceding decade, come to assume that policy would change. Unfortunately, the course of expected future policy is hard to ascertain and could be manipulated in the estimating process by result-oriented policymakers and econometric researchers. While this is no criticism of generational accounting relative to the cash-flow budget deficit—which simply sweeps problems of this sort under the rug—it does indicate the difficulty of devising a reliable measure in practice.

More generally, for purposes of subjective estimation, Kotlikoff's dismissal of the deficit's reliance on "mere labels" is overstated. When the government calls a cash inflow a "loan" on which it owes "repayment" rather than a "tax" that it plans later to offset through a "transfer," it expresses a more definite commitment to make the later payment. People therefore may tend to discount future payments called "transfers" more than those called "repayments," thus preventing the distinction from being wholly meaningless.

Further problems relate to defining current policy. Discretionary spending aside, does it simply equal the set of policies currently on the books? Sometimes the policy on the books is misleading, because of implicit agreements to enact specified changes. Consider popular tax benefits with expiration dates—added deliberately to improve official deficit forecasts—that there is widespread consensus about extending. Moreover, sometimes, no matter what is on the books, further negotiations will be required before anything can be implemented. Consider multiyear budget plans, adversarially negotiated between Congress and the president, that provide for unspecified out-year spending cuts, any version of which is likely to provoke intense political conflict and possible deadlock. Should these cuts be deemed part of current policy before they have been specified? While one can always prepare alternative computations, this may leave one somewhat at sea, faced with too many alternative measures to know where one stands.

Kotlikoff is on shakiest ground, however, in assuming that discretionary spending. will grow in real terms to match the growth of the economy, thus largely eliminating the net fiscal benefit of increased productivity. Official Social Security projections, by contrast, treat increased growth as aiding system solvency, because, with law on the books to provide a reference point, they do not assume that benefits will grow with the economy (although in practice Congress might respond to economic growth, as it did through the early 1970s, by enacting benefit increases).

One could argue that Kotlikoff's assumption makes better-case scenarios for the economy look unrealistically gloomy. The principle of declining marginal utility suggests that as national income grows, government spending may tend to decline, all else being equal, as a percentage of such income, since the most urgent needs and political demands have increasingly been satisfied. While government spending has grown more rapidly than national income during much of the twentieth century, this may reflect political and ideological trends that are in the course of exhausting themselves. Moreover, while a relative spending decline would yield no net fiscal benefit if tax revenues commensurately declined, the latter decline may be less likely, given the relative painlessness to Congress of using automatic revenue increases from economic growth to reduce currently projected fiscal shortfalls.

Once again, this criticism does not extend to generational accounting in principle. The system can be adapted to employ any set of assumptions about future policy, and cash-flow budget deficits never even reach the issue. Yet the inherent difficulty of the task that generational accounting laudably sets for itself affects the determinacy and usefulness of any answers that it can provide.

Intertemporal budget constraint. The other most controversial feature in generational accounting is its intertemporal budget constraint: the assumption that total revenue must ultimately equal total expenditure in present value terms (government net wealth aside), and thus that deferring taxes does not reduce their present value. Robert Eisner argues that, to the contrary, public debt need never be repaid, since the government is infinite-lived, can borrow in its own currency, and can indefinitely reassure lenders given its power to raise taxes. Thus, the notional day of reckoning, in which substantial tax increases or benefit cuts will be necessary, need never come. Eisner concludes that generational accounting's most dramatic finding—the unsustainable lifetime net tax rate for future generations—is incorrect.

While Eisner is literally correct that the national debt may never need to be repaid, his rejection of the intertemporal budget constraint does not follow. A perpetual stream of market interest payments to finance federal borrowing would have, by definition, the same economic value as immediate repayment of the loan principal. Thus, taxes must pay for spending in the long run (treating default as a kind of tax) even if they lag behind, requiring taxpayers perpetually to pay the ongoing interest charges for past and current spending. Similarly, corporations do not avoid paying for capital by issuing perpetual bonds or nonredeemable stock.

The Eisner argument has one more step, however. Suppose that the government could perpetually borrow enough to pay not only for current spending but also for all interest charges on its prior borrowing. Under this scenario, taxes would indefinitely remain deferred and the burden never felt. This generally would require, however, that the debt not grow relative to the economy, which in turn would require that the rate of economic growth at least equal the interest rate on the debt and that the "primary" budget deficit (excluding interest costs) do no more than eliminate any excess.

These conditions would in effect permit one to run a burden-deferring Ponzi scheme indefinitely. However, while Ponzi schemes can in theory work forever, in practice they never do. Some economists have therefore described basing fiscal policy on acceptance of the intertemporal budget constraint as akin to buying "generational insurance" rather than gambling that the burden can be passed on indefinitely (see Ball, Elmendorf, and Mankiw 1995; Congressional Budget Office 1995, 54).

In any event, however, the precondition that the national debt not grow relative to the economy is not expected to hold under current policy. Recent fiscal projections suggest that under current trends, not long after the year 2000, the cash-flow budget deficit would rise from 2 or 3 to 15 or 20 percent of GDP, causing public debt to grow far more rapidly than the economy. Borrowing at this level might quickly prove hard to sustain—or at least be assumed so by policymakers, who might therefore act to avoid it—given the dangers of overly crowding out domestic private investment and of increasing the debt's perceived riskiness, thus necessitating the payment of higher interest rates (see, e.g., Stein 1996).

While the intertemporal budget constraint therefore seems correct, Kotlikoff's treatment of it is (deliberately) highly stylized. He allocates the entire unprovided-for net tax burden to future generations, although this is an ever-shifting group of people over time. For example, as of today, those to be born in the year 2000 are members of future generations, but they will soon join present generations. When they do, a recalculation of table 2, in the absence of any major policy or economic changes, would show them bearing a lifetime net tax rate closer to the 34 percent now shown for people born in 1990 than to the 84 percent now shown for future generations. They will have joined the group to which none of the unprovided-for burden, rather than all of it, is being assigned.

Taken literally, this jump in results at the moment of birth would not be plausible. Being just born rather than about to be born cannot have so large an effect. Kotlikoff's "future generations," however, are a notional category, deemed to bear the entire unprovided-for burden because we cannot tell how it will actually be allocated, given current policy's failure to provide any clues.

Suppose we were to conclude that the unprovided-for net tax burden will in fact be addressed very soon. This conclusion would enable us to begin guessing how the lifetime net tax rates that different age groups actually will bear differ from those that they would bear under current policy. Disregarding such details as different age groups' relative political power, and which specific policy changes are presently being discussed, the general implication is that the younger one is, the more one's lifetime net tax burden is likely to increase. Greater youth implies that, on average, more of one's life will be lived after fiscal policy has changed to begin addressing the unprovided-for burden.

Thus, just as no one really thinks that people born in 2000 will pay a lifetime net tax rate as high as 84 percent, so, perhaps, no one should expect people born in 1990 to pay as little as 34 percent. By contrast, those born in 1930 may well come close to achieving the table 2 projection of 30.4 percent, unless the policy changes are surprisingly sharp, sudden, and aimed at them. Once again, therefore, while generational accounting is highly informative—and far more so than the cash-flow budget deficit—the long-term, inherently indefinite nature of what it is examining eliminates any prospect of precision. The problem lies not in generational accounting as such but in the inherent difficulty of determining where our fiscal policy is truly heading and how people perceive its effects on their wealth.

Use of lifetime perspective. One factor that probably impedes widespread acceptance of generational accounting is its use of a lifetime perspective. As Thomas Barthold has put it, many policymakers intuitively do not feel "that a retired couple with social security, pension, and asset income of $35,000 and a backup shortstop in the major leagues making $200,000 should be lumped together because they [each] have a permanent income of $50,000 [per year]" (1993, 292). While one might say so much the worse for these policymakers, their intuition receives some empirical support from studies suggesting that people tend to smooth out their consumption over a time horizon of only a few years, rather than over their entire lifetimes, and to let current consumption spending vary more with current income than one might expect from the lifetime perspective (see Carroll and Summers 1991).

Thus, at least for macroeconomic and size-of-government purposes, the effects of a policy change that alters the average lifetime net tax payment for people currently, say, age twenty may depend on when during their life spans their gross taxes or receipt of transfer payments changes. Generational accounting may take too long a view for these purposes, just as the budget deficit takes too short a view, although in principle one could incorporate the discount rates and time horizons that people actually apply.

Broader dynamic effects of fiscal policy. An inherent problem with fiscal forecasting, faced at present by government revenue estimators, concerns the extent to which one should take into account the broader dynamic effects of proposed policies, such as on societal levels of consumption and investment. Government revenue estimators often are criticized for applying too static an analysis, by, for example, ignoring the effects on economic growth that adherents of a tax incentive for investment claim their proposal would have. The estimators defend their position on the ground that while some types of dynamic behavioral response can be assumed (for example, more frequent capital gain realizations if the tax rate on capital gains is reduced), other responses are too speculative and should be ignored.

As practiced by Kotlikoff, generational accounting similarly disregards broader dynamic effects. It looks at government fiscal policy only in a global or aggregate sense, ignoring the possible generational significance of the details of the particular taxing and spending programs that the government adopts. Consider, for example, the claim that an income tax, by taxing some of the economic return to investment but none of the psychic return to immediate consumption, discourages saving and reduces its amount, whereas a consumption tax generally is neutral with respect to when one consumes.[16] This suggests that income taxation, by reason of its effect on private saving, may be worse for future generations than consumption taxation, even if the two alternative systems would generate equal revenues from current taxpayers. Or consider the argument that estate taxation greatly increases consumption by present generations and discourages leaving large bequests (McCaffery 1992). Generational accounting not only makes no adjustment for the possible behavioral effects of such taxes (holding who pays them constant) but might mistakenly treat as benefiting future generations an income or estate tax increase that, on balance, reduced national saving to their detriment.

This problem has no good answer. On the one hand, dynamic effects that actually will occur *should* be taken into account. In principle, one should respond to uncertainty by discounting for probability, not by ignoring a prospect altogether. On the other hand, economists often disagree, not only about what is certain but even about what is probable. Even the direction of possible dynamic effect may be unclear, as with budget deficits, which Keynesians such as Eisner consider stimulative but many others regard as reducing saving and economic growth. If estimators can choose among the various speculative adjustments that arguably are plausible, then they are free to manipulate the inquiry, and reach whatever bottom-line outcome they happen to prefer.

Kotlikoff makes two main points in defense of his ignoring broader dynamic effects. First, the broader dynamic effects of policies, such as on the level of investment, tend to emerge gradually and thus may have relatively small present value effects. Second, the main dynamic effect that he thinks current policy, considered in the aggregate, has—reducing saving and therefore the rate of economic growth by

16. See, e.g., Andrews 1974, 1168–69. A graduated consumption tax would distort the timing of consumption by encouraging people to try to consume roughly the same amount each year, in order to minimize their exposure to higher rates.

reason of the government-induced shift of consumption to present generations—would only strengthen his core conclusion of dispropor-tionate impact on future generations (Auerbach, Gokhale, and Kotli-koff 1994, 88–89). More generally, to counter the risk of manipulation, he urges that the government's official generational accounting com-putations be prepared by independent experts. He notes that Social Security's long-term forecasts—which often have direct political con-sequences, such as their stimulating the 1983 reforms—are prepared by independent actuaries whose reputation for steering clear of politi-cal manipulation is excellent (91).

b. The Limits of a Mere Fiscal Policy Measure

Thus far, I have emphasized the difficulties inherent in generational accounting's task of measuring the likely course and macroeconomic effects of fiscal policy. A second set of problems that require dis-counting the system's findings involve the limits of fiscal policy itself. Fiscal policy is only a subset of everything the government does, which in turn is only a subset of everything that present generations do.

Transfers in kind between individuals and the government. By fo-cusing only on transfers of cash between individuals and the govern-ment, generational accounting (like any fiscal policy measure) ignores transfers in kind. Thus, with respect to government expenditures, it makes no adjustment for the value of goods and services such as roads, national defense, education, and police protection. It thereby leaves out roughly half of government spending in its computation of benefits that offset gross tax payments.

Recognizing the omission, Kotlikoff concedes that even if pure public goods (such as defense) cannot meaningfully be allocated, many government goods and services have generation-specific primary beneficiaries. While expressing the hope that future research will per-mit adding the value derived from such expenditures to future compu-tations, he argues that the omission is not critical to the assessment of post—World War II policy, because government spending (in contrast to who pays for it) has remained fairly constant relative to total na-tional output during this period (Kotlikoff 1992, 168). This may unduly ignore the significance of changes in the composition of government spending, such as shifts between defense spending and various kinds of nondefense spending. It also leaves open the possibility that generations born before World War II, despite paying lower estimated life-time net tax rates, have not really benefited relative to their juniors from government's operations overall.

On the other side of the ledger, in measuring transfers to the government, generational accounting does not include the value of services contributed by members of different age cohorts. For most government employees, whose salary receipts are ignored as well, this omission seems justified. The arm's-length nature of the exchange supports treating the offsetting transfers as presumptively equal—although where, say, a patronage appointee fails to render genuine services, one might want, in principle, to treat the salary payment as a transfer by the government. However, people who perform services involuntarily, such as military draftees during most of our major wars, presumably have made a transfer in kind that generational accounting disregards. Indeed, where by reason of being drafted, one loses earnings and thus pays less tax than one would have otherwise, generational accounting in effect treats one as having been made better off. (Indeed, dying in battle before one's main tax-paying years is the ultimate "benefit.") Even today, when we have an all-volunteer army, the inaccuracy may be important to the extent that generational accounting is applied on a lifetime basis (not just a forward-looking basis) to veterans of World War II and the Korean and Vietnam wars.

Similarly, in measuring transfers to the government, generational accounting disregards the excess burden of taxation or detriments borne by taxpayers that, unlike the burden of paying tax, do not result in the transfer of value to the government. Examples include the costs to taxpayers of income tax compliance and the lock-in effect on appreciated capital assets of the tax system's reaching capital gain only upon the occurrence of a realization event, such as a sale. Tax writers increasingly recognize that such costs are relevant and important to measuring the distribution of overall tax burdens. For example, if one ignores excess burden, then a revenue-raising reduction in the capital gains tax rate, which makes the relatively old holders of appreciated capital assets better off on balance, is mistakenly treated as making them worse off, because it induces them voluntarily to pay more overall tax on the increased volume of transactions (see, e.g., Shaviro 1993a, 407–8).

The point about excess burden applies with equal force to the costs to private individuals of complying with government regulations and mandates outside the tax area. Some such items—for example, the costs (as well as the benefits) resulting from compliance with the Age Discrimination in Employment Act, which bars employers from disfavoring the elderly by reason of their age—plainly have strong generational implications. Generational accounting does not at present reflect these costs, however.

Value of targeted or compensatory transfers from government. In general, one would think it clear that transfer payments from the government are worth their face amount to the recipients. For example, a $10 Social Security check that I receive today is worth $10 to me. Thus, all else being equal, one would think it plain that those receiving larger transfers from the government are being treated better.

For two reasons, however, this is not always certain. First, where government transfer payments are targeted to a particular use, disparities in expenditure may not indicate disparities in value received. Suppose, for example, that successful, comprehensive health-care reform made medical care cheaper yet no less effective and thereby reduced the government's expected Medicare and Medicaid costs, without either harming program participants' health or shifting costs to them. The computational result would be to increase lifetime net tax rates for all groups born since 1920. People's net taxes would increase as the amount that the government spent on their Medicare and Medicaid benefits declined. By definition, however, they would be no worse off, since their health and the quality of their health care would have remained constant. People benefit from the value of what they actually get, not from the number of dollars that the government spends on their behalf.

Second, suppose that the government has a neutral policy ex ante of providing greater payments to those experiencing greater need or hardship. In effect, the government provides insurance on equal terms to all. Those who subsequently experience greater need or hardship, and therefore ultimately receive larger payments, arguably have been treated the same as others, not better. Similarly, one would not say that a company offering earthquake coverage had discriminated among its customers in favor of those who ended up needing to file a claim. We saw this problem at work in table 1, where women seemingly fared better than men as an indirect consequence of their living longer and having lower annual income. (Table 2, if computed by gender, would reduce the disparity, by computing the tax rate in light of women's lower income.) A further example could involve an age cohort's suffering from unusually high unemployment and therefore receiving greater unemployment insurance payments.

Distinction between nominal tax payments and real tax burdens. The transfers to the government that generational accounting measures generally omit what are called implicit taxes, such as the reduced pretax return on municipal bonds by reason of the federal tax exemption. Suppose, for example, that a taxpayer with a marginal federal income tax rate of 30 percent and $100 to invest has a choice between buying (1) a 10 percent corporate security earning $10 before tax and $7 after tax, and (2) a 7 percent municipal bond that resembles the security in its risk and term features but pays $7 both before and after tax because of marketplace capitalization of the value of the tax benefit. If the taxpayer buys the latter, one could describe the taxpayer as having paid a $3 "implicit tax." The taxpayer accepted a $3 reduction in pretax return and thus is in the same after-tax position as one who bought the corporate security. Moreover, the taxpayer thereby served the government purpose that presumably underlies the tax exemption—reducing municipalities' cost of borrowing—to the same extent as if he or she had paid $3 in taxes directly to the federal government to finance the direct payment of a subsidy to the bond issuer. While the two cases arguably are identical in substance, only the former would be included by generational accounting.

While tax-exempt bonds, considered alone, may seem a minor case, tax benefits that affect prices and thereby lead to implicit taxation are rife throughout the Internal Revenue Code. Consider, for example, tax subsidies for employer health care, the estimated annual cost of which exceeds $50 billion. In any case, measuring implicit taxes is only one example of a broader problem. Economists have long struggled to determine the incidence not merely of nominal tax payments but of real tax burdens and have often been unable to achieve consensus regarding the latter. Kotlikoff's focus on nominal tax payments, however necessary computationally, lowers one's confidence in the significance of his analysis given the aggregate generational differences between such groups as owners of capital and consumers. It also may lead to overstatement of the elderly's relative benefit, if implicit taxes pertain mainly to capital income, which the elderly receive disproportionately owing to their greater per capita wealth.

Ricardian offsets by present generations to the generational effects of government fiscal policy. A finding of complete Ricardian equivalence would make generational accounting meaningless. Whatever the government did, households would reverse by adjusting their bequests and other intergenerational transfers. While such a strong Ricardian claim is implausible, surely some offsetting private adjustments occur, moderating the real generational effects of government fiscal policy. Suppose, for example, that one accepted some researchers' finding that about 20 percent of the increase in public debt is compensated for by increased private saving (see Altonji, Hayashi, and Kotlikoff 1992; Holcombe, Jackson, and Zardkoohi 1981). Generational accounts would need to be adjusted accordingly in order to reflect fiscal policy's actual net effects on generational distribution and perhaps perceived wealth.

The amount of appropriate adjustment for Ricardian offsets cannot easily be measured. One problem is that the degree of offset may vary with the kind of policy. Suppose, for example, that the government increased its spending on health care for children and that generational accounting could measure the new benefits even to the extent that they were provided in kind. One would still need to determine in whose generational accounts to include them. To the extent that parents' direct spending on their children remained constant, one might want to credit the children's accounts. To the extent that such spending declined, one might want to credit the parents' accounts. While a similar adjustment would be appropriate in principle even if the parents were handed cash (potentially inducing them to spend more on their children, as well as on themselves), the degree of net benefit to children might be greater in the case of targeted in-kind benefits. Generational accounting cannot easily incorporate such subtleties.

c. Generational Accounting versus the Cash-Flow Budget Deficit as a Focus of Public Political Debate

Thus far, my criticisms of generational accounting have been of two kinds. First, certain of Kotlikoff's assumptions and conventions can be questioned. However, this merely indicates revising generational accounting, not rejecting it or preferring the budget deficit as a measure. Second, the questions that generational accounting requires us to ask are so difficult that we cannot answer them confidently—although they are the right questions. However, this merely calls for viewing all findings cautiously and realizing that no system of measurement can overcome the limits to our knowledge. Thus, neither criticism undermines Kotlikoff's claim to have devised a better, more meaningful, more informative measure of fiscal policy than the budget deficit.

Yet Kotlikoff does not merely argue that generational accounting provides a better measure than the budget deficit. He argues that the latter measure is utterly meaningless and should be discarded for all purposes, including as a focus of public political debate. Here he exaggerates. The deficit is neither so devoid of economic content nor so worthless as a fiscal policy guidepost as he maintains.

An initial point is that cash flow can matter for some purposes. It is not theoretically impossible for the level of current U.S. government borrowing to affect interest rates. On the econometric data itself, a sympathetic commentator recently complained that "the evidence is more mixed than Kotlikoff presents. [A] fair reading . . . does not offer firm conclusions" (Cutler 1993, 64). The 1980s were the only era of large, noncyclical peacetime deficits in American history, and they featured too many other changes for deficits' effects to be isolated.

In addition, the deficit is not completely meaningless as a policy guide, despite the fact that it ignores economic accrual and depends on mere terminology. If it were completely meaningless, then even large-scale, multiyear deficit reduction, conducted without offsetting changes to Social Security or Medicare, would affect generational distribution randomly. This is not the case, however. Instead, holding entitlements constant, large-scale, multiyear deficit reduction generally does reduce the unprovided-for net tax burden that Kotlikoff allocates to future generations—as his own computations show.[17]

The main factors that made the deficit such a misleading measure in the past—its short time horizon and disregarding long-term fiscal trends in entitlements programs—are increasingly widely understood. Today, deficit reduction efforts typically involve multiyear forecasts and attention to Social Security and Medicare financing. If policy has not changed as much in the direction of restoring fiscal balance as Kotlikoff and many others would like, it is mainly because present voters prefer a policy that offers them large benefits that they need not pay for, not because they are confused.

While Kotlikoff believes that better information will inevitably

---

17. See, e.g., Kotlikoff 1995, table 1, showing that adoption of a balanced budget proposal would reduce future generations' net tax burden from 84.4 percent to 72.5 percent.

produce what he considers better policy, he ignores the political reasons for fiscal policy's having so long benefited older Americans at the expense of younger and unborn Americans (see, e.g., Elliott 1985, 1091–92). To illustrate these reasons, it is convenient, if oversimplifying, to divide Americans into three groups: those older than sixty-five, who often are retired or close to retirement; those between the ages of eighteen and sixty-five, most of whom are actually or potentially in the workforce; and those younger than eighteen or unborn, who cannot vote. The first of these groups, although currently only 12 percent of the population (Kotlikoff 1992, 54), has several great advantages in exercising political power. Its members, generally having more leisure, can more easily learn where their interests lie and act to pursue their interests. Their relatively high voting rate comes as no surprise. Moreover, their economic interests are more internally consistent and focused on generational issues than those of younger voters with workplace affiliations. The occasional residential concentration of the elderly further increases their internal cohesion and political effectiveness, as does the existence of powerful lobbying groups such as the American Association of Retired Persons (AARP). Thus, one would expect them to do best in influencing the government's distributional policies.

Those between the ages of eighteen and sixty-five are next best-off politically. They can at least reflect upon their interests and vote, although they have less leisure than their elders and may focus on professional and occupational interests that divide (as well as distract) them. One is hardly surprised by the evidence from generational accounting that they do better than those younger than eighteen or as yet unborn but not as well as the elderly.

Against this background of unequal power and participation, generational accounting data, while welcome, may prove to be of only limited value. Indeed, in some cases, it may even tilt power still further toward the elderly. Consider Kotlikoff's findings that older generations gain from tax benefits for existing investment, while losing from tax benefits for new investment and from taxing consumption. The elderly might make better use than younger voters of such information. One could imagine, for example, AARP-financed television commercials denouncing proposed legislation that had been estimated to cost the average elderly person a specified dollar amount.

In such an environment, the deficit, despite its clear analytical inferiority to generational accounting, has certain advantages as a focus for political debate. At present, many accept what Kotlikoff sarcastically calls the " 'Golden Rule of Deficits,' according to which the only good deficit is a zero deficit" (7). As long as this is true, reliance on it has clear implications for policy: reduce spending or increase taxes until the accepted target of zero is reached, or at least avoid going in the opposite direction. The "Golden Rule" is backed by centuries of popular concern about deficits and by the intuitive analogy between public and private borrowing. In recent years, it has repeatedly influenced the legislative process. Consider the Gramm-Rudman-Hollings Act of 1985, the budget agreements of 1990 and 1993, and the competing Republican and Democratic plans of 1995 and 1996 to balance the budget within seven years. Moreover, the antideficit movement, however limited its success, may have constrained interest group activity at the margin. For example, on the tax side, the norm of requiring proposed changes to be revenue-neutral has been widely credited with discouraging unmeritorious giveaways (see, e.g., Gramlich 1990, 80; White and Wildavsky 1989, 458–60).

The long-term financing problems presented by Social Security and Medicare may likewise be more politically tractable when they receive distinct treatment. Long-term fiscal estimates for these programs, premised on the objective of close actuarial balance over the long term, have already attracted significant attention and motivated major policy changes. Indeed, the programs' popularity is such that emphasizing their expected long-term inability to pay for themselves may be essential to persuading politicians and voters to consider fiscally necessary changes to them sooner rather than later.

Generational accounting presents no such clear target for fiscal policy as that of "balance." Moreover, it is not as intuitive, salient, or historically rooted a measure as the budget deficit. In a world of irrational or shortsighted actors, responding haphazardly to sound bites or the crisis du jour, the paradoxical effect of replacing the budget deficit as a focus for public debate might be to *reduce* political pressures either to lessen the fiscal burden on future generations or to address in advance problems of policy sustainability.

Accordingly, discussion of the budget deficit ought not to disappear from public political debate, even if generational accounting increasingly supplements it. For purposes of intellectual inquiry, however, generational accounting plainly represents a major step forward. One can disagree with any number of Kotlikoff's decisions in constructing his version of it or doubt that the system will ever be precise enough to inspire as much confidence as one might like, but its two core features—applying economic accrual principles and focusing on *who* pays taxes and receives benefits—significantly advance our understanding of fiscal policy.

F. Summing Up the Last Twenty Years of the Deficit Debate among Economists

1. Conclusions from the Literature Review

The deficit debate among economists over the last twenty years has had two great virtues. The first involves revival more than innovation. Macroeconomic debate is once again joined by generational and size-of-government debate. The second, more innovative virtue, responding to changes since the 1930s in the federal government's size and scope of operations, involves how one should measure the effects of fiscal policy. The cash-flow budget deficit is no longer blindly accepted as a canonical measure.

My review of this debate has yielded a number of conclusions, including the following, that are crucial prerequisites to addressing the substance of the issues raised by budget deficits.

The budget deficit is deeply flawed as an economic measure. It ignores economic accrual, gives undue weight to whether one uses the terminology of "loan" and "repayment" or that of "tax" and "transfer" and does not address who pays taxes or receives government benefits. There is, however, a meaningful underlying economic phenomenon. I will henceforth use the term *tax lag* to describe a fiscal policy (such as our present one) in which, over the long term, (1) tax revenues will be inadequate to pay for government spending absent a policy change, and/or (2) under present policy, future generations and younger individuals seem likely to pay higher lifetime net tax rates than current generations and older individuals. These two variants—underspecification of long-term net revenues under present policy, and the imposition of higher lifetime net tax burdens on younger individuals and future generations—are closely linked as a practical matter, despite being intellectually distinct. Underspecification of needed net revenues implies that change will be necessary in the future, very likely to the detriment of younger individuals and future generations when they become the main taxpayers and the main beneficiaries from government spending. Such underspecification therefore strongly implies generational burden-shifting.

Tax lag can be reduced in two ways. The first is to increase the present value of the taxes expected over the long term under present policy, or to be paid by current generations and older individuals. The second is to reduce the present value of the government spending expected over the long term under present policy, or that will benefit current generations and older individuals. Since the term *tax lag* describes the relative timing of taxes and spending, it could just as accurately be called *spending acceleration*.

The Ricardian equivalence theorem, stated in strong form to assert that tax lag has no first-order consequences, is incorrect. Ricardian offsets, or adjustments to bequests and lifetime transfers between members of different generations to achieve preferred distributions no matter what the fiscal policy, are incomplete as a result of fiscal illusion, the prospect of leaving a "negative bequest," and strategic behavior and impure altruism both within and between households. Ricardians are right, however, to emphasize that fiscal policy is but one of the arenas in which the generations interact; that the household is a second important arena, in which internal altruism plays a role; and that private behavior can offset apparent effects of government policy.

Tax lag tends to increase current market consumption relative to saving and to shift lifetime consumption from future to current generations. This results from its generally increasing aggregate perceived wealth, because people tend not to weigh the implied future taxes at their present value equivalent in current taxes. Greater perceived wealth should lead to greater lifetime spending on market consumption (which is another way of saying that Ricardian offsets are incomplete).

Traditional Keynesian claims about budget deficits can be modified to relate instead to tax lag (as subjectively perceived by current consumers). From such a modified Keynesian perspective, one could claim that, short of full employment, tax lag not only is stimulative but also increases total market consumption over time (through a shift from nonmarket consumption), rather than merely shifting market consumption from the future to the present. However, this claim is subject to the following qualifications: tax lag generally induces both types of shifts; increasing market relative to nonmarket consumption is not necessarily desirable, especially in nonrecessionary circumstances; fiscal stimulus can only address cyclical, not structural, unemployment; and the president and Congress cannot be trusted to run an actively countercyclical fiscal policy in a principled or effective fashion.

Tax lag tends to increase government spending by reducing its perceived (and real) cost to current voters. Yet it is unclear to what extent reducing tax lag would lead to a smaller government, even if (as seems likely) it reduced government spending. The actual size of government is a much more elusive concept than the number of dollars being spent, since it is a function of government policy's actual effects. Same-dollar tax levies or spending programs can have radically different magnitudes of effect on, say, resource allocation or wealth distribution. Moreover, regulations, while substantively equivalent and to some extent interchangeable with tax-financed spending programs, are off-budget. Thus, limiting tax lag would not affect them directly and might even lead them increasingly to replace explicit taxes and spending.

The most intuitive way to measure tax lag would be through a measure that (purely as a thought experiment) I call the "economic accrual budget deficit." This would measure the increase in present value, during the current fiscal year, of the amount by which taxes seemed inadequate to pay for government spending over the long run under current policy. Suppose, for example, that at the beginning of the fiscal year, the national debt stood at $2 trillion, and the present value of all expected future budget deficits (construed to include all "off-budget" items) under current policy stood at $3 trillion. Tax lag would therefore total $5 trillion, in present value terms, at the start of the year. (This would be the "economic accrual national debt.") Next, suppose that during the fiscal year, there was a $100 billion cash-flow budget deficit and that the present value of all expected future deficits rose by $150 billion. The economic accrual budget deficit would equal the sum of these two figures, or $250 billion, as the present value of the tax lag would have increased by that amount to $5.25 trillion in the course of the fiscal year.

Although the economic accrual budget deficit provides an intuitive measure of tax lag, generational accounting is ultimately more informative, because it addresses who pays taxes and receives government benefits. Yet Laurence Kotlikoff's particular version of it can be questioned in various respects. For example, he may underestimate the tendency of economic growth to reduce tax lag. Moreover, he treats tax lag as significant only when it shifts tax burdens to future generations, whereas in a world of limited information, it may increase one's perceived wealth even if one is likely to pay added taxes later in one's life. In addition, the accuracy and value of any generational accounting computations are limited by our inevitable uncertainty about the future, by the difficulty of discerning people's subjective expectations, and by fiscal policy's including only a portion of what the government and present generations do.

Generational accounting computations suggest that modern fiscal policy generally has transferred wealth from younger to older Americans and will continue to do so under its present course. Lifetime net tax rates have risen fairly steadily throughout the twentieth century and may, if present policy continues, reach levels for future generations that seem severe and even prohibitive.

2. The Problem of Policy Sustainability

Generational accounting's findings, however one discounts them for uncertainty and omitted variables, raise concern about all three of the main issues involving tax lag: generational distribution, macroeconomic policy, and the size of government. The next three chapters will explore these issues at length—particularly with regard to whether the consequences are regrettable and, if so, what should be done about them. First, however, I will briefly discuss a fourth implication of generational accounting's findings: that current fiscal policy is likely to prove unsustainable fairly soon.

If current policy is unsustainable, it must and will change. The direction in which it ought to change depends on the three main issues raised by tax lag, as well as on other issues such as those related to wealth distribution within generations. Yet the prospect of policy change also has an important prudential focus that merits brief discussion.

Government policy changes all the time. When it changes, different individuals win and lose on what is essentially a windfall basis. Even if they in effect have bet in the marketplace on whether policy would change—as when I buy a home for a high price, reflecting my belief that Congress will not enact a "flat tax" eliminating the deduction for home mortgage interest—there is a windfall gain or loss as the uncertainty is resolved.

Why—and when—should we care about these windfall gains and losses, given that government policy must and often should change? Consider three examples of windfall loss from policy change. The first is a permanent federal government default on particular bonds. (Or one could make it expropriating someone's property, after repealing the constitutional requirement that government takings of property be compensated.) The second example is changing Social Security policy so that workers near retirement, who have made decades of mandatory contributions to the system, will never receive the benefits that current policy seemed to promise them. The third example is surprising me, after I bought my home for a high price in the example above, by repealing the mortgage interest deduction that I had thought would be retained.

Although all the examples are conceptually similar, many would agree that they should not be viewed the same way. The first policy change (in both its bondholder and property-owner variants) seems most troubling, the second intermediate, and the third most innocuous. Yet the distinction, however important, is essentially prudential. After all, bondholders bet against default (and property owners against expropriation), no less than I, as a home buyer, bet against a tax law change. Even the Social Security participants "placed bets" by deciding how much to save. Moreover, in each case, the market price at which the bets were placed reflected a widespread societal belief that policy change was unlikely.

Three main factors create the powerful prudential distinction among the three cases. The first is backward-looking and involves actual or reasonable *reliance*. To what extent did people assume, or should they have assumed, that government policy would not change? Here the bondholder and the property owner have strong claims. The worker near retirement who is facing a loss of expected Social Security benefits has an intermediate claim, given that Social Security policy frequently changes (and is clearly on the current political agenda) but that to some extent there has been a promise of general policy continuity, such that contributors will later benefit. The amount that the worker saved for retirement may have reflected an implicit government promise not to change Social Security too much. My conscious knowledge that major tax changes were being discussed, and in any event happen all the time, makes my reliance interest the weakest among this group, although the Social Security reliance claim of a still-young worker might be weaker still.

The second distinction among policy changes is forward-looking and involves future *expectations*. Here, once again, powerful considerations suggest protecting the bondholder and the property owner. A bond default might raise the interest rate that the federal government must pay on its bonds for decades to come. A policy shift to permitting expropriation might make people reluctant to invest in socially valuable ways that left them vulnerable to uncompensated seizure. As we move to the Social Security and home-buyer cases, these concerns, while they do not disappear, grow weaker if one is less concerned about opportunistic government behavior. In addition, the offsetting advantages of retaining policy flexibility may grow stronger.

The third distinction among policy changes is present-oriented and involves *transitional shock*. Suppose that repealing the home mortgage interest deduction would cause a wave of mortgage defaults, leading to bank failures and general economic disruption. This prospect might suggest, at the least, providing transitional relief or phasing in the repeal gradually, even if one thought that buyers and their banks ought not to have relied and bet as they did. This is essentially a point about implicit insurance. Losses often inflict the least harm if they are spread widely rather than being highly concentrated.

For each of the three distinctions, one could argue that if people are averse to the risk of policy change, they can simply buy private insurance against it. Why have the government act as implicit insurer if private insurance markets, which tend to be more efficient, are available? The government, however, is the optimal insurer against the risk of its reneging on its own definite commitments. Thus, the argument for private insurance, in lieu of policy continuity as a form of implicit public insurance, makes sense only when one is not overly concerned that the government will renege opportunistically.[18]

Generalizing from these three distinctions, policy continuity and policy flexibility have competing benefits, the relative weight of which

18. Compare Kaplow 1986 (arguing for only private insurance against the consequences of legal change) with Logue 1996 (arguing that the government is the best insurer against its own opportunistic reneging on implicit promises of policy continuity).

varies with the setting. Some policies should be more fixed while others should be more flexible, and shared understandings should (and generally do) enable people to tell these policies apart. As it happens, the practicalities of government borrowing dictate locating near the pole of continuity, while those of running an income tax system dictate locating nearer the pole of flexibility, with Social Security lying somewhere in between (and moving toward the continuity pole for older as compared to younger participants).

As a general matter, however, gradual and widely expected change is better than sudden and surprising change. Moreover, distributing the costs of change as widely as possible is often desirable on insurance grounds. This suggests that if a set of policies is unsustainable, it should be changed as soon and as gradually as possible (all else being equal). Changing it sooner and more gradually gives greater notice, facilitating people's adjustment. In addition, it permits the costs of change to be spread among more people, since older generations, approaching the end of their lives, will share the cost either now or never. Finally, the choice of policy changes should reflect the relative strength of continuity and flexibility interests in different areas. This is why bondholders generally should be repaid and retirees who receive Social Security and Medicare benefits treated in light of their possible reliance, even if they are required to bear some of the cost of change.

At present, generational accounting computations—as well as more conventionally framed estimates regarding budget deficits, Social Security, and Medicare—indicate that the problem of policy sustainability is quite acute. Ever-increasing tax lag is inherently a kind of Ponzi scheme, and the rate of increase that generational accounting shows indicates that collapse of the scheme is imminent. Yet which precise changes we should adopt depends less, in the end, on these problems of transition than on matters of long-term substance, including generational policy, macroeconomic policy, and size-of-government issues. I turn to those three issues next.

FIVE

Tax Lag and Generational Equity

So far, the analysis in this book has mainly been positive rather than normative. On the issue of generational distribution, while we have seen that tax lag tends to benefit present generations at the expense of future generations, we have not yet considered whether there is anything wrong with this. To put it more broadly, how *should* fiscal policy affect the relative well-being of members of different generations? Can we define a norm of generational equity?

Many may share Laurence Kotlikoff's view that our current fiscal policy, as measured by generational accounting, is grossly unfair. Indeed, the picture that generational accounting presents is bad enough to have policy implications wholly apart from any appeal to moral principles. Lifetime net tax rates on future generations in excess of 80 percent would seem practically and politically unsustainable even if one had no objection to them in principle.

Yet Kotlikoff goes beyond noting the sustainability problem to set forth an affirmative principle of generational equity, which he calls "generational balance," under which avoiding confiscatory rates is not enough. Rather, Kotlikoff asserts, members of each generation should pay the same lifetime net tax rate. When lifetime net tax rates continually rise, he believes that lifetime consumption opportunities are being unfairly transferred from future to present, and younger to older, generations.

Although, as we will see, Kotlikoff has technical reasons using this precise definition, the underlying norm could be stated more intuitively as disfavoring large-scale intergenerational wealth transfers through fiscal policy. Such a norm underlies as well the commonly expressed view that we are "robbing" future generations by leaving them the bills to pay for our government spending. I therefore begin the normative analysis of generational equity by evaluating first this no-transfer principle and then Kotlikoff's principle of generational balance.

A. A No-Transfer Norm for Generational Policy?

Opposition to a fiscal policy that transfers lifetime consumption opportunities between generations is a subset of opposition to government-induced wealth transfers generally. The belief that government should minimize its compulsory wealth transfers, at least where they lack strong justification, has widespread appeal. It resonates in individual liberty, in property rights, and in a kind of equal treatment if one thinks it somehow invidious to take from one person in order to give to another. A no-transfer norm reflects the practice of expecting people to pay their own way, rather than being supported by or asked to support others, which we follow in most of our dealings with strangers, neighbors, and even close friends.

Classical principles of benefit taxation, which hold that people should pay the government only for the value of the benefits that they themselves get back from it, reflect the no-transfer norm. So does the view among some economics-minded conservatives that permissible government policies should be restricted to the Pareto superior: those that help someone and hurt no one, leading to a requirement that even a policy yielding societal gains in excess of losses not be adopted unless the losers receive full compensation.

One can ground the no-transfer norm in prudential considerations, no less than in moral first principles. Some argue, for example, that a no-transfer norm tends to promote efficiency in the sense of societal wealth maximization. Redistribution tends to be costly, not only because of its transaction costs and effects on incentives but also because of its encouraging the range of socially nonproductive activities, designed to procure or resist wealth transfers, that the public choice literature calls "rent-seeking."

The no-transfer norm is nonetheless, and quite rightly, highly controversial. In tax policy, the benefit theory of taxation has long since given way, in most quarters, to a belief that tax burdens should be allocated based on ability to pay (see, e.g., Seligman 1931, 71–74;

Simons 1938, 3; Groves 1974, 29)—thus transferring wealth from the better-off to the worse-off if the better-off do not receive commensurately greater benefits from government spending. A range of moral theories, from utilitarianism to Rawlsianism to communitarianism, can be invoked to support compulsory wealth transfers that involve progressive redistribution.

In addition, writers such as Cass Sunstein argue that a no-transfer norm is inherently arbitrary because it adopts as a baseline the "pre-political" distribution of wealth that ostensibly would prevail absent whichever government policies one is evaluating. Sunstein's argument is twofold. First, the no-transfer norm requires assuming the prevailing distribution's superiority to any other. Second, given the pervasive effects of government on *all* private activity and wealth—not only through explicitly redistributive programs but in light of such core functions as protecting private property—the no-transfer norm is incoherent. There *is* no identifiable starting point to treat as a baseline; the implicitly assumed pre-political distribution does not exist to begin with (see Sunstein 1987).

These arguments, whether one accepts them or not, help to show the inherently controversial nature of a no-transfer norm. In the setting of generational policy, however, one need not decide whether or not the arguments are correct. The no-transfer norm, even if persuasive in other settings, is peculiarly artificial and question-begging here. What makes it so is the pervasiveness of transfers between members of different generations, acting outside the realm of government fiscal policy. Ordinarily, when one is comparing two groups—say, the rich and the poor or urban and rural Americans—one can assume that there will be a relative paucity of gratuitous transfers between the groups. Exchange transactions are the expected norm. Thus, without absurdity, one can isolate for analysis a proposed wealth transfer between the groups—although, to be sure, there is always the argument that a seeming transfer from group A to group B merely reverses a preexisting separate transfer from group B to group A. The claim that fiscal policy improperly favors one group at another's expense is not inherently myopic.

A comparison of overlapping generations, for purposes of assessing government fiscal policy, is quite different. Even accepting that fiscal policy has generational consequences given the incompleteness of Ricardian offsets, a no-transfer norm for fiscal policy appears strangely blinkered and formalistic given the other gratuitous transfers between the generations that are always taking place. Why care about one particular route of accomplishing something that is pervasive, and that mostly goes in the opposite direction, from older to younger generations?

The existence of bequests is only a small part of the broader picture—commonly emphasized because it is the part most obviously subject to Ricardian adjustment. Consider that numerous members of older generations devote enormous resources—above all, their own personal efforts as parents—to support and train for adulthood the members of younger generations. Every diaper changed, every moment spent driving one's child to school, could be termed an intergenerational transfer of consumption, or at least a positive spillover if the parent enjoys it for its own sake.

Yet even the transfers within a single household capture only a portion of the whole. Consider the occurrence throughout society of net capital formation, or the increase over time in net social resources, generally resulting from saving and productive investment. Or consider the fact that at no time (as yet) have living generations wholly depleted or degraded existing real resources, despite by now possessing the physical power to do so. Resource nondepletion and, beyond that, net capital formation depend in large part on the willingness (whether or not altruistically motivated) of members of present generations to forgo consumption during their lifetimes, to the potential benefit of their descendants. Such decisions are functionally equivalent to transfers to future generations, even if the word *transfer* seems inapposite given its implication that everything now available is rightfully ours to dispose of as we wish. A "transfer," for this purpose, need only mean a decision not to allocate wholly to oneself a resource that is subject to one's physical power.

Transfers from present to future generations through resource nondepletion and net capital formation are so huge that a principle barring transfers in the opposite direction from the narrow area of fiscal policy seems absurd. In addition, such a no-transfer norm might be contrary to all generations' preferences. Suppose, as Allan Drazen has posited, that parents would increase their investments in their children's education, given the enormous return that such investment may yield in the form of increased future earnings, but for the difficulty of ensuring that the children will share the benefits with them. One cannot, after all, create a legally enforceable debt running from one's minor children to oneself (repayable at adulthood), or require them to repay one's debts at death, or, as a practical matter, even borrow against their expected future earnings. Given these imperfections in capital markets, a selfish parent might decline, say, to borrow for a child's education at 8 percent for a return of 20 percent, absent any mechanism for making the child share this return. Debt-financed government spending for education, to be repaid when the children are tax-paying adults, has the potential to correct this gap in the capital markets and thus to benefit members of both generations despite its violating the no-transfer norm (see Drazen 1978). Under the right conditions, therefore, all generations would reject the norm and instead support the use of fiscal policy to transfer money from younger to older generations.

One could also extend this argument for universally acceptable generational transfers to more controversial circumstances. Suppose that one generation saved too little because its members reasonably failed to anticipate an extraordinary one-time improvement in medical technology that would enable them to live longer lives at a greater cost in medical treatment. Arguably, under these circumstances, the benefit that wealthier younger generations could convey to them through a one-time wealth transfer would support or perhaps require a departure from the no-transfer norm, even if it were otherwise compelling.

Or suppose that societal preferences shift regarding the treatment of different age groups. In the 1930s, for example, the enactment of Social Security reflected a deliberate decision to benefit the elderly, on the ground that they were past their prime earning years and thus could not be expected to escape poverty. More recently, the view has spread that we should focus on helping children, because of their helplessness, the decline of the traditional nuclear family, and the payoff to society from "investing" in them. One could argue that neither of these two views ought to have been rejected simply because of the transitional effects on lifetime outcomes for different age cohorts.

Against all these weighty objections to the no-transfer norm for fiscal policy, only one good argument weighs strongly in favor of it. The norm may be well suited to minimize fiscal illusion and thereby to enable members of present generations to achieve the desired relationship between their own consumption and the wealth that they make available to their heirs through bequests or otherwise. Even Ricardians, who necessarily reject fiscal illusion, might concede that a no-transfer norm for fiscal policy could lower the cost of making an accurate long-term assessment.

This argument is far from trivial if one believes that as a result of fiscal illusion, present generations are saving too little relative to their own intergenerational preferences. It would imply that both present and future generations suffer when generational policy is imbalanced. Present generations fail to accomplish their own objectives—although they may never learn that they have left their descendants less than they intended. Future generations end up receiving smaller net bequests than they would have if their forebears had correctly understood the effects of government policy.

Nonetheless, the argument falls short of establishing that the no-transfer norm should be accepted despite its many problems and limitations. Alternative and less sweeping responses to the fiscal illusion problem are possible. One such response would be simply attempting to promote greater public understanding and debate regarding the generational consequences of government policy. A second possibility would be to encourage saving and investment by alternative means. For example, one could extend more favorable tax treatment to saving and investment or alter government spending to place greater emphasis on long-term investment.

Moreover, at bottom, the fiscal illusion argument relies on a claim of harm to present, rather than future, generations. Although future generations are harmed if present ones mistakenly save too little, only the departure from what present generations really want makes this appear unambiguously bad rather than a potentially indeterminate tradeoff. Accordingly, I will postpone further discussion of the fiscal illusion problem until chapter 6, where I discuss the claim that national saving is too low from the perspective of present generations.

Even if one nonetheless accepted the no-transfer norm for fiscal policy, one would run into the problem of its being avoidable through purely formal policy changes. Consider a hypothetical example of two generations, each containing the same number of individuals. The average member of generation 1 pays taxes in the amount of $40 and receives a $15 transfer payment from the government (financed by members of generation 2), leaving the individual a lifetime net tax payment of $25. The average member of generation 2 pays taxes in the amount of $45 (including the $15 paid to members of generation 1) and receives no transfer payments from the government. Thus, that person's lifetime net tax payment is $45. Under a no-transfer norm, generation 1 is unduly benefiting at the expense of generation 2.

Suppose, however, that one changed the tax and transfer systems so that the average member of generation 1 simply paid $25 in tax to begin with, rather than paying $40 and receiving $15. Under this change, the average member of generation 2 would continue to pay $45 in taxes, with the extra $15 now making up the revenue loss from the generation 1 tax cut rather than going directly to members of generation 1. Nothing would have changed in substance, yet there would no longer be so explicit a transfer.

What seems to matter, therefore, is relative lifetime net tax payments, not explicit, traceable transfers in the fungible medium of cash. Yet perhaps even lifetime net tax payments do not tell us enough. Suppose, in the above example, that the average member of generation 1 has lifetime income of $100, while the average member of generation 2 has lifetime income of $300. This would lead to lifetime net tax rates of 25 percent for generation 1 and only 15 percent for generation 2—perhaps suggesting that generation 2 has been treated better after all, even with the explicit transfer. What arguably matters is neither explicit transfers nor relative lifetime net tax payments, but relative lifetime net tax *rates*. This is Kotlikoff's position, and I examine it next.

B. A Fiscal Policy Norm of Generational Balance?

Kotlikoff does little to defend or even explain the norm of generational balance, defined as equalizing the lifetime net tax rates of at least some present generations and future generations. Perhaps he means to rely on the standard tax policy norm of horizontal equity, defined as extending equal treatment (in the form of a uniform net tax rate) to persons who are deemed relevantly equal.

The argument that a principle of horizontal equity requires applying the same lifetime net tax rate to average members of different generations depends on a number of narrower claims. For example, it requires asserting both (1) that members of a single generation are sufficiently alike that one should group them together for purposes of determining the effect of government fiscal policy on an average member of the group, and (2) that members of different generations, while not appropriately grouped together, are equals in a morally relevant sense.

In *Generational Accounting*, Kotlikoff defends only the first of these two claims. He states that generational groupings make sense because people born at around the same time tend to act more alike than people born at very different times, reflecting their degrees of common experience (1992, 107–8). This point has more obvious relevance to using generational groupings for purposes of predicting the effects of government policy than for purposes of measuring equity.

Suppose, however, that we accept generational groupings and average-member comparisons for purposes of measuring horizontal equity. An additional preliminary problem worth noting is that the horizontal equity standard is controversial in the public finance literature. Louis Kaplow argues that horizontal equity lacks a clear normative basis and conflicts with better-grounded utilitarian and social welfare norms. It can indicate reducing overall social welfare, as in the case where, since A is being treated better than B but ought to be treated the same, it could support harming A even if B does not benefit from the change (Kaplow 1990).

Even if one accepts the principle of horizontal equity, however, its capacity to support equalizing lifetime net tax rates in the generational setting is extremely weak. For one thing, why should we regard the members of different generations as relevantly alike? In the tax policy literature, likeness often is thought to depend on the amount of one's income or consumption. Such an assumption seems implicit in generational accounting's lifetime net tax rate computation, which uses lifetime income as the denominator. Most tax writers regard horizontal equity as in principle consistent with applying different tax rates to people whose incomes (or consumption) differ. Comparisons between persons at different levels therefore are said to require consulting the far less determinate standard of *vertical* equity, or appropriately differentiated treatment of those who in a relevant sense are not the same. Anyone who supports any significant degree of rate progressivity in the income tax system should reject the claim that in the generational setting, horizontal equity requires equalizing lifetime net tax rates —unless one expects lifetime income henceforth to be constant over time, in contrast to its long-standing historical trend of steady increase.

Suppose, however, that one rejects rate progressivity. Even so, the principle that equals should be treated equally provides at best limited support for equalizing different generations' lifetime net tax rates. An initial problem is that the norm seems powerful, if at all, only as applied to overlapping generations. To illustrate, consider two generations that do not overlap at all. Suppose that one generation, born in 1800, had a lifetime net tax rate of only 10 percent, while another generation, born in 1950, is expected to have a lifetime net tax rate in excess of 30 percent. The claim that the 1950 age cohort has been treated inequitably relative to the 1800 age cohort is implausible. Even if we accept the unlikely assumption that the two age cohorts received government services of equal value—and thus that the 1950 generation truly did worse in its relations with the government than the 1800 generation—the two sets of lifetime net taxes reflect wholly separate sets of political decisions made by different people at different times, with no direct interaction. Thus, even if the 1800 group fared better than the 1950 group in its fiscal transactions with the government, this seems morally irrelevant. Similarly, one would term it merely unfortunate, not unfair, that modern generations have the polio vaccine and earlier generations did not.

Even with overlapping generations, however, the norm of holding lifetime net tax rates constant has limited power at best. In other writing about horizontal equity, I have noted that when it is evaluated by looking only at a subset of the government's actions, it "suffers from ineradicable second-best problems. Where the treatment of two individuals may differ in numerous respects, equalizing how they are treated under one set of government rules does not necessarily have any tendency to equalize their treatment by the government overall, and may as plausibly reduce overall equality of treatment" (Shaviro 1993a, 410). This criticism may seem less relevant to generational accounting than to income taxation, since the former captures a broader subset of government rules by looking in full at both the tax and transfer sides. Still, generational accounting is limited to fiscal policy and thus mostly cannot adjust for generational differences in benefit from the noncash goods and services that the government provides, in detriment such as regulatory burden, and in noncash contributions to the government such as conscripted military service. The size and scope of these items may vary sharply over time, for such reasons as the historical growth of government, the sporadic nature of foreign wars (and use of the military draft), and the enactment or revision of regulatory legislation (such as the Age Discrimination in Employment Act) that may have disparate effects across age cohorts. In addition, generational accounting cannot adjust for all of government's indirect generational effects. Consider how the tax system's generational effects might differ, holding constant the revenue received from current taxpayers, depending on whether it encouraged saving (to the benefit of future generations) or discouraged it (to their detriment). Given these omissions, it is hard to be certain that age cohorts with higher lifetime net tax rates have actually fared worse vis-à-vis the government than age cohorts with lower rates.

Yet even focusing purely on the overall activities of the government provides too narrow a focus for assessing generational equity. As I noted in criticizing the no-transfer norm, government policy embraces only a small portion of the total interaction between present and future generations. What matters most in the end is the overall level of well-being that different generations experience, which depends in good part on present generations' net capital formation and productivity of investment. A generation that benefits from substantial tax lag but nonetheless saves a lot and invests it productively, is treating future generations better than one that, despite avoiding tax lag, saves less and invests it less productively. A focus purely on lifetime net tax rates can thus severely mislead one regarding the overall picture.

The following hypothetical examples help to show the weakness of the relationship between tax lag and succeeding generations' relative well-being. All dollar totals are in present value terms from birth, all generations have the same number of individuals, and what I for convenience call "bequests" include transfers made by older generations (as for child support) during their lifetimes.

> **Example 1.** The average member of generation 1 has $100 of lifetime income, pays $30 in lifetime net taxes (which buys $30 worth of consumption), spends $60 on private lifetime consumption, and bequeaths $10 to generation 2. The average member of generation 2 has lifetime income of $120 (including the average $10 bequest) and pays $36 in lifetime net taxes.

Under these facts, no deferred taxes were handed down from generation 1 to generation 2, and both generations have lifetime net tax rates of 30 percent. Here lifetime net tax rates may appear meaningful: they seem to illustrate the policy of generational balance that Kotlikoff advocates.

> **Example 2.** Same as example 1 except that generation 1 uses debt financing to pay for one-third of its government-provided consumption. Hence, the average member of generation 1 pays only $20 in taxes. Generation 1 is completely Ricardian, however—or else has a higher propensity to save than in example 1 for unrelated reasons. Its average member therefore continues to spend

$60 on lifetime consumption and to bequeath $20 gross—$10 net of deferred taxes—to generation 2. The average member of generation 2 uses the extra $10 bequest (relative to example 1) to pay the $10 of deferred taxes, thus increasing lifetime net taxes to $46.

While this example is identical in substance to example 1, generation 2's lifetime net tax rate rises to 46/130, or 35.4 percent, while generation 1's rate falls to 20 percent. Suppose that we changed example 1 to have generation 1 pay no taxes, using instead 100 percent debt financing, yet still make full Ricardian adjustments. Now generation 2's lifetime net tax rate would rise to 66/150, or 44 percent, while generation 1's rate would be zero, despite the lack of any true change in end result.

Or suppose we changed example 1 still more, to convert an additional $30 of the average member of generation 1's private consumption into government-provided consumption that was debt-financed but fully offset by a $30 increase in the gross bequest. Now generation 2's lifetime net tax rate would rise to 96/180, or 53.3 percent, although it would still be faring just as well as it did in example 1.

The underlying point is that later generations are neither benefited nor burdened on balance when they are bequeathed both additional gross assets and additional deferred tax obligations. Yet lifetime net tax rates treat this breakeven transaction as yielding additional lifetime income that is taxed at 100 percent—thus increasing the recipients' lifetime net tax rate despite the lack of any true change.

This example is significant even if one agrees that full Ricardian offsets generally do not occur. Examples 1 and 2 could simply be different societies (or the same society at different times) that happen to differ in their savings rates as well as in their use of tax lag. The point remains that lifetime net tax rates can provide a misleading picture of one generation's actual net effect on the next generation.

Example 3. Same as example 2 (in the main variant, where the average member of generation 1 leaves $10 of deferred taxes) except for two changes. The first is that the level of Ricardian offset for the change of fiscal policy from that in example 1 is more realistic. The average member of generation 1—feeling wealthier than in example 1 despite the implied future taxes and a willingness to leave a positive bequest—now spends $68 on lifetime consumption rather than $60 as in examples 1 and 2. The generation 1 member thus bequeaths $12 gross, or $2 net of deferred taxes. The second change from example 2 is that, while generation 2 still spends 30 percent of its lifetime income (net of deferred taxes) on taxes to pay for its government-provided consumption, the amount thus determined now equals only $33.60.

The average member of generation 2 therefore has lifetime income of $122 (reflecting the gross bequest) and pays $43.60 in net taxes (including $10 in deferred taxes). The lifetime net tax rate is 35.7 percent, as compared to generation 1's rate of 20 percent.

Here, a focus on lifetime net tax rates correctly shows that generation 2 has been adversely affected by generation 1's tax lag. Yet such a focus misconceives the adverse impact as resulting from the deferred taxes themselves rather than from the reduction in the net bequest. In addition, it invites one to overlook the fact that generation 2 is better off than generation 1 despite the tax lag. Its lifetime income, net of deferred taxes to pay for generation 1's consumption, is $112 compared to generation 1's $100.

Example 4. Same as example 1 except that generation 1 spends $68 on lifetime consumption (as in example 3) even without the goad of debt financing. Now generation 2 receives a $2 gross (and net) bequest and has lifetime income of $112. Assuming that generation 2 still chooses to use 30 percent of net lifetime income to pay for its own government-provided consumption, its average member will pay a net tax of $33.60 and have a lifetime net tax rate of 30 percent—the same rate as that on generation 1.

Here, lifetime net tax rates imply that the case is equivalent to example 1, whereas in fact generational distribution is identical to that in example 3. Again, what matters is not deferred taxes but the net bequest, which depends on generation 1's saving rate. Deferred taxes matter only indirectly, since they tend to induce members of generation 1 to consume more than they would otherwise.

Example 5. Same as example 1 except that during the middle of generation 1's life span, a technological change increases the extent to which in-kind consumption is most efficiently supplied by the government. Accordingly, a permanent policy change is adopted under which lifetime net tax rates will henceforth be 50 percent. Since generation 1 is already midway through its life span, however (and on a course to pay only 30 percent), its average member ends up paying a lifetime net tax rate of only 40 percent.

Now, even though no deferred taxes were handed down from generation 1 to generation 2, the latter has a much higher lifetime net tax rate–50 percent instead of 40 percent.

Example 6. In society A, generation 1 leaves generation 2 zero gross assets and zero deferred taxes. Generation 2 has average lifetime income of $100 and pays lifetime net taxes of $20 that finance its own consumption. Society B is identical to society A, except that generation 1 leaves generation 2 both gross assets and deferred taxes (which generation 2 pays) in the amount of $900. Accordingly, in society B, generation 2's gross lifetime income is $1,000 (although net of deferred taxes, it is only $100), and it ends up in the same position as its counterpart in society A after paying $920 of lifetime net taxes (including $20 for its own consumption). Each generation 2 fares about the same in material terms, even though in society A its lifetime net tax rate is 20 percent, while in society B the rate is 92 percent.

Example 6 shows again that high lifetime net tax rates need not indicate a generational equity problem, even if they indicate a sustainability problem. While generation 2 has been treated no worse in society B than in society A, we may suspect that a 92 percent lifetime net tax rate will be politically and practically impossible to apply. The problems are twofold. First, tax distortions will likely be far higher at a 92 percent rate than at a 20 percent rate, although in principle one could imagine the use of nondistortive lump-sum taxes to provide the extra revenue. Second, generation 2 may well resist the imposition of higher taxes in society B, because its higher gross resources may give it a different set of expectations. Its members were not in a position to agree in advance to the deferred taxes as a condition of receiving the gross assets.

In sum, one simply cannot state a meaningful norm regarding how different generations' lifetime net tax rates ought to compare. Even a predicted 84 percent lifetime net tax rate on future generations would not necessarily be generationally unfair. Such a rate should indeed be viewed with concern, but on sustainability grounds. If current fiscal policy suggests a lifetime net tax rate on future generations that we know will be politically and practically impossible to apply, then fiscal policy is bound to change, and this change may prove disruptive. I next turn to the question of how one *could* give meaningful content to the principle of generational equity.

C. Developing Alternatives to the Unpersuasive No-Transfer and "Generational Balance" Norms

If both horizontal equity and the no-transfer norm for government fiscal policy are unpersuasive, where does this leave us? The immensity of transfers (broadly conceived) from present to future generations does not establish that we are entitled to get something back through fiscal policy. We obviously owe everything, even our existence, to past generations that similarly made transfers to us. The point, rather, is that fiscal policy is merely one integral part of a larger whole. What matters, for purposes of determining the allocation of consumption between present and future generations, is the *overall* nature and amount of what we take and what we leave. This, in turn, depends in part on saving rates and net capital formation, construed to include human capital and all changes to depletable and degradable resources. Yet this broad perspective merely describes the scope of our normative inquiry; it does not immediately suggest any answers.

Fortunately, normative inquiry about generational equity can draw on a rich economic and philosophical literature. An oft-quoted starting point for considering the claims of future generations on current ones is Edmund Burke's famous statement that the state is a partnership among all members of the society, and that "[a]s the ends of such a partnership cannot be obtained in many generations, it becomes a partnership not only between those who are living, but between those who are living, those who are dead, and those who are to be born. Each contract of each particular state is but a clause in the great primeval contract of eternal society" (Burke 1989). This view states our obligation toward future generations in the strongest possible terms yet arguably diminishes its independent importance by placing it in a broader framework of stasis, continuity, and equal obligation to the past and its traditions. Implicitly, our descendants will be much like us and will not need different goods and institutions from those that we have, or more of them. While the implications for tax lag are unclear, Burke might support honoring the debts we inherit and not leaving excessive debts for our descendants, although perhaps tax lag could grow absolutely while staying constant relative to national income or wealth.

A less frequently quoted, but American, starting point is provided by Thomas Jefferson's claim that, because "the earth belongs always to the living generation," no generation should bind its successors in any way. Thus, we should not even expect our descendants to observe the same constitution and laws, much less honor our private debts, public debt, or other fiscal obligations.

Jefferson's view has stood the test of time considerably worse than Burke's. After two centuries of armed revolutions less benign than our own, the notion of reinventing civil society every twenty years seems neither realistic nor attractive. Moreover, past generations cannot avoid fundamentally shaping the world in which future ones come to live, no matter how hard they try to avoid doing so (and there is no reason to believe that they should try). Thus, a norm of total autonomy for each generation is implausible. At best, as James Madison recognized when he replied to Jefferson that future generations could rightfully be asked to inherit obligations alongside benefits, the underlying intuition decomposes into a no-transfer norm.

However, Burke's view has suffered over time as well. In the twentieth century, the worldwide pace of technological, political, and cultural change—along with, perhaps, a greater historical understanding of the pace of change even in the past—has tended to discredit his belief in continuity, suggesting that our descendants may live (if at all) as very different people in a very different world.

The rapid pace of contemporary change has helped to stimulate two separate stages in the development of the generational equity literature. First, since the 1920s, welfare economists have addressed the question of how to determine the optimal rate of saving, given saving's effect on the relative material well-being of present and future generations. Second, in philosophy, a new genre of examining generational justice emerged in the 1970s, largely in response to widespread fears that people are degrading the global environment and depleting the earth's finite resources. The fear of collective catastrophe and potential species extinction, newly generalized beyond the threat of nuclear war, encouraged philosophers to examine the moral claims of persons who do not now exist, who may never exist, and whose identities as individuals (if they come to exist) will depend on inherently unpredictable future happenstance, such as the chances governing which ova, fertilized by which sperm, happen to develop into living people. Neither of these two literatures has yet, to any significant degree, been brought to bear on the generational debate among economists who are concerned about budget deficits and tax lag.

If these literatures permitted one to reach firm normative conclusions, then in principle one could define, for any given moment, the optimal rate of saving in light of the expected productivity of investment. One could then, by comparing the optimal rate to the actual rate, determine whether present generations were saving too much, too little, or just the right amount. This, in turn, could tell us whether increasing or reducing tax lag would bring us closer to the proper level.

Even to speak of the "optimal rate of saving" sounds too narrow. It tends to downplay the level of human capital transfer and factors such as environmental degradation or depletion or, for that matter, the threat of nuclear war. A change in something like the divorce rate, given its well-documented effect on children's well-being, ought in principle to be part of the generational analysis as well.

Moreover, once one recognizes this undue narrowness, one can begin to question the entire framework of analysis. For example, why care about the timing of material consumption when there is so much doubt about its relationship to actual subjective well-being? Are wealthier societies or individuals generally happier than those less wealthy, who may live in totally different circumstances and adopt wholly different sets of expectations? How does one even measure consumption, which sophisticated economists have long recognized is "fundamentally . . . a flow of satisfactions, of intangible psychological experiences" (Haig 1959, 55)? Not even the person having such experiences can quantify them. Using a single implicit metric, such as "satisfaction," ignores qualitative differences and is at best a convenient organizing metaphor.

The economist's familiar tool of revealed preferences provides no help in this regard. That tool also is useless in distinguishing between consumption and saving, since this distinction turns on the actor's motive or on the timing of the actual or expected return from what one chooses to do. If I change my child's diaper instead of watching television, then while tautologically I have done what I preferred, it does not follow that I have maximized my present consumption. I may have subjected both my child and myself to a few unpleasant moments because I think that our increased satisfaction tomorrow, when the child does not have diaper rash, will exceed our mutual disgruntlement today. Yet how does one distinguish this from the possibility that I am acting to ease my pangs of conscience or anxiety about the future, and thus to please myself, today?

In the multigenerational household context, identifying the incidence of benefit is no easier than specifying its timing. Evolution has equipped parents with a measure of altruistic empathy for their children's pleasures and pains, and children with a talent for nudging this empathy. Even the core decision to have children resists classification:

> [F]rom the viewpoint of parents, children are themselves akin to consumer goods. Most parents have children because they want them, and they want children even though they know that children are expensive and present problems in other ways. If adults choose to spend their money on children rather than on steak, this may be because they find eating hamburger with their children more satisfying than eating steak alone. It is not obvious, therefore, that having children makes adults worse off in any meaningful sense, even if it reduces their consumption of "luxury" goods, reduces a previously two-earner family to a one-earner one with less income, and increases the fraction of their income that they allocate to "necessities." (Palmer, Smeeding, and Jencks 1988, 19)

The incidence and timing of benefit resist classification even outside the household context. What looks mainly like investment may really (or also) be consumption. A costly weapons development program, ostensibly (but ineffectively) strengthening our national defense for years to come, may serve mainly as a source of national pride or to benefit local defense workers. Likewise, what looks like consumption may also be investment. A government program that provides free meals to schoolchildren may look like current consumption yet involve investing in human capital. Or consider progressive wealth redistribution among members of living generations. While it may increase current consumption as conventionally measured given poor people's generally greater marginal propensity to consume, it might, if successful in reducing poverty, permit some individuals to live longer and more productive lives (an investment-type result).

The only way to defend the myopic conventions that underlie a standard examination of the optimal rate of saving is to argue not only that a more sophisticated analysis would be difficult or impossible but also that the standard analysis is meaningful enough to merit attention. While this is unprovable, surely people often act as if they believe that wealth and material consumption tend to correlate with happiness and view the decision whether to spend money now or later, or nominally on themselves or others, as a choice of when to consume and who gets to consume. One may therefore be justified for present purposes in reluctantly leaving the broader methodological problems to one side. With that in mind, I now turn to the questions that ought to replace the no-transfer and generational balance norms in evaluating our fiscal policy: how does one evaluate the optimal rate of saving, and where do we presently stand in relation to it?

D. Is the Current Rate of Saving Too Low, Given the Interests of Future Generations?

1. Defining the Problem

One often hears the complaint that people in the United States are saving too little, both individually and collectively. For example, economist Benjamin Friedman, in his antideficit tract *Day of Reckoning,* compares us to

> a man on a binge who asks why it matters? Flush with cash from liquidating his modest investment portfolio and from taking out a second mortgage on the inflated value of his house, he can spend seemingly without limit. The vacation cruise his family has dreamed about for years, the foreign sports car he has always wanted, new designer clothes for his wife and even his children, meals in all the most expensive restaurants—life is wonderful. What difference does it make if he has to pay some interest [and ultimately liquidate the rest of his assets]? [But] Americans have traditionally confronted such questions in the context of certain values, values that arise from the obligation that one generation owes to the next. (1988, 3)

As Friedman emphasizes, the main implications of a claim that we as a society save too little are intergenerational. To be sure, the claim has some relevance for present generations as well, even under the assumption that people generally do what is best for themselves. I discuss a number of different *intra*-generational arguments for increasing national saving in chapter 6.

The primary implications of the claim are intergenerational for two reasons. First, what we do to ourselves generally raises less serious moral problems than what we do to others who cannot affect our behavior because they have not yet been born. Second, an unduly low national saving rate, to the extent that it reduces the rate of growth in overall societal wealth, affects our descendants more than ourselves, given the long time lag that is needed for it to have a significant impact. Suppose, for example, that per capita GDP grew each year by 3 percent, rather than 4 percent, owing to insufficient saving. Five years from now, per capita GDP would still be more than 95 percent of what it "ought" to have been had we saved more. Fifty years from now, it would be a bit more than 60 percent of what it "ought" to have been.

So far, while agreeing with Friedman that the main implications of his claim that we are saving too little are intergenerational, I have not questioned the claim itself. Yet it plainly requires justification. Friedman, perhaps sensing the deep waters into which attempting to establish it would drag him, or else because *Day of Reckoning* is written for a popular audience, oversimplifies the issue by arguing from an inapt analogy. His man on a binge is dissaving, and thereby dissipating his wealth—not merely saving too little and thereby increasing his wealth too slowly. The United States, by contrast, still has a positive saving rate and a GDP that is growing per capita in real terms.

The one thing that *is* clear in support of Friedman's position is that in recent years the national saving rate in the United States, as conventionally measured, has been unusually low by both international and our own historical standards. Since around 1980, our national saving rate has generally been last, and always at least close to last, among major industrialized nations. After averaging 7.1 percent in the 1970s, it has averaged only 3 percent since 1980 and stood at only 1.7 percent in 1993. While this partly reflects the growth in federal budget deficits, which are counted as public dissaving, it also reflects a decline in the private rate of saving, from 8.1 percent for the 1970s to a low of 4.5 percent in 1989, albeit with more recent increases (see Vogel 1996; Wang 1994).

This evidence of unusually low saving may, however, be an artifact of how saving is officially measured. Some economists argue that the measure errs in excluding asset appreciation, such as on homes and stock investments, that people can use (no less than money deposited in a bank) to finance future consumption. By this measure, savings rates since 1980 (a period of substantial stock market appreciation and, on balance, of home appreciation) have been reasonably robust after all (see Bradford 1991; Vogel 1996).

Still, even if one accepts the conventional measure and thus that our recent saving rate has been unusually low, no normative implications need follow. Perhaps other societies, including the United States in the past, save excessively or simply have different tastes. Or perhaps we now have good reason to save less—for example, because the size and vigor of our economy and the stability of our political institutions make it relatively easy for us to attract foreign investment.

A low saving rate tends to slow economic growth and the upward path of productivity. Even if a reasonable level of domestic investment is sustained by foreign investment, the profits presumably will inure to foreigners, thus reducing, although not eliminating, domestic benefit from the foreign investment. Short of dissaving, however, a low national saving rate does not create any inherent sustainability problem for the present level of consumption. While obviously a higher growth rate is preferable if all else is equal, all else is *not* equal given the general tradeoff between current consumption and saving for future consumption. Surely we are not obligated to live like hermits, toiling unceasingly so that future generations can live a lot better than us, any more than, at the other extreme, we should make no provision for the future at all.

Hence the claim that there is an optimal rate of saving, defined as the rate that would lead to the optimal allocation of consumption between present and future generations. One needs to know whether the actual saving rate is above or below the optimal saving rate before one can tell whether tax lag, by reducing our saving rate, is making things better or worse.

Unfortunately, as Amartya Sen (1961) commented more than thirty years ago, "the search for the 'optimum' rate of saving has not yet been vastly more successful than that for the holy grail." John Rawls agrees that it "seems to admit of no definite answer" (1971, 286). E. J. Mishan notes that while a number of well-developed economic models purport to determine the appropriate rate of economic growth (permitting one to deduce the optimal rate of saving, with the help of additional information), "the models are 'cooked up' so as to give the imprimatur of science to what is, after all, no more than a popular ethical judgment" (1977, 383). Mishan attributes this failing less to the particular economists who have designed the models than to the inherently limited capacity of economics, as a discipline, to derive strong welfare conclusions about complex social issues from its conventional starting point of revealed preferences.

The problems in determining the optimal rate of saving are both empirical and philosophical. As examples of the former, what real growth rate should we expect from our saving, and how well-off will our descendants otherwise be relative to us? Real growth rates in the U.S. economy have varied substantially over time and conceivably could vary still more in the future. Are we on the verge of an unprecedented technology-fueled wealth explosion? Might we instead be approaching reversal of the centuries-old trend of generally steady growth, under the strains of an aging population, overall population growth, environmental disasters, and growing resource shortages? Might we even be approaching a catastrophe, caused by war or environmental and demographic strains, such that significant saving for the future serves little purpose?

While such questions are close to unanswerable, the philosophical issues are no easier. As Jan Narveson puts it, answers to the question of what we are morally obligated to do for future generations "range all the way from Nothing to Everything—which would be no cause for alarm, except that both answers, and some in between, have rational support" (1978, 38). Do we owe future generations everything? Rawls argues that this could follow logically from utilitarianism if one prefers to maximize aggregate rather than average happiness, allows no time discount for future relative to current consumption, and assumes that future generations, in the aggregate, will be far more numerous than ourselves (1971, 289). Alternatively, do we owe future generations nothing because they have done nothing for us and lack the moral status of presently living individuals?[1] Derek Parfit (1984) suggests that we might owe them nothing whenever our choices change the precise identity of who comes to be born. He notes that given the biological facts of human reproduction, including monthly ovulation of a distinct egg, very little is needed for a collective social choice to bring about such change. Those who would not have been born but for such choices cannot complain, he argues, as long as they are glad, on balance, to be alive, and those who never come to be born surely have no moral status. As an intermediate alternative to the positions noted by Rawls and Parfit, is what we owe future generations a function of what

---

1. Narveson notes that this arguably follows logically from viewing morality as based on at least implicit contract between independent rational agents (1978, 38).

past generations have done for us? Benjamin Friedman asserts this, implicitly relying on something like Edmund Burke's view of an eternal chain-linked contractual partnership. Or does what we owe future generations depend on satisfying John Locke's proviso for the legitimacy of private property acquisition: that there be "enough and as good left . . . for others"?[2] The proviso's implications in the generational context (as elsewhere) are subject to dispute.[3]

This only hints at the range of philosophical questions that can be (and have been) asked in the generational setting. Ought one to apply a social rate of discount, treating future harms as less weighty than present ones? Or are a billion catastrophic deaths in one hundred years, if certain to occur, as bad as a billion catastrophic deaths today? If one adopts a utilitarian perspective, should one seek to maximize future generations' average happiness or their aggregate happiness? As various philosophers have noted, either definition seems to invite absurd consequences—such as killing everyone but the happiest person (assuming that person would not mind) under the former definition or massively increasing the human population to a Malthusian level of bare sustenance under the latter. Is the norm of generational justice simply incoherent, as Terence Ball (1985) argues, on the ground that "justice" is a socially contingent concept that future people are almost certain to view completely differently from how we view it? Ought we simply to rely on our own norms, either because it does not matter whether they will be held in the future or because one can assume that they will? Or ought we to hark back to Thomas Jefferson's view that, because "the earth belongs always to the living generation," no generation should try to bind its successors to any set of practices, whether embodied in an ongoing constitution or in a commitment to repay public debt or keep Social Security in place?

While these are weighty questions about which reasonable people disagree, the choice of standard is fundamental. For convenience, and because it fits my generally utilitarian intuitions, I will adopt a modified version of John Rawls's approach (albeit that Rawls rejects utilitarianism). Rawls famously describes the original position, a hypothetical

2. Locke 1967, sec. 27. See Nozick 1974, 174–82, for a discussion of Locke's proviso as limiting (but not greatly) the right to private property in a libertarian system.

3. Compare Attfield 1983, 96 (arguing that Nozickean justice implies only minimal obligations toward future generations), with Elliot 1986 (arguing that Locke's proviso, as interpreted by Nozick, may generate extensive obligations to future generations).

state from which people decide on appropriate principles of justice, social institutions, and the like in light of the consequences that their choices will have but behind a veil of ignorance concerning who, and how well-off, they will be in the resulting society (1971, 12). While the original position and veil of ignorance provide a useful heuristic, I reject Rawls's accompanying ad hoc assumption of apparently infinite risk aversion, which leads him to derive a "maximin" principle under which those making choices from the original position would conclude that nothing matters but maximizing the well-being of the worst-off person or people. The arbitrariness of this assumed extreme risk aversion can be shown in many ways—for example, by asking whether in practice very many people would (or should) buy a lottery ticket for $1 if it offers a 1 percent chance of no return and a 99 percent chance of earning a billion dollars. In the generational setting, the "maximin" principle has the peculiar implication—which Rawls steadfastly but (as many commentators agree) unconvincingly denies—that no generation should save if, in consequence, the next generation will be better off (since maximin focuses exclusively on the well-being of the worst-off individuals).[4] Rawls himself recognizes that our moral intuitions, on which he often relies, rebel at the notion that per capita economic growth should be regarded as an evil reflecting undue sacrifice by present generations.

In place of maximin, I will assume a general utilitarian norm, on the ground that a decision maker in the original position wants to maximize his or her likely well-being as a randomly placed person. I will also assume that the Rawlsian decision makers know that we have gotten to where we are today and thus do not attempt to operate from the highly abstract original position. The question they face, asked from behind a veil of ignorance regarding who they will be and when or even if they will live (where different potential people are possible), is what to do next.

I will ignore the difficult issue of population size and thus of average versus aggregate utility. This issue, in addition to being all but insoluble, is not directly implicated by questions of the optimal saving rate, since the causal linkages are unclear. Does increased saving imply fewer children because it requires reducing current household con-

---

4. See, e.g., Ackerman 1980, 223–25 (criticizing Rawls's rejection of this implication of maximin); Solow 1974 (developing an economic model that deduces a norm of equal consumption by all generations from applying maximin).

sumption? Or does it imply more children because greater societal wealth ultimately makes raising children more affordable? Likewise, does increased tax lag, to the limited extent that it affects family planning, predominantly motivate people to have fewer children, so that their households' likely shares of future taxes will not increase, or more children, because paying less in current taxes tends to make one feel wealthier?

Among the consequences of my choice of norm is that I can ignore the Burkean claim that generational policy should depend on explicitly or implicitly contractual reciprocity between the generations. The same goes for any claim that parents have a duty to treat their children's well-being as more important than their own (rather than equally important). While such moral claims cannot be logically disproven, they derive from different moral premises from those I choose. On the same ground, I disregard Parfit's distinction between choices that change exactly who will be born in the future and those that do not. The modified Rawlsian approach also has the consequence of eliminating the social discount rate as between present and future lives and suggesting that, say, severe material deprivation is equally regrettable whether it occurs today or in five hundred years (assuming equal certainty of its occurrence). Discounting is appropriate only within a person's life, since only then can one imagine deferral as reducing the value of a satisfaction or the cost of a harm.

These specifications still leave the analysis alarmingly open-ended. The modified Rawlsian approach does not support a norm of monetary wealth maximization, which might imply that present generations should toil like slaves, consuming as little as possible, so that per capita social wealth can grown as fast as possible. If one assumes a generally declining marginal utility of wealth, then a present person does not necessarily increase aggregate well-being by depriving himself or herself of x units of consumption so that an already wealthier descendant can enjoy $x + y$ units of consumption. The proper tradeoff between these two consumption alternatives would be difficult to evaluate even if one could quantify x and y (and the wealth of the alternative consumers) in constant dollar terms.

One would like to find a shortcut to avoid the many empirical and philosophical imponderables. Three main possibilities come to mind. First, drawing on the economic literature concerning growth, one could adopt a standard called dynamic efficiency, which, as John Seater explains, "is a kind of Pareto optimality; an economy is dynamically efficient if it is not possible to improve one generation's welfare without reducing the welfare of another. In particular, an economy is dynamically inefficient if it has overaccumulated capital" (1993, 150) such that it could consume more without reducing future generations' consumption. As Seater notes, however, we are far short of the dynamic inefficiency frontier, at which we would self-defeatingly be saving too much (158).

Second, one could try to reconcile the generations' interests by treating living people's preferences as changeable. Suppose that the question one asked was whether it would be better, from the modified Rawlsian perspective, if present generations could be induced to enjoy saving and therefore to engage in far more of it. Such enjoyment might reflect the influence of what Keynes called "pure miserliness, i.e., unreasonable but insistent inhibitions against acts of expenditure as such" (1964, 108). Or it might reflect the pleasure of performing what one deems a virtuous action that promises to increase future individual, household, or national wealth. Assume that the alternative was for people to dislike saving and therefore engage in as little of it as their prudence and altruism would permit. It seems clear that a positive taste for saving would be better for society over time, since it would permit present generations' preferences and those of possibly more materialistic future generations to be more consistent and mutually fulfillable. Accordingly, one could imagine a benevolent government seeking through education to instill such a preference. The argument is similar in form to one for having the government discourage, say, racial hatred or sadistic enjoyment of inflicting pain on other people—tastes that create even greater conflicts between the satisfaction of one person's preferences and that of another's.

Yet such an argument for shaping current preferences has several problems. It does not guide behavior prior to the change in preferences, and the hoped-for change may be hard to accomplish. Moreover, relying on the feasibility of changing preferences, rather than working from revealed preferences, makes the whole analysis rather open-ended. Why not posit instead that future generations can be educated to be less materialistic, so that they will not mind our leaving them less in the way of material goods? One also could debate how far people's psychological flexibility extends: not only what sets of preferences are possible but also whether different sets are, in truth, equally enjoyable. Keynes, for example, in discussing the taste for "pure miserliness," probably believed that this taste was not only socially destructive (given the societal need for greater spending on consumption) but personally unsatisfying and constricting as well[5]—a view that, while perhaps psychologically plausible, is hard to test empirically.

One more ground exists, however, for arguing that we need not evaluate a set of difficult tradeoffs in order to conclude that present generations ought to save more. This ground is perhaps the most promising, and certainly the most popular, of the three. Various writers (mainly lawyers and economists; see, e.g., Elliott 1985; Buchanan and Wagner 1977) have argued on what one might term procedural grounds that the level of saving in society is generally likely to be too low. When present generations decide how much to save, they are engaged in a one-sided transaction that has two-sided consequences. Future generations are affected by what we do, but they cannot bargain or even plead with us. At a minimum, as Sen notes, this shows that we cannot rely upon the standard economic norm of consumer sovereignty and assume that the current level of saving, in light of the market interest rate, is appropriate (1961, 486). However, one could take the argument a step further and assert, with Arthur Pigou, that the level of private saving will inevitably be too low and that the government therefore must act to increase national saving. Or based on James Buchanan's skepticism about government, one could argue that the government is likely to be part of the problem rather than the solution. This might suggest either despair or the need for a constitutional response such as a balanced budget amendment (or a generational accounting equivalent thereof). The following section assesses the argument that, on procedural grounds, the national (or at least the private) saving rate is likely to be inadequate from the standpoint of generational justice.

2. Does the One-Sided Nature of Decision Making by Present Generations That Affects Future Generations Suggest That the Level of Saving Will Be Too Low?

The claim that the national saving rate must be too low, relative to what it would be if all affected parties' interests were fairly represented, is familiar in form. Benefit to future generations from saving seems a standard externality that present actors might be expected to

5. See Skidelsky 1976 (discussing Keynes's rebellion against Victorian prudence and future-mindedness).

undervalue, both in their private behavior and through the political process. Contemporary political practice and preferences concerning tax lag seem to provide rich anecdotal confirmation. The Ricardian claim of multigenerational altruism within the household may give one temporary pause, but perhaps the incompleteness of Ricardian offsets shows that at the margin, even if not unlimitedly so, present generations are selfish rather than altruistic. The procedural argument that we tend to save too little does not require assuming that we are indifferent to future generations' well-being, only that we value it unduly less than our own well-being.

An initial problem with the procedural argument concerns the implicit norm of genuinely two-sided decision making, involving future as well as current generations, that it seems to assume would be appropriate if only such a process were physically possible. Even as a thought experiment, this norm is hard to put in persuasive form. Before assessing the modified Rawlsian original position, it is useful to begin by considering two settings for coordinating conflicting interests that are more realistic and less abstract: the marketplace and public decision making through politics.

Starting with the marketplace setting, one might imagine that if only future generations could be brought here for the limited purpose of expressing their demand and affecting market prices, they would bid up the interest rate to a sufficient level to increase saving and enable them to consume more. This is incorrect, however. The theoretical loan transaction between present and future generations involves a trade, whereas the reality involves an either/or choice. Saving past our own life spans involves a one-way transfer of lifetime consumption from us to our heirs. Thus, a theoretical marketplace negotiation between present and future generations could not give rise to a mutually agreeable allocation, any more than the poor could negotiate with the rich in such a setting to determine the proper distribution of presently existing wealth.

The political setting may appear more promising as a thought experiment, since in principle future generations could vote to require us to save more and thereby increase their lifetime consumption relative to ours. Here, however, the difficulty lies in assuming that one can use the political setting to decide, as a normative matter, who ought to transfer wealth to whom. Since voting necessarily disregards the intensity of people's preferences, majority rule can yield transfers that are unjust or that reduce collective well-being. Hence the concern with

minority rights that dates back, within the American political tradition, at least to Madison. Thus, even if we are quite right, as a general
matter, to allow wealth transfers through the political process on the
grounds that no better means of decision making exists and that a no-
transfer norm is arbitrary, one cannot assume in any given case that
the actual (or, under the future-generations thought experiment, hypothetical) wealth-transfer outcome is normatively appropriate. For example, what if future generations were to mandate, at the hypothetical
ballot box, our toiling like slaves for their benefit?

Thus, fixing procedural defects in the two main settings in which
we decide how to coordinate people's interests would not yield a
clearly better answer, even as a thought experiment. Perhaps the modified Rawlsian setting does more to make the case, since one might find
plausible the claim that moving from membership in present generations to the original position would enhance most people's concern for
the interests of future generations. Yet this line of reasoning seems to
yield a false prediction. Suppose one made the plausible assumption
that we current individuals have some generational altruism but attach greater weight to our own well-being, especially relative to that
of distant generations and perhaps even relative to our own children
with respect to experiences they will have in the future when we can
no longer observe them. This might suggest the likelihood of negative
real saving, leading to the gradual depletion of existing resources, such
that the standard of living would continually decline, even if only modestly. In effect, one might expect to observe at least a moderate version
of Benjamin Friedman's depiction of the man on a binge. This is counterfactual, however, given the lengthy period during which we have had
a positive national saving rate and real per capita economic growth.
While it remains possible that present generations still undervalue future generations' interests if a modified Rawlsian perspective would
lead them to make future generations better off still, it is difficult to
condemn very strongly, on grounds of insufficient altruism, those who
permit others to be somewhat better off than themselves.

How can one explain each recent historical generation's apparent
willingness to save enough so that the next generation would do better,
other than by positing what might seem an implausible level of altruism? At least four different but complementary explanations are possible. First, the pressures of evolutionary survival, as a species and a
society, may select for future-mindedness beyond one's life span—in
effect, as a kind of automatic reflex, even if at various margins we are

selected to act selfishly. Second, and more mundanely, as has been discussed in the Ricardian literature, imperfect annuity markets may induce people to oversave against the "risk" of living too long, and thus to leave behind substantial unconsumed wealth when they die accidentally or prematurely. Third, the existence of constantly overlapping generations may be significant. Multigenerational hypotheticals, for convenience, often abstract to a setting where two distinct groups live at different times and never meet. In practice, however, living generations have a range of expected life spans, continually extending into the future as the population turns over. This may help to discourage the strategy of drawing down present resources, by making it potentially disadvantageous to a large percentage of the living. Fourth, technological advances offer new opportunities to later-born generations that cannot be transported backward with a time machine and that earlier-born generations may repeatedly underestimate because the advances cannot be imagined. Surely few in the mid-nineteenth century foresaw that we would possess items such as cars, television, supersonic jets, and personal computers. In addition to being unimaginable, and thus perhaps systematically underestimated, technological advances appear to have made a significantly greater contribution than has capital accumulation through saving to economic growth during the twentieth century (see, e.g., Schumpeter 1934; Solow 1957; Scherer and Ross 1990, 613; Denison 1967, 297–300)—although there still would be no growth if present generations dissaved sufficiently.

Whatever the reason for earlier generations' willingness to save at a rate that permitted later generations to enjoy greater lifetime consumption, the long-standing occurrence of this trend suggests that the basic picture, in which the living have all the power and the unborn therefore bear unpleasant consequences, is inaccurate. After all, unborn generations have power, in a sense, whether because we unthinkingly and instinctively provide for them or because, by being born later, they get to live at a time when more has been accomplished and more is known. The situation is analogous to that of a hypothetical society where the poor have all the political influence, but the government lacks the power or will to levy high taxes or engage in takings, with the result that the rich, despite being political outcasts, are nonetheless better off.

Thus, the procedural argument fails to establish that present generations save too little, and thereby end up consuming too much relative to future generations, from the modified Rawlsian standpoint that

I have posited. For one reason or another, present generations may even, as best we can tell and depending on unpredictable circumstances, end up saving too much. Thus, impossibly hard though it may be to do, we must look at the actual merits after all.

3. The Tradeoff between Consumption by Present and Future Generations: Maximizing Total Consumption versus Equalizing Its Distribution

Again, the actual merits of the tradeoff between present and future consumption are exceptionally hard to assess. Even apart from the theoretical ambiguities that lie buried in my choice of a modified Rawlsian standard—for example, how steeply the marginal utility of wealth should be assumed to decline (when we cannot measure it)—there is pervasive empirical uncertainty concerning how the future will look compared to the present, under different scenarios regarding the amount of present saving.

Still, the analysis need not be unstructured, even if it is ultimately indeterminate. Three main points come to mind. The first is the absence of a social discount rate across life spans, given that a decision maker behind the Rawlsian veil of ignorance would not know when he or she was going to live. Thus, all else being equal (and ignoring any uncertainty about whether future generations will in fact be born), one would prefer to trade x units of consumption by people today for $x + y$ units of consumption by people in the future.

The second point to keep in mind is that such an uneven tradeoff is in fact presented if saving generates a real positive return. The argument starts from the point that profitable investment, by definition, increases the amount of wealth available for consumption—in effect, permitting $x + y$ units of consumption later in lieu of x units now, where y is the real interest rate, or rate of growth for the economy, over the period of deferral. Within the life of an individual, the potential for real growth does not establish that deferring consumption is desirable, given the time value of consuming sooner to avoid impatience. However, if present value discounting is inappropriate for future consumption by the unborn since they do not yet experience impatience, then net capital formation tends to increase aggregate utility, by increasing future generations' consumption by more than it reduces current generations' consumption.

Indeed, the real interest rate may understate the increase in the actual subjective value of the increased consumption that ultimately results from deferring consumption to pay for profitable investment. Later consumption may provide more utility than earlier consumption, even without an increase in its dollar value, if technological advances increase consumer surplus. To illustrate, suppose that one person living in the 1920s and another living in the 1990s have identical wealth, measured in constant dollars, except that the latter owns a television, videocassette recorder, compact disc player, and computer (plus all the accessories needed to enjoy them) with a total market value of $5,000. If the former person would have paid more than $5,000 to own and enjoy those assets and the latter would not renounce them for $5,000, then surely the latter is more than $5,000 better off, all else being equal. As evidence that the products created by technological advances provide enormous consumer surplus, consider a recent survey suggesting that nearly half of all Americans questioned said they would refuse to give up television for the rest of their lives for less than $1 million[6]—obviously far in excess of its lifetime cost to the consumer.

These two points would seem to suggest that present generations should save more than they in fact do—indeed, should save to the very limit of dynamic efficiency, at which so much capital has been invested that its marginal efficiency declines to zero. The third point has opposite implications, however. It concerns the generally declining marginal utility of wealth. These factors tend to limit the amount of net capital formation, beyond that necessary to maintain constant per capita wealth, that is desirable. At some unknown point, as net capital formation increases beyond the maintenance level, the lifetime consumption opportunities of members of future generations become sufficiently greater than our own to suggest that our descendants will derive less utility from $x + y$ additional units of consumption (or even $x + y + z$, including increased consumer surplus) than we would from x units. Thus, a decision maker in the modified Rawlsian setting would face a tradeoff between optimizing the total amount of material consumption and optimizing its distribution. This tradeoff is inherently difficult to resolve.

In what remains the best-known (although the earliest) economic

6. See "$1 Million Not Enough to Make Some Give Up Television," *Chicago Tribune*, October 5, 1992, p. 3 (46 percent of those surveyed would require a payment of at least $1 million).

model designed to determine the optimal rate of saving, Frank Ramsey (1928) deduced from the declining marginal utility of wealth that the optimal rate of economic growth might constantly decline, as increasing societal wealth reduced the marginal utility of consumption. Indeed, it eventually might reach zero, at the point he termed "bliss," where additional consumption had lost all marginal utility and where merely maintaining the existing wealth level would therefore be optimal. More generally, in Ramsey's model, under the assumptions that the rate of return on capital declines as more is invested and that the marginal utility of consumption declines as overall consumption increases, one could specify that the amount of capital investment should be set at precisely the level where its rate of return would equal the percentage rate of decline in marginal utility.

Even if one considers this specification to lack practical usefulness and Ramsey's state of "bliss" to be practically or even theoretically unattainable, his model helps to show, within the welfare economics tradition, the significance of the offset between long-term wealth maximization and equality of distribution. The rhetorical significance of future generations' assumed increasing wealth may be even greater than its real significance in Ramsey's rigorous social welfare terms. As Gordon Tullock notes, people who are making charitable gifts tend to have little interest in increasing the welfare of those better off than themselves, and generally make gifts only to those who appear worse off (1964b, 334). Thus, the case for having the government play Robin Hood in reverse, by changing its fiscal policy in a regressive direction so as to shift consumption from present to future generations, may have little appeal to many of us once we understand it in these terms, despite the utilitarian case for conveying benefits to our better-off descendants that exceed the detriment to ourselves.

Should we assume increasing per capita wealth, however? Such an increase does not follow logically from net capital formation alone, since in principle the population could grow more rapidly from the economy. An expectation of increasing per capita wealth does follow, however, from the admittedly controversial assumption that long-standing historical trends will continue. In both the United States and western Europe, per capita wealth and lifetime consumption have been increasing fairly steadily, and in the aggregate dramatically, for many centuries (subject to various troughs caused by recession and war). The continuing rapid pace of technological development provides some ground, at least, for believing that this trend will continue.

At a minimum, surely long-standing history and the course of technology create enough of an inference of increasing per capita wealth to require an explanation of why one should expect anything different in the future. Moreover, such an explanation must fall into a broad middle ground in order to support the conclusion that present generations should save more. Suppose, for example, that the world is headed for an imminent nuclear catastrophe, given the seemingly inevitable dissemination of nuclear weapons. Increasing saving would make little sense under this scenario. The lack of a significant future would suggest consuming all the more while we can.

The middle-ground pessimism that would support increasing saving is not wholly implausible, however. A number of present trends arguably, although controversially, may support it. Consider the relative aging of the U.S. population, owing to long-term demographic trends along with the effects of new medical technologies that can keep sick people alive for longer (although, perhaps, not always making them better off) at enormous expense. Or consider arguments that top-soil erosion and the effects of maximum-yield farming will lead soon to a reversal of recent enormous increases in farming productivity (see, e.g., Pimenta et al. 1976; Brink et al. 1977). Some have argued that humans are reaching the point of exhausting the earth's finite fuel resources and at the same time are generating toxic waste products in volumes that will soon exceed the tolerance of a well-functioning (from our perspective) global environment (see, e.g., Meadows et al. 1972). The threat of global warming, potentially resulting in widespread flooding of densely populated coastal areas and desertification of areas that at present are agriculturally productive, is only one example of such dangers. The staggering pace of world demographic growth, particularly in impoverished Third World nations, excites understandable concern as well (see, e.g., Boulding 1984, 222). A further set of threats relates to war, social breakdown, and the possible worldwide effects of evil regimes, akin to those in Hitler's Germany or Stalin's Russia (or any number of contemporary examples, from Cambodia to Iraq to Rwanda to Haiti), that might do enough harm to make our descendants worse off than ourselves, yet without rendering present investment futile.

These fears have tended to excite greater skepticism in the economics profession than elsewhere. Many economists recall how frequently such fears have been expressed from time to time (yet never fulfilled) since the days of Thomas Malthus. Under the optimistic view that some economists prefer, population growth merely increases the stock of human capital, which Julian Simon (1981) terms the "ultimate resource" and which increases the attainable scale efficiencies in providing people with goods and services. Moreover, resource limitations have frequently been solved in the past by the advance of technology, driven by marketplace incentives, as well as by market-driven increases in resource substitution, recycling, and intensity of search for resources as they become more costly (see, e.g., Barnett and Morse 1963). Yet the optimistic view does not necessarily extend to political and social dangers, and even for scarce material resources it is unprovable as applied to the future, however frequently it has been correct in the past.[7]

Thus, one surely could make the case for increased saving on behalf of future generations, based on the view either that things will generally get worse (but not so bad as to eliminate the future benefit from saving) or that while growth will continue, the benefit of increasing it still more outweighs the detriment of regressive redistribution from us to our descendants. Yet making the case with any great sense of certainty would require either obtuseness or unfounded confidence in one's intuitions about the future.

The most defensible stance, from a modified Rawlsian perspective, appears to be one of skepticism concerning *any* strong claims about the proper level of saving. One might nonetheless accept or even welcome people's voluntary decision to save more, whether expressed in the private saving rate or in political demands for changing fiscal policy, on the ground that present generations presumptively are not injured by something that they do voluntarily. This is an argument, however, for exhorting increased saving and accepting it if it arises, not for requiring it outright.

Given the range of empirical and philosophical uncertainties that impede evaluating the tradeoff between present and future consumption, one could powerfully argue that generational policy should not be at center stage in current politics—other than perhaps as a device for demonstrating the separate point that present fiscal policy may be unsustainable and thus should be changed as gradually and smoothly

7. See, e.g., Georgescu-Roegen 1971 (discussing the significance of material entropy, or our ongoing diffusion of concentrated natural resources and conversion of productive resources into waste products); Smith and Krutilla 1984, 227–30 (discussing theoretical and practical challenges in the economic literature to the optimistic Barnett and Morse analysis).

as possible. Decisions about efficiency, distribution, and the like among present generations, while hardly lacking their own imponderables, at least concern matters that we can observe more directly.

Thus, if generational policy were the only substantive issue raised by tax lag, one would be tempted to conclude that tax lag does not merit nearly the level of attention that it has received in the political process in recent years. If it is as important as many have believed, it must be so for other reasons, including both the prudential concern for sustainability and the macroeconomic and size-of-government issues that I examine next.

SIX

Macroeconomic Issues Raised by
Tax Lag and Budget Deficits

A. The Econometric Literature

Assessing the macroeconomic issues raised by tax lag has both an empirical and a normative component. Empirically, what are its effects on such phenomena as the rates of saving and unemployment, the interest rate, and the U.S. balance of payments? Normatively, are these effects good, bad, or indifferent?

At least for the empirical issues, one might expect the econometric literature to provide considerable help. Unfortunately, however, this literature, while extensive concerning budget deficits (though not tax lag more broadly), is plagued by a radical lack of consensus. Ricardian, Keynesian, and neoclassical economists each make their own empirical claims, brandishing in support their own empirical studies. Yet no school succeeds in persuading the others, any more than it is persuaded by them.

This is all too common in econometrics, a field in which little consensus has emerged after years of research about such extensively researched questions as the effects of income taxes on saving, of capital gains rates on tax revenues, and of minimum wage laws on employment levels. Empirical proof is inherently difficult in a field so far removed from the conditions of a physical science laboratory. The national economy is an immensely large and complicated system, aggregating the behavior of hundreds of millions of unpredictable and imperfectly observable human actors facing ever-changing circumstances. In this setting, it is hard to conduct or observe a controlled experiment or to adjust properly for independent variables. Often, one cannot even be certain that one's basic economic data are meaningful. Consider the dispute, which I noted in chapter 5, about whether the savings rate should include asset appreciation. Or consider the official unemployment rate, which counts only people who are classified as actively searching for jobs, and thus ignores those who have stopped looking out of discouragement.

Against this background, definite empirical proof of even the most elementary propositions is close to impossible. Econometric results are extremely sensitive to researchers' design choices on matters about which there often is enormous discretion and no clear correct answer. One need not be acting in bad faith to make choices that reflect one's underlying beliefs and help the data to "make sense." Perhaps this explains why economists from across the intellectual spectrum so frequently end up deriving the results that we know they expected or preferred in advance. Somehow it always seems that Robert Barro finds evidence confirming Ricardianism, and Robert Eisner finds it for Keynesianism, while Martin Feldstein but not Lawrence Summers detects large disincentive effects from redistribution through the tax and transfer systems.

While there are better and worse econometric studies, the field at best engages in an art, not a science. In determining what weight to give any results, one should avoid the false dichotomy between the real-world empirical evidence that econometrics purports to provide and "mere" theoretical argument based on abstract reasoning. The claim that econometric data establish an empirical correlation (or the lack thereof) in the past and that this correlation should be expected to persist in the future is itself a theoretical claim, requiring one to rely on extensive unprovable assumptions regarding how an infinite range of variables actually have affected or could affect the result.

All these are general problems of econometrics. Measuring the effects of tax lag raises a host of area-specific problems as well. Almost all studies of tax lag are based on variants of the budget deficit and thus fail to use an economic accrual framework or one that, like generational accounting, reflects who is likely to pay what net taxes (or expects to pay them) on a lifetime basis. The sheer number of different variants of the deficit increases the risk of finding spurious correlations, since one can keep changing the measure until one finds something. Moreover, despite the large number of studies, the historical evidence concerning deficits is surprisingly limited. Peacetime, nonrecessionary deficits and national debt were small compared to GDP until the 1980s, making any effects harder to detect. The more recent data are still too time-limited to permit confidence that any accompanying changes in macroeconomic aggregates resulted from the deficits rather than from other unique conditions during the last two decades.

While the use of a more economically meaningful framework, such as generational accounting, would seem more promising, little work has been done using it to date. Such work would in any event raise the difficulty of requiring, in principle, the construction of generational accounts that reflected people's actual subjective expectations regarding future policy, as opposed to the objective course of present policy (however defined). Yet subjective expectations are hard to reconstruct, and relying on assumed reconstructions of them would invite manipulation.

Fortunately, however, the econometric studies using budget deficits are not completely indeterminate or lacking in value. When one adds to them the force of logical reasoning based on more general empirical observation, one can derive broad answers to many of the key empirical disputes. This, in turn, permits one to draw normative conclusions concerning tax lag in macroeconomic fiscal policy, or at least to understand the main tradeoffs.

In this chapter, I draw on the existing economic literature, including econometric research, to examine the main aggregate economic measures that tax lag arguably might affect. First I consider a set of items that, while relatively tangential to the main analysis, are of considerable interest both substantively and as subjects of econometric debate: interest rates, the trade deficit, and the inflation rate. Then I turn to the core macroeconomic issue raised by tax lag and budget deficits: whether they, as claimed, tend to increase current consumption. This claim underlies both lauding tax lag as a tool of Keynesian stimulus and condemning it as injurious to long-term economic growth.

B. The Effects of Tax Lag and Budget Deficits on Various Macroeconomic Aggregates

1. Interest Rates

The standard view in much of the economic literature has been that budget deficits should have a short-term effect of increasing domestic real interest rates, all else being equal. The argument goes as follows.

When current government spending is debt-financed, the government is forced to enter capital markets as a borrower (assuming it does not simply print money). By so doing, it shifts upward the demand curve for borrowing money, thereby increasing the equilibrium market price (the interest rate).

Under one variant of this view, cash-flow budget deficits, rather than tax lag in an economic accrual sense, would be the determinant of interest rates. The government's cash-flow needs would determine how much it actually borrowed at any given time in the capital markets. One could also base the view on tax lag, however, by arguing that greater tax lag implies greater present and expected near-term future government borrowing, thus increasing the long-term borrowing demand that market participants expect without regard to cash flow at any given moment.

Ricardians are the most unequivocal in rejecting the standard view. They argue that any deferral of taxes relative to spending will cause taxpayers to save more, as they adjust their behavior to ensure that their descendants will still receive the right-sized bequests after taxes. In effect, then, government borrowing fails to shift the demand curve for the use of funds to the extent that people respond by curtailing their own consumer borrowing, or else it induces an offsetting shift in the supply curve as people increase their private saving.

One might think that the Ricardian claim would lead to a simple empirical test of the degree of correlation between nominal cash-flow deficits and interest rates. Unfortunately, however, things are not so simple, in practice or even in principle. Empirically, the evidence concerning deficits' effect on interest rates is mixed (see Seater 1993, 175–77; Bernheim 1989, 70), although those denying the existence of a detectable positive correlation have somewhat the better case.[1] Anecdotally, consider the general decline in interest rates in the early 1980s, as nominal cash-flow deficits were growing to unprecedented levels. Although such an observation cannot support a definite conclusion, given the possibility that other factors were responsible and that interest rates would have declined still more but for the deficits, it should at least give one pause in assuming that deficits affect interest rates all that powerfully.

---

1. Kotlikoff, for one, regards the evidence as strongly rebutting the standard view (see 1992, 72–73). A largely sympathetic reviewer has criticized him, however, for ignoring contrary findings in the empirical literature (Cutler 1993, 64).

Even more importantly, however, failure to observe a significant interest rate effect of deficits would fail to support Ricardianism against alternative explanations. To Laurence Kotlikoff, this failure simply shows the deficit's economic meaninglessness. He notes that even on its face, the standard claim seems to assume a small closed economy, where the government's level of borrowing can strongly affect overall demand for the current use of money relative to the supply. For a large open economy that is integrated with world capital markets, even the demand of as large a borrower as the U.S. government may have no discernible effect, since national interest rates will remain pegged to world interest rates, which reflect worldwide supply and demand. Thus, even if the deficit was an economically significant measure to begin with, it would not discernibly affect interest rates.

If the U.S. government were a large enough borrower for its financing needs to matter, then Kotlikoff would presumably expect tax lag, rather than the deficit, to be the significant measure. Farsighted participants in world capital markets would respond not just to the government's borrowing demand today but also to its expected borrowing needs in the future. Tax lag's effect on interest rates would still be hard to observe, given the crucial role played by subjective expectations concerning the course of our fiscal policy. Such expectations are likely to shift with the political winds, in a manner that may be hard for econometricians to reconstruct.[2]

Adding further complications, interest rates reflect changes in both actual price inflation and inflationary expectations. Given inflation's influence on nominal interest rates, observations concerning them may misdescribe the effects on real interest rates. Yet even observing real interest rates is not wholly satisfactory, since their fluctuation reflects unexpected changes in the inflation rate that leave the real return either higher or lower than the market had anticipated.

A further barrier to empirical observation relates to the role of the Federal Reserve Board in managing the money supply and interest rates. If the Fed anticipates and offsets the effect of deficits or tax lag (for example, by expanding the money supply so as to moderate the government's interest costs), then any effect on interest rates may be hard to observe. Still greater observational difficulty results if the Fed's

2. See, e.g., Evans 1986 (attempting to take account of people's fluctuating estimates regarding future deficits under several different assumptions).

responses are inconsistent. Empirical research suggests that the Fed does not respond to deficits in a consistent manner. Sometimes it expands the money supply to accommodate government borrowing, while at other times its response is contractionary (see, e.g., Dwyer 1985, 668–74). This inconsistency should come as no surprise. As Alan Blinder puts it, "[p]olicymakers come and go bringing with them different preferences [and applying changing economic theories to changing conditions]. For example, the objective function that is being maximized by the Fed changed, I think, when Paul Volcker replaced William Miller" (1985, 687).

So far, the discussion has been purely empirical and concerned with whether tax lag's effect (if any) on interest rates tells us anything that is of separate interest—for example, as a test of Ricardianism. One might further ask whether interest rates have any independent relevance for fiscal policy. Suppose, for example, that tax lag does tend to increase interest rates and that countervailing action by the Fed is generally incomplete. Is there any reason why we should consider one possible interest rate better than another? After all, the interest rate merely states the price relationship between two goods—present consumption against rights to future consumption. One could argue that as a general matter, economists and policymakers should not treat any particular market price ratio—such as that between, say, the prices of housing and food—as inherently preferable. One might prefer simply to let the marketplace decide, absent strong grounds for second-guessing it.

Some argue, however, that interest rates' possible broader macroeconomic effects—for example, on inflation or economic growth—justify public policy concern. Yet this raises the question, which generally lacks a clear answer, of what these effects actually are. An increase in real interest rates may either stimulate inflation by adding to the costs that economic producers need to recover or deter it by reducing consumer demand for goods (given the increased return to saving). Indeed, if both explanations are correct but the latter takes place over a longer period, then an increase in real interest rates may be inflationary in the short run and deflationary in the long run.

As for economic growth, Keynesians often argue that low interest rates play an important role in encouraging investment by reducing the cost of obtaining loan capital. However, this claim reflects the characteristic (and controversial) Keynesian skepticism about markets' capacity to clear rapidly. One might alternatively predict that, at least in the long run, higher interest rates, by prompting increased saving and thereby shifting consumption from the present to the future, will yield, after an unspecified transitional period, an equilibrium with higher investment.

Two broader points seem clear, however, if one assumes that tax lag can affect interest rates. First, stable interest rates, whether high or low, may encourage economic activity by reducing the risk of un-predictable interest rate change. Thus, any tendency of fiscal policy to increase interest rates' oscillation would be undesirable. While fiscal policy could in principle aim to stabilize rather than destabilize them, in practice this might require an unrealistically high level of discipline and coherence in the politically driven budget process.

Second, lowering interest rates tends to improve the government's fiscal position as a new borrower (although, on the other hand, raising interest rates tends to lower the market value of outstanding fixed-rate government debt). Reducing the government's interest rate is socially desirable, holding all other government spending constant, insofar as it reduces the level of inevitably distortive taxation that is necessary to finance bond payments. Yet reducing interest costs may also cause substantive government spending to increase. If one joins the Virginia theorists, such as James Buchanan, in viewing such spending as likely, at the margin, to be wasteful or even actively harmful, then one might prefer to force the government to spend as much as possible on inter-est costs. Such a view relies, however, on strong claims regarding both the constancy of the overall budget constraint and the degree of harm caused by government spending programs.

When one adds together all the empirical uncertainties and norm-ative ambiguities, there seems to be little basis for basing the appro-priate degree of tax lag in our fiscal policy on concern about interest rates. Other considerations should control, unless they prove equally unhelpful.

2. The U.S. Balance of Payments

The standard view of budget deficits makes a prediction regarding their effect on the U.S. balance of payments that is the counterpart, for an open economy and integrated worldwide capital markets, to the prediction that they will increase interest rates in a closed economy. Again, under the standard view, interest rates may fail to change appreciably in an open economy because foreign capital inflows accommodate the government's increased demand for the use of money, without thereby greatly altering the overall worldwide relationship between supply and demand. If this is so, however, then budget deficits should have two related effects. First, they should increase the country's balance-of-payments deficit, since capital inflows count as a debit for purposes of that measure. Second, by increasing the balance-of-payments deficit, they should increase the national currency's exchange rate against other currencies. Since foreigners who wish to invest in the United States (whether in government bonds, corporate stock, or real estate) generally must pay in dollars, their investment decisions tend to increase their demand for dollars and thus to raise the dollar's price in terms of other currencies.

The main reasons for not expecting budget deficits to have these two effects resemble the reasons for not expecting the predicted interest rate effects. Ricardians see no need for foreign capital inflows to finance increased government borrowing, since private domestic saving automatically increases as people make provision to pay the expected future taxes. To Laurence Kotlikoff, while the standard view is correct regarding tax lag, deficits provide too poor a measure of it to have any systematic effects (1992, 71).

A further problem with drawing definite conclusions from any lack of detected correlation between budget deficits and the balance-of-payments deficit is that here, as in the interest rate area, there are overwhelming "noise" problems. These may range from the actions of various governments to the effects of inflation or inflationary expectations (which weaken a currency that is subject to them); to problems of lag, as people in businesses in one country gradually respond to currency fluctuations by changing their purchasing patterns and relationships; to broader changes in worldwide patterns of production, trade, and domestic consumption.

Accordingly, it is not surprising to find that here, as in the interest rate area, the empirical evidence is mixed. Many regard the evidence of the early 1980s as strongly supporting the standard view. Increased budget deficits were followed by increased balance-of-payments deficits (including an increased current account trade deficit) and a stronger dollar. Indeed, Martin Feldstein had predicted the "twin deficits," which he regarded as reason for reducing the budget deficit, before they occurred (see, e.g., Krugman 1990, 42). However, a recent econometric study based on quarterly U.S. data from the early 1980s failed to show that budget deficit and balance-of-payments changes tracked each other closely in the short term, thus ostensibly supporting Ricardianism (see Evans 1986). In another study based on more than a century of English data, Ricardianism was ostensibly either confirmed or disconfirmed, depending on what assumptions one thought appropriate regarding how well people forecast war-related government expenditure before it occurred (Ahmed 1986, 220).

The standard view, however, surely is correct on logical grounds—at least as applied to tax lag. As long as one accepts the core anti-Ricardian conclusion that deferring taxes tends to increase private consumption relative to saving—since people feel wealthier, as shown by their political aversion to current taxes—deferring taxes should, at the margin, increase net capital inflows (or reduce net outflows). Given the need, purely as an arithmetic matter, for capital inflows to make up the difference between domestic investment and domestic saving (since one cannot invest more than the amount that savers make available), the trade deficit necessarily reflects the relationship between these two aggregates (see, e.g., Krugman 1990, 94). More generally, trade deficits tend to be owed by countries with low saving rates to those with high saving rates. Since tax lag generally reduces national saving (Keynesian slack aside), it should increase the trade deficit or reduce the trade surplus.

This brings us to the normative question of what we should think about these probable empirical effects. Once again, few clear implications for policy emerge. While trade deficits are no less of a popular bogeyman than budget deficits, this reflects a comparable lack of public understanding. Trade and balance-of-payments deficits, whether they reflect foreign purchases of our financial assets or foreign investment in property and businesses in this country or simply an excess of our imports over our exports of consumer goods, are in effect a loan from foreigners to us. We receive a present net inflow of real or financial assets that, for now, permits consumption and investment in the United States to exceed national income—just as one can consume and invest more than one's income if one borrows money from a bank.

Eventually, disregarding the prospect of unanticipated default or expropriation, we will owe our foreign lenders repayment of their principal plus notional interest (including both literal interest and the profits on American properties or businesses that they own). Such repayment shifts real goods and services away from domestic use. Yet if the opportunity to make current use of others' assets had no value, then one would not, as a general matter, observe loan transactions in which borrowers agreed to pay interest. The transactions that give rise to the trade deficit may turn out to be either a good or a bad bargain for Americans, depending on how one compares the benefit of the current use of foreign resources to the cost. Yet at least the transactions are reciprocal and result from voluntary private and governmental decisions that one should not automatically assume are misguided. (Indeed, even if our trade deficits result in part from foreign exclusionary practices toward our commercial products, a long-standing free trade tradition among economists holds that we would not benefit from seeking to eliminate the trade deficit through reciprocal or retaliatory protectionism.)

In addition, it seems clear, given the low level of domestic saving over the last fifteen years, that only foreign capital inflows have permitted the level of domestic investment (which provides Americans with jobs), enhanced production and productivity, and the like to remain high. Absent such inflows, either such investment would have been many hundreds of billions of dollars less, or else its maintenance would have required, through the mechanism of higher interest rates, a significant curtailment of current consumption. The United States would certainly be far worse off if, like Haiti and North Korea, it had great difficulty in attracting foreign investment (see Stein 1989a).

One reason for popular unease about budget deficits in the international context is the concern that we are giving foreign lenders a dangerous degree of leverage over American policy or economic well-being. The most obvious fear—that foreigners, for political reasons, will exploit their position as owners and ongoing purchasers of the national debt—seems unrealistic, given the size and diversity of worldwide capital markets, and most lenders' profit motive. The holders of existing debt do not so much exercise power over us as we do over them, in the sense that we can threaten to default (albeit at enormous long-term cost to ourselves). Any group of prospective investors who refused, for noneconomic reasons, to purchase newly issued U.S. government debt would surely find that others were willing to take their place, especially if the offered yield were even minimally greater than that offered by alternative investments.

To be sure, the feared exercise of leverage by foreign investors with respect to their investments in the United States generally (not just in government bonds) might also be economically motivated. Here a stronger argument for public concern can be made. Many have argued that a one-way net flow of capital into the United States cannot go on forever. This is not literally true. Just as public debt may remain outstanding indefinitely, so may U.S. public and private debt owed to foreigners. As long as our present output and expected future output remain sufficiently large relative to the level of debt and our reputation as trustworthy borrowers who will not willfully default or expropriate remains intact, investment in our economy may remain attractive. Still, there are limits to any country's capacity to absorb foreign invest-ment without eventually prompting concerns about repayment. At some point—when lenders become uneasy, or when other investment opportunities begin to seem more attractive—one might expect repay-ment through net capital outflow to become necessary.

The replacement of trade deficits by trade surpluses need not be painful. Consider, after all, that until the early 1980s, the United States had generally experienced trade surpluses for a lengthy period without evident resulting hardship. However, the replacement of deficit by sur-plus can be painful when prompted by a sudden loss of foreign invest-ors' confidence. Much of Latin America learned this during its debt crisis of the early 1980s, when foreign investors successfully demanded the adoption of austerity programs that required severe domestic sac-rifice, at least in the short term. One could argue that the programs served the long-term interests of the countries that adopted them un-der duress, and that the duress permitted these countries to overcome shortsightedness or politically caused policy irrationalities. Yet the people living in those countries surely disliked not only the short-term effects themselves but also the feeling that they had lost their auton-omy in setting national economic policy.

The prospect of something similar happening in the United States is considerably more remote, given our economy's vastly greater size and strength. Still, it cannot be dismissed altogether. Respectable economists have occasionally predicted an imminent "hard landing," resulting from a sudden collapse of foreign investors' confidence. While, to date, all definite predictions of a hard landing have been falsified, this could change someday. A hard landing could result not only from worsened economic performance but also from a change in the political environment such that willful default or expropriation began to seem possible.

Perhaps a more serious potential problem with the trade deficit is that it tends to increase domestic political pressures for protectionism. Such pressure is regrettable as long as one agrees that free trade tends to benefit its practitioners on balance even if other countries decline to reciprocate. Paul Krugman notes the "old saw in trade theory: Saying that my country should be protectionist just because other countries are is like saying that, because other countries have rocky coasts, I should block up my own harbors" (1990, 129–30).

Simply as a symbol, the trade deficit strengthens the hand of those who wish to blame American economic problems on nefarious foreigners who ostensibly decline to trade on free or fair terms. Economists generally agree that such arguments are bogus, despite the conceded existence in various foreign markets of import barriers and subsidies for home producers. The United States has extensive import barriers and home producer subsidies as well. More important, however, unfair foreign trade practices cannot credibly be blamed for more than a tiny portion of the trade deficit. Relative saving rates, as between the United States and countries such as Germany and Japan, have a far greater impact.

Still, the political symbolism of a high trade deficit can potently influence an ill-informed public that wants scapegoats and easy answers to economic problems. The budget deficit helps to show the political power of a norm of balance, since its own potent symbolism helped to produce the budget agreements of 1982, 1984, 1990, and 1993, which raised taxes despite general public aversion to them. Moreover, as Krugman notes, trade deficits do not merely have symbolic effects but also tend to correlate with increased interest group clamor for protectionism. While, in general, the influence of domestic producers who want protection is countered by that of exporters who support free trade, a sizable trade deficit suggests that the former group will be larger and thus potentially more powerful (102).

Accordingly, the case for reducing tax lag in order to reduce the trade deficit cannot wholly be dismissed. In general, the trade deficit involves the same tradeoff between present and future consumption as public borrowing, or any private loan transaction, and thus is indeterminate in the abstract. Arguably, however, the two special risks of a hard landing and of encouraging protectionism are especially significant. To the extent that these risks are significant (and there is no clear evidence that they are), one might attach some value to reducing tax lag in order to increase national saving.

What about concern with the exchange rate, which one generally would expect to be higher when there is a substantial trade deficit? Again, this presents a tradeoff and perhaps even a net benefit of the trade deficit. While a strong dollar impedes exports by raising the cost to foreigners of our goods, the American economy may not lose jobs on balance. Most economists argue that labor supply, not demand, determines domestic job levels and that unemployment will tend toward the "natural rate" without regard to the level of our exports (Krugman 1990, 37–39). Moreover, a strong dollar makes imports cheaper and thus raises the real standard of living in the United States, at least in the short term. It also restrains inflation by providing cheap foreign competition for domestically produced goods.

In summary, trade deficits present a slightly stronger case than interest rates for concern about tax lag. However, the speculativeness of the possible dangers impedes drawing strong inferences for government fiscal policy. Macroeconomic concern about tax lag must rest on other issues if it is to be regarded as of central importance.

3. The Inflation Rate

Regarding inflation, the standard view of budget deficits turns once again on the presumption that debt financing, by increasing perceived wealth relative to tax financing, increases current consumer demand. This, in turn, suggests that increasing budget deficits (or, more properly, tax lag) will have some tendency to induce price and wage inflation. To what extent this will happen, however, depends on a number of variables.

One of the main variables, related to the Keynesian distinction between the conditions of full employment and economic slack, is how quickly and easily producers can increase output—for example, by restarting idle factories and rehiring skilled workers who have been laid off, as opposed to the slower responses of building new factories and training new workers. A second variable is the degree to which worldwide markets for consumer goods and services are integrated. Just as an increased domestic demand for the current use of money will lead to capital inflows rather than to increased interest rates if worldwide capital markets are sufficiently large and integrated, so increased consumer demand may only increase imports, without noticeably affecting prices, under similar circumstances. At present, worldwide market integration is far less advanced for consumer goods than for capital and is least advanced of all in markets for providing services. Nonetheless, many believe that when a strong dollar encourages cheap imports, the inflation that one otherwise might expect is dampened significantly (see, e.g., Feldstein and Elmendorf 1989, 2–3, 15–21).

A third important variable is the extent to which the Fed responds through monetary policy to the potential inflationary pressure resulting from increased demand. The best empirical test of tax lag's independent effect would be provided if the Fed simply ignored it and continued its preexisting policy. An accommodating monetary policy of expanding the money supply to ease federal policy would tend to increase inflation, but arguably for mainly monetary reasons. Economists since at least the time of David Hume have noted that expanding the money supply tends to cause inflation, because it makes each available unit of money less valuable relative to whatever stock of real goods and services is held for purchase (again, subject to the qualifications regarding international markets and the ease of expanding output). By contrast, a contractionary monetary policy, designed to counter the inflationary pressures created by tax lag, would tend to reduce or eliminate the observable effects.

Suppose, however, that none of these factors dampens inflation: there is little Keynesian slack, imports fail to play a significant role in constraining prices, and the Fed does not respond through monetary policy. Assuming that tax lag therefore causes inflation, would the effect, under the standard view, be short-term only or more permanent? The question has no simple answer. On the one hand, the picture of increased consumer demand pushing up prices, to the extent that production cannot keep pace fast enough absent idle factories and unemployed trained workers, is purely short-term. One would expect production ultimately to catch up with consumer demand and moreover for such demand, by reducing saving and investment and thus lowering economic growth, to prove self-correcting. On the other hand, inflationary expectations play such an important role in wage and price trends that once inflation got started, it might persist or accelerate. The course of such expectations cannot, however, be modeled or predicted in the abstract. Thus, the standard analysis, in addition to yielding no definite prediction that short-term inflation will always result, also yields no definite prediction regarding the persistence of any such inflation.

As usual, Ricardians would reject the entire standard analysis, including even its short-term component, on the ground that debt financing does not increase perceived wealth relative to tax financing and therefore that budget deficits do not increase overall demand. Kotlikoff rejects the standard analysis regarding budget deficits but presumably would accept it regarding tax lag.

One might further argue that a one-time transfer to present generations from increasing tax lag will have only limited effects on current consumption, making observable inflation relatively unlikely. If people base their consumption decisions on expected lifetime income, then an increase in perceived wealth will cause one to increase one's spending only gradually. Monetarists such as Milton Friedman argue on this ground that fiscal policy is generally a weaker macroeconomic tool than monetary policy for reducing inflation.

Recent econometric literature has paid little attention to the degree of correlation between budget deficits and inflation. This reflects the widespread understanding that given the wealth of separate factors affecting inflation, one cannot use the relationship between inflation and tax lag as a meaningful test of Ricardianism. A more casual examination of the last few decades reveals precisely the mixed evidence that one might expect. On the one hand, many blame the start of the inflationary spiral of the early 1960s on President Johnson's decision, several years earlier, to seek both "guns" and "butter" (the Vietnam War and Great Society domestic spending) without a tax increase. In addition, many blamed the increasing deficits of the late 1970s for contemporary inflation. Yet the evidence of the 1980s shows that higher deficits can be accompanied by reduced inflation—at least when the Fed pursues a severely contractionary monetary policy and succeeds in significantly lowering inflationary expectations.

Accordingly, even if the assumed relationship between tax lag and inflation is correct in theory, one can largely ignore it in practice, at least as long as the Fed continues to make aggressive use of monetary policy. Thus, the normative question of to what extent inflation fears should enter into fiscal policymaking seems relatively unimportant. I nonetheless will briefly examine the question of inflation's social costs, because it is relevant to the tradeoff that tax lag or budget deficits may present between inflation and unemployment.

While the magnitude of inflation's costs and dangers is disputed, there is basic underlying consensus about their character. First, everyone agrees that hyperinflation, as experienced, say, by Weimar Germany or post-Soviet Russia, can work disastrous harm by causing a breakdown in the use of money. However, this is not really a danger even at rates of inflation that we would nonetheless consider quite high—say, 10 to 20 percent annually. At such rates, the problem takes the lesser (although not trivial) form of making people bear a cost when they decide to hold money, thus potentially burdening liquidity and requiring people to engage in additional transactions to lessen this cost.

Second, under some circumstances and assumptions, inflation below the "hyper" level could be nearly, or indeed wholly, irrelevant. As long as the inflation rate can be predicted with reasonable accuracy in advance or measured after the fact, economic actors can make all sorts of adjustments for it, such as agreeing to interest rates that are indexed to inflation (or at least reflect plausible assumptions about it) and providing for regular cost-of-living wage increases in long-term employment contracts. The main problem with such adjustments is their cost and complexity, especially when price increases are differentially distributed across the economy. Inflation adjustments can be burdensome to apply, and inflation increases the level of costly information that people need in order to make sound decisions.

Such cost and complexity can be particularly high for adjustments after the fact. A borrower and a lender, for example, may need to know exactly what nominal amount the former will repay on a given date and thus may strongly prefer to base the terms of their transaction on an expected inflation rate. To the extent that this is true, fluctuating and unpredictable inflation can expose economic actors to unwanted risk of windfall loss that impedes long-term planning, rewards the otherwise unnecessary skill of predicting inflation, and perhaps diminishes the long-run efficiency of the economy by increasing the extent to which competitive outcomes reflect luck rather than superior performance.

Third, absent comprehensive adjustments, a high rate of inflation can cause problems in the operation of the income tax system, both by enabling Congress, through the mechanism of rate bracket creep, to raise taxes without explicit or visible action and by increasing the system's mismeasurement of capital income. Congress eliminated the former problem in 1981 by indexing the rate brackets, but the latter problem remains. In a high inflation environment, "lock-in" of appreciated capital assets is accentuated through the taxation of inflationary gains, economic income is mismeasured as between lenders and borrowers who may be in different rate brackets, and tax depreciation allowances may lag behind economic depreciation.

Fourth, as the Virginia theorists have noted, granting government the power to cause unexpected inflation or deflation can lead to socially wasteful rent-seeking behavior. Creditors and debtors, for example, may compete to use government policy as a tool for changing the real value of the latter's repayment obligations. Or "Leviathan" may use unexpected inflation, in effect as a hidden tax on the holders of public debt.

Fifth, under some circumstances, apparently acceptable inflation may feed on itself and turn into damaging hyperinflation. Most economists today accept Milton Friedman's and Edmund Phelps's argument that if the government, through expansionary fiscal or monetary policy, aggressively pursued an artificially defined "full employment," the cost in inflation would grow steadily higher rather than remaining relatively stable as suggested by the Phillips curve. Once rampant inflationary expectations have been established in the economy, they are difficult to dampen, other than through a severe recession such as that which the Fed, through its contractionary monetary policy, imposed between 1979 and 1982.

Again, at present, these problems are not strongly raised by tax lag, at least as long as the Fed uses monetary policy to control inflation. Yet they would be relevant to any attempted revival of the use of fiscal policy for broad macroeconomic purposes, such as under Robert Eisner's proposal vastly to increase the budget deficit (and tax lag) in the effort to stimulate economic expansion and reduce unemployment.

C. The Effects of Tax Lag and Budget Deficits on the Level of Consumption Relative to Saving

The question of whether tax lag affects current decisions to consume or to save is fundamental. As we have seen, most of the other claims concerning the effects of fiscal policy depend on it. Tax lag (and budget deficits) should not be expected to increase interest rates, the trade deficit, or the rate of inflation unless they increase current consumption relative to saving.

In addition to being important as a marker of other likely effects, the margin between consumption and saving is important for its own sake. The empirical claim that tax lag increases current consumption underlies the view that it can be used to combat recession, or more broadly to reduce unemployment, as a tool of Keynesian stimulus. This empirical claim also underlies the seemingly opposite view that tax lag impairs economic growth by reducing the amount that is saved and invested. These two views are intellectually reconcilable, in that the former assumes slack in the Keynesian sense, while the latter assumes its absence.

1. Does Tax Lag Have the Claimed Effect of Increasing Current Consumption Relative to Saving?

Only Ricardians dispute that tax lag tends to increase current propensities to consume rather than save. In one respect, the empirical issue that the Ricardians raise seems an appealing one to study. Whatever effects tax lag has on the level of domestic consumption (or saving) should not be concealed by international asset or capital flows. If Americans begin consuming more as tax lag increases, measurement is not thrown off by their consuming foreign-produced goods.

Two recent studies in which Laurence Kotlikoff participated tend to rebut Ricardianism. First, a generational accounting study suggests that fiscal policy transferring wealth to older generations (and benefiting all living generations relative to the unborn) has in fact reduced saving (see Gokhale, Kotlikoff, and Sabelhaus 1995). Second, a study using household-level data collected at periodic intervals from the same extended families since 1968 finds that the studied households did *not* more than slightly adjust intergenerational consumption for the effects of government fiscal policy (Altonji, Hayashi, and Kotlikoff 1992, 1196). However, more studies like these two and studies conducted by researchers not known to be anti-Ricardian are obviously needed.

With respect to budget deficits, the evidence is disappointingly (although perhaps not surprisingly) indeterminate. Some believe that Ricardian equivalence is sharply contradicted by the experience of the 1980s, when deficits greatly increased yet private saving significantly declined. However, a one-time rough empirical correlation is hardly conclusive. Turning to econometric studies of the effects of budget deficits, John Seater calls them a "mishmash, yielding wildly different results from one to the next" (1993, 164). Robert Barro agrees that "the results are all over the map, with some favoring Ricardian equivalence and others not" (1989, 49). Barro finds inherent methodological shortcomings in most of the tests, relating to how changing income affects consumption and how the business cycle affects both budget deficits and private decisions to consume or to save.

Even if one could filter through the "noise" and obtain more definite empirical conclusions from the deficit studies, the significance of one's findings would be unclear. Again, given the weak relationship between cash-flow budget deficits and tax lag, a finding of no correlation might support Kotlikoff's position as much as Barro's, while a finding of positive correlation would likewise be suspect. Recall, for example, Kotlikoff's finding that government fiscal policy did far less to transfer wealth from future to present generations in the high-deficit 1980s than in the low-deficit 1950s—thus showing that over a given period where other variables are fluctuating, deficits can actually correlate negatively with tax lag.

An additional problem with evaluating the significance of even clear-cut econometric evidence involves the main disagreement among non-Ricardians concerning how fiscal policy affects decisions to consume or to save. This disagreement concerns the time horizon within which fiscal policy affects private behavior. In illustration, consider a hypothetical increase in the budget deficit that results from a tax cut, unaccompanied by any change in the level of government spending. A traditional Keynesian would expect the beneficiaries to spend their extra cash relatively quickly, whether because they were cash-constrained and had wanted to spend more all along or because they applied short time horizons and were myopic about the possibility of offsetting future tax increases. By contrast, neoclassical economists ranging from Milton Friedman to Laurence Kotlikoff generally would assume more rational long-term planning, in keeping with the lifetime or permanent income hypothesis. Thus, while a neoclassical economist might agree that the tax cut will increase perceived wealth (unless people expect an offsetting tax increase during their own life spans), he or she would expect the resulting effect on consumer spending to be far more gradual. Just how gradual would depend on whether people thought that the tax cut was permanent or merely a one-time windfall.[3] While the neoclassical view differs from the Keynesian view only in degree, it makes far more plausible the concern that the current year effect will be buried by statistical "noise."

In the end, therefore, one must return to the theoretical debate. I have argued that Ricardianism is theoretically implausible for a num-

3. See, e.g., Reid 1985, an econometric study that emphasizes the distinction between permanent and transitory tax changes and finds the evidence that it studies in light of this distinction inconsistent with Ricardian equivalence.

ber of reasons. It fails to account for strategic behavior and impure altruism within the household and unduly downplays the significance of rational ignorance, fiscal illusion, and rent-seeking behavior between households. In particular, it ignores and cannot explain voters' special aversion to current taxes, relative to the future taxes implied by tax lag. Eliminating deficits would not be as difficult politically if this were not so.

Indeed, a Ricardian who really believes his or her own theory would be well advised to enter politics and run for president on a platform of painless deficit elimination (painless because the candidate can explain that paying current taxes is no worse than deferring them). While voters' aversion to current taxes is hard to "prove" rigorously in econometric form, the real experts on the subject of what people think—politicians and campaign consultants, as opposed to economists—evidently believe in it. When they forget or try to act more Ricardian—as with Walter Mondale's pledge in 1984 to raise taxes or George Bush's agreement to do so in 1990—they generally pay a stiff political price. We therefore essentially have empirical proof, if not of a conventional kind, that tax lag, when viewed as credible and sustainable, increases perceived wealth and thus should be expected to increase current consumption at the expense of saving.

2. Tax Lag as a Tool for Combating Recession and Unemployment

a. Assessing the Keynesian Case for Countercyclical Stimulus

As we have seen, the Keynesian view of the business cycle retains some validity. People's decisions to reduce current market consumption can reduce it permanently, not just shift it to the future. Moreover, reduced market consumption can reflect a collective action problem, in which individuals decline to buy because they are afraid they will be unable to sell. This collective action problem may yield a low-market-consumption equilibrium at which it is plausible that people are less satisfied than they would have been at a high-confidence, high-market-consumption equilibrium. Increasing perceived wealth can address the collective action problem by inducing large numbers of people to believe that they can afford to spend more.

In addition, changes in demand can prompt surprisingly slow responses by sellers. Consider the "menu costs" of changing prices, along with regulatory and contractual rigidities. In addition, certain markets, such as labor and housing, may adjust to changing conditions particularly slowly. On the one hand, a person who is offering a relatively fungible asset, such as corn or the use of money, can be expected, in most cases, to observe that the price has shifted or that no sale is possible at the prior price. Even one offering a relatively unique asset, such as a particular make of car or the meals in a distinctive restaurant, can be expected to observe promptly that sales are unduly low. Yet the seller of a unique asset who enters the marketplace only on special occasions—such as a worker seeking a job or a home owner selling a house—may have greater difficulty pricing realistically in light of current conditions, especially given the possibility of windfall success in finding a highly motivated buyer. Failure to perceive the shift in one's "lottery" odds regarding such a one-time event would be a subtle and unsurprising type of error. Under these circumstances, Keynesian stimulus may eliminate the waste that results from people's failure to adjust their expectations rapidly. In effect, the mountain comes to Muhammad. Obsolete, unadjusted expectations regain their accuracy once the level of demand changes back to its prior level.

Nonetheless, the limits of Keynesian countercyclical policy should be kept clearly in mind. The further one departs from a severe recession, the less convincing is the assumption that increasing GDP will increase people's subjective well-being. Moreover, the most that one can reasonably expect from the policy is shorter and less severe recessions. "Full employment" in Keynes's sense is close to useless as a technical term and cannot generally guide government macroeconomic policy. Given the inevitability of human decision-making error, some productive resources will always be mistakenly underutilized, but Keynesian stimulus does not enable one regularly to reach such resources (or to know that one has done so) rather than prompting either inflation or shifts in people's preferences that do not necessarily increase their aggregate satisfaction.

Nothing resembling full employment, in the loose sense that everyone who really wants a job gets one, is attainable through Keynesian stimulus. The best that one can hope for is a speedier return to the nonaccelerating inflation rate of unemployment (NAIRU), whatever it may be at any given time, when the economy suffers some sort of shock that creates temporary displacement. Attempting to reduce unemployment still more is likely either to prove ineffective or to prompt spiraling inflation. To achieve more durable reductions in unemployment, one must somehow reduce the NAIRU—for example, by reducing the burdens that taxes and regulation place on the employment relationship. Possibilities include (1) providing governmental wage subsidies to marginal or low-wage workers, (2) reducing the legally mandated minimum wage, (3) eliminating other regulatory mandates that affect employers or employment, (4) reducing Social Security taxes, (5) reducing income taxation of marginal workers' wages, and (6) reducing the "tax" that one may incur by working, in the form of reduced welfare or unemployment benefits.

The claim of traditional Keynesians such as Robert Eisner that permanent fiscal stimulus through ever-greater tax lag will increase not only current consumption and employment but also long-term economic growth, is incorrect. Eisner's policies would likely result in a permanently lower saving rate that would reduce long-term economic growth and thus shift consumption from the future to the present. While this does not necessarily mean that his proposed policies are wrong, given the indeterminacy of normative generational policy, it does establish the existence of a tradeoff that he fails to recognize. Yet, no matter how one evaluates this tradeoff, his proposed policies cannot do as much as he would like about unemployment, the main problem that he wants to address, given the extent to which it is structural rather than cyclical.

Finally, the limited case that I have been making for Keynesian countercyclical policy relates only to its theoretical potential, not to the effects that one should actually expect from it in practice. The degree of benefit (if any) that it will yield in practice depends on how it is administered. This depends in part on how well the available tools, fiscal and monetary policy, would work under the best of circumstances, where well-informed experts with the right motives and incentives were applying them. It also depends on real-world decision makers' motives, incentives, and level of information. The next section examines the prospects for Keynesian stimulus through tax lag, such as manipulating budget deficits, with appropriate comparison to monetary policy.

b. Assessing the Case for Keynesian Fiscal Policy

As Joseph Minarik puts it, the case for Keynesian countercyclical policy is strongest if one assumes that it is administered by

[a] Socratic economist-king [who] sits, ever alert, with his hands on the fiscal and monetary policy dials [ready to respond w]henever news of an economic shock hits—or rather, whenever an economic shock hits, because the economist-king is omniscient and need not wait for the news. . . . [F]ortunately, the economist-king is non-ideological as well as omniscient. He or she is a pure scientist, and has no political ax to grind. Therefore, all policy steps promote the long-term good of the society, and follow established and accepted principles. (1991, 251–52)

Obviously, these conditions for the optimal execution of Keynesian policy are rather restrictive. In the real world, the case for such policy is far more contingent, although not hopeless. However, the real-world case for calling on Congress and the president to manipulate the budget deficit, in particular by enacting tax cuts or spending increases during recessions, is by now well known to be particularly weak.

The most widely recognized problem with responding to recessions through fiscal policy is that of implementation lag (Okun 1970, 65). First an impending recession must be observed. Then someone, typically the president, must make a legislative proposal to stimulate the economy through tax cuts or spending increases. Inevitably, the process of enactment, by a Congress that typically likes to make its own decisions even if it is controlled by the president's party, takes time. Even once the stimulus program is enacted, implementation may take additional time—for example, if government contracts must be bid out or if taxpayers must await the filing of their income tax returns or if market mechanisms must be developed for widely disseminating the use of new tax preferences.

Monetary policy does not involve comparable lag. The Federal Reserve Board can both reach and implement a decision to change the discount rate that it charges banks, or the cash reserve ratio that it imposes on them, overnight. Although the full economic effects take somewhat longer to be felt, the timing difference between the two types of policy remains substantial.

Especially with respect to fiscal policy, implementation lags may prevent the stimulus from arriving until economic recovery has begun. When this happens, the policy's effect may be to heighten, rather than moderate, the business cycle. Recall the metaphor of a thermostat that detects cold temperatures during the winter but does not succeed in turning the heat on until the summer—thus, in the end, destabilizing indoor temperatures. While one can attempt to reduce fiscal policy lag, this has costs of its own. Policymakers may find it necessary to "jump the gun" by relying on early-warning economic forecasts that carry a high risk of being incorrect. Or, once they start implementing new programs, they may face what Minarik calls the "timing/quality trade-off." Programs that need to be implemented swiftly to create effective stimulus would need to be implemented slowly in order to use resources effectively (Minarik 1991, 254).

In one respect, this pessimistic view of fiscal policy lag may be overstated. If consumer spending is based on people's perceived wealth rather than merely their cash on hand, then fiscal stimulus may start to take effect (through both increased consumer spending and business anticipation thereof) before full implementation, and indeed as soon as the policy change begins to be anticipated. This is most plausible, however, when the legislative outcome is relatively certain—hardly a quality of recent major policy debates in Washington. Uncertainty about what Congress will do may actually have the effect of *slowing* any decisions by businesses to invest or by consumers to spend.

An additional problem with fiscal policy that becomes apparent once one focuses on attempting to increase people's perceived wealth concerns the time frame in which one should expect consumer spending to increase. Again, the traditional Keynesian claim that people tend to spend a large proportion even of a one-time tax cut requires assuming that a significant portion of the population is either cash-constrained (a more plausible premise in the 1930s than today) or myopic about the likely future course of their taxes. Under the lifetime income hypothesis, such a one-time increase in perceived wealth may have relatively little immediate effect on the level of consumer spending. Whatever short-term effect there is may depend on such elusive variables as people's confidence about the economy and their expectations about the future course of fiscal policy.

Monetary policy may tend to have a greater short-term effect on output, as long as demand for loan capital is reasonably elastic. If it is, then even slightly reducing the interest rate should immediately lead to increased private expenditure. Only if such demand is relatively inelastic should monetary policy fail to have short-term effects and thereby justify the traditional Keynesians' disparagement of responding to recessions through monetary policy as akin to "pulling on a string." Given the likely differences in short-term responsiveness to fiscal and monetary policy, the Keynesians had it precisely backward— if not during the 1930s, then at least as applied to our well-functioning capital markets, where the demand for money seems robust.

Admittedly, monetary policy has problems of its own, which arguably have grown worse in recent years. The increasing integration of world capital markets tends to counteract, or else to dissipate throughout the world economy, the impact of the Fed's money supply and interest rate interventions. (This is a problem for fiscal policy as well.) In addition, the difficulty of measuring and controlling the money supply has increased over time, with the growth of modern financing arrangements such as the extensive private use of credit card debt. Still, most economists agree that monetary policy can continue to be used as an effective device for economic stabilization (see, e.g., Krugman 1994, 118–23; Lightfoot 1994).

The special problems with fiscal policy would raise concern even under the best of circumstances, where one assumed that policymakers had the right motives and incentives. Looking at the actual decision makers, the elected politicians in Congress and the presidency, only increases one's concern. Politicians tend to find—at least to the extent permitted by fear of deficits—that increasing the voters' perceived wealth through tax cuts or new spending programs benefits them politically without regard to the stage of the business cycle. Moreover, given voters' limited attention and short memories, election pressures often induce politicians to adopt inappropriately short time horizons.

Finally, a set of political rigidities impede the continuing implementation of countercyclical fiscal policy. Tax increases and spending cuts during times of inflation are generally less popular than their opposites in times of recession. Moreover, once expansionary tax cuts and spending increases have been enacted, they are hard to repeal. People get used to them, and they acquire interest group constituencies. This is all the more regrettable if the provisions, their countercyclical effects aside, are allocatively inefficient, as special tax concessions and pork-barrel spending appropriations often are. Monetary policy is far easier to reverse than fiscal policy—as the Fed proved between 1979 and 1982, when it combated inflation through a severely restrictive policy that no Congress, and perhaps no president, would have found politically sustainable.

For these reasons, the only strong case for countercyclical fiscal policy concerns that which takes place automatically, without requiring the enactment of new legislation. Purely under the fixed terms of current policy, recessions tend both to reduce the government's income tax receipts and to increase its expenditures under programs such as welfare and unemployment insurance. Economic expansion tends to have the opposite effect. These automatic countercyclical aspects of fiscal policy involve considerably less implementation lag than seeking and implementing new enactments, and they also self-correct without requiring politically unpopular policy changes.

The main ground on which one could criticize automatic countercyclical fiscal policy relates to the potential for misuse. Politicians can mislabel as merely countercyclical a fiscal policy that is tax-lagged over the long term. Hence the argument that even if temporary tax lag is harmless or indeed beneficial, only a norm of rigorously avoiding it can prevent it from growing uncontrollably.

3. Tax Lag and Budget Deficits as Reducing the Rates of Saving and Economic Growth

Aversion to tax lag for reducing the rate of saving, and thereby slowing the rate of long-term economic growth, is the flip side of support for it as a tool of countercyclical stimulus. Holding income constant (and ignoring Keynesian slack), people necessarily will save less if they consume more and will save more if they consume less. Thus, a growth advocate's aversion to budget deficits for reducing saving may initially appear to differ only in sign from a Keynesian's support for countercyclical budget deficits because they increase current consumption. That is, the two positions make identical assumptions about the effect of tax lag and seem to disagree only about the effect's desirability.

In fact, however, the two positions have an important difference. Keynesian countercyclical policy calls for increasing the propensity to consume, not as a general matter but during a particular stage in the business cycle. By contrast, the claim that the government, through fiscal policy, ought to increase the level of national saving by reducing the tax lag, looks to the long term rather than to what stage in the business cycle we are in.

Accordingly, the pro-growth position is not subject to several of the empirical objections to Keynesian fiscal policy. Its feasibility is affected neither by the problem of implementation lag nor by the implication of the lifetime income hypothesis that consumption will adjust to perceived wealth only gradually. Moreover, it does not require assuming that as a political matter, fiscal policy can be adapted from year to year.

It suggests instead a consistent course designed to increase national saving.

The view that tax lag should be reduced as a means of increasing saving therefore rests on empirical claims that are quite resilient once one rejects Ricardianism. The only plausible objection to it is the normative one that there is no particular reason for assuming that saving ought to be increased. With regard to present generations, the principle of consumer sovereignty—at least if one applies it to political as well as private choices—suggests that our present collective choices reflect our preferences and interests at least as well as any alternative that one could posit in the abstract.

Nonetheless, even without considering the interests of future generations, one could argue on a number of different grounds that the rate of national saving ought to be increased. The remainder of this section examines several such arguments.

a. Increasing Saving as a Paternalistic Response to People's Tendency to Save Too Little for Retirement

Neoclassical economic theory generally assumes that people act rationally and make the best possible decisions for themselves. The claim is not that people are too smart to err but rather that such rationality should generally be presumed on two grounds. First, under the notion of revealed preferences, people's behavior provides the only reliable evidence of what their preferences actually are. Second, even if one could identify the preferences or personal utility that underlie behavior and show that people are making mistakes, it is plausible that over the long run, they will make better decisions for themselves than anyone can make for them. The fact that people are flawed decision makers applies just as much to the paternalist who offers to intervene as to the target of that intervention, and the target may have better information and incentives regarding his or her own preferences than does the paternalist.

Nonetheless, one can perhaps support paternalism in cases where error seems both systematic and clear-cut. Suppose, for example, that people systematically underestimate the risk of death that driving a car involves relative to taking a plane. The decisions they consequently make may be both provably erroneous, assuming that we care only about the percentage likelihood of a fatality, and erroneous in a systematic direction. Therefore, a paternalist who wants to make them fly more and drive less stands on relatively strong ground—at least if the alternative of simply providing better information is ineffective or overly costly. The paternalist need not claim to be a better decision maker for other people in general, just to be better informed in this case.

On this type of ground, it has been argued that people often tend to save too little for their retirement and therefore that a paternalistic government policy of inducing or requiring them to save more, or else of saving on their behalf, would make them better off. Deborah Weiss, for example, argues that people may save too little out of myopia, impulsiveness, or impatience rather than simply experiencing changing preferences. She notes empirical research by psychologists showing both that people's preferences tend to be inconsistent and that people often regard themselves as struggling unsuccessfully to achieve self-control so that they can act in their own best interests (1991, 1285–86, 1300–1311). If people save too little because they are unable to pursue what they recognize all along as their true self-interest, then a paternalistic government policy of increasing saving might be desirable.

b. Increasing Saving in Response to Its Discouragement by Income Taxation

Numerous commentators since John Stuart Mill have noticed that an income tax, by "double taxing" (as he put it) income that is saved and invested but not that which is immediately consumed, disfavors saving. Though the point is often argued in "fairness" terms, one can make it more clearly in efficiency terms. Consider two individuals, X and Y, each of whom earns $100 in year 1 in a country where income tax is levied at a flat 40 percent rate. Both X and Y pay $40 of tax in year 1. Suppose, however, that X immediately consumes his after-tax income of $60, while Y invests her $60 in a perpetual bond that earns 10 percent, or $6, per year, which amount she consumes annually. (X had the same opportunity to make this investment but chose not to do so.) X will owe no further tax with respect to the original $100 that he earned. Y will owe additional tax in the amount of $2.40 per year on the investment income from the bond.

Whether or not one chooses to follow Mill semantically in calling this a double tax, the conclusion that Y is being taxed more heavily than X seems clear. Each pays the same amount in year 1, and thereafter Y pays additional tax. Yet the only posited distinction between X and Y was that they had different preferences regarding the timing of their consumption.

If X's and Y's timing-of-consumption decisions were wholly inelastic, the disfavoring of saving under the income tax would have no obvious efficiency consequences. In practice, however, many people's decisions regarding when to consume presumably are somewhat flexible. Thus, when one is deciding whether to act like X or like Y, the fact that the tax system will levy a greater aggregate charge in the latter case than in the former may influence one's decision. Even if market interest rates adjust to some extent, offering a greater pretax return than they would have absent the income tax burden on saving, the new market equilibrium should be one with less saving and investment than had there been no income tax—just as a tariff on an item typically will decrease its sales even if sellers bear part of it. To the extent that the tax system's treatment of saving yields a substitution effect—that is, people save less and consume sooner in response to the extra charge on saving—national saving will be too low relative to people's preferences absent the tax distortion.

But does the income tax actually have this overall effect? While one might think this obvious given the substitution effect, economists recognize the possibility of an offset from what is called the income effect. Suppose that I am determined to accumulate savings of exactly $20,000 so that I can afford to buy a particular car. Holding pretax rates of return constant, taxing my interest income will lead me to *increase* the amount that I save, by forcing me to replace the portion that I have lost to the tax collector. Some argue, based on the offset between income and substitution effects, that it is indeterminate whether the income tax, by disfavoring saving, increases or reduces saving on balance. Predictably enough, econometrics fails to provide a consensus answer, although many studies suggest that saving would increase substantially if the income tax were replaced by a tax that lacked this distorting effect (see, e.g., Summers 1981; Auerbach and Kotlikoff 1983; Fullerton, Shoven, and Whalley 1983; Bernheim, Scholz, and Shoven 1991).

Despite these uncertainties, the substitution effect seems, as a logical matter, highly likely to predominate. To illustrate why, consider a world where the main foods were oranges and bread, where most people bought some of each, and where suddenly the price of oranges went up. The substitution effect would yield a shift in consumption from oranges to bread. The income effect would work in the opposite direction, to the extent that consumers who were determined to continue purchasing roughly the same number of oranges now found that they had less money left to spend on bread. Under these circumstances, it is hard to be certain that the substitution effect would predominate. Suppose, for example, that people needed to maintain their prior levels of orange consumption in order to avoid vitamin C deficiency.

Once one moves from bread versus oranges to current versus future consumption, however, the predominance of the substitution effect over the income effect seems far more likely. What makes the bread-versus-oranges hypothetical relatively indeterminate is its stylized, rigid assumption that there are only two choices. Such rigidity makes the income effect more likely to prevail, by permitting a fixed requirement for one item that has little elasticity. Yet in the real world, the forms that both current and future consumption can take are almost infinitely varied. Even if one is saving for a particular type of item, the demand for which may be relatively inelastic—such as a car, a home, or a college education—one often can vary the expensiveness of the item that one chooses to buy. For example, the choice between buying a Corvette or a plainer car in a few years can be traded off against taking a vacation now, as can the choice between a four- and a five-bedroom house. As a general matter, it seems plausible that people frequently will scale up or down their future wishes in terms of the extent to which current wishes must be sacrificed, rather than pursuing narrow goals rigidly without regard to broader tradeoffs.

Accordingly, it seems highly likely that the income tax reduces private saving. Moreover, while the effect's magnitude is unclear, we are talking about a system that raises hundreds of billions of dollars per year through tax rates that approach 40 percent, albeit with a variety of ad hoc rules reducing the real tax rate borne by various kinds of investment income. The overall effect therefore might well be significant.

If one dislikes the effect of the income tax on saving, the most direct and obvious response would be to replace it with some other system, such as consumption taxation that generally is neutral with respect to the timing of consumption. However, this not only seems politically unlikely but also could be undesirable if (as is disputed) the income tax has other, offsetting advantages, such as a more progressive incidence at any given level of rate graduation. If we decide to accept as given that the income tax cannot or will not be replaced, then we may want to search for other means of increasing national saving. Reducing tax lag is one possible response, although many others are possible as well, such as increasing the investment component of government spending.

c. Increasing Saving in Response to Present Generations' Fiscal Illusion regarding the Generational Consequences of Government Policy

A third argument for considering national saving too low from the perspective of present generations involves the possibility that because of fiscal illusion, tax lag leads us to save less than we actually want to save and think we are saving. This argument, first made by David Ricardo, is the macroeconomic, household counterpart to the micro, public policy argument, first made by Adam Smith and discussed below in chapter 7, that tax lag encourages wasteful government spending.

In the household context, however, even if people are induced by fiscal illusion to save too little relative to their true preferences, it is unclear to what extent they are harmed thereby. Obviously, they *are* harmed to the extent that they fail to anticipate future taxes on themselves. However, to the extent that they merely fail to leave as much to future generations as they wanted and expected, there is a teasing philosophical question. Am I harmed by a state of affairs that would cause me displeasure if I knew about it but that does not otherwise affect me if I never come to know about it? Or is ignorance bliss, in the sense that present generations are better off if they can consume more without realizing that they are having undesired effects on their descendants? If the latter, then the effect of fiscal illusion on national saving presents a tradeoff between the well-being of present and future generations, rather than harming both.

d. Increasing Saving in Response to Aggregate Economies of Scale That Cause the Social Return to Saving to Exceed the Private Return

A further argument for increasing national saving relies on the claim that it generates positive externalities, or returns to the society in excess of the return to the saver. (In effect, this is the opposite of the Keynesian claim that increasing current consumption has positive externalities resulting from interdependent preferences for current marketplace consumption.) If the claim that saving has spillover benefits is correct, then one would expect collective action problems to result in a suboptimal level of private saving. That is, people who in principle would be willing to increase their own saving as long as others reciprocally did so would see no point to doing so in isolation.

The government could respond to such a collective action problem through any number of different measures designed either to increase private saving or to make up the shortfall through public investment. Reducing tax lag would be an obvious possibility, although others could include replacing income with consumption taxation, increasing savings incentives in the income tax, using fiscal policy to transfer wealth from low-saving to high-saving groups among present generations, and increasing public investment expenditure on durable physical assets such as roads and airports or on human capital development as through education.

Unfortunately, it is hard to prove the claim that saving generates positive externalities in any standard economic sense. Perhaps the main argument for the claim, made recently by James Buchanan (1993), is that economic growth creates increasing economies of scale. Several considerations support this view. Where production costs are fixed rather than variable, increasing scale may lower unit costs or increase the level of investment in increased capacity that is economical. Human and physical capital can become more finely specialized if greater capacity exists (along with the marketplace demand to make use of the capacity). Technological innovation, which is a crucial source of long-term productivity growth but one tending to be reduced in practice by the difficulty of capturing all the gains from one's innovations, may be greater in absolute terms in a larger economy. New technologies may need to be broadly applied, so they can benefit from support networks and interact with complementary technologies, before they can yield significant productivity gains. As computer networks grow, for example, new users may benefit others in ways for which they are not directly compensated.

The problem with these claims, despite their eminent plausibility, is that they may represent only part of the picture. Increasing scale may have diseconomies as well as economies. Consider pollution and its growing total impact on the environment as the scope of economic activity increases. Scarce resources may be depleted more rapidly if the economy grows faster. Or economic growth may yield a quantum increase in the size and complexity of the state regulatory regime, thus potentially making the regime both costlier and less effective. Accordingly, one cannot be certain that, on balance, the full set of scale externalities makes saving more valuable to society than the individual rather than less. As David Friedman has put it, Buchanan's argument for increasing saving amounts to mere "special pleading" that adds up the positive externalities to growth while ignoring the negative ones (1993, 288).

e. Increasing Saving to Enhance the Long-Term Economic and Political Strength of the United States compared to Other Countries

The previous section noted the argument that saving has positive externalities in a narrow economic sense. One could also argue that it has broader societal benefits. In particular, the rate of saving in the United States, by affecting our wealth and productivity growth, may have long-term effects on our prosperity, not only absolutely but also relative to that of other countries. All else being equal, a richer country is likely to be more powerful and influential. Increasing the relative power and prosperity of the United States over the long term could be important for any of three reasons.

First, continued national power could be an end in itself: a consumption good, pleasing to our patriotic sentiments. We may enjoy thinking of America as powerful and prosperous, observing foreigners' deference, and hearing news about American military, diplomatic, or economic triumphs. While this is a matter of taste, the taste is widespread. Concern about national decline has given the deficit debate an anxious edge that it would not otherwise have. Budget deficits excite the fear that the United States, like England in the first half of this century, is entering a period of prolonged relative economic stagnation that will ultimately strip it of its status as a leading world power.

Second, continued national power could bring Americans tangible benefits. Militarily, it may enhance our ability to respond to international threats and to protect valuable allies and supplies, as during the Cold War, when we were prepared to defend Western Europe against Soviet invasion, or the Gulf War, when we wrested Kuwait and its oil supplies from Iraq's grasp. Even among allies, national power may increase our bargaining power over matters such as trade or global environmental protection. On the other hand, one could argue that the great relative power of the United States causes us to bear various costs. It may make us more prone to delusive ambitions to control the rest of the world, leading to wasteful imperial overreach. Or it may enable countries with whom we have common interests to count on us to bear disproportionately the costs of shared enterprises, such as mutual defense, because only they can credibly threaten to shirk bearing a proportionate share.

Third, our continued national power could benefit the rest of the world, if one views the United States as a benevolent force, at least relative to the forces that otherwise would prevail. Suppose, for example, that one believed the United States tends to act with at least moderate effectiveness in favor of human rights, political freedom, economic development, and peaceful coexistence between neighbors. Under such a view, as Lea Brilmayer has argued, altruism might dictate, or moral duty even require, that we preserve our capacity to act as a benevolent hegemon.[4] This view rests, however, on a high and perhaps unrealistic level of confidence regarding both the motives and the effectiveness of the United States on the world stage.

Accordingly, concern about long-term national power provides some support for the proposition that national saving ought to be increased, although how much support is debatable and unclear. The argument rests on a combination of a priori personal taste and controversial empirical claims regarding the consequences, for us and for others, of such power as we now do, or in the future could, enjoy.

Overall, there is something to be said for the claim that we ought to reduce tax lag as a means of increasing national saving. However, this requires defending both the end and the choice of means. The end is plausible but contestable. The choice of means is likewise plausible but only one of several given that we could alternatively shift from income taxation to consumption taxation or increase productive public investment.

On balance, this leaves the case for reducing tax lag in stronger shape than when we considered only generational distribution. Nonetheless, the case is not overwhelming. Recall the evidence suggesting that during the twentieth century, technological advances have made a much greater contribution to economic growth than has capital accumulation through saving (see, e.g., Schumpeter 1934; Solow 1957; Scherer and Ross 1990; Denison 1967). This suggests that the importance of saving to long-term economic growth, while significant, can be exaggerated.

4. See Brilmayer 1994, discussing the more limited claim that as long as America has the power to act as a benevolent hegemon, it may be morally obligated to exercise this power under appropriate circumstances.

Moreover, even if one focuses on increasing saving, one could argue that tax lag (albeit in the mismeasured form of budget deficits) is receiving too much public attention. Why not focus directly on increasing national saving, thus encouraging the consideration of alternative means to the same end and lending the debate far greater clarity than it has had to date? A strategy of fudging this issue in order to rely on the public's simplistic and symbolically based deficit aversion may help in the short run but over time could amount to continually crying wolf, especially if it is couched in the form of predicting imminent calamity that continues not to arrive.

SEVEN

Issues of Government Size and Structure

So far, the analysis in this book, while paying attention to the political setting in which fiscal policy is made, has done so, for the most part, only in relationship to matters of separate concern. Thus, we have considered how interest group politics promotes wealth transfers through fiscal policy from younger to older generations, and the political reasons that explain why an actively countercyclical fiscal policy may work poorly in practice.

Tax lag, however, raises an important set of issues that relate more directly to the political process and that only James Buchanan and the Virginia theorists have discussed at any length in the economic literature. These issues concern the claim that tax lag, by concealing or deferring the costs of government spending, promotes undesirable government growth and the adoption of unmeritorious spending programs. The Virginia theorists argue that a balanced budget amendment would be a constructive response to these problems, although one who accepted their basic analysis might call instead for any number of alternative responses. This chapter first examines the claim that tax lag is problematical for the public choice reasons identified by the Virginia theorists and then analyzes various possible responses, starting with the balanced budget amendment.

A. Do Government's Shortcomings Make Tax Lag Undesirable?

1. Tax Lag's Tendency to Impair Rational Political Decision Making and/or to Increase Government Spending

In general, the main question raised by government spending is how well the money is being spent. Are scarce societal resources being used in an optimal or at least minimally helpful fashion? From this perspective, the mode of financing is distinctly secondary. No good government spending program becomes bad simply because it lacks current tax financing. Likewise, no bad program becomes good simply because current taxpayers are paying for it.

Yet the choice of financing mechanism matters as well, not only because it is itself a government program with various effects (as on efficiency and distribution), but because it is not wholly endogenous to the spending choice. Once one rejects Ricardianism, it becomes clear that tax lag, by reducing the perceived or actual cost of government spending to current voters, should tend to increase the amount of such spending.

One could regret this effect of tax lag on either of two grounds. First, if one regards the decision-making process in politics as generally well-functioning but imperfect, then one may think that promoting underappreciation of costs will yield worse decisions over time. This relatively optimistic and process-based view suggests a preference for current tax financing and visible rather than concealed taxes, without regard to whether the long-term result is reduced spending and/or a smaller government.

Second, if one more deeply distrusts the political process, then one may regret tax lag's tendency to conceal the costs of government spending for reasons of result rather than process. This view differs from the first in that it looks to the bottom line and considers tax lag undesirable precisely to the extent that government spending (or at least its undesirable components) would be lower, rather than current taxes higher, if current tax financing were required.

One who viewed the political process as basically irrational or poorly functioning could also applaud, rather than condemn, the effects of debt financing and fiscal illusion. Recall Abba Lerner's claim that the military spending necessary to "protect [future generations] from nuclear war and/or totalitarian domination" depended, as a practical matter, on public acceptance of the claim that debt financing was innocuous (1964, 95). Lerner presumably considered people too myopic or too lacking in altruism toward their heirs to fund national defense at an adequate level if they actually had to pay for it currently. Analogously, Robert Eisner argues that if people were less deficit-averse, they would support increased spending on government programs, such as for poverty relief, constructing infrastructure, and education, that he believes are inherently worthwhile.

The Lerner-Eisner view that fiscal illusion, by increasing government spending, leads to better collective decisions can be generalized in respectable economic terms by arguing that voters, because of collective action problems and rational ignorance, demand too little from government in the way of valuable public goods. Or they may oppose desirable wealth redistribution because they are insufficiently altruistic toward their fellow citizens. Thus, creating a level of ignorance on the cost side that offsets ignorance or disregard on the benefit side may yield a "second-best" solution to certain defects of collective decision making. Given this argument that ignorance of the cost of government spending is desirable as an offset to underestimation of its benefits, we cannot determine whether the fiscal illusion created by tax lag is good or bad without first addressing whether, in its absence, government spending would be too low or too high.

2. Arguments for Regretting the Tendency of Tax Lag to Increase Government Spending

a. Is Government Spending Too Low or Too High?

The claim that government spending tends to be too low and the opposite claim that it tends to be too high have an important shared attribute: both are clearly correct in certain settings. Distortions or irrationalities in the political process both block approval of desirable government spending and promote approval of undesirable spending. Which is the greater effect—or, more precisely, whether the particular spending cuts that reducing tax lag would induce would be good or bad on balance—can neither be deduced in the abstract nor convincingly demonstrated as an empirical matter. Plainly, massive expansions in the scope of government, as in the former Soviet Union compared to the United States, often have disastrous effects. Yet this does not prove that lesser expansions, in the context of a democratic and mainly free-market society, would be undesirable (or contractions desirable). There is no way to be sure, for example, whether the United States would be better or worse off today if the federal government expansion that began in the New Deal era had never occurred.

Even if something close to proof one way or the other about the proper size of government were possible, probably few people on the "wrong" side would end up being persuaded. Views about government, while including a strong component of implicit empirical prediction that could in principle be falsified, tend in practice to be closely interwoven with strong ideological presumptions. People's beliefs regarding the likely effectiveness of government in promoting particular objectives often inappropriately reflect their underlying sympathy for, and degree of interest in, the objectives. Most of us have met both conservatives who are all too swift to dismiss the prospect that various social programs will advance stated objectives and liberals who are equally swift to conclude that the programs will be effective. With military spending, the sides often are reversed, even though the particular pathologies (as of bureaucracy and pork-barrel congressional politics) that might cause both types of programs to fail are highly similar. Perhaps people, when thinking about public issues as distinct from their own lives, care more about symbolism than about substance. Or they may simply enjoy believing that goals they consider important can, in fact, be pursued effectively, since an alternative view would prompt feelings of impotence and frustration.

Given the difficulty of proof or persuasion, I must settle for baldly stating my own belief: the spending reductions that would likely result from reducing tax lag would probably be good, assuming no offsetting changes in government activity (such as a shift to greater use of regulation). Or, to state it more generally, reducing the size and scope of government would probably be good on balance.

I should emphasize that this does not make me a conservative Republican, any more than it makes me a liberal Democrat, in the conventional political sense. Indeed, since becoming aware of politics, I have more frequently supported the Democrats than the Republicans, in part because the differences between the two camps often relate more to what the government should do and whom it should help than to how much it should do. Notwithstanding their rhetoric, many Republicans and self-styled conservatives support a large government in various forms. For example, they may variously favor automatic defense spending increases without regard to the merits of particular programs; expanding the government's national security powers and ability to act in secrecy; using the power of the national government to dictate morality and culture to the society; redistributing wealth from poorer to richer Americans; and subsidizing favored constituencies, such as farmers and various business groups. These are neither goals I find attractive nor indicia of a smaller government.

Even though I cannot prove the correctness of my underlying skepticism about the merits of government activity at the margin—or even, in all likelihood, persuade many readers who do not already share it—I will briefly try to explain and justify my view. I do not believe that one can intelligently base support for a smaller government on a high level of confidence in the desirability of private market outcomes. Market failures and externalities are rife, various public goods that the market cannot supply are desirable, and the market has no inherent tendency to distribute wealth in an optimal or equitable fashion. Thus, at any time, there is much that government ought to do (assuming it could act effectively enough) yet is not doing.

The real issue is a comparative one. Does politics tend to work even worse than private markets, or at least badly enough to suggest that one's hope of improving market outcomes will often be disappointed? At least, is aggregate harm likely at the margin where government spending is likely to change if one increases its perceived cost by reducing tax lag? The margin is important, since it is plausible that the most plainly meritorious government spending would be unaffected by a requirement of current tax financing. Despite the fears of Lerner, surely the United States would not unilaterally disarm or disband all national and local police forces, support for education, and the like if greater use of current tax financing were required. The following section explains and develops the proposition that the political process works badly enough to support skepticism about the merits of government spending at the margin.

b. Pathologies of the Political and Regulatory Processes

The belief that, increasing (or not decreasing) government spending is more likely to make things worse than to help rests on two main types of concern. First are the standard set of public choice problems with the political process, broadened to recognize important attributes of what one might term voters' and politicians' consumption functions. Perhaps the core public choice problem is that in a world where voters have limited time and information, hidden and widely distributed costs often have less political impact than visible and concentrated benefits. Given the costs of information and political activity, collective action problems tend to yield substantive outcomes that reflect interest group politics.

This problem is exacerbated by the organization of Congress, which empowers locally elected representatives, deferred to by their colleagues because of logrolling, to control national policy. When a Congressman Rostenkowski or Gingrich, or a Senator Byrd or Dole, along with each member of the majority coalitions that he assembles, can obtain nationally funded benefits for his district, the standard efficiency norm of fiscal federalism, which holds that policies with national effects should be decided nationally and those with local effects decided locally, is effectively violated. Given the 435 congressional districts, a program need scarcely be worth one 435th of its cost in order to be enacted. Although voters in all 435 districts might benefit from reciprocally forgoing all such programs, collective action problems impede reciprocally opting out. This is the core theoretical reason explaining why *pork barrel* is such a term of opprobrium. It also helps to explain the public's long-standing tendency, shown by countless opinion polls, to despise Congress but support local representatives, who are fighting for a local share of the pork.

Yet interest group behavior and localist legislation, driven by logrolling, are far from the whole problem.[1] The level of pork-barrel spending has been estimated at less than $10 billion annually, an amount that represents barely half a percent of annual federal outlays and less than 5 percent of a typical recent budget deficit. To be sure, pork-barrel spending is only one component of localist legislation. Consider agricultural price support programs, which also cost an estimated $10 billion annually (see Georges 1994). Or consider such localist components of defense spending as weapons programs that serve to provide jobs in the districts of influential members of Congress and unneeded domestic military bases—a number of which are presently being closed, at an estimated saving of $4 billion per year, except that the closings have mysteriously been proceeding far more slowly than expected (see, e.g., Schmitt 1994). Still, the importance of the localist aspect of excessive federal spending can easily be exaggerated.

1. See Shaviro 1990. Important works by political scientists that support the themes in the next few paragraphs include Edelman 1964; Mayhew 1974; Fiorina 1977; Fenno 1973; Manley 1970; and Kingdon 1984.

It has relatively little to do with the main cause of tax lag, which is the explosive growth of entitlement programs such as Social Security and Medicare.

Despite the problems with interest group behavior and localist legislation, political outcomes might even improve on balance if the behavior of voters and politicians were driven more purely by narrowly defined self-interest. As many have noted, the assumption of narrow self-interest cannot explain core features of the political system, including even the fact that in each election, a significant portion of the eligible population actually votes. The decision to vote in a mass election is almost never "rational," in a narrowly self-interested sense, even if one strongly prefers one of the candidates, given the extreme unlikelihood that one's vote will change the outcome. Even if one cares about the winning candidate's margin of victory on the ground that it will affect the winning candidate's power, a solitary vote cannot have a significant effect. For this reason, it seems clear that people vote, for the most part, either out of a sense of duty or as an expressive activity best described as a form of consumption.

Whether one terms the motive "duty" or "consumption," it is in a sense done casually. People generally know that their individual voting decisions will not have the same level of consequences for their own lives as, say, buying a car. This encourages ill-informed decision making or even outright frivolity. Symbolic behavior by politicians and the false intimacy created by television frequently outweigh the substantive effect (if any) that a politician or the outcome of an election is likely to have on one's material well-being. People often vote for a candidate who flatters them, seems likable, or makes factual claims that they hope are true. Politicians' substantive effects on one's life would be difficult to untangle in any event, amid the complexity of events and the confusing dispersion of responsibility among the many levels and branches of American government. Yet the disconnection between one's own decision and the likely outcome strongly discourages any strong effort to grapple with these difficulties.

Politicians' behavior is strongly affected by this environment of casual and symbolically driven decision making by voters, as well as by politicians' own complex set of motivations in public life. In practice, the goal of reelection leads not only to the application of short time horizons and the cultivation of monied and well-organized interest groups but also to an elaborate focus on position taking, credit claiming, and blame avoidance, all aimed at the casual observer and often only weakly related to the real empirical effects of government decisions (see Mayhew 1974).

Decision making by politicians also tends to reflect an inherent bias in favor of exercising power and showing that one is important. As a member of Congress once put it in confidential conversations with a political science researcher, "Congress exists to do things. There isn't much mileage in doing nothing" (Kingdon 1984, 41). This "mileage" pertains alike to reelection, to the frenzied competition for prestige within the political and social world of Washington, and to the desire, through influence on public policy, to build legislative monuments to oneself. Many observers have noted that "politicians generally are motivated to an unusual degree by what is variously described as a 'desire for attention and adulation,' 'intense and ungratified craving for deference,' 'ache for applause and recognition,' and 'an urge for that warm feeling of importance' " (Shaviro 1990, 81). What Harold Lasswell termed the psychological "displacement" of these cravings onto public objects, "rationalized in terms of public interest" (1948, 38), often leads politicians to make only a facile inquiry, if even that, into their proposals' real merits and likely empirical effects.

Given both political self-interest and these underlying motivations, a Bill Clinton or a Newt Gingrich wants salient proposals on hand without awaiting the results of tedious social science research concerning the proposals' likely effects over time. Nor does the politician's daily life experience, with its demands of perennial fund-raising, constituent outreach, boosterish public relations, and negotiating with one's peers, as well as the perpetual risk of meeting with public rejection and the loss of one's job, encourage serious reflection. Prominent politicians also face a "screening-out" problem. The people they consult may tend to tell them what they want to hear, making it all the easier for them to dismiss unpleasant accounts. Given the difficulty of concretely proving anything rigorously about the merits and real-world effects of alternative policies, there may be little prospect that accurate information about the larger effects of the proposals they consider will break through the "screen."

All of these factors adversely affect the quality of legislation and broader political decision making. Once legislation has been enacted, however, a second set of problems comes into play. Much legislative policy is neither fully worked out in its details nor self-executing. Bureaucracies often are needed both to continue writing the law and to administer it on an ongoing basis. Yet, as William Niskanen has put it, "there is nothing inherent in the nature of bureaus and our political institutions that leads public officials to know, seek out, or act in the public interest" (1971, vi). The economic literature on bureaucracies emphasizes the ways in which their incentives and performance tend to depart from those one might prefer from a public interest standpoint (see, e.g., Stewart 1975; Niskanen 1971; Tullock 1965; Aranson, Gellhorn, and Robinson 1982, 47–52).

For this purpose, a comparison of public agencies to private firms is instructive. Surely the profit motive has some beneficial effects on the behavior of private firms, at least if they can be forced to internalize the main consequences of what they do. It induces them to produce goods that people actually want, and to try to do so relatively cheaply. While many firms are poorly run, make bad decisions, or fail to engage in rational profit maximizing because of their internal cultures and politics, such firms are subject to loss of market share or even bankruptcy. However imperfect Darwinian competition in the marketplace may be, corporate titans as huge and powerful as U.S. Steel, General Motors, and IBM have learned in recent decades that they are not exempt from it. The U.S. government and its various agencies do not face similar constraints.

In bureaucracies, the lack of a profit motive has several adverse consequences. One is a tendency to substitute power for profit as the main goal, leading agencies to try to maximize their budgets, breadth of jurisdiction, and managerial perquisites, often at the expense of cost-effectiveness and appropriate policy. Consider the perennial resistance to integrating and rationalizing the functions performed by different branches of the armed services. In addition, the lack of a clear bottom line (akin to profit in the private sector) makes bureaucratic performance, both individual and collective, harder to gauge and encourages a compensating reliance on awkward and unwieldy centralized management by pervasive regulation. The lack of a clear bottom line also protects agencies that are hopelessly inefficient in a performance sense from suffering the same marketplace sanctions as a mismanaged business, as long as they have the political resources to continue receiving congressional funding.

Additional problems arise to the extent that bureaucracies seek to promote substantive goals. Agencies that are charged with reducing specified risks often have incentives to minimize visible errors rather than the total costs of error. Thus, it is a commonplace that the Food and Drug Administration, in monitoring new drugs, has more to lose by licensing a drug that proves harmful than by unduly delaying authorization for one that proves beneficial. Agencies charged with regulating particular industries are subject to capture by the very groups they are supposed to be regulating. Agencies with well-defined regulatory missions often ignore tradeoffs between these missions and other valuable objectives, whether it is the Environmental Protection Agency imposing costly and rigid environmental standards or the Treasury Department undervaluing the significance of taxpayer compliance costs.

For reasons such as these, to paraphrase what Churchill said about democracy, the profit motive seems the worst possible way to organize human behavior outside the household, except for all of the others. While the problems with bureaucracy do not establish that pure market outcomes are always, or even usually, preferable, these problems should influence one's judgment at the margin concerning the relative merits of alternative approaches. Moreover, such problems provide some support for the view that the size of government tends to be too great. While distrust of bureaucracy plainly influences political decision making to some extent—consider, for example, the influence on the 1994 health-care debate of public aversion to creating a large new health-care bureaucracy—the effect is sporadic, and bureaucracies once established cannot easily be pruned or eliminated. Their visibility can be low and their political clout, along with that of any private interests that they serve, formidable.

Even when a bureaucracy aggrieves voters, members of Congress often benefit from its existence and feel no motive to reduce its jurisdiction. Grievances generate congressional casework or opportunities for winning gratitude through particularized intervention on behalf of constituents. As Morris Fiorina has put it, "the more decisions the bureaucracy has the opportunity to make, the more opportunities there are for the Congressman to build up credits" with voters through intervention (1977, 48). And even if Congress is not quite so cynical, or at least farsighted, as to deliberately establish large and powerful bureaucracies for this reason, it often has other reasons for doing so. As Roger Noll has noted, when areas in which there is a political demand for regulation are characterized by ineluctable conflict either between groups (such as consumers and manufacturers) or between desired objectives (such as high quality and low cost, or environmental protection and economic growth), Congress often settles for statutes that provide "fatuous, self-contradictory wish-lists" rather than specific mandates. That way, it can claim credit for seeking to advance all of the conflicting interests or objectives, and the bureaucracy that must be created to answer the hard questions can take the blame for making hard choices, in addition to generating future casework (Noll 1971, 101).

Do all of these problems with the legislative and regulatory processes firmly establish that at the relevant margin of decision, increasing the size of government tends to make things worse? This would greatly overstate the case that I have made. Merely showing that governmental processes have serious flaws does not prove the comparative claim that markets, with their own externality and collective action problems, generally work better. One could argue, however, that market outcomes need not be very attractive in order for flawed regulatory solutions to be more likely to worsen than improve them. The underlying point, embodied, for example, in the law of unintended consequences, is one of entropy. Since desired states of affairs are highly organized, changes (such as those mandated by government policy) that function, in effect, as random shocks are considerably more likely to do harm than good. By analogy, a person suffering from a chronic illness who decided to ingest at random substances from the environment would more likely harm than help that person's medical condition. Or consider how twentieth-century governments have most powerfully affected the economic well-being of their societies. From a stable starting point where physical security, basic property rights, and the like are protected, surely no government ever has done, or could ever hope to do, as much good to the economy as recent regimes in, say, Haiti and North Korea have done harm. Entropy significantly limits the gains that one can reasonably expect from centralized planning, even when such planning is directed by capable people with good information and the right incentives.

The analysis thus far has emphasized efficiency, or whether the benefits of government programs are likely to be worth their costs. Concern about distribution provides an alternative basis for favoring a larger government. Overall, taxation and government spending are probably at least modestly progressive, at least as far as those on the bottom of the income scale are concerned. The poorest individuals pay little in the way of taxes and do receive benefits, through both transfer programs and government goods and services. These benefits may also be sufficiently vulnerable politically to be the first ones to go when the size of government is reduced. Thus, concern about the effect on poor people of reducing the size of government is real, legitimate, and not to be wholly dismissed.

Nonetheless, one should not place too much weight on the argument that progressive redistribution supports having a larger rather than a smaller government. The progressive redistributive content of government spending can easily be exaggerated. In particular, its overall impact may be regressive in some ranges above the income level necessary to incur significant income tax liability. Even at the bottom of the income scale, spending on programs such as welfare and unemployment insurance—programs with middle-class as well as poor beneficiaries—constitutes only a small percentage of the federal budget. Thus, for fiscal 1993, direct federal aid to the poor totaled about $140 billion—less than the cost of certain major tax breaks that mainly benefit the middle class and the wealthy and less than 20 percent of the amount spent on entitlement programs with mainly middle-class and wealthy beneficiaries (Wines 1994).[2]

This relative lack of progressivity in government spending should come as no surprise. In general, people who are poorer and therefore less powerful are not well situated to become the main recipients of government largesse or to influence policy. The balance of power in a democratically elected government is likely to reflect that in the society. Organized interest groups that are active in Washington disproportionately represent the relatively well-off, such as business owners or professional groups and skilled employees, rather than, say, poor children or unemployed welfare recipients.

Thus, even if one supports progressive redistribution in principle, one should not too readily conclude that greater government spending helps significantly. While initial budget cuts may tend to target the poor, far more money is available from larger programs with more affluent beneficiaries, such as middle-class entitlements and pork-barrel-driven defense spending. Thus, even if a slight reduction in government spending would be regressive, a more significant reduction has some chance of being progressive.

A final point about progressive redistribution is that the effect on

2. The three tax breaks being counted for this purpose are deductions for retirement plans, deductions for home mortgage interest, and the exemption of health insurance premiums that companies pay on behalf of their employees.

poor people's well-being of reducing government spending on their behalf may be considerably less than the amount by which such spending was reduced. This could follow from observing that various programs, such as public housing, convey low-quality goods and services that cannot be traded in for cash, and the value of which to the recipients (given government waste) may not equal the budgetary cost. Or it could follow from accepting the controversial arguments of conservative writers, such as Charles Murray, who claim that welfare spending on the poor generally reduces the recipients' well-being by weakening incentives to work and creating a culture of dependence (Murray 1984).

B. A Balanced Budget Amendment

The previous section discussed why one might believe that the size and reach of the federal government ought to be reduced. Given the likelihood that requiring current tax financing would reduce the political appeal of government spending programs, this could involve enacting an amendment to the U.S. Constitution that was designed to reduce tax lag—although, as we will see, this is only one of many possible responses.

1. A Generational Accounting Version of the Balanced Budget Amendment

Proposals to amend the Constitution with the aim of reducing tax lag have invariably taken the form of a balanced budget amendment (BBA), based on the cash-flow budget deficit. Given that measure's flaws, the question arises about whether a better measure of tax lag would be more suitable for this purpose.

Two alternatives come to mind. The first would be to base the BBA on generational accounting. One could require, for example, that the estimated lifetime net tax rate for future generations not unduly exceed, or grow compared to, the estimated lifetime net tax rate for newborns, or perhaps persons at age eighteen. For this purpose, one would require use of Laurence Kotlikoff's convention assigning the entire unprovided-for net tax burden to future generations. While such an amendment would essentially implement Kotlikoff's norm of generational equity that I have argued is unconvincing, the reason for its adoption would be different. Increasing net tax burdens on future generations would be disfavored as an indicator that today's voters were ignoring a portion of the costs of current government policy (and thus making bad decisions) rather than for generational reasons as such.

The second alternative would be to convert the budget deficit into an economic accrual measure, without taking generational accounting's additional step of estimating *who* would pay what net taxes under present policy. Thus, instead of being restricted to current cash flow, it would measure the accrual of future expected taxes and government spending under current policy. The arguments for this alternative would be twofold: it makes the restriction on tax lag more salient and recognizable than does generational accounting, and tax lag may promote fiscal illusion even if it operates purely within, rather than beyond, current generations' life spans.

Both alternatives would face serious difficulties. For example, would one need to constrain the definition of "current policy" for purposes of the rule? Suppose Congress passed a law that purported to eliminate undue tax lag by providing that all current newborns (or eighteen-year-olds) would owe the government $1 million in inflation-adjusted dollars when they reached age seventy. One might imagine Congress winking when it passed the law, neither intending nor envisioning that the tax would ever be collected. It is inherently difficult to define "current policy," and the laws on the books can be manipulated if they are its sole touchstone.

Or consider the manipulability of the long-term estimates that would determine how either alternative applied. Alan Auerbach, who collaborated with Kotlikoff in designing generational accounting, agrees that "in cynical hands . . . [it] can be distorted, through the use of inappropriate economic assumptions about the future. While budget enforcement rules based on generational accounting would represent an improvement over the current practice, I am unconvinced that policymakers who lack the will to make hard decisions can rely on such rules to make them do so" (1993, 522).

A final point, however, is that there appears to be no prospect of enacting an anti-tax lag constitutional amendment based either on generational accounting or on an economic accrual version of the budget deficit. Accordingly, while these alternatives would be worth considering if the prospect arose, the more realistic question for now is whether a rule based on the cash-flow budget deficit is better than doing nothing at all. In making this determination, while the weak relationship between the deficit and actual tax lag should be kept in mind, it is not dispositive. For example, even Kotlikoff's estimates suggest that dramatic movement in the direction of annual budgetary balance would tend to reduce tax lag significantly.[3]

2. Problems with a Balanced Budget Amendment Based on the Cash-Flow Budget Deficit

The arguments against a BBA can be divided into two categories: those that assert that it is inherently inappropriate and those that more modestly show its drawbacks and limited effectiveness. The former arguments mainly do not succeed, although they raise legitimate concerns. The latter arguments succeed in making one highly skeptical about the amendment.

a. Is a Balanced Budget Amendment Inherently Inappropriate?

Two main arguments suggest that a BBA is inherently inappropriate. The first holds that no particular budgetary policy should be enshrined in the Constitution. Laurence Tribe argues:

> As Justice Holmes wrote at the turn of the century, "a Constitution is not intended to embody a particular economic theory. . . ." [U]nlike the ideals embodied in our Constitution, fiscal austerity—however sound as a current goal—speaks neither to the structure of government nor to the rights of the people. . . . Because the Constitution is meant to express fundamental law rather than particular policies, it should be amended only to modify fundamental law—not to accomplish policy goals. (1979, 628–29)

Tribe adds that since Congress has the power to adopt a balanced budget whenever it wishes, "there is *no need* to amend the Constitution to make the pursuit of that policy the law of the land" (630). He also notes—failing in 1979 to anticipate the irony these words might later evoke—that statutory cures to budget deficits already are "surging" in Congress and that "President Carter has worked to serve the objectives

3. See Kotlikoff 1995 (estimating that a plan to eliminate the deficit within seven years would eliminate about one-fourth of the gap between the tax rates of the youngest living Americans and those of future generations).

of fiscal restraint as well—and he has stressed to the public his contin-uing commitment to them" (630).

Obviously, the vast growth of budget deficits in the years since Tribe wrote these words, despite widespread agreement in principle among most politicians and voters that they ought to be eliminated, challenges the realism of his claim that Congress can balance the bud-get whenever it wishes. More importantly, however, Tribe's character-ization of budgetary balance as a contingent "policy" too dependent on current circumstances to belong in the Constitution seems wide of the mark. While he may correctly describe the ephemeral nature of contemporary concerns about generational policy or the rate of na-tional saving, tax lag's tendency to conceal the costs of government spending, and thereby to prompt undue government growth, arguably is "fundamental" and based on "structure" in the sense that he invokes.

Rational voters who were concerned about undue government growth conceivably might tie themselves to the mast by requiring con-stitutionally that revenues generally equal outlays on an annual basis. The whole point of having a Constitution that prevails over ordinary laws, and that is hard to change, is to permit voters to bind themselves (and their descendants) when they do not trust their own collective behavior under the circumstances of ordinary politics. This is the very reason why one who generally liked majority rule might nonethe-less welcome, say, the First Amendment's impeding the enactment of speech restrictions. Thus, whether or not a BBA is a good idea, it is not inherently miscast as a constitutional rule.

A second argument that a BBA is inherently inappropriate relies on its claimed ill effects on the political process. This argument has three main components. First, concern about budget deficits prevents us from focusing on issues that ultimately matter a great deal more. As Joseph White and Aaron Wildavsky complain:

> The debate and politics of the deficit have been among the most stultifying experiences in our political history. From one year to the next we heard the same arguments, fought the same battles, prophesied the same doom. Nobody seems to have learned anything. . . .
>
> This is bad policy and worse analysis; it has paralyzed our political system. Fixated on the deficit, we ignore other ques-tions. Do we want more savings or more job training? Should we forget about full employment, define it as what we have

already achieved, or try to lower unemployment further? What is a sensible defense policy—as opposed to a convenient way to fit into [budgetary constraints]? What is, or should be, our place in the world economy? (1989, 575)[4]

Second, the argument goes, a goal of deficit reduction or elimination leads to foolish policy decisions driven purely by short-term revenue concerns. Examples include forgoing desirable fiscal policy changes because of their current revenue effects and employing smoke-and-mirrors manipulation of current revenues and expenses. Third, given the opportunities for such manipulation, the exercise might fail to reduce tax lag (and the extra spending that it causes). In the end, manipulations aside, Congress might not have to change significantly the real tenor and substance of its fiscal policy.

This three-part argument is not so much wrong—indeed, it is at least partly right—as it is premature and overstated when used to dismiss a BBA out of hand. Starting with the last point, a BBA, if given sufficient rigor, could hardly fail to be significant. With recent deficits typically exceeding $200 billion per year, and presently projected to remain in that range or higher indefinitely, smoke-and-mirrors accounting alone cannot make up the gap. Rather, a rigorous BBA would almost certainly require major substantive changes in fiscal policy, probably including spending cuts as well as tax increases.

As for the argument's first two points, one can accept the basic contentions without the conclusion. That a balanced budget constraint distracts Congress from matters of substance and often induces it to make particular decisions that are foolish does not rebut the possibility that on balance it would be desirable. The whole point would be to limit Congress's power and inclination to make bad choices as well as good ones. Tying oneself to the mast has inherent disadvantages, but the merits of a BBA depend on its overall effects, not on a subset of its effects. The case for the amendment rests on a second-best claim: that further distorting a flawed decisional process, in such a way as to respond to preexisting distortions, may improve decisions overall. Such second-best arguments are hard to evaluate but generally cannot be dismissed out of hand.

In order to assess the second-best claim that underlies the case for

4. While the quoted text discusses the recent national preoccupation with budget deficits rather than the effect of a BBA, it has obvious application to the latter.

a BBA, I will proceed in two stages. First, would the amendment in fact be likely to reduce significantly the size of government, or at least improve the decisional process by making the costs of government decisions more obvious? Second, what offsetting disadvantages would it have? The former would have to be worth the latter in order for the amendment to be a good idea.

b. Would a Balanced Budget Amendment Significantly Reduce the Size of Government?

The fact that a rigorous BBA would inevitably be significant, in an environment where budget deficits typically approximate $200 billion per year, does not necessarily mean that it would yield a smaller government (or even permit voters to assess the costs of government spending more realistically). In a number of respects, it might merely alter the form of government activity.

Initial support for this concern comes from the observation that tax lag is not a unique cause of undue government growth or bad cost-benefit decisions, and thus that limiting its use is not a unique response. Indeed, the relative importance of tax lag as a cause of such growth can be questioned. Robert Barro, for example, observes that over the last fifty years, federal tax revenues have grown more rapidly than the national debt (see, e.g. Barro 1976, 348)—although he ignores for this purpose "implicit debt" in the form of unfunded Social Security and Medicare commitments.

Perhaps more crucial to undesirable government growth is the malfunctioning or even breakdown, under modern conditions, of Madisonian limitations on interest group activity and the growth of government. As I discussed in section C of chapter 4, Madison and his colleagues, fearing majoritarian tyranny, relied on disaggregating the government's decision-making powers. The Constitution's carefully drawn distinctions between the executive, legislative, and judicial branches, its establishment of a bicameral legislature, and its preserving an important continuing role for state governments were all meant to hamstring concerted action by interests invidious to the general welfare. Even the decision to transfer as much power as the Constitution initially did from the state governments to a strengthened national government reflected, at least for Madison, the hope that in a large republic no set of parochial interests could easily dominate.

While Madison's thinking is vindicated to some extent by the endurance of constitutional government, with relatively stable policy and without sectarian tyranny, in many respects his prescription has been undermined by events or its own internal defects. The events of the last two centuries have lessened both the internal decentralization of the federal government and the regional disaggregation of interest groups on which he relied. Moreover, in two respects his analysis proved to be incorrect on its own terms. First, minority factions proved far more potent than he expected, because of their organizational advantages over dispersed majorities sharing diffuse interests. Second, logrolling by interest groups to assemble legislative majorities proved more feasible than he had expected. Madison had argued that forming large and diverse factional coalitions would be difficult because "where there is a consciousness of unjust or dishonorable purposes, communication is always checked by distrust in proportion to the number whose concurrence is necessary" (in Hamilton, Madison, and Jay 1961, no. 10). Today, consciences are so elastic, or the ability to be at once self-interested and self-righteous so great, that this argument sounds naive and quaint.

Accordingly, even if budget deficits were eliminated, one still might expect substantial government growth. The deficit's mismeasurement of tax lag provides only part of the reason for concluding that the constraint would be quite porous. A further point is that tax lag can be reduced by raising current taxes, as well as by cutting spending. Despite the present political atmosphere of tax aversion and hostility to government, it is highly plausible that, if a rigorous BBA were in place, current tax increases would be used to some extent. Government spending for such purposes as national defense, entitlement programs such as Social Security and Medicare with middle-class constituencies, and honoring the terms of existing public debt has such powerful political support that Congress, if deprived of all menas of evasion, might well conclude, up to a point, that current tax increases were the lesser political evil.

Current tax increases would be only one likely congressional response to a balanced budget amendment, however. A second response, more on the part of groups that seek government spending than on the part of Congress itself, would be to shift activity to state and local governments, which presumably would not be affected by a federal balanced budget amendment. Spending reductions by the national government can fail to have the intended effect on overall government size if they prompt offsetting spending increases at the state and local levels.

Perhaps the most important point, however, is that—even holding taxes constant over the long run and taking account of all levels of government—the level of spending is not the sine qua non of the level of undesirable government activity. As discussed in chapter 4, government spending correlates only very crudely, at best, with the level of its activity or the magnitude of its effects. Same-dollar tax or spending programs can have radically different levels of effect on personal freedom, economic efficiency, or wealth distribution. Moreover, the level of government spending tells us nothing about the government's effects on private behavior through regulation. Constraining spending programs through a requirement of greater current tax financing can simply lead to their conversion into regulatory mandates, the implicit "taxes" and "spending" from which are entirely off-budget.

If mandates were perfectly substitutable for government spending, then BBA would have *no* significant effect on the size of government in either the efficiency or the libertarian sense. In practice, however, mandates are only somewhat substitutable for government spending. Consider President Clinton's 1994 health-care reform plan. Since neither current tax financing nor debt financing was politically feasible at the levels that were needed to finance the program, it relied in large part on requiring employers to make certain health insurance options available to their employees. In this case, however, as distinct from the case of the Americans with Disabilities Act, the proposed mandates prompted vigorous political opposition. Part of the reason may have been rhetorical. Employers could complain about increasing their labor costs with less embarrassment than they would feel complaining about eliminating bars to access by the handicapped. In addition, as it happened in the health-care case, the groups that would have borne the cost of complying with the mandate were both sufficiently well informed to view it as a tax and quite well organized and powerful politically. Small business, the main source of opposition in 1994 since larger national businesses often were already providing many or all of their employees with tax-favored health-care benefits, tends to have great political influence, reflecting its presence in virtually every congressional district.

Thus, health-care reform shows how restricting tax lag (in this case, because it had already approached politically acceptable limits) can impede government expansion—whether for better or for worse. Yet there are many counterexamples. It is hard to know in practice to what extent government spending is substitutable, and a BBA therefore avoidable, by shifting to the use of regulatory mandates.

A final problem with assuming that a BBA would reduce undesirable government activity concerns the problem that one might term "targeting." Suppose, for example, that government spending were 20 percent too high and that suddenly it had to be reduced by 10 percent. Would the reduction necessarily represent a step in the right direction? It would depend on what spending was cut. The point is to reduce bad spending, not simply the aggregate amount of spending, and much bad spending might turn out to have strong political support. Even a rule that required spending reductions of a specified level (as the BBA does not) would leave in place the political power disparities, such as the strength of organized interest groups, that drive and distort government policy.

In practice, this problem may be quite serious. Suppose that spending on behalf of the poor or for education or to encourage valuable research and development is desirable yet politically vulnerable. Or suppose that the military budget is grossly bloated but that if it were cut, needed manpower training, rather than wasteful weapons programs responding to localist politics, would go first. In either case, despite the existence of enormous quantities of wasteful spending, the actual spending cuts that Congress would adopt under the pressure of a balanced budget rule might be undesirable.

c. What Other Effects Would a Rigorous Balanced Budget Amendment Likely Have?

The previous section suggested that, at least to a large extent, a BBA would merely change the forms of government activity rather than reduce its real scope. In addition, the amendment might have a range of independent effects, some ambiguous at best and others clearly bad. I have already mentioned substitution of mandates for explicit spending. Other important side effects are likely as well.

Effects on regulation aside, perhaps the most important side effect of a rigorous BBA would be eliminating the automatic countercyclical effect of fiscal policy as recession decreases tax revenues and increases various welfare and social insurance payouts. Indeed, a rigorous BBA would require Congress to worsen the business cycle by enacting spending cuts or tax increases during recessions. One wonders what level of constitutional rigor would be needed to make this politically feasible, even apart from its undesirability; yet allowing countercyclical deficits would risk encouraging Congress to treat the economy as forever in recession.

A BBA might also, depending on its structure, create greatly increased public uncertainty about the course of government policy, thus impeding business and personal planning. Suppose that tax increases or spending cuts would be imposed automatically in the event that an unprojected budget deficit began to emerge over the course of the fiscal year. Private parties would continually have to account for this contingency in their planning rather than merely asking themselves whether the enactment of any policy changes with retroactive effects seemed likely.

Again depending on its structure, a BBA might also cause shifts in power over spending within the federal government. If power did not merely shift within Congress to committees that were responsible for maintaining budgetary balance, then it might shift away from Congress, either to the president, to independent experts (such as economists charged with preparing revenue estimates), or to the courts. None of these changes is necessarily desirable. For example, a shift of power to the courts would raise concerns about the costs, delays, and uncertainty of litigation and about the institutional competence of courts in the area of fiscal policy.

Overall, the case for a balanced budget amendment becomes weaker the more closely one looks at it. Even if it reduced government spending significantly, it might not succeed in reducing the real size of government. If it would not even do much to government spending, the case for it would virtually evaporate.

While some of the empirical issues that the BBA raises are unresolvable, one can perhaps test empirically the its likely effect on government spending. The best evidence comes in two main forms. The first pertains to state governments, nearly all of which have balanced budget requirements of some kind. The second pertains to the Gramm-Rudman-Hollings Act, first enacted in 1985 to limit federal deficits (and ostensibly eliminate them within five years). Gramm-Rudman-Hollings was repeatedly modified thereafter, in keeping with its merely statutory status, but never wholly eliminated. The next two sections examine these two sources of evidence concerning the likely effectiveness of a BBA.

3. Evidence from the States' Experience with Balanced Budget Requirements

Forty-nine states—all except Vermont—have rules limiting budget deficits or the issuance of public debt in one way or another. (Perhaps Vermont is too inherently frugal to need any such thing.) Of these forty-nine states, forty-three have constitutional, rather than merely statutory, rules, although a number have both. The states therefore provide a rich lode of experience that one can bring to bear on the federal constitutional issue.

To some observers, the near universality of debt or deficit limitations at the state level makes an implicit case for a federal amendment, by showing that the national government diverges from the predominant pattern. In fact, however, the prevalence of balanced budget rules at the state level reflects important differences between the federal and state governments. One could argue that the use of debt financing is both more tempting and more dangerous at the state level than at the federal level, suggesting a greater (self-interested) need for a constitutional bar.

The fact that states cannot print money, and therefore cannot borrow in their own currency, is part of the difference. It suggests that the states present a greater risk to prospective lenders of explicit default, perhaps motivating the states to give greater assurance that this will not happen. To be sure, the federal government, by printing money and borrowing in its own currency, merely substitutes for a portion of this explicit default risk a threat of implicit default: that is, using unexpected inflation to devalue the existing public debt in real terms. However, this threat may tend to alarm lenders less than the threat of explicit default by the states, because of what one might term a "hostage" problem. Unexpected inflation does not merely hurt lenders to the federal government; it has a host of other effects as well, many of which may be unpopular with voters. To the extent that inflation is politically costly, or even unacceptable, as a result of these other effects, politicians cannot use it despite the benefit (from a narrow Leviathan perspective) of debt devaluation. The short-term effects of an explicit default, such as by a state government, are far more concentrated on the lenders than is societywide inflation.

Equally importantly, since states are smaller than the country as a whole and must maintain open domestic borders, they are far more subject to voter entry and exit, and far more integrated into an economy extending past their jurisdictional boundaries. This may strengthen the state voters' incentive to shift lifetime consumption from future to present generations, since exit increases the likelihood that the future taxes will be borne by households other than one's own. To be sure, the voters may not so benefit to the extent that voter-owned property within the state loses value by reason of the expected future taxes. However, this prospect may be even better concealed from their understanding by fiscal illusion than the prospect that if they remain in the jurisdiction, their descendants will bear the taxes to repay outstanding public debt.

The states' relatively small size and open borders also impedes their ability to repay public debt by raising taxes. People and businesses can simply leave if taxes grow too high relative to current services. This problem, alongside the restriction on money issuance, again makes state governments far more subject to explicit default than is the federal government. Even short of default, states are far more prone to face bad credit ratings, which force them to offer lenders substantial risk premiums. This may motivate them, more strongly than the federal government, to seek balanced budget amendments as a means of reassuring lenders, thereby lowering their interest costs.

While the adoption of state constitutional rules to prevent default therefore makes sense—and indeed, as a historical matter, responded to the default wave of the 1830s—the rules may not have been as responsible as one might think for the states' subsequently improved performance as debtors. One could argue that the states benefited more from a learning curve concerning the need for fiscal prudence, as well as from the growth of their economies and finance systems, than from the constraints imposed on them by the amendments. In support of such a view, the move to constitutional limitations beginning in the 1840s apparently did not, at the time, observably constrain either spending or debt issuance by state governments (see Savage 1988, 117–18). Nor has it had an observable effect more recently. Total outstanding state debt has continued to grow steadily over the years, from $353 million in 1870, to $21.6 billion in 1962, to $315.5 billion in 1990 (see Kiefer, Cox, and Zimmerman 1992, 24). In all likelihood, however, this evidence would not disappoint those who, in the nineteenth century, supported the enactment of state constitutional limitations on budget deficits and debt issuance. Their concerns centered not on the level of public spending but on default and debt repudiation, most of which had related to bonds issued to help finance privately owned capital investment such as roads, canals, and rail-roads (24).

Further reason for skepticism about the significance of the state balanced budget rules comes from their limited scope. In several respects, the state rules fall far short of what has been proposed on the national level. A majority of the rules merely require some mix of gubernatorial submission of a balanced budget to the legislature and legislative approval of such a budget. Fewer than one-third of the state rules have an enforcement mechanism—mostly provisions for mandatory expenditure reduction, although in a few cases requiring mandatory tax increases.

In addition, the state budgets that are subject to a balance requirement differ from the federal budget in that they include only what are deemed current operating expenses. Capital outlays are not expensed; they are not even amortized. Rather, they are disregarded altogether, along with the revenues from special funds that are used to pay for them directly or through debt service.

This treatment of capital outlays does not merely, or perhaps even primarily, exist to facilitate evasion of the balanced budget rules. In principle, capital budgeting makes sense economically. Moreover, for states, as compared with the federal government, the ease of entry and exit may make it all the more important. Requiring taxpayers to pay for durable assets in full upon acquisition would tend to penalize current residents (especially those who were planning to leave) and to reward those who subsequently moved into the jurisdiction, absent sufficient capitalization of the expected future tax-benefit ratio into the value of in-state property owned by voters.

Yet notwithstanding the good reasons for distinguishing capital outlays from current expenses, the inevitable result of doing so is to facilitate evasion of state balanced budget rules. On average, the general operating fund that is subject to a state's balanced budget rule covers barely more than half of its total annual expenditures. The sheer range of variation—from more than 70 percent coverage in Connecticut to a bit more than 20 percent in Wyoming—has been cited as suggesting that some states must aggressively misclassify a portion of their current expenditures as capital (Kiefer, Cox, and Zimmerman 1992, 21). In difficult economic times, such as those presented by the 1982 recession, various states have achieved nominal budgetary balance by the subterfuge of shifting general fund obligations into off-budget special funds. They also have relied on such devices as underfunding or even raiding their employee pension funds, accelerating tax collections to the current fiscal year, postponing the payment of tax refunds until the next fiscal year, and even extending their fiscal years by one to three months so that "annual" balance could be achieved (see Lubecky 1986, 573–74).

The states' use of capital budgeting puts supporters of a federal balanced budget rule in the enviable debating position of being potentially helped, but not hurt, by examining what the state rules accomplish. If one could show that despite capital budgeting, the state rules tend to constrain spending or debt issuance, then the case for a federal balanced budget amendment would be strengthened (although still subject to the objection that spending levels are not the sine qua non of government activity). Yet a failure to show any effect could be dismissed as showing no more than the abuses that result from capital budgeting.

As it happens, the state level evidence is mixed. Of three recent studies, only one finds a significant tendency for relatively stringent state constitutional rules to restrain spending (Rowley, Shughart, and Tollison 1987, 279). The other two find that state balanced budget rules, considered in isolation, have had either no discernible effect on spending or else a fairly insignificant effect.[5]

There also are two recent studies finding that states with stringent antideficit rules tend to respond more rapidly to fiscal shocks (such as recession) that suddenly yield unexpected deficits (Alt and Lowry 1994; Poterba 1994). However, this point relates only to short-term fiscal management, not to long-term spending trends. Moreover, such increased responsiveness is less important at the federal level than at the state level. The federal government faces a lesser default risk than any state and thus is not endangered to the same degree by short-term deficits resulting from a shock such as recession. Moreover, the federal government may justifiably be less eager than any state to act swiftly to eliminate deficits that result from recession, given that it can more effectively engage in Keynesian countercyclical policy.

---

5. See Abrams and Dougan 1986; Crain and Miller 1990. Abrams and Dougan find no correlation between state constitutional limits and the level of state spending, while Crain and Miller find a 1 percent restraining effect on the rate of state spending growth. This seems too trivial to give much heed, since if transposed to the federal level it would imply an effect on spending growth of less than $1 billion per year. Crain and Miller do, however, find that the effect of a balanced budget rule depends on its interaction with other aspects of the institutional environment (1042).

In the end, therefore, evidence from the states reveals disappointingly little about the extent to which a balanced budget amendment would likely reduce federal spending. It does, however, confirm something we already knew: legislators, faced with balanced budget rules that hinder satisfying the political demand for spending in excess of current taxes, search aggressively and creatively for smoke-and-mirrors avoidance techniques, among which the misuse of capital budgeting is important but not unique.

4. Evidence from the Gramm-Rudman-Hollings Act and Related Federal Statutory Deficit Limitation Rules

Although the national government has never been subject to a constitutional limitation on budget deficits or debt issuance, one could argue that the history of the Gramm-Rudman-Hollings Act of 1985 (GRH),[6] along with its statutory precursors and successors, provides some evidence bearing on the question of how well such a limitation would work. In many respects, GRH resembled a balanced budget amendment, although with the important difference that it was merely statutory and thus could be redrawn and superseded at any time. GRH plainly failed on its own terms—it was supposed to eliminate the federal budget deficit by 1991—but its history provides grist for both mills in the debate concerning the merits of a balanced budget amendment. A more neutral evaluation should start by placing it in historical context.

At the time of its enactment, GRH looked like the culmination of a long-term trend of centralizing and rationalizing the federal budgetary process. From the enactment of the Constitution through the first two decades of the twentieth century, there had been no such process in any formal or comprehensive sense. During the course of a legislative session, Congress would simply act in sequence on whatever revenue and appropriations bills happened to come before it. However, the twentieth century's two world wars, with their increased spending and budget deficits, made this lack of a comprehensive budget procedure begin to seem antiquated.

Apparently in response to the deficit and spending effects of World

---

6. GRH was formally known as the Balanced Budget and Emergency Deficit Control Act of 1985, Title II of P. L. 99–177 (Increase in the Public Debt Limit), 99 Stat. 1038–1101 (December 12, 1985).

War I, Congress enacted the Budget and Accounting Act of 1921, directing the president to submit a proposed annual budget, and to include recommendations for "new taxes, loans, or other appropriate action" to finance a projected deficit.[7] Yet there remained no formal process for considering the president's budget or adopting a legislative version of it. In the aftermath of World War II, Congress adopted the Legislative Reorganization Act of 1946, which finally provided for the adoption of a comprehensive annual budget. Yet this provision was long ignored, and Congress finally repealed it in 1970.[8]

Stronger demand for comprehensive budget procedures emerged only in the early 1970s. It had two main causes: the era's growing budget deficits and weakening economy, which made the lack of such procedures seem newly unacceptable, and a series of bitter budgetary battles between President Nixon and the Democratic Congress. Nixon repeatedly vetoed domestic spending programs in areas where he disagreed with Congress politically. In several cases where his vetoes were overridden, he attempted to prevail anyway by impounding, or refusing to spend, appropriated funds. Nixon also took the battle to the public with veto messages and speeches that accused Congress of fiscal irresponsibility and secret postelection plans to increase taxes. He denounced Congress, not only for its more liberal policy views but also for what he called the "hoary and traditional procedure [that] permits action on the various spending programs as if they were unrelated and independent actions" (see Penner and Abramson 1988, 9–11; Makin and Ornstein 1994, 155–58).

This criticism found a receptive audience. Congressional leaders not only could not defend the traditional procedures in an era of greater concern about budget deficits but also realized that adding structure and centralized control to the budgetary process would permit them to compete more effectively with the presidency. Shortly before Nixon resigned from office, when he was too weak to continue the institutional struggle, Congress enacted the Congressional Budget and Impoundment Control Act of 1974.[9] This legislation, in addition to "serving as the final nail in the coffin of the constitutional prerogative to impound" (Abascal and Kramer 1974, 184), already battered by a

7. Budget and Accounting Act of 1921, P. L. 67–13, 42 Stat. 21 (June 10, 1921).

8. Legislative Reorganization Act of 1946, chap. 753, sec. 138, 60 Stat. 812, 832, repealed in 1970 by sec. 242(b), 84 Stat. 1172. See Stith 1988, 601.

9. P.L. 93–344, 88 Stat. 297 (July 12, 1974).

series of court decisions, established procedures designed to permit Congress to engage in comprehensive budgetary planning based on its own staff's analysis.

To this end, the 1974 act created the House and Senate Budget Committees, provided them with access to expert independent staff by establishing the Congressional Budget Office, and specified a detailed structure and timetable for the new congressional budget process. Under the direction of the budget committees, Congress ostensibly would pass a concurrent resolution by May 15 of each year that set a target floor for total revenues, as well as target ceilings for total outlays, the budget deficit, and total public debt. Each congressional committee would then have an allocated level of budget authority, although in practice the committees might have little difficulty in reporting out (or Congress in adopting) costlier legislation. By September 15, at which time all committee action was supposed to have been completed, Congress would pass a second concurrent resolution on the budget that ostensibly was binding. If the legislation that already had been enacted resulted in exceeding the deficit or spending limits contained in this resolution, then this second concurrent resolution would include reconciliation instructions, in the form of suggested tax increases or spending cuts, so that budgetary targets could be met. Congress would act on these proposals by October 1. Any subsequent legislation for the year that would cause the second resolution's limits to be violated could be objected to and ruled out of order.

Some supporters of the 1974 Budget Act hoped that it would bring about deficit reduction, and even more hoped that it would help restrain the growth of federal spending (see Ellwood 1983, 73). Moreover, the act seemed well conceived to advance these goals. It not only permitted Congress to budget more coherently but also attempted to address the diffusion of power within Congress. Such diffusion can lead to increased deficits because it encourages extensive logrolling, permitting each member of a majority coalition to demand a narrowly targeted set of spending programs or tax benefits. In response to such diffusion, the budget committees seemed well equipped to identify specific budgetary targets and the means of meeting these targets.

In the event, however, deficits only increased—from less than $5 billion in 1974 to an average of more than $50 billion per year over the next seven years. The rate of nominal spending growth also greatly increased (although partly as a result of inflation) (see Savage 1988, 290–91). In large part, these increases reflected independent factors, including the effect of other contemporaneous changes in congressional procedure that greatly decentralized the effective exercise of legislative authority and thus intensified disaggregated logrolling (see Shaviro 1990, 102–3). Congress, in its eagerness to spread particularized benefits, repeatedly declined to adhere to the budgetary procedure specified in the 1974 legislation, for example, by missing timetables for adopting budget resolutions and then ignoring the targets that the resolutions established. However, to the extent that the 1974 Budget Act mattered at all, it seems to have made things even worse. According to Kate Stith:

> [T]he comprehensive budget process prescribed by the 1974 Act . . . increased Congress' opportunities to scrutinize individual expenditures annually. Ironically, this enhanced scrutiny made it more difficult politically to achieve [centralized] legislative control of the budget. By making every program vulnerable every year, the process required Congress to expend more effort on negotiation, logrolling, and the making of alliances. The increased conflict and interdependence among various interest groups and members of Congress merely entrenched existing programs and led Congress to ignore its self-proclaimed aggregates, instructions, and deadlines. (1988, 620)

Stated abstractly, the problem was as follows. Suppose that one-third of the legislature supports spending program A and is indifferent to spending program B; one-third supports B and is indifferent to A; and one-third opposes both programs. If program A is effectively entrenched and only B is up for legislative consideration, then B may lose. If both are up for consideration, however, then the supporters of A and B may be more likely to agree to a logroll whereby both are adopted. By this mechanism, the 1974 Budget Act, placing more spending programs politically at risk, perversely strengthened the dynamic that led Congress to adopt unfunded spending programs.

Again, deficits remained stable at about the $50 billion level for the seven-year period beginning in 1975. In 1982, however, prompted by the 1981 tax cuts and increased defense spending, the deficit exceeded $100 billion for the first time in American history. It continued to grow. The perceived crisis that this created, alongside the broader resulting sense of political impotence and the 1974 Budget Act's manifest failure to advance its deficit reduction objective, prompted the view that only a truly radical change in congressional procedures could yield a change in budgetary outcomes. This view, in turn, made GRH politically possible.

GRH was a good example of "policy entrepreneurial" legislation that gains enactment despite lacking an interest group constituency, because its sponsors can claim credit for acting boldly in a perceived general interest, and their colleagues fear criticism if they do not go along (see, e.g., Shaviro 1990, 93–94; White and Wildavsky 1989, 431). The enactment of tax reform in 1986 is a similar example. What made GRH so seemingly radical—typical descriptions of it at the time ranged from "budgetary terrorism" and "doomsday machine" to "fundamental . . . amend[ment of] our implicit 'fiscal constitution' " (White and Wildavsky 1989, 431–32; Stith 1988, 597)—was its mechanism for seeking to ensure that Congress would not revert, after its enactment, to ignoring the deficit reduction principle.

As an initial matter, GRH set deficit reduction targets that would have not merely strained but overwhelmed credulity—especially after practice under the 1974 act—without some form of attempted guarantee. It purported to require that the budget deficit, projected at nearly $180 billion for 1986, be reduced to zero over five years by equal annual increments of 20 percent, or $36 billion. The deficit would not be permitted to exceed $144 billion in 1987, $108 billion in 1988, $72 billion in 1989, $36 billion in 1990, and zero in 1991. In part, these targets were to be met by strengthening the 1974 procedures in various ways, such as requiring the president to submit a budget within the applicable deficit limit, accelerating the timetable for congressional consideration of budget measures, increasing the constraints on committees to honor their allocated limits, and prohibiting deficit-increasing floor amendments to proposed legislation.

However, out of concern that these conventional measures were not enough, GRH provided a procedure for automatically eliminating excess deficits, without requiring the enactment of budget reconciliation legislation. The procedure involved sequestration, or automatic, across-the-board spending cuts in all government spending programs except for those (such as entitlements and interest payments on the national debt) that it partly or wholly exempted. In practice, only about 46 percent of federal outlays were subject to sequestration, but this included both defense spending presumed dear to President Reagan and domestic spending presumed dear to congressional Democrats (White and Wildavsky 1989, 460).

Under GRH as initially enacted, sequestration was to be administered by the comptroller general, pursuant to a rigid formula whereby outlays for each affected "program, project, or activity" would be reduced on a uniform percentage basis as necessary to achieve deficit reduction targets (although different percentages would apply to defense and nondefense spending). When the Supreme Court struck down this rule in 1986 for giving executive powers to a legislative official,[10] Congress surprised many observers by reauthorizing the first round of sequestration cuts that the comptroller general had identified. It then amended GRH in 1987 to meet the Supreme Court's constitutional objection by assigning the sequestration power to the executive Office of Management and Budget. However, Congress also used this occasion as an opportunity to soften GRH's short-term deficit reduction targets and push back the date of projected deficit elimination by two years, to 1993.

Proponents of GRH fully recognized the inefficiency and disruption that could result from sequestration's sledgehammer across-the-board spending cuts, adopted in the middle of a fiscal year and without regard to specific programs' merits or people's reliance interests. Sequestration could interrupt important government services, require irregular employee furloughs, and lead to breaches of contracts with private individuals. The prospect of such disruptions apparently caused various private vendors to refuse government business, or else to charge more because they expected to be paid late (White and Wildavsky 1989, 518). In some instances, it was unclear how sequestration could even be applied. Commentators noted such conundrums as "[h]ow do you cut 10 percent of an aircraft carrier?" (456).

Sequestration's relatively uniform spending reductions were nonetheless favored for three main reasons. First, they eliminated the need for Congress to agree, either in advance or at the time of sequestration, on which specific programs should be reduced by how much. Second, they avoided giving discretion to the implementing officials, thus preventing a revival of Nixonian impoundment in pursuit of policy goals distinct from those of the congressional majority. Third, they ostensibly would serve a hostage function. Even warring parties that strongly disagreed about how (or even whether) to reduce the deficit, such as the Reagan White House and Democratic congressional leadership, were expected to find sequestration so mutually unpalatable, and yet

10. Bowher v. Synar, 478 U.S. 714 (1986).

Table 3 Original and Revised Deficit Targets, and Actual Results, under the Gramm-Rudman-Hollings Act of 1985 and Successor Legislation (in billions of dollars)

Fiscal Year	Original Target	1987 Target	1990 Target	Actual Deficit
1986	171.9	—	—	221.1
1987	144	—	—	149.8
1988	108	144	—	155.2
1989	72	136	—	153.5
1990	36	100	—	220.5
1991	0	64	327	268.7

Source: Keith and Davis 1992, tables 1 and 2. Keith and Davis note that Social Security trust fund surpluses and the results of the Postal Service are excluded from the original and 1987 target numbers but included in all other numbers.

so difficult to avoid without courting public condemnation by repealing GRH, as to compel agreement on a more nuanced set of deficit reduction measures.

Sequestration took place five times within the six years after the initial enactment of GRH. In most of these cases, it was changed substantially or even rescinded by subsequent legislation. Congress's most dramatic response to the sequestration threat was its ending a major budget crisis in 1990 by substantially amending, and in effect largely repealing, GRH in connection with a one-time round of spending cuts and tax increases. The 1990 changes eliminated GRH's fixed deficit targets in favor of adjustable ones that would soon make sequestration a thing of the past. In effect, the result of these changes was to grandfather, and abandon any hope of eliminating, the existing structural deficit and to convert GRH mainly into a more conventional 1974-style procedural statute that required future legislative changes to be revenue-neutral by subjecting them to points of order.

Did GRH nonetheless significantly affect deficits or government spending while it was relatively fully applicable? Table 3 shows how actual fiscal results for the years 1986 through 1991 compared to the changing GRH targets.

As the table shows, budget deficits were significantly lower for the years 1987 through 1989, when GRH imposed the strongest constraints, than immediately before or afterward. Moreover, even in 1990, when the deficit increased as a result of broader economic trends, GRH arguably had an effect, in the sense that it was "traded in" for the one-time deficit reduction measures, including tax increases that proved controversial enough to help end President Bush's political career two years later.

It is far from clear, however, to what extent one should credit GRH with altering the course of fiscal policy in any real or substantial sense, even during the years when it was most fully in force. For one thing, Congress, in order to meet deficit targets to the extent that it did, relied in large part on smoke-and-mirrors accounting devices. On one occasion, for example, it "saved" $2.9 billion by moving a military payday back one day to place it in the next fiscal year. On another, it "saved" $19.9 billion through the adoption of intentionally overoptimistic economic assumptions for forecasting purposes (see Stith 1988, 638; White and Wildavsky 1989, 568). Maneuvers such as these inspired widespread public cynicism and led some commentators to dismiss GRH as having merely created "substantial pressure on the ingenuity of accountants" rather than for genuine spending reduction (Makin and Ornstein 1994, 185).

Nonetheless, the rate of spending growth genuinely declined for the years 1987 through 1989, suggesting that more than smoke and mirrors was involved (see Gramlich 1990). Even here, however, GRH may not deserve the credit. In 1990, economist Edward Gramlich—plainly not voicing anti-GRH polemical motives, since he supported its retention and complained that it was "coming under vicious attack" —concluded that this slowdown was "largely coincidental—defense spending had lost its political constituency anyway, nondefense spending was drifting down anyway, and taxes were going up anyway. Budget bargaining, or any changes in the process due to GRH, seemed to have little to do with the improvement" (75, 80). Gramlich argued that if GRH had contributed meaningfully to spending restraint, it had done so only indirectly, through its effect on the general political atmosphere. Any such effects were potentially significant but unverifiable.

Thus, it is hard to say whether GRH reduced spending commensurately with the level of disruption and uncertainty that resulted from its sequester mechanism. Moreover, it clearly did prove somewhat more disruptive of government operations than most of its proponents had anticipated. Again, the ostensibly unthinkable "doomsday threat" of sequestration took place no less than five times in six years. The main proponents had not expected this—in part because both congressional Democrats and Republican presidents miscalculated that the other side would find sequestration more intolerable and cave first. In practice, however, the threat of sequestration seems to have discouraged and delayed offers to compromise, because no matter what one gave up now, one was likely to have to give up still more later when sequestration was immediately at hand. Hence, GRH, while perhaps eventually facilitating negotiation and compromise, would do so, if at all, only after a period of encouraging stalling and brinksmanship (see White and Wildavsky 1989).

What should one finally make of the history of GRH and preceding structural budgetary legislation? To supporters of a BBA, GRH's ultimate failure shows only the need to proceed by constitutional amendment, so that budget targets cannot be scrapped when they prove politically painful. A tougher rule might require a lot more than merely smoke and mirrors and perhaps would indirectly affect the political climate as well by discouraging large spending initiatives.

To opponents of a BBA, however, the GRH experience suggests considerable skepticism about how well such an amendment would work. Congress, in attempting to satisfy political demands for spending in excess of current taxes, would surely work hard to evade the applicable limitations by all possible means. Smoke-and-mirrors deficit reduction might be not merely irrelevant but also harmful if it involved irrational substantive policy and increased public cynicism. Congress might also be able to flout even express commands of a BBA—unless they were judicially enforceable, which would raise problems of its own—without paying a political price if the public was not strongly committed to the principle of balance. Moreover, to the extent that a BBA relied on automatic sequesters, however enforced, the sequesters might end up being used so frequently as to create pervasive uncertainty in people's dealings with the federal government.

The latter set of concerns is sufficiently imposing to make the actual terms of a BBA crucial. Surely the case for such a provision is extremely weak unless close analysis of its provisions tends to support the view that at least it is likely to require significant spending reductions. Indeed, given the many ways in which a BBA would likely fail to work as intended—for example, by encouraging tax increases, greater reliance on regulatory mandates, smoke-and-mirrors accounting, and frequent disruptions of government operations—a high level of confidence that it would significantly reduce spending seems necessary, although not sufficient, to support any reasonable case for it. To this end, the following discussion takes a close, section-by-section look at the BBA that Congress nearly approved in 1995 and evaluates how it would likely work in practice.

5. The Balanced Budget Amendment That Nearly Won Approval

Much talk about a BBA is based on the assumption that it would actually require annual balanced budgets, except perhaps in times of war or severe recession. In principle, such an amendment could be drafted, although it would probably have to rely on automatic tax increases or spending cuts that were beyond Congress's power to countermand, other than under narrow and precisely defined circumstances, and perhaps that were judicially enforceable. In practice, however, the enactment of such an amendment seems highly unlikely. Thus, it is useful to examine the version of early 1995, which gained the necessary two-thirds approval in the House of Representatives and fell only one vote short of doing so in the Senate as well.

This version of the BBA plainly provides no clear assurance that the budget will actually end up being balanced. Indeed, even though it would be constitutional rather than statutory in status, in the end it would be about as porous as GRH. Whether it would reduce government spending, absent continual strong backing from public sentiment, is unclear, and it might even end up increasing spending. The best case for its effectiveness rests less on its substantive legal content than on the hope—or perhaps blind faith—that it would transform the atmosphere of political discussion.

Sections of the BBA that establish rules other than a balanced budget requirement—relating, for example, to the national debt ceiling and the procedural requirements for enacting tax increases—will be noted here, but I will mainly defer discussing them until later parts of this chapter dealing with the merits of such rules. After completing a section-by-section analysis, I will ask whether the whole has attributes that the particular sections, considered in isolation, would lack—for example, as a result of its tendency to frame political discussion in terms of deficit reduction.

Section 1. Total outlays for any fiscal year shall not exceed total receipts for that fiscal year unless three-fifths of the whole number of each House of Congress shall provide by law for a specific excess of outlays over receipts by a rollcall vote.

On its face, this provision seems to require that the federal budget be balanced each fiscal year unless 60 Senators and 261 members of the 435-member House of Representatives are willing to go on record as approving of a budget deficit. It also seems to require these account-able individuals to specify the allowable budget deficit and to bar any larger one from being incurred. As we will see, appearances may be deceiving; it may require no such thing in practice. One can begin the analysis, however, by asking what effect it would have if this interpre-tation were correct.

Kathleen Sullivan (1994) has complained that this provision is un-duly countermajoritarian, because under it "40 percent of the Con-gress could hold the legislative agenda hostage." This result is not nec-essarily bad, however. The drafters of the Constitution recognized as much in establishing other countermajoritarian rules, such as the two-thirds requirements for overriding vetoes, proposing constitutional amendments, approving treaties, and convicting officials who have been impeached. Sullivan distinguishes such rules on the ground that most of them serve to "prevent tyranny by protecting the executive branch [or the Constitution] from Congress," whereas the above three-fifths rule is "designed to protect Congress from itself" (12). Why should this distinction matter, however? Either form of protection might make sense, especially given the modern Congress's apparently inescapable tendency to respond to the political pressures it faces by approving spending in excess of current tax revenues.

A more telling question goes to the 60 percent rule's likely effect in practice. The sanction of accountability for voting to approve a budget deficit can be no stronger than public opinion—and evidently has not prevented the incurrence of large budget deficits, or for that matter periodic approval of increasing the statutory limit on the national debt, up to the present. We have budget deficits in large part because they are less unpopular than tax increases and spending cuts. The amendment does not require any particular preconditions or grounds for approving a budget deficit. Thus, not only does it make Congress's discretion unreviewable, but it does not include even a hortatory state-ment of the grounds on which deficits are acceptable.

Would requiring 60 percent approval of a budget deficit, rather than the 50 percent required for most congressional actions, even tend to discourage deficit spending? This is far from clear, for a reason resembling that which underlay the tendency of the 1974 Budget Act to increase, rather than reduce, the deficit. The need to assemble a 60 percent coalition might increase the amount of logrolling that was necessary. Suppose that 51 percent of the House was willing to approve a $200 billion deficit, which in fact would result from the programs in place, but that getting to 60 percent required the leadership to woo extra votes by agreeing to additional spending programs and targeted tax cuts.

This is not to say that *no* move toward requiring a greater supermajority (or, at the limit, unanimity) would deter approving deficits. Logrolling may become more difficult as the size of the winning coalition increases, to the extent that voting members have inconsistent preferences rather than simply different wish lists. For example, if members of the 51 percent coalition in support of a prospective deficit strongly dislike the spending that would be necessary to attract the support of an additional 9 percent, then it may prove impossible to form a 60 percent coalition in support of any particular deficit. Moreover, to the extent that members of Congress vote on straight party lines, a supermajority requirement may tend to deter approval of deficits, by making approval impossible unless either both parties agree to it or one party has a very large margin in both houses of Congress (and is willing to take the public onus for approving a deficit). Still, the effect of the 60 percent rule is indeterminate, as is the answer to the question of what level of supermajority requirement would be necessary (if 60 percent is not enough) to make deficit reduction more likely than deficit expansion.

Returning to the text of section 1, since the 60 percent majorities in each house must authorize the budget deficit "by law," the president can veto their decision and bar approval of a deficit unless the veto is overridden by two-thirds of those voting in each house. This, however, could similarly lead to increased spending, if that were the price either of the president's approval or of the votes needed for the veto override. Perhaps the president is relatively likely to support limiting the deficit, since he can take more credit for deficit reduction than an individual member of Congress and is appealing to a broader political constituency. However, nothing inherently limits what the president could demand in exchange, and once again an effect of increasing deficits cannot be ruled out.

If Congress and the president found the requirement of section 1 inconvenient, they could evade it in a number of ways. One would be to approve a deficit limit far in excess of anything that was likely to be necessary and explain this to the public as simply a worst-case scenario rather than the outcome they really wanted. Or all sides could agree to authorize large deficits—much as the Democrats and Republicans have occasionally agreed in the past to share the responsibility for unpopular reductions in Social Security benefits, in order to ensure that no one in particular would bear the blame.

The discussion so far has assumed, however, that in the end no deficit could be incurred without congressional approval. Yet this is not the case. To begin with, what do "total outlays," "total receipts," and "fiscal year" mean? The first two are defined in section 6 of the proposed amendment, and I will discuss them when I get there. It is worth noting, however, that section 1 may permit Congress to disregard particular outlays in determining whether a deficit is allowable. This depends not on the term "outlay" itself—which, as we will see, section 6 attempts, not very successfully, to make comprehensive—but on the term "specific" in section 1. Again, section 1 bars a current fiscal year deficit unless "Congress shall provide by law for a specific excess of outlays over receipts by a rollcall vote." Does "specific" mean "numerically specified," however? Or does it have a broader meaning, such as "determinate"? Would a 60 percent vote to disregard all Social Security outlays (but not receipts), in computing the relationship of outlays to receipts, be "specific" enough to pass constitutional muster?

"Fiscal year," unlike "outlays" or "receipts," is not defined anywhere in the text of the amendment. This suggests that it is open-ended unless one presumes that the courts will police its meaning. Recall that states with BBAs have at times lengthened their fiscal years by up to three months in order to evade the requirement of fiscal year balance. Might Congress do the same if necessary to avoid violating the balanced budget requirement? Or might it deliberately structure the twelve-month fiscal year in such a fashion as to leave the overall fiscal results unclear for as long as possible? For example, Congress could adopt a fiscal year that ended on April 30, so that until annual income tax returns began arriving after April 15, one could plausibly deny that there was going to be a budget deficit.

This, in turn, leads to a host of broader questions. What in fact happens if outlays for the fiscal year end up exceeding receipts? The provision merely says that they "shall not" do so, but this is no more self-executing than the enactment of a law stating that when there are budget deficits, the sky must turn orange. At what point is the excess to be determined? How is the excess of outlays over receipts to be eliminated? What recourse, if any, exists once the fiscal year has ended? When must the three-fifths vote authorizing the deficit be taken, relative to the fiscal year as a whole? These questions might be answered by enabling legislation, enacted pursuant to section 5 of the amendment, but, as we will see, this raises problems of its own.

The effects of enabling legislation aside, is the president allowed, or even constitutionally obligated, to prevent an unauthorized shortfall from occurring by impounding funds? One could argue that an impoundment power follows from his sworn obligation to "faithfully execute" the laws and Constitution, which upon adoption would include the BBA. The committee report that accompanied an earlier year's draft of a textually identical amendment dodged the question of whether the president would be authorized, or even required, to impound funds for this reason. On the one hand, the report states that "Congress and the President, pursuant to legislation or through exercise of their powers under the first and second articles of the Constitution, shall ensure that outlays do not exceed receipts for a fiscal year." This appears to strengthen the case for impoundment. On the other hand, the report states that the above duty "neither anticipates nor requires any alteration in the balance of powers between the legislative and executive branches, but merely imposes an additional responsibility upon each, to be fulfilled through the exercise of existing authorities" (Senate Report 1993, 8). This arguably suggests that no new impoundment power would be created—although the mention, near the end, of an "additional responsibility" may weaken this conclusion. Litigation might well be necessary at some point to resolve the impoundment issue.

A further question raised (but not answered) by section 1 is whether judicial enforcement of the balanced budget requirement is contemplated or authorized. Moreover, if it is, then who has standing to sue, and what, if anything, would the federal courts be empowered to do if they found a violation? The prospect that the courts would end up administering and enforcing the BBA has excited widespread concern. Robert Bork, for example, raises the prospect of

> hundreds, if not thousands, of lawsuits around the country, many of them on inconsistent theories and providing inconsis-

tent results. By the time the Supreme Court straightened the whole matter out the budget in question would be at least four years out of date and lawsuits involving the next three fiscal years would be climbing toward the Supreme Court. (cited in Saturno 1989, 9)

Yet precisely because this prospect seems so unappetizing, judicial intervention to enforce the amendment seems unlikely, absent express legal grounds requiring it. The federal courts, and ultimately the Supreme Court, would probably be highly reluctant to take on the responsibility for actively enforcing a balanced budget requirement. They lack both the expertise and the institutional capacity to implement budgetary balance. They have no clear power to require tax increases or spending cuts. Finally, they seem unlikely to gain institutional prestige by embroiling themselves in political controversies over the details of taxes and spending. This suggests a strong likelihood that they would steer clear of enforcement controversies under the amendment if at all possible.

It is clear, moreover, that the courts would have powerful doctrinal grounds for steering clear. They could hold that disputes about the budget deficit are not justiciable or present political questions that must be left to the executive and legislature, or that no plaintiff has standing to bring suit concerning a violation of the BBA (see, e.g., Crosthwait 1983). For such reasons and on such grounds, state courts have mostly declined to involve themselves in enforcing balanced budget rules from state constitutions (see Lubecky 1986, 574–79). All this is not to deny, however, that the federal courts would end up playing a role in interpreting the BBA—for example, in resolving disputes between the president and Congress regarding whether the amendment authorizes or requires executive impoundment of appropriated funds. Moreover, in the event that enabling legislation attached specific consequences (such as spending sequesters) to an unauthorized excess of outlays over receipts, the Supreme Court might need to define "outlays" and "receipts" under a host of ambiguous circumstances.

If the federal courts decline to get involved, Congress would have a host of options to make its own noncompliance less subject to criticism. Suppose that the words "specific excess of outlays over receipts" *do*, as properly interpreted, require specifying a dollar amount rather than exempting specific outlays. Even if this is true, there might never be an authoritative statement about it. The Supreme Court generally does not issue opinions that are merely advisory. Congress could therefore choose to violate the amendment by misinterpreting "specific," rather than by passing no legislation that authorized an excess of outlays over receipts.

Even if one disregards this point, the lack of any obvious legal consequences to an unauthorized deficit is especially significant in relation to the supermajority requirement. While that requirement's likely effects are indeterminate in the abstract, the one thing that does seem clear is that a 60 percent majority is more difficult to assemble than a 51 percent majority. Thus, there may be cases where requiring the higher threshold to be reached will mean that no prevailing coalition can be assembled. If this meant that in effect there would be no deficit, then perhaps section 1 would hold out significant hope of requiring balance after all. However, if the default outcome is simply that the deficit remains unauthorized, the provision may become a virtual dead letter, at least where neither party has a 60 percent majority and each can blame the other for the failure to reach an agreement. As the amendment stands, members of Congress might generally ask themselves, "Why should I take a potentially unpopular vote to authorize a budget deficit, and risk having this vote used against me in the next election, when the legislative outcome makes no substantive difference? Why should I not prefer an unauthorized deficit to one that I have publicly voted to authorize?"

> *Section 2.* The limit on the debt of the United States held by the public shall not be increased, unless three-fifths of the whole number of each house shall provide by law for such an increase by a rollcall vote.

This provision is discussed in subsection C.1 below.

> *Section 3.* Prior to each fiscal year, the president shall transmit to the Congress a proposed budget for the United States government for that fiscal year, in which total outlays do not exceed total receipts.

This provision, while on its face merely hortatory, seeks to make the president share with Congress the responsibility for finding ways to achieve budgetary balance. Indeed, in one sense one could argue that it limits the president more severely than section 1 limits the Congress, since no circumstances permit the president to propose and justify a deficit. Nonetheless, even the hortatory force of this provision appears quite weak. Not only is there no sanction for noncompliance, but presidents can avoid the need to propose tough political choices in any number of ways. One possibility is to achieve projected balance through the use of unrealistic economic forecasts. A second is to issue a budget proposal that explicitly relies on unspecified revenue enhancements or spending cuts, to be determined by the Congress, in order to achieve budgetary balance. The committee report states that it "anticipates good faith on the part of the President with respect to projected economic factors" (Senate Report 1993, 9), but this language is no stronger than it sounds.

> *Section 4.* The Congress may waive the provisions of this article for any fiscal year in which a declaration of war is in effect. The provisions of this article may be waived for any fiscal year in which the United States is engaged in military conflict which causes an imminent and serious threat to national security and is so declared by a joint resolution, adopted by a majority of the whole number of each house, which becomes law.

This section adds to the grounds for waiver from section 1, except that it sets no limit on the allowable deficit. Indeed, there is not even a requirement that the allowable deficit be limited to the costs of the war or other military conflict that led to the waiver. Its main practical significance would appear to be twofold. First, by separately stating the wartime exception, section 4 strengthens the inference that a section 1 waiver can, without violating the BBA's spirit, rest on any grounds at all. Second, section 4 permits a deficit to be incurred based only on a majority vote of each house and without requiring a rollcall vote, although admittedly on a specific ground that could not easily be fabricated without embarrassment. One would hope that the president and Congress would not deliberately seek military conflicts as a device for avoiding section 1, although that section's very weakness gives some hope that this would not happen.

> *Section 5.* The Congress shall enforce and implement this article by appropriate legislation, which may rely on estimates of outlays and receipts.

An earlier year's committee report emphasizes that this language "underscores Congress' continuing role in implementing the balance budget requirement [thus] preclud[ing] any interpretation of the amendment that would result in a shift in the balance of powers among the branches of government" (Senate Report 1993, 11). While this statement seems designed to discourage both presidential impoundment and judicial activism, it might not prevent such responses from being considered appropriate fallbacks if Congress failed to enact significant enabling legislation.

The committee report also emphasizes the "flexibility" that this provision gives to Congress: "For example, Congress could use estimates of receipts or outlays at the beginning of the fiscal year to determine whether the balanced budget requirement of section 1 would be satisfied, so long as the estimates were reasonable and made in good faith" (11). These are elastic terms, and what would be the legal recourse if they were not? The report goes on to state that "Congress could decide that a deficit caused by a temporary, self-correcting drop in receipts or increase in outlays during the fiscal year would not violate the article" (11).Does this mean that countercyclical deficits, or deficits misportrayed as countercyclical, would not even need section 1 authorization? The committee report continues that "Congress could state that very small or negligible deviations from a balanced budget would not represent a violation of section 1" (11). Again, these are elastic terms. Finally, it states that "Congress can require that any shortfall must be made up during the following fiscal year" (11). Or perhaps Congress can decide never to make up the shortfall once the fiscal year is over. Perhaps it can also provide a considerably longer period than one year for making up budgetary shortfalls.

Two additional points about section 5 are worth making. First, while relying on estimates is unavoidable if a balanced budget rule is to have any effect before the end of the fiscal year, estimates can be fudged or based on overoptimistic assumptions. Nothing apart from public opinion or the hortatory force of the committee report's mention of good faith would constrain Congress in deciding what estimates to use. For example, there is no requirement that the estimates be made by independent experts.

Second, the fact that the BBA would be ineffective absent meaningful enabling legislation leaves it, in the end, no less avoidable through superseding legislation than GRH. The amendment's incompleteness as it stands suggests the riddle: "When is a constitutional bar not really a constitutional bar?" The answer: "When it needs to rely on enabling legislation." Only by placing more of the operating features of the rule in the Constitution itself, as part of the amendment—admittedly at the expense of subsequent flexibility—could Congress truly bind itself to the mast, as it was not bound when it enacted the merely statutory GRH.

> *Section 6.* Total receipts shall include all receipts of the United States government except those derived from borrowing. Total outlays shall include all outlays of the United States government except for those for repayment of debt principal.

Here the amendment supplies two missing definitions from section 1. While this language looks comprehensive, arguably it is not. Even apart from the fact that it would count the proceeds of asset sales as deficit-reducing and ignore the present value of future obligations, it probably can be avoided by establishing entities that nominally are distinct from the federal government itself to engage in what is substantively public spending.

The earlier year committee report attempts to block this evasion by stating that "outlay" would cover "all disbursements from the Treasury of the United States, either directly or indirectly, through Federal or quasi-Federal agencies created under the authority of acts of Congress, and either 'on-budget' or 'off-budget.' " It clarifies, however, that "[a]mong the Federal programs that would not be covered . . . is the electric power program of the Tennessee Valley Authority [since] the financing of that program is solely the responsibility of its own electric ratepayers" (12). Yet the TVA is only one such program. Might any government program that purports to charge service fees, however inadequate, or that ostensibly is an independent public corporation, rather than a "Federal or quasi-Federal agency," qualify as well?

Additional methods of evasion might also be possible. One would be for Congress to exploit the ambiguity of what constitutes "borrowing" and "debt principal." Perhaps, for example, when Social Security payouts began exceeding current revenues, they could be redefined as loans that included an element of principal repayment. Or "borrowing" could be construed narrowly by offering lenders variable returns that did not look like standard debt. Or a portion of what constitute interest payments under current usage could be redefined as repayments of debt principal. Suppose, for example, that the government were to offer only a 3 percent return on its borrowing but compensated lenders for inflation by indexing the debt principal so its value would remain constant in real terms. The committee report states only that "[d]ebt principal . . . refers to a capital sum due as a debt" (12) but does not require that debt principal remain constant in nominal terms.

Some types of federal subsidy could avoid inclusion altogether. Suppose that the federal government provides loan guarantees, permitting the beneficiaries to borrow at lower interest rates. Arguably, a guarantee is not a current "outlay." Or suppose that the government provided benefits in the form of low-interest, contingent-repayment loans. While section 6 states that "total outlays shall include all outlays of the United States government except for . . . repay[ing] debt principal," and here the government would be advancing, rather than repaying, loan principal, one could anticipate the argument that loans are not "outlays" to begin with, given the borrower's repayment obligation.

A final point, of great significance under present circumstances, is that the definition of receipts and outlays evidently would require inclusion of any current cash flow surpluses from Social Security, Medicare, and other trust funds and entitlement programs. Such surpluses would reduce the measured deficit in the short run despite pertaining to programs that are expected to be insolvent over the long run. For fiscal 1993, the effect of including the Social Security cashflow surplus along with that from other, similarly situated government trust funds would have been to reduce the reported deficit by an estimated $120 billion (see Kiefer, Cox, and Zimmerman 1992, 19).

> *Section 7.* This article shall take effect beginning with fiscal year 2002 or with the second fiscal year beginning after its ratification, whichever is later.

Allowing ample time before the BBA would take effect serves two main purposes. It facilitates enactment by encouraging members of Congress with short time horizons to ignore any constraints that it would ultimately impose; and it permits Congress to change fiscal policy, in response to the amendment, less suddenly and jarringly. These concerns seem reasonable enough, although given the amendment's likely ineffectiveness, they might not end up mattering very much.

It is worth noting, however, that Congress would not necessarily adjust to the approach of the amendment's effective date by gradually reducing the budget deficit (even to the extent that such reduction would be necessary after the effective date). Instead, one might see a sharp increase in the pre—effective date budget deficit, as Congress frantically sought to shift as much spending as possible to before the effective date and as much tax collection as possible to afterward. This could involve a combination of smoke-and-mirrors devices with one-time spending binges. One could also imagine pre—effective date program expansion that was designed to create powerful constituencies with strong expectations of continued spending, in order to ensure that future spending cuts would be more difficult or would have to take place elsewhere.

In summary, the more closely one looks at the text of an actual BBA, the less likely it seems to accomplish very much—even under the controversial assumption that reducing government spending would in fact make the government smaller. Nonetheless, one could still perhaps argue that the amendment would prove greater than the sum of its parts. In particular, might its symbolic significance or influence on the structure of the budgetary process and public discussion thereof cause it to have greater effects than one would otherwise expect?

This possibility cannot be ruled out. To some extent, the BBA would stand as a statement of the principle that the federal budget ought, as a general rule, to be balanced annually. Moreover, one could imagine the enactment of enabling legislation (establishing timetables, a role for revenue estimates, and the like) that, even if porous and readily changeable, would increase the public relations pressure not to deviate too far from the principle of balance. Politicians who wanted to cut particular programs that retained significant political support would now have a better pretext for doing so. They could argue that the BBA mandated the cuts, rather than that they were hostile to the programs. Politicians opposing such program cuts would be under additional pressure to identify alternative spending cuts, since otherwise it would appear that only their opponents were acting responsibly and constitutionally.

Two points should be kept in mind, however. First, the history of the 1974 Budget Act and GRH counsel against placing too much reliance on bulwarks of this kind. The political pressures to spend in excess of current tax revenues are simply too strong, and the balanced budget principle's hold on the public simply too weak, for the latter to constrain the former more than marginally. Second, some such constraint already exists, because of existing public sentiment and budget legislation. Consider the existing post-GRH rules of congressional procedure that subject proposed floor amendments to a point-of-order objection unless they are revenue-neutral. Or consider the extent to which proponents of costly legislation—be it President Clinton seeking health-care reform or House Republicans in 1995 seeking substantial tax reductions—must respond, in the realm of public debate, to opposition based on budgetary concerns. If the public sentiment behind these constraints were to weaken, then having memorialized it in the form of a BBA that was technically ineffectual would be unlikely to help very much.

Thus, the case for a BBA rests in large part on the claim that it would tend to lock in the public sentiment that supports relative budgetary balance. Such a claim is hard to evaluate but not inherently very persuasive. Moreover, one could question whether it is any stronger than the claim that the amendment's main effect, given the political difficulty of achieving its aim, would be instead to increase public cynicism about politicians and the budgetary process. On balance, the prospect of slightly reinforcing public sentiment in favor of budgetary balance may be worth something but not a lot.

Yet the downside is arguably modest as well. To be sure, one hardly welcomes the prospect of encouraging additional smoke-and-mirrors accounting to meet newly specific budgetary targets, against a background of constitutional wrangling and litigation between the president and Congress and perhaps frequent disruptive sequesters or threats thereof. Still, if one subscribes to the view that the government does too much because politicians tend to make bad decisions reflecting bad information and bad incentives, then these are not necessarily serious costs (the disruption of private expectations aside).

In the end, the most persuasive conclusion is not that the BBA would do great harm but that it is unlikely to do much good. Thus, its advocates, to the extent that they are motivated by the hope of reducing the size of the federal government, probably ought to make more productive uses of their effort. Moreover, if they do procure the amendment's enactment, they should not deceive themselves that they have accomplished very much.

6. A More Rigorous Balanced Budget Amendment

The analysis above suggested that the BBA would fail to reduce the size of government significantly for four main reasons. It might merely shift the form of government activity; it would use a noneconomic measure that relates only crudely to tax lag; it would have little direct legal effect absent enabling legislation that could be revised at any time; and its general requirement of balance could be overridden by a

60 percent coalition that might be assembled through logrolling. In principle, one could revise the amendment so as to mitigate at least some of these problems.

This raises the questions of what such a revised BBA would look like and whether it would be desirable. In considering possible revisions, however, some of the alternatives that are most likely to be effective can be disregarded as politically out of the question. Suppose, for example, that members of Congress were made personally financially liable for all budget deficits during their tenures or that a randomly selected 10 percent were required to resign whenever a deficit was incurred. While such provisions would create powerful incentives to achieve budgetary balance, there plainly is no prospect of their being adopted. The question of what an effective amendment would look like is best confined to rules of a more familiar and politically plausible kind.

In considering how the BBA could plausibly be made more effective, the history of GRH provides useful information. Clearly, what made it most effective—albeit at the cost of continual brinksmanship and uncertainty—was its automatic sequester mechanism. What hurt its effectiveness most, apart from being merely statutory and thus subject to revision at any time, was Congress's ability to comply in form but not substance through smoke-and-mirrors accounting. Such accounting took two main forms: deliberately relying on bogus revenue estimates and making trivial policy changes (such as paying government workers a day late) that exploited the deficit's limitations as a cash-flow measure.

This seems to indicate that a maximally effective BBA would have three main attributes that the present version lacks. First, it would include GRH-style automatic enforcement mechanisms as part of a broader, tightly structured annual budgetary process. Second, it would protect the independence and integrity of the revenue estimating process and permit improvement of the deficit measure. Third, even if it did not bar budget deficits altogether, it would attempt to restrict more stringently the conditions under which they could be authorized.

Although one could attempt to compromise at any number of intermediate points, it is worth considering briefly what a relativley effective BBA might look like. The following version, which draws on the features of GRH and the 1974 Budget Act, seems as plausible as any:

(1) By express constitutional provision, an independent agency would be established and given responsibility for making all legally

relevant estimates of government revenues and outlays. This agency would be at least partially insulated from the political process in much the same fashion as the Federal Reserve Board (except that the rules creating and insulating it would be constitutional rather than statutory). For example, the estimating agency's directors could be appointed by the president subject to congressional approval, and then protected from removal until their terms had expired. Their terms could be structured to extend past that of the appointing president. While in office, the directors could be given a degree of autonomy over their own staffing and deliberations comparable to that presently possessed (under statute) by the Fed.

(2) The agency would be empowered to make administratively feasible changes to the applicable definitions of government revenues and outlays. At a minimum, these adjustments would be designed to negate smoke-and-mirrors manipulations, such as selling government assets or moving paydays back a day. The agency could also be empowered to consider adjustments that moved more ambitiously in the direction of economic accrual accounting, such as taking into account changes in the present value of expected future government liabilities. The use of capital budgeting would not be permitted, however, given the danger of abuse.

(3) By a specified date near the beginning of the fiscal year, the president would officially be required to submit to Congress a proposed budget that the estimating agency agreed was balanced. To satisfy the spirit of this requirement, the president would be expected to detail the specific provisions, such as spending cuts and tax increases, through which he proposed to achieve budgetary balance.

(4) By a specified date in the early middle of the fiscal year, Congress would be officially required to enact a comprehensive budget that the estimating agency agreed was balanced. Failure to comply— either by enacting a budget with a projected deficit or by not enacting a comprehensive budget—would lead to the imposition of automatic spending cuts by means of a GRH-style sequester. The estimating agency would determine the amount of spending cuts (if any) that were necessary, through calculations based on the assumed continuation of prevailing policy. Some other independent agency or official would administer the cuts, pursuant to a formula limiting the inevitable discretionary elements (which Congress by law could change, as long as the overall level of spending cuts remained adequate).

(5) By a specified date later in the fiscal year (but not too close to

the end), the estimating agency would reestimate the year's expected fiscal results and impose revised sequesters. After that date, a two-thirds majority in both houses of Congress would be required to enact tax cuts or spending increases (as defined by the estimating agency). Budget deficits that resulted from such late changes, or from the estimating agency's making what proved to be inaccurate projections, would have to be made up within a short period, such as the next one to five fiscal years, under the same mandatory requirements as those employed with respect to annual balance.

(6) Despite all of the above, budget deficits (both estimated and actual) could be permitted under specified circumstances. For example, certain expenditures in relation to a declared war, or to other overseas military engagements, could be exempted, perhaps subject to their being made up within, say, five years either of their being incurred or of the end of the crisis to which they related. Or the estimating agency's projections of balance could be adjusted to the business cycle, allowing limited recessionary deficits but requiring surplus during periods of economic expansion. Or Congress could be permitted to authorize deficits—perhaps by a two-thirds rather than a 60 percent vote—but only if it made specific findings, such as that a military or economic crisis required deficit spending. The need for such findings might, as a political matter, deter incurring deficits on spurious grounds, even if the findings were not judicially reviewable.

Would such a BBA work? Up to a point, it might. Unless the estimating agency was subverted, or its findings illegally ignored, the amendment could result in drastically reduced budget deficits and perhaps significantly reduced government spending. Yet would such a rule be desirable? This is far less clear, in part for the very same reasons that it likely would be effective. The essential features for its success—the establishment of a rigid, cumbersome process; the use of automatic sequesters; the creation of a powerful independent estimating agency; the greatly reduced flexibility to incur deficits when there is a better case for them—all are troubling in many respects. The very flexibility and direct political control of taxes and spending that make deficits seem so difficult to avoid are not wholly bad, especially compared to the alternatives of perpetual disruptive sequesters and delegating enormous powers to an agency that was not directly politically accountable (and that presumably would embody many of the flaws of bureaucracy).

In one sense, the independent estimating agency might still not be

powerful enough under this structure. Its weapon of requiring sequesters would not only create increased uncertainty about the course of
government policy but also prompt various planning responses that
would be undesirable yet hard to control. For example, agencies might
learn to spend their annual appropriations as fast as possible, so that
less of their budgets would be subject to sequester. This could lead to
lack of planning, bad purchases, shoddy construction, and undesirable
prepayment for goods and services.

More fundamental, however, is the question of how much power
over taxing and spending—along with regulation, the substance of discretionary government policy—one would want to assign to a body
of independent experts. Despite the attempted political insulation, the
estimating agency might, from time to time, raise suspicions that it
had a conscious political agenda. Even if it did not, however, the sacrifice of democratic political control might prompt concern.

Historical experience with the Fed—which is insulated from direct
political control only by statute—is not completely reassuring. As discussed earlier, the Fed and its independence are highly popular today
because of the Fed's successful war on inflation under Volcker, along
with its subsequent success in maintaining a high measure of economic stability. This has not always been the case, however, and may
not continue indefinitely. Either a costly mistake in macroeconomic
forecasting or an instance of apparent political intervention as egre-
gious as the 1972 monetary expansion that helped reelect President
Nixon could lead to a renewed appreciation of the risks inherent in
trusting an independent agency run by "experts."

One also could argue that, even as things stand, the Fed's lack of
political accountability is troubling. It may lead, for example, to macroeconomic policy that attaches too little weight to the risk of increased
cyclical unemployment relative to the risk of increased inflation, simply because Fed officials' associations and career paths make them
more sensitive to the concerns of Wall Street investors than to those of
marginal workers with tenuous job prospects. The prospect of creating
such bias by limiting the Fed's direct political accountability surely
would not be tolerated were direct political control of monetary policy
not so strongly (and justifiably) distrusted.

On balance, however, the case for the Fed's autonomy seems
clearly stronger than that for an independent estimating agency that
would effectively determine the need for and level of sequesters. Again,

the estimating agency would be affecting the very core of government policy—specific tax and spending provisions—rather than simply setting interest rates, bank reserve requirements, and the like. Its determinations would directly override decisions made by elected officials, rather than occupying a separate decisional realm. Moreover, this would take place in pursuit of nothing as tangible as managing the business cycle. Again, one could not even be confident, after the fact, that the regime really was making the government smaller in a meaningful and desirable sense.

The dilemma, in the end, is that while *any* political discretion is likely to be exploited to satisfy the overwhelming political taste for spending in excess of taxation, and thus to frustrate the principle of reducing tax lag, political discretion has some value in a democratic system. Limiting direct legislative control over taxes and spending goes far beyond, not only leaving monetary policy to the Fed but practice in other discrete areas where we have tied ourselves to the mast constitutionally, such as by providing in the First Amendment that Congress shall make no law abridging freedom of speech or burdening or establishing a religion.

The problem, ultimately, is akin to trying to legislate virtue. Public sentiment in support of reducing tax lag has value given its tendency to increase awareness of the costs of government spending. Such sentiment, if sincerely and deeply held, may even tend to limit the use of smoke-and-mirrors accounting and to promote some focus on items that the budget deficit ignores, such as the long-term solvency of Social Security and Medicare. Yet one cannot easily replicate, through a binding legal rule, the effects that such public sentiment would have.

Moreover, such sentiment is not wholly absent today. Even though large budget deficits have become politically acceptable, public sentiment seems to discourage increasing them greatly and to generate some ongoing pressure to reduce them. Problems such as Social Security solvency also receive attention and prompt significant legal changes from time to time. In a sense, then, we have something that resembles a balanced budget constraint imposed by public sentiment, except that it treats, say, a $200 billion deficit, rather than annual balance, as the target. A BBA that promoted either cynicism by permitting easy evasion or resentment by preventing all evasion might perversely serve to weaken, rather than strengthen, the force of this public sentiment.

C. Other Fiscal Policy Responses to Undue Government Growth

One could argue that focusing on tax lag unnecessarily complicates the use of fiscal policy to limit the size of government. After all, it concerns the relationship between two items—taxes and spending—that may each be easier to measure absolutely than comparatively and that could be jointly ratcheted up, in response to a rule limiting tax lag, in lieu of reducing either.

If the problem is measurement, one could instead design a rule addressing the issuance or enforceability of federal debt. If the problem is joint ratcheting up, or else comparative as distinct from absolute measurement, one might want to consider rules that limit only taxes or only spending, without regard to the relationship between the two.

1. Limiting the Issuance or Enforceability of Federal Debt

The idea of constitutionally limiting federal debt, as an alternative or supplement to addressing tax lag, is not new. Section 2 of the 1995 BBA provided that the statutory public debt limit "shall not be increased, unless three-fifths of the whole number of each House shall provide by law for such an increase by a rollcall vote." While this provision attempts to limit debt issuance, one could alternatively address the legal enforceability of newly issued federal obligations, thus obviating the need to define "debt" judicially.

A constitutional rule limiting debt issuance or enforceability would impose constraints resembling those from a BBA with GRH-style enforcement teeth. It thus would share the disadvantage of encouraging the equivalent of disruptive sequesters. The federal government, whenever it ran out of money, would be legally unable to pay for anything. Government employees' salaries, electric bills, and progress payments on government contracts might all go unsatisfied until new tax revenues arrived or Congress took appropriate action, except insofar as people could be paid with IOUs that were deemed not to constitute explicit (or enforceable) debt. One might also expect the government to engage in triaging, deciding which obligations were most important as its fiscal resources began to run low. At the same time, there might be a rush by various agencies and personnel to spend their budget authorizations as fast as possible, lest the debt limit take priority before these amounts had been spent in full. Finally, one would expect to see extensive adjustments by private parties in their dealings with the government, including prepayment demands, security interests if legally permissible, and demands for extra risk-adjusted compensation in the event of late payment. Viewed optimistically, these disruptions and costly adjustments would be the price of forcing Congress to authorize a lower course of spending over the long run.

Would the rule have this long-term effect, however? We saw in 1995, during the standoff between President Clinton and the Republican Congress concerning legislation to increase the debt limit, that financial maneuvers can keep the government operating for a considerable time, even once the limit has seemingly been reached. Moreover, the prospect of default or serious disruption of government operations can create pressures for those who are demanding reduced spending to moderate their demands and accept a compromise. The question, therefore, is whether the compromises that are reached are likely, over time, to involve lower spending than they would have in the absence of debt limits. In this regard, it is useful to examine historical evidence from the states.

More than three-fourths of the states limit public debt issuance through one mechanism or another. The rules range from altogether barring debt issuance, to limiting outstanding state debt (either to a flat dollar amount, or as a percentage of annual revenues or assessed property values), to conditioning its issuance on approval in public referenda or by legislative supermajorities (see Sterk and Goldman 1991, 1315–17). States also treat certain debts as not guaranteed by their full faith and credit, or as not to be repaid using general tax revenues.

From the standpoint of likely effectiveness at the federal level, the evidence concerning how these state provisions operate is not encouraging. Empirical research suggests that the debt limits do not discernibly affect state spending levels (see Abrams and Dougan 1986). The limits have not prevented the continuing immense growth in state debt, from $21.6 billion in 1962 to $315.5 billion in 1990 (Kiefer, Cox, and Zimmerman 1992, 24).

An important reason for the ineffectiveness of state debt limits is the use of a host of avoidance techniques. One is nonguaranteed borrowing, which, instead of being supported by the state's full faith and credit (and thus counting for constitutional purposes), is supported only by particular nontax revenues, such as highway tolls or other user fees. This has been a major growth area in recent years—evidently despite any reluctance one might expect from lenders absent suitable compensation for the added risk. Nonguaranteed debt grew from 14.2 percent of outstanding state debt in 1942, to more than 50 percent in 1962, to 76 percent in 1990. During the 1980s, it grew more than six times as fast as full faith and credit state debt (25).[11] The feasibility of using nonguaranteed debt has obvious implications for the claim that making certain federal debt nonguaranteed would affect government spending.

Other popular techniques in avoiding the force of state constitutional rules include (1) shifting borrowing activity from state to local governments, in states where the latter are not subject to the constitutional limits, (2) establishing independent quasi-governmental authorities to issue debt, (3) using other off-budget special funds, (4) issuing "tax anticipation notes" that in effect sell the right to specific forthcoming tax revenues, and (5) substituting leasing arrangements for explicit borrowing. As an example of the latter, a state, instead of borrowing $100 million to purchase a building, may instead persuade the putative lenders to purchase the building and then lease it to the state. If the lease is sufficiently long-term to cover the building's useful life, the economic result may be the same as if the government had purchased it through debt financing, but for formal legal purposes its annual payments to the putative owner may constitute rent rather than principal plus interest (see Sterk and Goldman 1991, 1330–34).

State courts' responses to such evasion techniques vary. In most states, the courts construe the debt limits narrowly, apparently reflecting sympathy for legislative evasion. Commentators attribute this in part to the courts' relative lack of political independence in states where the judges are elected and do not have life tenure—unlike federal judges. However, the state courts' permissiveness apparently also reflects a widespread view among state judges that the political branches should not be second-guessed on the details of their spending where the issuance of debt does not appear fiscally imprudent, in the sense of risking default. Such a motive might comparably influence federal judges (1358–59).

11. Statement by Louis Fisher, Congressional Research Service, House Committee on Budget, May 11, 1992, Balanced Budget Amendment, p. 3 (between 1981 and 1984, nonguaranteed state debt for long-term borrowing grew by 57.4 percent, while full faith and credit debt grew by only 9.1 percent).

At the federal level, one additional evasion technique would be available. The federal government can pay for deficit spending, not only by issuing debt but also by printing money. This eliminates the need to make interest payments while creating the off-budget equivalent of a tax in the form of inflation. Yet expanding the rule to address money issuance might disrupt the generally well-functioning monetary policy regime.

The federal government also might have less difficulty than any state government in selling explicitly nonguaranteed debt instruments without a large risk premium. Its ability to raise revenue is less subject to doubt, and it could establish a course of dealing confirming that even explicitly nonguaranteed debt instruments would in fact be honored. After all, even today, when federal debt is perceived by lenders as virtually risk-free, trust based on the course of dealing, not a legal guarantee, is what really matters. If the U.S. government decided to default, lenders would have no legal recourse. However, even if there were some additional perceived risk, requiring the payment of higher interest rates, it is hard to know to what extent this would yield reduced substantive spending rather than the imposition of additional distortive taxes.

A final problem with debt limits is that various smoke-and-mirrors devices, resembling those that Congress used to meet GRH targets, can be effective. One option would be federal asset sales, perhaps followed by leasebacks of the assets. Another would be deferring contractual obligations such as salary payments until specified revenues had been received or offering taxpayers discounts (thus applying an implicit interest rate) to accelerate their tax payments.

In sum, constitutional debt limits have a number of inherent problems—although, if the limits were strict enough, they might have some effect. It seems clear, however, that section 2 of the 1995 BBA would matter little. Again, it bars increasing the statutory federal debt limit without approval by 60 percent of the members of each House in a rollcall vote. This supermajority requirement might be no constraint. It is true that in recent years, increases in the statutory national debt limit have often caused political difficulty, and ultimately only barely passed, despite requiring a mere majority of those voting (see, e.g., Hill 1992). Yet not only may requiring a larger winning coalition lead to increased logrolling, but close votes often reflect posturing. Conceivably, a large majority of those in Congress recognize that an increase in the debt limit is politically necessary, but many of them prefer to vote against it as long as their votes in support are not needed. Freeing unneeded potential members of a majority coalition to vote against controversial legislation is a familiar legislative tactic.

Section 2's likely effect is also greatly weakened by its failure to constrain the frequency of votes to increase the national debt limit, or the amount of each increase. If votes to increase it are politically unpleasant, particularly in light of the 60 percent rule, one might expect them to be undertaken less frequently and to involve a larger increase each time. Or one might even see repeal of the statutory debt limit—justified politically on the ground that it would eliminate disruptions to the governing process and the orderly functioning of the bond markets. Section 2 may not bar such a change, although it presumably would require the repeal to receive a 60 percent rollcall majority.

2. Tax Limits

A second alternative or supplement to addressing tax lag would be imposing a constitutional limitation on some aspect of taxation. Some versions of the proposed BBA—although not the main 1995 version— have contained a modest tax limit, providing that "no bill to increase revenue shall become law unless approved by a majority [or, in other cases, 60 percent] of the whole number of each House by a rollcall vote." In addition, a recent House of Representatives rule requires income tax rate increases to receive 60 percent support or else be ruled out of order.[12]

A basic problem with this approach is that the line between "tax increases" and "spending cuts" is far less definite than most people realize. To illustrate, consider the alternatives of reducing Social Security benefits or increasing the extent to which the benefits are includable in taxable income. While the two alternatives would have similar effects on Social Security recipients in the aggregate, the former would be a "spending cut" and the latter a "tax increase."

Or consider "cutting spending" through the "Bradford plan" discussed in chapter 4, with its three linked changes: eliminating, say, $50 billion of military appropriations, enacting a $50 billion "military supplier tax credit" that went to the defense contractors that had pre-

12. H.R. Res. 6, 104th Cong., 1st Sess., sec. 106 (1995).

viously received the eliminated appropriations, and enacting a general $50 billion tax increase (see Bradford 1988). This would formally constitute a spending cut plus offsetting, revenue-neutral tax changes. In substance, however, it would be identical to increasing taxes by $50 billion. A focus purely on "taxes" would not work to the extent that imaginative politicians exploited opportunities of this kind—although perhaps there are built-in political limits to how far they could go.

To date, tax limitations have been considerably more popular at the state level than at the federal level. The best-known example is California's Proposition 13, which was adopted by popular referendum in 1978. Proposition 13 amended the California state constitution to impose various restrictions on the taxing power. In particular, it placed a ceiling on property tax rates and annual valuation increases, and for all other tax increases required legislative supermajorities or popular referenda.

Initiatives of this sort have remained prominent in state constitutional debate, although their political success has varied. In 1994, six states voted on such initiatives by referendum. In two, constitutional tax limitations were approved. Nevada voters gave preliminary approval (subject to a second vote in 1996) to a rule requiring tax increases to receive either approval by popular vote or a two-thirds majority in both houses of the legislature. Florida voters approved an initiative generally limiting state revenue collections to the prior year's level adjusted for growth in personal incomes in the state. Voters rejected constitutional tax limitations in four states. South Dakota voters rejected Proposition 13—style property tax limits; Oregon and Montana voters rejected a voter approval requirement for tax increases; and Missouri voters rejected a proposal requiring voter approval for state revenues to increase by more than 0.2 percent annually (see Douglas and Hamilton 1994).

As these examples help show, tax limits pose two main types of design question. First is what to limit. The possibilities include revenue-increasing legislation (as under some versions of the BBA), applicable tax rates or bases (as under Proposition 13), and the overall level of tax revenues, either in absolute terms or as a percentage of some measure such as GDP. Second is how to limit the affected tax provisions. They can be barred altogether, required to meet some extra threshold such as a legislative supermajority or approval in a public referendum, or, at the low end, merely required to win a rollcall vote.

a. Limiting Tax Increase Legislation

Attempting to impede the enactment of tax increase legislation raises a number of design problems. If a single enactment contains many provisions, should it be tested as a whole for whether it is a tax increase, or should the test apply separately to each part (however defined)? How does one determine whether taxes are being increased? Should this depend on legislative purpose, as in a section of California's Proposition 13 that addresses "changes in State taxes enacted for the purpose of increasing revenues collected"? Purpose is inherently ambiguous and can be concealed behind purported independent aims. Should it depend instead on revenue estimates? These, too, are manipulable and often genuinely ambiguous. Consider the ongoing dispute concerning the revenue effect of cutting capital gains rates. Would a capital gains rate cut be treated as a tax increase if the applicable estimate portrayed it as increasing revenue? For that matter, would a capital gains rate increase be exempt from the rule if revenue estimators determined that it would lose revenue? What if a tax change were estimated to have one direction of revenue effect over the next year or several years but an opposite overall effect as determined in a present value sense?

A rule limiting the enactment of tax-increasing legislation could also be evaded to the extent that effective tax increases were possible without new legislation. In the 1970s, for example, before federal income tax brackets were indexed for inflation (and when they were relatively highly graduated), many people's taxes increased automatically each year with inflationary bracket creep, without any need for new congressional action. If Congress's power to legislate tax increases were limited constitutionally, one might expect it to rely more on such opportunities to increase taxes automatically.

Even if both legislated and automatic tax increases became less frequent, tax revenues might not be reduced over the long term. Instead, each of the rarer enactments might simply bring about a larger tax increase. A tax limit (such as a supermajority requirement) cannot easily be calibrated to apply with greater rigor as the size of the tax increase grows greater, except in the sense that voters may be more hostile to a larger increase. If voters are relatively ill informed, however, then a measure's bare status as a tax increase may be more clearly perceived than its magnitude.

There is evidence that many voters exaggerated the extent (if any) to which the 1993 tax changes increased their own tax liabilities.

Underestimation is possible as well, however. Suppose that federal income taxes were increased on balance, but through a mix of nonobvious increases (such as lowering the point at which higher rate brackets become applicable) with visible tax cuts (such as increasing widely applicable personal deductions). Suppose as well that the real tax increase was less than the increase in withholding from paychecks, leading to greater refunds at tax filing time. Given the "withholding illusion" (see, e.g., Burnham 1989, 28), whereby people confuse changes in the balance due or receivable upon filing with changes in their overall tax liabilities, voters might easily be led to underestimate the increase, if indeed they realized that it had occurred at all.

b. Limiting Tax Rates and/or Tax Bases

A second tax limit approach would limit legislative discretion with regard to particular tax rates and bases. In illustration, suppose that a constitutional amendment prohibited the application of marginal income tax rates in excess of 30 percent, as well as the enactment of a federal property tax, wealth tax, sales tax, or value-added tax. Such a rule might significantly limit Congress's revenue options, apart from broadening the income tax base and raising lower-tier marginal rates.

The most prominent recent example of this approach is provided by California's Proposition 13, which, among other provisions, limited "any ad valorem tax on real property" to 1 percent of the "full cash value" of such property, except to the extent necessary to meet pre—Proposition 13 public debt obligations. Proposition 13 also defined "full cash value" in a way that ensured it would often be less than fair market value. Except where real property is newly constructed or changes hands (as through sale), "full cash value" was defined as "the County Assessor's valuation . . . as shown on the 1975–76 tax bill," subject to annual appreciation of no more than 2 percent, and even to that extent only as necessary to adjust for inflation. For new construction and property that changed hands, "full cash value" would increase to fair market value but then, once again, could not increase by more than 2 percent per year until the next such change occurred.

Had Proposition 13 contained no other tax limits, it might have led merely to the increased use of other kinds of taxes. Thus, it also required that revenue increases enacted by the state legislature receive two-thirds approval in each house. In addition, it required local governments to receive two-thirds approval from their electorates before imposing "special taxes." Under no circumstances, however, could the state or localities impose higher real property taxes or taxes of any sort upon the sale of real property.

Proposition 13 has remained in force since its enactment, and there is no significant move afoot to repeal or even weaken it. Not surprisingly, however, local governments have responded strategically. They now make greater use of debt and charge more fees for particular services, such as "benefit assessments" to pay for such things as fire protection, park upkeep, and street lighting. Realizing that under the post—Proposition 13 regime, sales taxes offer them greater revenue potential than property taxes, they compete aggressively for development in the form of strip malls and shopping centers, at the expense of middle-class housing (see Schodolski 1994). They also, as in the case of the recent Orange County bankruptcy, may employ overly aggressive investment strategies that might have been less tempting under weaker revenue constraints.

At times, spending decisions have been distorted by consideration of whether fees can be used instead of taxes. Sacramento County recently bought a new public golf course, at the same time as it was telling its sheriff's deputies that it lacked the money to offer them pay increases, because the former expense, but not the latter, could be recouped through fees (see Schrag 1994).

In addition, Proposition 13 induced the state government to supply additional financial assistance to localities, reflecting its greater resources, possession of a budget surplus at the time of enactment, and newfound responsibility for allocating revenues from the now-uniform real property tax. The result was a massive, although apparently unintended, shift of power over local taxing and spending decisions to the state government—arguably violating the principle of fiscal federalism that jurisdictions should make their own decisions when they mainly internalize the effects.

Has Proposition 13 nonetheless had some significant constraining effect on the size of state and local government in California? An initial problem is that even if spending was constrained, distortions such as deterring home sales (which generally cause the property tax to increase) are themselves a form of "big government." Yet even purely with regard to spending levels, analysis is impeded by the difficulty of disentangling Proposition 13's effects from those of a constitutional spending limit, Proposition 4, that was enacted in 1979. Proposition 4 limited all local governments' appropriations out of taxes and grants from the state to the prior year's appropriations limit, adjusted for changes in population and inflation. Efforts to isolate Proposition 13's effects also are impeded by such complicating events as the one-time $7 billion revenue loss that resulted from rolling back property assessments to 1975–76 levels, the offsetting existence of a large budget surplus at the state level at the time, and the nationwide recession that began shortly after the proposition was approved (see, e.g., Stocker 1991, 12; California Joint Legislative Budget Committee 1988, 12).

Nonetheless, the evidence seems to support the view that Proposition 13 (or, at least, the two propositions together) significantly constrained state and local taxes and spending. In the first ten years after enactment, special taxes sought by local governments passed only 27 percent of the time—although requiring a simple voting majority would have permitted them to pass 64 percent of the time (see Break 1991, 176). (This reflects the unfeasibility of logrolling among a general electorate that votes in secrecy and is too numerous for vote trades to be workable.) Between 1977 and the mid–1980s, state and local taxes in California declined from 20 percent above the national average to 2 percent below. During the same period, using indices computed by the Advisory Commission on Intergovernmental Relations (ACIR), California's "tax effort" fell from 17 percent above to 6 percent below the national average, even though its "tax capacity" rose from 14 percent above to 20 percent above.

On the spending side, what the ACIR calls the "direct general expenditure ratio" fell from 9 percent above the national average to less than 1 percent above (from Break 1991, 178). Not surprisingly, less spending meant less services. California now provides no more than an average level of government services, whereas in the 1970s it was well above average (see Schrag 1994). Observers generally agree that the level of services being provided by government in California has declined virtually across the board. The quality of public education from the grade school through the university level has apparently declined, as has maintenance of public infrastructure. Services that voters apparently cared more about, such as garbage collection and police and fire protection, were affected less. There is reason to believe, however, that even from the standpoint of general voter preferences, the "wrong" spending has often been curtailed. For example, reflecting the power of state employee unions, California's public employees remain among the highest paid in the nation, at the same time as "libraries can't buy books, [and] schools [are] curtailing programs and laying off counselors" (Schrag 1994, B–10).

Accordingly, even if Proposition 13 was a success in its own terms, its overall merits are unclear. Discouraging home sales, imposing unequal property taxes on people who own homes of the same value, cutting the "wrong" spending because of interest group power, centralizing authority over local decisions, and inducing local governments both to compete with each other for less restricted tax bases and to prefer fee-generating services to those that provide indivisible public goods are all costs that must be weighed in the balances. While many of these problems reflect peculiar features of California's post—Proposition 13 public finance regime, similar problems are hard to avoid when one is imposing strict constitutional restraints on legislative discretion regarding taxation.

c. Imposing a Ceiling on National Tax Revenues

A further possible approach to limiting federal tax revenues would be the most direct and comprehensive. Instead of focusing on tax increase legislation or on particular features of the federal tax system, one could simply impose a ceiling on annual federal tax revenues. This approach could also be expanded to limit all federal revenues, including those derived from charging fees. For example, the Constitution could be amended to provide that except under specified conditions such as war, total revenues for a fiscal year could not exceed a given percentage of GDP. Or one could limit the allowable increase in such revenues from year to year—for example, by barring any increase except to the extent of inflation, increased population, and/or GDP growth.

Such rules would be more comprehensive than limiting particular taxes—although they would not affect the use of regulatory mandates—and would retain legislative flexibility concerning what taxes to levy. The main administrative problems that they would pose (other than distinguishing taxes from spending) concern how to detect violations and what consequences a violation would have. Presumably, except to the extent that manipulable revenue estimates were used, one would not know until after the end of the fiscal year that excess revenues had been levied.

At that point, one could either mandate tax cuts for the next available fiscal year by formula or require the payment of explicit tax refunds. State rules provide some guidance on how this could be done. In Florida, under a recently voter-approved state constitutional amendment, excess taxes are allowed to accumulate, up to a point, in a "budget stabilization fund" that goes first to pay for future tax or budgetary shortfalls. Once this fund reaches capacity, the legislature must decide how to provide refunds.[13] California's Proposition 4—technically a spending limit, but one that functions more like a tax limit since it limits only the spending of tax revenues—provides additional illustrative guidance. Under Proposition 4, excess revenues that cannot lawfully be spent must be returned to taxpayers within two years, but through reductions in tax rates or fee schedules rather than explicit refunds. The Proposition 4 limits are enforceable through lawsuits by taxpayer associations and other interested parties.[14]

d. Conditions That Tax Limitation Rules Could Impose

Whether one limited legislative tax increases, the imposition of tax rates above specified levels, or overall tax revenues, a question would arise concerning how firm the limitation should be. Completely banning the offending taxes might prove overly restrictive in the event of future fiscal crises or changes in societal needs and preferences. One might consider settling for a constitutional rule that simply imposed preconditions, procedural or otherwise, on the imposition of otherwise barred taxes.

Perhaps the most timid such proposal is provided by the 1995 BBA, which would merely have required a rollcall vote and approval by a majority of the members of each House (rather than simply a majority of those present). Possible alternatives include requiring supermajority approval; requiring voter approval in a nationwide referendum; conditioning the tax increase on specified circumstances, such as war; or making excess taxes refundable. While none of these proposals is completely unworkable, each is subject to some objections. As I noted earlier, the general effects of requiring supermajority approval are ambiguous—although at least here, the failure to assemble a supermajority coalition would matter, since it would cause the tax laws to remain as they were. (In the balanced budget context, by contrast,

13. See H.R.J. Res. 2053, from General Acts, Resolutions, and Memorials Adopted by the Thirteenth Legislature of Florida under the Constitution as Revised in 1968, vol. 1, pt. 3, 1994.

14. See, e.g., San Francisco Taxpayers Association v. Board of Supervisors of San Francisco, 2 Cal. App. 4th 1159, 273 Cal. Rptr. 503 (1990); Oildale Mutual Water Co. v. North of the Pier Municipal Water District, 215 Cal. App. 3d 1628, 264 Cal. Rptr. 544 (1989); Santa Barbara County Taxpayers Association v. Board of Supervisors of Santa Barbara County, 209 Cal. App. 3d 940, 257 Cal. Rptr. 615 (1989).

failure to assemble a supermajority might lead only to the deficit's being officially unauthorized.)

The next possibility, requiring national referenda, would be a major and highly controversial innovation in federal constitutional practice. At the state level, there is some evidence that allowing the use of referenda encourages demagogic and poorly thought-out legislation. Finally, the refund course could involve difficulty in allocating refunds and locating the appropriate taxpayers, unless it took the form of mandatory tax cuts (subject, presumably, to reversal through tax increase legislation) in later years.

e. Overall Assessment of Tax Limitation Rules

Based both on the history of Proposition 13 and on the variety of forms that a tax limitation rule can take, it appears plausible, at the state level, that such rules can reduce government spending. Whether they reduce the size of government or better the government's net impact on society is less clear.

Is there any reason why such rules would be less effective at the federal level? Three main problems come to mind. First, the federal government can print money to pay for its spending. Second, the federal government is less constrained as a borrower than any state, given its greater economic power. Third, the pressures and opportunities to transfer wealth between segments of the voting public are greater at the national level than in any state or locality. Exit is less of an option, and the competing groups are more diverse and less linked. Thus, the political pressures to increase taxes in spite of any limitations might prove greater at the federal level than at the state level.

Perhaps for these reasons, recent empirical research into federal fiscal practice has found little evidence for the proposition that tax increases tend to stimulate spending increases and thus presumptively that limiting the former would tend to limit the latter. Rather, the causal relationship seems to run in the other direction. Spending increases generally come first (often after crises that change public attitudes about the proper size of government), with tax increases following later on grounds of fiscal necessity.[15] This is precisely the rela-

---

15. See von Furstenberg, Green, and Jeong 1986. For a pair of dueling studies prepared by congressional staffers and reaching predictable conclusions, see Vedder, Gallaway, and Frenze 1987 (study prepared for Senate Republicans that concluded, unsurprisingly, that tax increases fail to reduce the deficit because they prompt increased spending); and Hakken and Nielsen 1987 (study prepared for the Democratic

tionship that one would expect, given fiscal illusion and the greater popularity of government spending than taxation. This suggests that tax limits, to have any chance of being effective, would need to be linked to other complementary and comprehensive limits, such as on debt issuance and government spending.

3. Spending Limits

Spending limits are a final fiscal policy alternative to addressing tax lag. For example, one could adopt a constitutional limitation on federal spending as a percentage of GDP. Or one could limit annual spending growth, perhaps with allowances for such factors as inflation, population growth, and GDP growth. Or one could limit each year's spending to the prior year's revenue. Any such rule could have exceptions for military crises, severe recessions, and the like.

The most fundamental problem with spending limits is that, like tax limits, they address only one form of government activity. Positive spending can all too easily be converted to take the form of tax reduction. The "military supplier tax credit" example described above is no mere hypothetical. Politicians routinely advocate what are in substance spending programs through the mechanism of special exclusions, deductions, and credits in the Internal Revenue Code—"tax expenditures," in common (though controversial) parlance. One also can evade spending limits (or at least their underlying substantive goal) by shifting to the use of regulation. Consider once again the adoption of a minimum wage in lieu of wage subsidies, or of health care provided through employer mandates in lieu of explicit government spending.

In addition, spending limits would raise various practical problems. Appropriations often cannot have fixed dollar signs attached to them. A variety of programs, from building a new post office, to sending soldiers abroad, to providing benefits to all persons meeting specified qualifications, have costs that are not known in advance and yet could not very sensibly be shut down while in progress if their authorized funding ran out. Thus, an effective spending limit probably would have to be based on what actually took place, not just advance authori-

---

chairman of the House Budget Committee that, equally unsurprisingly, rebuts the Republican study). For a study of English fiscal practice that reaches the same broad empirical conclusion as von Furstenberg, Green, and Jeong, see Peacock and Wiseman (1979).

zations or estimates. Enforcement of a spending limit might require disruptive sequesters and lead to a variety of smoke-and-mirrors responses, such as postponing payments until just after the end of the fiscal year.

A further question posed by spending limits is whether anything should be exempt from them. California's Proposition 4 exempts payments for debt service from local governments' appropriation limits. This helps to protect lenders, and indirectly the local governments' credit ratings, but it also facilitates debt-financed spending. Moreover, the definition of "debt service" is elastic. In the federal setting, might it include government employee pensions—or perhaps even Social Security payments, either under present law or if benefits were tied more closely to contributions? In a recent California case under Proposition 4, the court held that the obligation to contribute to employee retirement plans constituted "debt service" and therefore could be ignored for purposes of computing the appropriations limit.[16]

D. Structural Alternatives within Political Institutions

Although both tax limits and spending limits may have some capacity to reduce the size of government, they are greatly weakened by their interchangeability both with each other and with alternative forms of government activity. Fiscal policy approaches inherently rely on overt dollar flows, whereas the size of government is intangible.

One might therefore want to act at a level more fundamental than fiscal policy, by addressing basic structures of political decision making. A structural political response could have the advantage, if successful, of affecting *all* government decisions comparably—decisions to regulate, no less than to tax or spend. While the possibilities are infinite, such a response could involve reconsidering the basic Madisonian structure of American government. Again, Madison and his fellow authors of the Constitution had thought to counter "faction"—a term that embraced ideological and religious, as well as economic interest group, activity—through two main prescriptions.

The first was strengthening the national government relative to the state governments. Madison predicted in the famous Federalist Paper Number 10 that such a shift would impede the formation of majority

16. *San Francisco Taxpayers Association,* note 14 above.

factions by increasing the range and diversity of interests in the electorate. The second prescription was disaggregating the exercise of power within the federal government, so that no group could swiftly or easily capture control of the whole. This involved (1) making the government tripartite, with separate executive, legislative, and judicial branches, each supreme within its realm; (2) creating a bicameral legislature, with different modes of election for the two houses of Congress; and (3) leaving the president, who presumably could act with more focused purpose than a multimember legislature, relatively weak in the key areas of legislating and control of the public purse. All taxing and spending decisions would be legislative, rather than executive, the veto power aside. Americans often do not realize how unusual this is, but, according to Joseph White and Aaron Wildavsky, "[n]o other nation has a legislature so strong [that] it actually dominates spending and taxing decisions" (1989, 1).

In short, the Madisonian response to faction involved spatial centralization of government alongside institutional decentralization. From a modern perspective, both prescriptions can be criticized. Spatial centralization may simply make politics more complicated and remote from the individual voter, increasing the opportunities for groups to seek wealth transfers or political control in their particular areas, while also adding to the costs of exit from the relevant jurisdiction. Institutional decentralization may simply promote logrolling between interest groups that are seeking distinct wealth transfers from the general population. It is worth considering whether either or both of these prescriptions could and should be reversed.

1. Centralizing Decision-Making Power within the Federal Government by Strengthening the Presidency

a. The Line-Item Veto

Strengthening the presidency is one obvious way to attempt increasing the centralization of power within the federal government. The president is a unitary official elected by vote of the entire nation, whereas Congress is a multiperson, bicameral body whose members are elected by local or statewide constituencies. The most commonly discussed device for strengthening the president's authority as it relates to the size of government—enacted in 1996[17] on an eight-year trial basis after

17. P.L. 104–130 (April 9, 1996).

years of discussion—is the line-item veto, under which the president can disapprove of part of a legislative bill while allowing the rest of it to become law. The power, as provided in the 1996 legislation, extends only to spending items (other than those under multiyear entitlements such as Social Security) and a narrow class of "targeted tax benefits" that are determined to benefit one hundred or fewer taxpayers.[18]

The enactment makes federal budgetary practice look more like that in the states, forty-three of which give their governors line-item vetoes. Of these, forty-two limit the power to legislative appropriations. Ten permit the governor to reduce as well as wholly disapprove an appropriation (see Briffault 1993, 1175–76).

For many years, it had been thought that a federal line-item veto was unconstitutional. Article 1, section 7 of the Constitution empowers the president only to approve or veto, presumably as a whole, "[e]very bill which shall have passed the House of Representatives and the Senate." The 1996 enactment largely avoids these constitutional problems—other than with respect to targeted tax benefits—by using a different formal approach: empowering the president to cancel spending subject to prompt congressional review. Congressional override of a line-item veto takes the form of enacting a "disapproval bill" with respect to the spending cancellation.

The line-item veto makes the presidential veto power a more nuanced, and thus powerful, weapon. The case for the line-item veto can be put either simplistically or sophisticatedly. Simplistically, one could argue that, as long as the president successfully uses the power even once to eliminate an appropriation, spending has been reduced. But this argument ignores the strategic element of political interactions between Congress and the president: different legislative provisions may be proposed in an environment with the line-item veto from one without it. Congress may, for example, enact more spending than it would otherwise, either so that more spending will survive more nuanced vetoes or because increased spending is the price the president sets for agreeing to approve legislation in full.

A more sophisticated argument for the line-item veto is twofold. First, the veto impedes logrolling within the legislature, since a veto-

18. A tax provision does not constitute a "targeted tax benefit" that is subject to the line-item veto if, among other things, it is deemed to extend the same treatment to all persons in the same industry, engaged in the same activity, owning the same type of property, or issuing the same type of investment.

proof president can unravel legislative bargains. Second, effectively shifting a quantum of legislative power to a unitary institution (the presidency) ostensibly reduces the overall legislative tendency to distribute particularized benefits to interest groups.

Even if one accepts these two points, however, the claim that the federal line-item veto will reduce government spending, the size of the government, or even the size of budget deficits can be questioned both empirically and theoretically. Econometric studies of relative spending levels in states with different types of gubernatorial veto powers have reached decidedly mixed conclusions. Some find that the line-item veto has no significant effect on spending,[19] while others find that it can be effective under specified circumstances, such as when the governor and the majority in the legislature belong to different parties or when the applicable rule permits the governor to reduce as well as wholly disapprove appropriations.[20] While econometric indeterminacy is neither surprising nor unusual, there are several reasons, all involving strategic behavior, for one to expect the line-item veto to have no significant effect on the size of government, even if presidents use it frequently and successfully.

On the executive side, it seems clear that a president who *wants* to reduce government spending can do so through the line-item veto, at least if his or her level of legislative support is intermediate, such that the president does not control the legislature yet has enough supporters to prevent veto override. Will presidents systematically use the power in this fashion, however? I noted above that the president can use the line-item veto to disrupt legislative logrolling. From another perspective, however, it simply adds one more party to the necessary logrolling coalition (or increases the president's bargaining power within the coalition). As Norman Ornstein puts it:

Presidential power—in whatever form—will be used to advance all Presidential interests. That means, ironically, that the

19. See, e.g., Holtz-Eakin 1988 (state budgets are not importantly altered by line-item veto); Zycher 1984 (finding no significant or consistent differences in spending between those states that have and those that lack the line-item veto). Arguably to similar effect, see Abney and Lauth 1985 (detailing results of mail-order survey suggesting that it was mainly used for partisan purposes that were distinct from fiscal restraint).

20. See, e.g., Alm and Evers 1991 (finding some tendency for the line-item veto to restrain spending when the governor and a legislative majority belong to different parties); Crain and Miller 1990, 1046.

line-item veto, over the long run, would probably *increase* spending, not cut it. Beyond any doubt, if the line-item veto had been available to President Reagan in 1984 when the MX missile was under fire in Congress, a number of calls would have been made to recalcitrant legislators from the White House, suggesting that a favored dam or federal building would be item-erased if the lawmaker did not reconsider and support funding for the MX. We would have paid for all those dams and buildings—along with more MXs. (1985, 331)

Even if one assumes that presidents will mainly use the line-item veto to restrain, not increase, spending, its potential significance is reduced by a degree of overlap with powers that the chief executive already has. Executive agencies, with varying degrees of presidential input, write regulations, follow discretionary enforcement policies, and make a variety of other decisions regarding how to implement laws and appropriations. A president also makes a variety of other decisions that legislators care about, such as on executive and judicial appointments or concerning the extent of presidential intervention (whether friendly or hostile) in legislators' reelection campaigns.

The exercise of these powers, just like the decision whether to exercise the line-item veto, can be traded for votes on particular legislative issues. If trading opportunities already were great enough, then adding one more power to the president's arsenal might make no difference. The president already has a highly nuanced ability to demand either higher or lower spending in exchange for other considerations.

In practice, however, while such trades no doubt are frequent, it seems likely that the line-item veto will add significantly to the president's arsenal. Unlike many of the discretionary tools the president possesses, the line-item veto power is both specific and easily disaggregated to the level of particular items. The president either vetoes or accepts specific appropriations, whereas a promise regarding general enforcement policy is both vaguer (and thus harder to monitor) and more difficult to connect, without legal impropriety, to particular beneficiaries whose interests a legislator wants to advance.

Thus, the line-item veto probably will marginally increase the president's bargaining power, although it remains ambiguous in what direction this power will most frequently be exercised. Still, Congress is hardly lacking in possible strategic responses. For example, it can respond in advance to likely line-item vetoes by padding the budget with added expenditure, both so that enough will survive the president's cuts and because, if it is not the last actor, its members may feel freer to be fiscally irresponsible in pursuit of a host of disaggregated short-term political gains (see, e.g., Devins 1990, 1005–6). Or it can make increased use of the tax code, rather than direct spending, to funnel benefits—perhaps without even having to avoid the "targeted tax benefit" rule, since that rule's constitutionality is unclear.

To be sure, a president who is sufficiently committed to reducing spending can respond to padding by simply increasing vetoes commensurately. Yet this may be politically unlikely. If both sides are mainly maneuvering to engage in plausible "credit claiming" before the audiences that matter to them politically, then the line-item veto may simply lead to a collaborative minuet. For example, a member of Congress may secure the inclusion in legislation of an unduly large local project (or two projects instead of one), fully expecting the president to scale it back (or veto one of the projects). The congressperson appears to have worked in the local voters' interests, and the president appears to have targeted legislative pork in view of the nation's interests; this posturing may contribute to the reelection of both, but it fails to reduce federal spending below what it would have been absent the line-item veto power.

Given these problems, the line-item veto should not be expected to yield significant reductions in government spending or the size of government. Only if the president's incentives, relative to those of Congress, systematically motivate him to prefer a smaller government, *and* if there is enough legislative backing to sustain vetoes but not enough to control initial legislative outcomes, will it even tend in the right direction. Even under those conditions, however, it will not accomplish very much.

b. Broader Impoundment Powers

Again, the line-item veto power granted in 1996 mainly enables the president to cancel certain spending, subject to congressional review that is analogous to veto override. The power could be made broader still by allowing the president to cancel authorized spending *without* congressional review. In the early 1970s, President Nixon claimed this power, referred to at the time as "impoundment," although he met with reverses both judicially and through the enactment of the Congressional Budget and Impoundment Control Act of 1974 (which the 1996 line-item veto legislation revises). Under Nixon's view, Congress not only was unable compel him to spend appropriated funds that he preferred to impound, but it did not even have a right to be informed that impoundment was taking place.

Nixon's claim of absolute impoundment power was widely, and perhaps appropriately, viewed as excessive, although one could argue that under established practice the president has roughly impoundment-like power in areas apart from spending. At least to some extent, the president can decide to "impound" a law, either by not enforcing it vigorously or by seeing to the issuance of weak regulations. It seems unlikely, however, that reviving unlimited presidential impoundment of authorized spending would significantly reduce the level of federal spending or the size of government. Just as under the line-item veto, the increased power might simply make the president more successful in demanding increased spending, or other policy initiatives, for favored purposes.

c. Other Possible Means of Shifting from Legislative toward Executive Budgeting

The line-item veto and impoundment only scratch the surface of the devices one could employ to increase the president's legislative power. Even in the area of fiscal policy, there are innumerable other alternatives. Yet many of these have a common theme of making the political system effectively more parliamentary, by moving in the direction of executive rather than legislative budgeting. Under such an approach, reversing that of present law, the president would mainly control the details of the budget, and Congress's power would extend little, if at all, past overall approval or disapproval.

While the president proposes a budget at the beginning of the fiscal year, this document has little practical significance. Legislators regularly declare it "dead on arrival." Even when the president's party controls Congress, the executive budget rarely serves as more than a starting point for extensive congressional deliberation.

In order to change these practices, one could give the president's budget greater legal significance and limit Congress's flexibility to depart from it other than by rejecting it altogether. For example, by constitutional amendment, one could deny Congress the power to initiate appropriations or to increase those in the president's budget. The Confederate Constitution of 1861—which also introduced the line-item veto to American practice—had such a rule, generally requiring expenditure proposals to originate with the president unless they were authorized by a two-thirds vote in both houses of the legislature (see Wells 1924).

Such proposals could more or less eliminate certain congressional strategic responses to a line-item veto or impoundment power, such as padding the budget with extra spending so that enough would remain or treating as many provisions as possible as the same "item." Yet the result might simply be role reversal, with the president now having the incentive to play games based on there being a subsequent actor. For example, in areas where the president preferred higher spending than did the congressional majority, he might propose still more spending than he really wanted in the hope that enough would survive the legislative process. Or the president might include spending provisions that he did not really want in exchange for a commitment by the congressional leadership to approve the spending provisions that he did want.

Accordingly, the claim that a shift toward executive budgeting, by whatever means, would reduce spending and the size of government depends crucially on the validity of the underlying claim that the president, as a unitary official elected by a national constituency, is likely to prefer lower spending than does Congress, as a multiperson, bicameral body whose members are elected by local or statewide constituencies. This claim is weaker than one might think.

d. Would Shifting Power from Congress to the President Tend to Reduce Spending and the Size of Government?

The claim that shifting power from Congress to the president would tend to reduce spending and the size of government stands on three main grounds, all of which relate to the two institutions' relative degrees of internal centralization. First, logrolling is more prevalent in Congress, where even powerful leaders may need to "buy" members' votes at retail. Second, the president, who serves a national constituency, may tend to be less dependent on any particular interest group. A Michigan politician has little choice but to support the automobile industry; a Texan the oil industry. The president can hardly ignore interest groups but is in a better position to pick and choose, making them compete for the privilege of allying with him.

Third, a president typically has much stronger political incentives than most members of Congress to pursue a broad general goal such as spending reduction (or, for that matter, deficit reduction), rather than to focus on providing particularized benefits to constituents. David Mayhew has explained how the electoral incentive for incumbent politicians to claim credit for legislative accomplishments often induces members of Congress to emphasize particularized benefits:

> [For an ordinary member of Congress], the prime mover role is a hard one to play on larger matters—at least before broad electorates. A claim, after all, has to be credible. If a Congressman goes before an audience and says, "I am responsible for passing a bill to curb inflation," or "I am responsible for the highway program," hardly anyone will believe him. (1974, 59)

Mayhew notes that even a congressman's truthful claims of responsibility for broad programs tend to be disbelieved, while false claims of responsibility for particularized benefits tend to be believed. The president, however, can plausibly claim credit even for broad developments that he did little to bring about, such as an economic expansion that reflected the business cycle and policies of the Fed. Restraining overall government spending is precisely the type of policy for which a president can plausibly claim credit.

Nonetheless, the claim that shifting power to the president would tend to reduce the size of government, government spending, or even the federal budget deficit, is fundamentally disputed in the political science literature. Some writers, such as Robert Inman and Michael Fitts, argue that a shift to congressional power, as well as increased decentralization within Congress, have yielded higher and more wasteful federal spending (see, e.g., Inman and Fitts 1990; Fitts and Inman 1992; Inman 1990). Yet many political scientists would agree instead with Norman Ornstein that "[o]ver time any executive-centered political system will almost certainly spend more than one with substantial legislative power" (1985, 331). Ornstein and others note that in recent decades, parliamentary democracies in western Europe and Japan generally have had higher government spending and larger budget deficits relative to GDP, along with more rapid growth in spending, than the United States (see Makin and Ornstein 1994, 265–68; Malbin 1984, 729; Ackley 1984).

Although those on the Inman-Fitts side could argue that this simply reflects our greater historical antipathy to a large national government, there are strong theoretical reasons why a more centralized and president-based system may tend to have higher government spending. They relate both to Mayhew's analysis of credit claiming and to the egoistic motivations that a politician must have in order to pursue so ambitious and laborious a goal as winning election to the presidency.

Most presidents both need and want to make a mark on the country in some significant way—whether it is Reagan seeking major tax cuts, domestic spending cuts, and a defense buildup, or Bush eager for the chance to play Churchill by confronting aggressive tyrants in the international arena, or Clinton pledging in 1992 that he will bring the American people fundamental "change," such as by "giving you health." Paul Peterson (1985) has noted that as a general matter, Republican presidents seek more defense spending and Democratic presidents seek more domestic spending than Congress wants.

The presidential ambition to make a mark on the country by doing something important is essentially a black box. Reducing the size of the federal government or the level of government spending is only one possible ambition. Other possibilities typically involve large-scale government expansion through the adoption of significant new programs. Indeed, for reasons of both political self-interest and electoral selection, an ambition to reduce the size of government—based on pledging to do less rather than to give people more—seems relatively unlikely among elected presidents unless a large portion of the electorate strongly supports this goal and can monitor the extent to which it is being accomplished. The goal of creating a massive new government program that will outlive one, and thus constitute one's lasting legacy, seems more natural and common.

As a historical matter, presidents have often contributed substantially to expanding both deficits and the size of government by playing the sort of dramatic policy-entrepreneurial role that few members of a disaggregated Congress would find feasible. As Paul Peterson and Mark Rom have noted:

> Deficit politics has proven to be a winning strategy for two popular presidents [Franklin Roosevelt and Ronald Reagan], both of whom had controversial agendas that shifted American policy in a new direction. . . . Overall, deficit politics became a vital component of the two strongest, most dramatic presidencies of the twentieth century. (1989, 179, 180)

Roosevelt clearly expanded the size of government, and Reagan arguably did so as well, at least in 1981, given that year's behavior-distorting tax act and the defense buildup that he oversaw. Moreover, to the list of important presidential deficit enhancers, one could add the names of both John Kennedy, who worked hard against congressional resistance to popularize 1960s-Keynesian tolerance of regular deficits, and Lyndon Johnson, who famously sought both guns and butter by simultaneously pursuing Great Society programs and the Vietnam War. No member of Congress, and indeed no Congress, has ever matched the government-expanding accomplishments of our most powerful and prominent twentieth-century presidents.

Given all this, one cannot easily reach a firm conclusion regarding the overall effect of presidential power on spending and the size of government. While Congress, because of internal logrolling, typically seeks to provide a greater volume of particularized benefits, presidents tend to be more interested in large-scale, internally coherent expansions of the federal government's role. Analogously, in foreign policy, nearly every president since Franklin Roosevelt has been interested in sending troops or other military and economic aid abroad in situations where Congress was reluctant to get involved.

e. Is Increasing "Gridlock" the Answer?

Even if presidents do not systematically prefer reduced spending and a smaller federal government, there is still one ground on which one could argue for increasing the president's budgetary or legislative powers. If Madisonian decentralization of power constrains, rather than expands, the size of government, and the presidency is currently significantly weaker than Congress in the legislative arena, then strengthening the president's role might reduce federal spending (and the size of government) by creating more frequent political deadlock. In effect, one would be adopting the widespread view that divided government leads to "gridlock" or legislative paralysis—except that one would view gridlock favorably and consider it presently insufficient given the president's limited budgetary powers.

Lloyd Cutler, among others, has claimed that gridlock systematically prevents deficit reduction (which might involve spending cuts) (see Mayhew 1991, 185). Yet he fails to explain why we should expect even a united president and Congress to be interested in deficit reduction or spending cuts. On the other hand, it is true that gridlock may promote tax lag by impeding reform of entitlement programs such as Social Security and Medicare. Increases in these programs take place automatically, without the need for new legislative action. Reforming entitlement programs to curb their runaway spending is easiest when one party controls the government. In a genuine two-party situation, each party is tempted to play chicken, leaving to the other the onus of arguing for painful but necessary spending cuts.

One clear result of gridlock is reduced accountability. Peterson and Rom point to American budget politics in the 1980s, in which both President Reagan and the Democratic Congress found blaming each other for the deficit more fruitful than trying to eliminate it through further unpalatable spending cuts or tax increases (Peterson and Rom 1989, 179). Accountability is another black box, however. One cannot easily tell what set of changes in policy it is likely to produce.

Making gridlock's significance murkier still, Mayhew argues that it is essentially a myth, and divided government is quite able to avoid legislative paralysis. His analysis of legislation from 1946 through 1990 suggests that the quantity of legislation—both overall and counting only what he deems important legislation—is unaffected by whether the president's party controls Congress (1991, 179). Divided government yields a more complicated legislative process and requires compromise among a larger group of political leaders, but it seems not, in the end, to constrain legislative activism.

One explanation that Mayhew offers for this finding is that the political parties are mere "policy factions," rather than strong and coherent political units, and that nominal party control often fails to correlate with effective control. In 1981, for example, the Republican President Reagan established a measure of working control in the House of Representatives despite its nominally Democratic majority. However, even effective control makes considerably less difference in the quantity of legislation than one might expect. Mayhew finds that legislative leaders, whether they are running for president or merely seeking acclaim as effective power brokers, often are no less motivated than the president to pursue major initiatives, and may be freer to do so if he is in the opposite party. Even when political foes control different stages of the legislative process, they often face shared pressures to produce visible accomplishments and avoid being blamed for what the media anoints as laudable "reform" efforts. The enactment of major tax reform in 1986, through cooperation between a Republican president, an independent-minded Republican Senate, and a Democratic House, provides a classic example.

In effect, a small oligopoly of leaders may produce no less legislative output than a one-person monopoly. This makes the question of what effect increasing presidential power would have even more indeterminate. As long as the number of influential actors remains small, strengthening any one actor's hand may lack systematic effects.

In the end, we know very little about how altering the extent of the federal government's institutional decentralization would affect the size of government. The one thing that *is* clear is that if the public sufficiently strongly preferred limited government, then greater centralization, such as by strengthening the president, would empower the public to demand it effectively. However, this is of purely hypothetical importance if the public's preferences regarding the size of government are mixed and changeable, or its ability to monitor too limited. Mayhew observes that "[n]othing we know about electoral behavior suggests that American voters, whatever the circumstances of party control, will reward a government for balancing budgets" (190). They may be equally unlikely to reward a government for reducing the scale of its operations, as distinct from better tailoring those operations to serve particular interests.

2. *Other Possible Centralizing Changes to the Federal Government*

If one nonetheless continues to prefer institutional centralization, strengthening the presidency relative to Congress represents only one possibility. Even short of adopting a full parliamentary system, other alternatives that would tend in the same direction include strengthening the role played by the political parties and increasing the power of the congressional leadership. The parties' power could be increased through campaign finance reform that gave them, rather than individual members, a central role in fund-raising. Or the parties could change their own rules to give leaders more say, and electoral primaries less, in nominating candidates for Congress and the presidency. What might matter most of all, but seems hardest to accomplish, would be a reversal of the ongoing decline in voters' party loyalties and affiliations.

As for increasing the power of the congressional leadership, this has already taken place in recent years. Although 1970s congressional reforms transferred much internal power from the leadership to subcommittees that, in alliance with the agencies and interest groups in their areas, formed tight "iron triangles" governing their areas, the leadership began regaining power in the 1980s (see Peterson and Rom 1989, 167). This trend has continued in the 1990s—as with Speaker of the House Newt Gingrich's 1995 decision to appoint committee chairs (with the concurrence of the Republican Party caucus) with only limited regard to seniority. Yet these changes have not had consistent effects on tax lag, government spending, or the size of government.

3. Shifting Broad Powers from the Federal Government to the States

Spatial decentralization is the second way to reverse the Madisonian prescription for limiting the size of government. Would shifting power to the states yield better and more definite results than increasing the federal government's institutional centralization?

Even if the answer to this question is yes, there is a question of means. Over a period of many decades, the courts have permitted the federal government's powers to expand far beyond anything contemplated by the authors of the Constitution, mainly through an elastic interpretation of the authority to regulate interstate commerce (and thus anything remotely pertaining to it). For better or worse, however, the battle to read the Commerce Clause narrowly is probably irrevocably lost—despite recent indications that the Supreme Court may attempt to narrow it slightly.[21] One also hears little talk of a constitutional amendment to limit the federal government's powers. Thus, devolution would probably need to be statutory and hence reversible.

The main advantages of shifting power from the national to the state and local levels are several. The latter governments, even in the aggregate, have less fiscal resources than the federal government. They cannot print money and are less able to increase tax revenues given the greater ease of taxpayer exit. Even when their fiscal resources are adequate, some policies are hard for them to pursue effectively without substantial cooperation from other states.

An important example is progressive wealth redistribution, which generally cannot be accomplished effectively below the national level. Wealthy residents need not stay in a jurisdiction that attempts to transfer significant wealth from them to poorer residents. Leaving the entire country tends to be considerably less feasible. When one considers as well the implications of ease of entry, it becomes clear that states and localities, if responsible for financing and setting the levels for social welfare payments to the needy, are likely to find themselves in a "race

---

21. See United States v. Lopez, 115 S. Ct. 1624 (1995).

to the bottom." The more a jurisdiction pays, the more it drives out wealthy taxpayers and attracts additional needy individuals.

The relative ease of entry and exit at the state and local levels has implications not only for the overall size of government (including the scope of progressive wealth redistribution policies) but also for government effectiveness in providing services to taxpayers. As Charles Tiebout (1956) first systematically explored, multiple small jurisdictions that must compete for residents and taxpayers may end up competing against each other much like private businesses, leading them both to specialize and perhaps to perform better. One can see this in the way jurisdictions devote different resource levels to public schools, and sometimes have extremely good ones. As a result of Tiebout competition, devolution of authority to the state and local levels can improve government's quality even absent any reduction in the overall size of government.

So much for the main ways in which devolution can either reduce the overall size of government or improve what remains. There also are a number of respects in which it can make government larger and more burdensome. When many small governments, rather than one large one, are engaged in doing something, each in a distinctive way—whether it is levying taxes, regulating advertising, setting product safety rules—the results may include inefficient duplication of government function and vastly greater compliance complexity. In the area of state and local taxation alone, I have very roughly estimated that overall administration and compliance costs might approach $20 billion annually (Shaviro 1993b, 31). Yet taxation is only one area in which these problems arise. In areas of substantive regulation, such as establishing product safety or pollution requirements, businesses may find it impossible to comply simultaneously with inconsistent state rules, potentially leading to the breakdown of national markets for goods and services.

While such harm may be inadvertent, state and local governments have two great temptations to enact affirmatively harmful rules. First, they often are politically motivated to discriminate against interstate commerce at the behest of local producers. Either taxes or regulations may be designed to function like tariffs, making goods produced outside the jurisdiction costlier or even unavailable. Even exclusionary policies that do not benefit the jurisdiction overall may prevail politically if consumers are less well organized and well informed than local producers.

Second, state and local governments often are motivated to engage in tax exportation, by designing their tax systems so that outsiders, rather than voters, will pay the taxes (or at least appear to do so). Jurisdictions are most likely to engage in government spending that is dubious in cost-benefit terms if the voters at least believe that outsiders are paying for it. It should be no surprise that the two states with the highest per capita spending are Alaska and Wyoming—hardly bastions, one would think, of "big government" but states that happen to derive most of their tax revenues from severance taxes on oil and coal. These are taxes that appear to be borne by outside consumers, although an economist might argue that in the long run they fall on local land or resource owners (39).

The federal government can exercise and sometimes has exercised its authority (either legislatively or judicially) to mandate the application of uniform legal rules, to eliminate instances of discrimination against interstate commerce, and to limit tax exportation. This helps to show that the exercise of greater authority at the national level may at times actually reduce the overall size of government. Thus, the strategy of devolution to the state and local level lacks consistent general implications. While it nonetheless merits case-by-case exploration in particular areas, the ultimate benefits would probably lie more in the area of fiscal federalism—locating authority at the "right" level in order to maximize efficiency and public satisfaction—than reducing the size of government.

E. Conclusions Regarding the Size of Government

In the end, concern about the size of government provides the most powerful reason for disliking tax lag. Tax lag tends to increase government spending because of fiscal illusion plus current voters' indifference to costs that they can pass forward. It thus exacerbates already-existing tendencies to adopt undesirable programs. Despite the empirical uncertainties, I am less agnostic about the claim that tax lag promotes bad government spending than about the claims that its generational or macroeconomic consequences are undesirable—albeit that in each case, one ultimately must make a leap of faith about a broad and indeterminate issue.

Nonetheless, concern about the size of government, no less than the other two concerns, fails to support the conclusion that reducing tax lag should be central to current debate and policy, much less mandated by a binding legal rule. There is simply too much reason to doubt the approach's effectiveness. The recently proposed BBA seems especially likely to have disappointing results if adopted.

Alternative fiscal policy approaches to restricting the size of government, focusing on debt issuance or enforceability or on either taxes or spending considered alone, appear no more promising. Proposals to reverse elements of our Madisonian political structure through institutional centralization within the federal government and/or spatial decentralization in favor of state and local governments also lack definite implications.

Perhaps if democratic government systematically, but in protean fashion, tends to overreach, there is little one can ultimately do, beyond arguing the merits of good policy both directly in broad philosophical terms and in each particular case. Moreover, despite the problem of democratic overreach, there is little reason to think that any other form of government, including rule by economists and other fiscal policy experts, would be better.

EIGHT

Conclusion

The underlying phenomenon with which budget deficits tend to correlate but that generational accounting measures more accurately is *tax lag:* the accrual of government spending in advance of tax revenues because of (1) underspecification of the tax increases or spending cuts that will ultimately be necessary and/or (2) burden-shifting to younger individuals and future generations. Our present policy of substantial and growing tax lag matters for three fundamental, long-term reasons and one prudential, short-term reason. The three long-term reasons—generational, macroeconomic, and effects on the level of government spending—all have the same cause. While all government spending must and will be paid for by someone at some point, tax lag reduces both its perceived and its actual cost to current consumers and voters. They either underestimate the implied future taxes or else are glad to shift the tax burden to future generations.

By increasing current generations' perceived and actual wealth, tax lag induces them to consume more than they otherwise would. It generally reduces saving and economic growth to the detriment of future generations, except in the case of Keynesian slack, where it can permanently increase market consumption that would otherwise have been permanently forgone. Tax lag also induces people to accept or even demand increased government spending, by reducing its perceived cost.

These effects do not have strong normative implications for policy, however. First, there may be nothing wrong with benefiting present at the expense of future generations. As long as our descendants will be wealthier than we are, reducing tax lag so that we will consume less and they will consume more may amount to playing Robin Hood in reverse. Or, if the future is sufficiently dark—owing, for example, to a pending nuclear or ecological calamity—then attempting to shift consumption from us to them might prove futile. Overall, the empirical and philosophical uncertainties concerning generational policy are simply too great to support concluding with any confidence that present generations are consuming too much rather than the right amount or too little.

Second, increasing current consumption at the expense of saving and investment is not necessarily bad. Even within a single generation, the choice between present and future consumption presents a difficult tradeoff. While there are some reasons for concluding that we are saving too little—such as the tendency of the income tax to reduce saving and the collective action problems that deter saving for general societal, as distinct from household, benefit—reducing tax lag is only one possible response. Moreover, it might be a partly or wholly self-defeating response if it involved increasing the income tax's deterrent effect on saving, or eliminating government spending that constitutes valuable long-term investment.

As for Keynesian fiscal policy, countercyclical tax lag may have some value when it takes place automatically, as when income tax revenues drop and welfare benefits increase during a recession. However, deliberate countercyclical fiscal policy, such as through enacting anti-recessionary tax cuts and spending increases, is likely to do more harm than good in a political environment rife with inappropriately short-term incentives and with slow response times. Deliberate management of the business cycle should generally be left to the Federal Reserve Board, acting through monetary policy.

Finally, while tax lag's effect on government spending levels seems undesirable if one thinks that the government is too large, in the end the amount that government spends correlates only very roughly with its size. The real size of government is a function of the magnitude of its effects. Two same-dollar tax levies or spending programs can have radically different effects on such underlying concerns as wealth distribution, efficiency, and liberty. Moreover, undesirable government activity need not involve explicit taxes and spending. Regulatory mandates, while equivalent in principle, are off-budget. At times, the costs that they impose may be even less visible than the future taxes implied by tax lag. Attempting to reduce the size of government by addressing only tax lag might prove, in the end, little better than trying to reduce the size of a balloon by pushing it in on one side.

Skepticism about the efficacy of seeking to reduce the government's size by reducing tax lag is made all the stronger by the difficulty of measuring tax lag properly. Generational accounting, while intellectually an enormous advance over the budget deficit, is too subject to estimating manipulation to provide a promising basis for a binding legal rule. The budget deficit, while more salient politically, is too myopic and manipulable through smoke-and-mirrors policy changes to provide a strong constraint.

The most recently considered version of the balanced budget amendment offers less hope still of restricting the size of government. It would have allowed any and all deficits that received 60 percent approval in Congress—thus potentially increasing deficits and spending because of the need for more extensive logrolling to assemble winning coalitions. In addition, it lacked a constitutional enforcement mechanism. Thus, deficits might simply cease to be officially authorized, while still continuing to occur.

Thus, while there are three fundamental, long-term reasons why tax lag matters, none has clear implications for policy or justifies keeping budget deficits at center stage politically. Yet there is also a prudential, short-term reason for our present policy of substantial and growing tax lag to have important implications for current policy. This is the problem of policy sustainability.

The best projections from a variety of sources—not just generational accounting but conventional deficit, Social Security, and Medicare projections—all indicate that the present degree of tax lag is not sustainable indefinitely, or indeed for very much longer. These projections might prove wrong if economic growth speeds up considerably. Yet they also could turn out to *under*estimate the speed with which present fiscal policy is becoming unsustainable, and with which a change of course will therefore be necessary.

Again, the term "tax *lag*" is appropriate because, over the long term, no government spending is free; all of it must and will be paid for by someone. Even if the national debt is never repaid but remains outstanding indefinitely, taxpayers bear it economically by paying interest. Even default—either actual or the implicit, partial default that results from using inflation to reduce the debt's real value—does not eliminate the need to pay for government spending. Instead, it merely shifts the cost from taxpayers to bondholders—functioning, in effect, as a one-time tax on the latter (perhaps to be handed back to taxpayers, over time, in the form of higher interest rates).

While in principle tax lag must ultimately be reversed through tax acceleration (taxes in excess of current and accruing government spending apart from interest), there is no theoretically necessary time when this must happen. Indeed, ever-increasing tax lag can be a stable policy as long as the unprovided-for tax burden—both explicit national debt and the value of accruing unfunded future spending obligations—is not becoming too great relative to the size of the economy.

Ever-increasing tax lag is conceptually a kind of Ponzi scheme (even when kept to sustainable levels). Paying each generation of investors by taking cash from the next is a zero-sum game, but one in which all participants come out ahead as long the scheme continues to work. In principle, Ponzi schemes can go on forever. In practice, they never do. When they collapse, societal wealth does not decrease— the schemes involve only cash transfers, not the creation or destruction of real societal wealth—but later investors suffer overall losses (paying for the earlier ones' overall gains) and have their expectations disappointed.

To call our fiscal policy over the last fifty years a giant Ponzi scheme is not hyperbole but precise analytic description. Each generation has come out ahead by passing on a larger deferred tax bill to the next. However, the growth of unfunded obligations—less from explicit debt than from Social Security and Medicare—relative to GDP indicates that the Ponzi scheme probably cannot be sustained in its current form for much longer. Those managing our fiscal and monetary policy already face a choice, which will only grow starker over time, among (1) tax increases, (2) benefit reductions, (3) debt issuance at a level that risks increasing interest rates and crowding out domestic private investment, and (4) printing money. Option 4 can indirectly implement options 1 through 3, if present law inflation adjustments, such as for income tax brackets and Social Security payments, are weakened or eliminated.

While this prognosis may sound grim, one should keep in mind that what we are talking about, at least in a direct, first-order sense, is for the most part simply cash transfers between different people through the medium of the government—not the actual, and so far ever-growing, level of our society's real economic resources. (The case of Medicare is more complicated, since it involves a particular use of real resources: providing subsidized medical care to certain individuals.) The main problem is one of disappointed expectations and reliance, although policy changes such as distortive tax increases or inflation could have indirect behavioral effects that reduced real societal wealth.

The problem is one of transition from unrealistic to realistic expectations about what government-provided benefits, at what cost in lifetime taxes, people can actually expect in a world where resources are finite. Fiscal policy must change, and therefore it will change—sooner or later, and in one way or another. At some point, it will likely find a more stable new equilibrium. Even during the transition period, our society's overall material well-being will probably continue to increase. Whether it does or not will depend more on technological, environmental, demographic, and political factors than on fiscal policy.

At the level of subjective expectations, the fiscal policy transition has already begun. Few younger Americans today expect from Social Security and Medicare even the benefits that present law seems to promise them. At the level of public policy, many are already calling for the transition to begin, and it is likely to prove all the smoother the sooner it begins.

Bibliography

Abascal, Ralph S., and John R. Kramer. 1974. "Presidential impoundment, part II: Judicial and legislative responses." *Georgetown Law Journal* 63:149.

Abney, Glenn, and Thomas P. Lauth. 1985. "The line-item veto in the states: An instrument for fiscal restraint or an instrument for partisanship?" *Public Administration Review* 45:372.

Abrams, Burton A., and William R. Dougan. 1986. "The effects of constitutional restraints on governmental spending." *Public Choice* 49:101.

Achenbaum, W. Andrew. 1986. *Social Security: Visions and revisions.* Cambridge: Cambridge University Press.

Ackerman, Bruce. 1980. *Social justice in the liberal state.* New Haven, Conn.: Yale University Press.

Ackley, Gardner. 1984. "Leviathan revisited: Macroeconomic evidence on the relative size of government." *Rackham Reports* (fall).

Ahmen, Shaghil. 1986. "Temporary and permanent government spending in an open economy." *Journal of Monetary Economics* 17:197.

Akerlof, George A. 1984. *An economic theorist's book of tales.* Cambridge: Cambridge University Press.

Akerlof, George A., and Janet L. Yellen. 1986. "A near-rational model of the business cycle with wage and price inertia." *Quarterly Journal of Economics* 100:823.

Alm, James, and Mark Evers. 1991. "The item veto and state government expenditures." *Public Choice* 68:1.

Alt, James E., and Robert C. Lowry. 1994. "Divided government, fiscal institutions, and budget deficits: Evidence from the states." *American Political Science Review* 88:811.

Altonji, Joseph G., Fumio Hayashi, and Laurence J. Kotlikoff. 1992. "Is the extended family altruistically linked? Direct tests using micro data." *American Economic Review* 82 (December): 1177.

Amacher, Ryan, and Holley Ulbrich. 1987. *Principles of economics.* 4th ed. Cincinnati: South-Western.

Andreoni, James. 1989. "Giving with impure altruism: Applications to charity and Ricardian equivalence." *Journal of Political Economy* 97:1447.

Andrews, William D. 1974. "A consumption-type or cash flow personal income tax." *Harvard Law Review* 87:1113.

311

Aranson, Peter H., Ernest Gellhorn, and Glen O. Robinson. 1982. "A theory of legislative delegation." *Cornell Law Review* 68:1.

Arrow, Kenneth J. 1963. *Social choice and individual values.* New York: Yale University Press.

Attfield, Robin. 1983. *The ethics of environmental concern.* Oxford: Blackwell.

Auerbach, Alan J. 1993. "Public finance in theory and practice." *National Tax Journal* 46:519.

Auerbach, Alan J., and Laurence J. Kotlikoff. 1983. "National saving, economic welfare, and the structure of taxation." In *Behavioral simulation methods in tax policy analysis,* ed. Martin Feldstein. Chicago: University of Chicago Press.

Auerbach, Alan J., Jagadeesh Gokhale, and Laurence J. Kotlikoff. 1991. "Generational accounts: A meaningful alternative to deficit accounting." In *Tax policy and the economy* 5, ed. David Bradford. Cambridge: MIT Press.

———. 1994. "Generational accounting: A meaningful way to evaluate fiscal policy." *Journal of Economic Perspectives* 8:73.

Bailyn, Bernard. 1967. *The ideological origins of the American Revolution.* Cambridge, Mass.: Belknap.

Ball, Laurence, Douglas W. Elmendorf, and N. Gregory Mankiw. 1995. "The deficit gamble." Working paper 5015. Cambridge, Mass.: National Bureau of Economic Research.

Ball, Terence. 1985. "The incoherence of intergenerational justice." *Inquiry* 28:321.

Barnett, Harold T., and Chandler Morse. 1963. *Scarcity and growth: The economics of natural resource availability.* Baltimore: Johns Hopkins University Press.

Barro, Robert J. 1974. "Are government bonds net wealth?" *Journal of Political Economy* 82:1095.

———. 1976. "Reply to Feldstein and Buchanan." *Journal of Political Economy* 84:343.

———. 1979. "On the determination of the public debt." *Journal of Political Economy* 87:940.

———. 1989. "The Ricardian approach to budget deficits." *Journal of Economic Perspectives* 3:37.

Barro, Robert J., and Glenn M. McDonald. 1979. "Social Security and consumer spending in an international cross-section." *Journal of Public Economics* 11:275.

Barthold, Thomas A. 1993. "How should we measure distribution?" *National Tax Journal* 46:291.

Bastable, C. F. 1922. *Public finance.* London: Macmillan.

Bernheim, B. Douglas. 1989. "A neoclassical perspective on budget deficits." *Journal of Economic Perspectives* 3:55.

Bernheim, B. Douglas, and Kyle Bagwell. 1988. "Is everything neutral?" *Journal of Political Economy* 96:308.

Bernheim, B. Douglas, Andrei Shleifer, and Lawrence H. Summers. 1976. "The strategic bequest motive." *Journal of Political Economy* 93:1045.

Bernheim, B. Douglas, John Karl Scholz, and John B. Shoven. 1991. "Consumption taxation in a general equilibrium model: How reliable are simulation results." In *National saving and economic performance,* ed. B. Douglas Bernheim and John B. Shoven. Chicago: University of Chicago Press.

Bittker, Boris. 1969. "Accounting for federal 'tax subsidies' in the federal budget." *National Tax Journal* 22:244.

Blinder, Alan. 1985. "Comment on 'federal deficits, interest rates, and monetary policy.'" *Journal of Money, Credit, and Banking* 17:685.

Boskin, Michael J. 1982. "Federal government deficits: Some myths and realities." *American Economic Review* 72:296.

Boulding, Kenneth E. 1984. "Sources of reasonable hope for the future." *American Economic Review* 74:221.

Bowen, William G., Richard G. Davis, and David H. Kopf. 1964. "The public debt: A burden on future generations." In *Public debt and future generations*, ed. James M. Ferguson. Chapel Hill: University of North Carolina Press.

Bradford, David F. 1988. "Tax expenditures and the problem of accounting for government." In *Tax expenditures and government policy*, ed. Neil Bruce. Kingston, Ontario: Queen's University, John Deutsch Institute for the Study of Economic Policy.

———. 1991. "Market value versus financial accounting measures of national saving." In *National saving and economic performance*, ed. B. Douglas Bernheim and John B. Shoven. Chicago: University of Chicago Press.

Break, George F. 1991. "Proposition 13's tenth birthday: Occasion for celebration or lament?" In *Proposition 13: A ten-year retrospective*, ed. Frederick D. Stocker. Cambridge, Mass: Lincoln Institute of Land Policy.

Brennan, H. Geoffrey, and James Buchanan. 1977. "Towards a tax constitution for Leviathan." *Journal of Public Economics* 8:255.

———. 1980. *The power to tax: Analytical foundations of a fiscal constitution.* Cambridge: Cambridge University Press.

———. 1981. *Monopoly in money and inflation: The case for a constitution to discipline government.* London: Institute of Economic Affairs.

Brewer, John. 1989. *The sinews of power: War, money, and the English state 1688–1783.* New York: Alfred A. Knopf.

Briffault, Richard. 1993. "The item veto in state courts." *Temple Law Review* 66:1171.

Brilmayer, Lea. 1994. *American hegemony.* New Haven, Conn.: Yale University Press.

Brink, R. A., et al. 1977. "Soil deterioration and the growing world demand for food." *Science* 197:625–30.

Buchanan, James. 1964a. "Concerning future generations." In *Public debt and future generations*, ed. James M. Ferguson. Chapel Hill: University of North Carolina Press.

———. 1964b. "The Italian tradition in fiscal theory." In *Public debt and future generations*, ed. James M. Ferguson. Chapel Hill: University of North Carolina Press.

———. 1964c. "Public debt, cost theory, and the fiscal illusion." In *Public debt and future generations*, ed. James M. Ferguson. Chapel Hill: University of North Carolina Press.

———. 1976. "Barro on the Ricardian equivalence theorem." *Journal of Political Economy* 84:337.

———. 1986a. *Liberty, market, and state.* New York: New York University Press.

———. 1986b. "Organization theory and fiscal economics: Society, state, and public debt." *Journal of Law, Economics, and Organization* 2:215.

———. 1993. "We should save more in our own economic interest." In *Justice across generations: What does it mean?* ed. Lee M. Cohen. Washington, D.C.: Public Policy Institute of the American Association of Retired Persons.

Buchanan, James, and Jennifer Roback. 1987. "The incidence and effects of public debt in the absence of fiscal illusion." *Public Finance Quarterly* 15 (January): 5.

Buchanan, James, and Gordon Tullock. 1962. *The calculus of consent: Logical foundations of constitutional democracy.* Ann Arbor: University of Michigan Press.

Buchanan, James, and Richard Wagner. 1977. *Democracy in deficit: The political legacy of Lord Keynes.* New York: Academic Press.

Buiter, Willem H., and James Tobin. 1979. "Debt neutrality: A brief review of doctrine and evidence." In *Social Security versus private savings*, ed. George von Furstenberg. Cambridge, Mass: Ballinger.

Burke, Edmund. 1989. *Reflections on the revolution in France*. Reprint, New York: Anchor Books.

Burnham, David. 1989. *A law unto itself: Power, politics, and the IRS*. New York: Random House.

California Joint Legislative Budget Committee. 1988. *Proposition 13, ten years later*. Sacramento.

Carroll, Christopher D., and Lawrence H. Summers. 1991. "Consumption growth parallels income growth: Some new evidence." In *National saving and economic performance*, ed. B. Douglas Bernheim and John Shoven. Chicago: University of Chicago Press.

Congressional Budget Office. 1995. "Who pays and when? An assessment of generational accounting" (November).

Cox, Donald. 1987. "Motives for private income transfers." *Journal of Political Economy* 95:508.

Cox, W. Michael, and Eric Hirschhorn. 1983. "The market value of U.S. government debt: Monthly, 1942–1980." *Journal of Monetary Economics* 11 (March): 261.

Crain, W. Mark, and James C. Miller III. 1990. "Budget process and spending growth." *William and Mary Law Review* 31:1021.

Crosthwait, Gay Aynesworth. 1983. "Article III problems in enforcing a balanced budget amendment." *Columbia Law Review* 83:1065.

Cutler, David. 1993. Review of *Generational accounting*, by Lawrence Kotlikoff. *National Tax Journal* 45:61.

Dale, Edwin L. Jr. 1973. "The security of Social Security: The young pay for the old." *New York Times Magazine*, January 14, pp. 8, 45.

Denison, Edward F. 1967. *Why growth rates differ: Postwar experiences in nine western countries*. Washington: Brookings Institution.

Devins, Neal. 1990. "Budget reform and the balance of powers." *William and Mary Law Review* 31:993.

Doernberg, Richard, and Fred C. McChesney. 1987. "On the accelerating rate and decreasing durability of tax reform." *Minnesota Law Review* 71:913.

Douglas, Carol, and Amy Hamilton. 1994. "State voters were cool to tax limits." *Tax Notes* 65 (November 21): 943.

Downs, Anthony J. 1957. *An economic theory of democracy*. New York: Harper and Row.

Drazen, Allan. 1978. "Government debt, human capital, and bequests in a life-cycle model." *Journal of Political Economy* 86:505.

Dwyer, Gerald P., Jr. 1985. "Federal deficits, interest rates, and monetary policy." *Journal of Money, Credit, and Banking* 17:655.

Edelman, Murray. 1964. *The symbolic uses of politics*. Urbana: University of Illinois Press.

Egol, Morton. 1986. "Deficit is worse than we're told." *New York Times*, June 13, p. 34A (letter to editor).

Eisner, Robert. 1983. "Social Security, saving, and macroeconomics." *Journal of Macroeconomics* 5:1.

———. 1986. *How real is the federal deficit?* New York: Free Press.

———. 1994. *The misunderstood economy: What counts and how to count it*. Boston: Harvard Business School Press.

Elliot, Robert. 1986. "Future generations, Locke's proviso and libertarian justice." *Journal of Applied Philosophy* 3:217.

Elliott, E. Donald. 1985. "Constitutional conventions and the deficit." *Duke Law Journal* 1077.

Ellwood, John W. 1983. "Budget control in a redistributive environment." In *Making economic policy in Congress,* ed. Allen Schick. Washington, D.C.: American Enterprise Institute for Public Policy Research.

Espenshade, Thomas, and Tracy Ann Goodis. 1987. "Demographic trends shaping the American family and workforce." In *America in transition: Benefits for the future,* Employee Benefit Research Institute. Washington, D.C.: Employee Benefit Research Institute.

Evans, Paul. 1986. "Is the dollar high because of large budget deficits?" *Journal of Monetary Ecomonics* 18:227.

———. 1993. "Consumers are not Ricardian: Evidence from nineteen countries." *Economic Inquiry* 31 (October): 534

Feldstein, Martin. 1974. "Social Security, induced retirement, and aggregate capital accumulation." *Journal of Political Economy* 82:905.

———. 1976. "Perceived wealth in bonds and Social Security: A comment." *Journal of Political Economy* 84:331.

———. 1988. "The effects of fiscal policies when incomes are uncertain: A contradiction to Ricardian equivalence." *American Economic Review* 78:14.

Feldstein, Martin, and Douglas W. Elmendorf. 1989. "Budget deficits, tax incentives, and inflation: A surprising lesson from the 1982–1984 recovery." In *Tax Policy and the economy* 3, ed. Lawrence H. Summers. Cambridge: MIT Press.

Fenno, Richard. 1973. *Congressmen in committees.* Boston: Little, Brown.

Ferguson, James M. 1964. "Introduction." In *Public debt and future generations,* ed. James M. Ferguson. Chapel Hill: University of North Carolina Press.

Field, Mervin. 1988. "The mood of California voters in 1987 regarding taxes and government spending." In California Joint Legislative Budget Committee 1988.

Fiorina, Morris P. 1977. *Congress: Keystone of the Washington establishment.* New Haven, Conn.: Yale University Press.

Fitts, Michael, and Robert Inman. 1992. "Controlling Congress: Presidential influence in domestic fiscal policy." *Georgetown Law Journal* 80:1737.

Flaubert, Gustav. 1965. *Madame Bovary,* trans. and ed. Paul De Man. New York: W. W. Norton.

Foell, Earl W. 1986. "Could the ancestral home of the potato ever turn out stereos?" *Christian Science Monitor,* June 24, p. 3.

Friedman, Benjamin. 1988. *Day of reckoning: The consequences of American economic policy under Reagan and after.* New York: Random House.

Friedman, David. 1993. "Comment on Buchanan: Do we save too little?" In *Justice across generations: What does it mean?* ed. Lee M. Cohen. Washington, D.C.: Public Policy Institute.

Friedman, Milton. 1969. "Has fiscal policy been oversold?" In *Monetary vs. fiscal policy,* ed. Milton Friedman and Walter Heller. New York: W. W. Norton.

Fullerton, Don, John B. Shoven, and John Whalley. 1983. "Replacing the U.S. income tax with a progressive consumption tax." *Journal of Public Economics* 20:3.

Georges, Christopher. 1994. "Clinton now faces a race with GOP Congress to cut taxes, budget while protecting his base." *Wall Street Journal,* November 14, p. A12.

Georgescu-Roegen, Nicholas. 1971. *The entropy law and the economic process.* Cambridge: Harvard University Press.

Gokhale, Jagadeesh, Laurence J. Kotlikoff, and John Sabelhaus. 1995. "Understanding the postwar decline in United States saving: A cohort analysis." Unpublished manuscript, April.

Goode, Richard, and C. Eugene Steuerle. 1994. "Generational accounting and fiscal policy." *Tax Notes* 65 (November 21): 1027.

Gramlich, Edward M. 1989. "Budget deficits and national saving: Are politicians exogenous?" *Journal of Economic Perspectives* 3 (spring): 23.

———. 1990. "U.S. federal budget deficits and Gramm-Rudman-Hollings." *American Economic Review* 80:75.

Griffith, Thomas. 1989. "Theories of personal deductions in the income tax." *Hastings Law Journal* 40:343.

Groves, Harold M. 1974. *Tax philosophers: Two hundred years of thought in Great Britain and the United States.* Madison: University of Wisconsin Press.

Gultekin, N. Bulent, and Dennis E. Logue. 1979. "Social Security and personal saving: Survey and new evidence." In *Social Security versus private saving,* ed. George M. von Furstenberg. Cambridge, Mass: Ballinger.

Haig, Robert M. 1959. "The concept of income—economic and legal aspects." In *Readings in the economics of taxation,* ed. R. Musgrave and C. Shoup. Homewood, Ill.: Irwin.

Hakken, Jon, and Rosemarie Nielsen. 1987. "The relationship between federal taxes and spending: An examination of recent research." Congressional Budget Office, August.

Hamilton, Alexander, James Madison, and John Jay. 1961. *The Federalist papers.* Reprint, New York and Scarborough, Ontario: New American Library.

Hayashi, Fumio. 1985. "The effect of liquidity constraints on consumption: A cross-sectional analysis." *Quarterly Journal of Economics* 100:183.

Heller, Walter. 1966. *New dimensions of political economy.* Cambridge: Harvard University Press.

———. 1969. "Is monetary policy being oversold?" In *Monetary versus fiscal policy,* ed. Milton Friedman and Walter Heller. New York: W. W. Norton.

Hill, Christopher. 1961. *The century of revolution 1603–1714.* New York: W. W. Norton.

Hill, Patricia. 1992. "Key budget official says an amendment to balance budget would be a 'hoax.' " *The Bond Buyer,* May 7.

Holcombe, Randall G., John D. Jackson, and Asghar Zardkoohi. 1981. "The national debt controversy." *Kyklos* 34:186.

Holtz-Eakin, Douglas. 1988. "The line item veto and public sector budgets: Evidence from the states." *Journal of Public Economics* 36:269.

Hume, David. 1764. "Essay IX: On public credit." In *Essays and treatises on several subjects,* vol. I, pp. 382–400. London: A. Miller in the Strand.

Inman, Robert P. 1990. "Public debts and fiscal politics: How decide?" *American Economic Review* 80:81.

Inman, Robert, and Michael Fitts. 1990. "Political institutions and fiscal policy: Evidence from the U.S. historical record." *Journal of Law, Economics, and Organization* 6:79.

Kahn, Douglas A., and Jeffrey S. Lehman. 1992. "Tax expenditure budgets: A critical view." *Tax Notes* 54:1661.

Kaldor, Nicholas. 1983. "Keynesian economics after fifty years." In *Keynes and the modern world,* ed. David Worswick and James Trevithick. Cambridge: Cambridge University Press.

Kaplow, Louis. 1986. "An economic analysis of legal transitions." *Harvard Law Review* 99:509.

———. 1990. "Horizontal equity: Measures in search of a principle." *National Tax Journal* 42:139.

Keith, Robert, and Edward Davis. 1992. *A balanced federal budget: Major statutory provisions*. Washington, D.C.: Congressional Research Service, Library of Congress (April 30).

Keynes, John Maynard. 1964. *The general theory of unemployment, interest, and money*. New York: Harcourt, Brace, and World.

Kiefer, Donald W., William A. Cox, and Dennis Zimmerman. 1992. "A balanced budget constitutional amendment: Economic issues." Congressional Research Service, Library of Congress, Report 92–458S (May 26).

Kimmel, Lewis. 1958. *Federal budget and fiscal policy 1789–1958*. Washington, D.C.: Brookings Institution.

Kingdon, John. 1984. *Agendas, alternatives, and public policies*. Boston: Little, Brown.

Kotlikoff, Laurence J. 1992. *Generational accounting: Knowing who pays, and when, for what we spend*. New York: Free Press.

———. 1993. "From deficit delusion to generational accounting." *Harvard Business Review* (May—June): 104.

Krugman, Paul. 1990. *The age of diminished expectations: U.S. economic policy in the 1990s*. Cambridge: MIT Press.

———. 1994. *Peddling prosperity: Economic sense and nonsense in the age of diminished expectations*. New York: W. W. Norton.

Lasswell, Harold. 1948. *Power and personality*. New York: Viking.

Leimer, Dean R., and Selig D. Lesmoy. 1982. "Social Security and private saving: New time-series evidence." *Journal of Political Economy* 90:606.

Lerner, Abba P. 1943. "Functional finance and the public debt." *Social Research* 10:1.

———. 1964. "The burden of the national debt." In *Public debt and future generations*, ed. James M. Ferguson. Chapel Hill: University of North Carolina Press.

Light, Paul. 1985. *Artful work: The politics of Social Security reform*. New York: Random House.

Lightfoot, Warwick. 1994. "The French miracle." *Wall Street Journal*, October 6, p. A–18.

Locke, John. 1967. *Two treatises on government*. 2nd ed., ed. Peter Laslett. Cambridge: Cambridge University Press.

Logue, Kyle D. 1996. "Tax transitions, opportunistic retroactivity, and the benefits of government precommitment." *Michigan Law Review* 94:1129.

Lord, William, and Peter Rangazas. 1993. "Altruism, deficit policies, and the wealth of future generations." *Economic Inquiry* 31 (October): 609.

Lubecky, David. 1986. "The proposed federal balanced budget amendment: The lesson from state experience." *University of Cincinnati Law Review* 55:563.

Lucas, Robert E., Jr. 1972. "Testing the natural rate hypothesis." In *The econometrics of price determination, Conference*, ed. Otto Eckstein. Washington, D.C.: Federal Reserve Board.

Lucas, Robert E., Jr., and Thomas J. Sargent. 1981a. "After Keynesian economics." In *Rational expectations and economic practice*, ed. Robert E. Lucas and Thomas J. Sargent. Minneapolis: University of Minnesota Press.

———. 1981b. "After Keynesian macroeconomics." In *Rational expectations and economic practice*, ed. Robert E. Lucas and Thomas J. Sargent. Minneapolis: University of Minnesota Press.

Macauley, Lord Thomas Babington. 1902. *The history of England from the accession of James the Second.* Vol. 4. New York: Harper Brothers.

McCaffery, Edward J. 1992. "Tax policy under a hybrid income-consumption tax." *Texas Law Review* 70:1145.

McChesney, Fred C. 1987. "Rent extraction and rent creation in the economic theory of regulation." *Journal of Legal Studies* 16:101.

———. 1989. "Regulation, taxes, and political extortion." In *Regulation and the Reagan era: Politics, bureaucracy, and the public interest,* ed. R. Meiners and B. Yandle. New York: Holmes and Meier.

McCormick, Robert, and Robert Tollison. 1981. *Politicians, legislation, and the economy: An inquiry into the interest-group theory of government.* Boston: M. Nijoff.

McCubbins, Matthew D., Roger G. Noll, and Barry R. Weingast. 1989. "Structure and process, politics and policy: Administrative arrangements and the political control of agencies." *Virginia Law Review* 75:431.

McDonald, I., and R. Solow. 1985. "Wages and employment in a segmented labor market." *Quarterly Journal of Economics* 100 (November): 1115.

Maddock, Rodney, and Michael Carter. 1982. "A child's guide to rational expectations." *Journal of Economic Literature* 20:39.

Makin, John H., and Norman J. Ornstein. 1994. *Debt and taxes.* New York: Random House.

Malbin, Michael J. 1984. "Plus ça change." *National Journal,* April 14, p. 729.

Malone, Dumas. 1951. *Jefferson and his time: Jefferson and the rights of man.* Boston: Little, Brown.

Malthus, Thomas Robert. 1968. *Principles of political economy, considered with a view to their practical application.* 2nd ed. New York: Augustus M. Kelly.

Mankiw, Gregory. 1990. "A quick refresher course in macroeconomics." *Journal of Economic Literature* 20:1645, 1656–1658.

Manley, John. 1970. *The politics of finance.* Boston: Little, Brown.

Mariger, Randall P. 1987. "A life-cycle consumption model with liquidity constraints: Theory and empirical results." *Econometrica* 55:533.

Marshall, Alfred. 1923. *Money, credit, and commerce.* London: Macmillan.

Mayhew, David R. 1974. *Congress: The electoral connection.* New Haven, Conn.: Yale University Press.

———. 1991. *Divided we govern: Party control, lawmaking, and investigations, 1946–1990.* New Haven, Conn.: Yale University Press.

Meadows, Donella, Dennis Meadows, Jorgen Randers, and William Behrens III. 1972. *The limits to growth.* New York: Universe.

Meltzer, Allan. 1981. "Keynes's general theory: A different perspective." *Journal of Economic Literature* 19 (March): 34.

——— 1983. "On Keynes and monetarism." In *Keynes and the modern world,* ed. David Worswick and James Trevithick. Cambridge: Cambridge University Press.

Menchik, Paul L. 1980. "Primogeniture, equal sharing, and the U.S. distribution of wealth." *Quarterly Journal of Economics* 94 (March): 299.

Mill, John Stuart. 1926. *Principles of political economy.* Bk.1. London: Longmans, Green.

Minarik, Joseph. 1991. "Countercyclical fiscal policy: In theory, and in Congress." *National Tax Journal* 44:251.

Mishan, E. J. 1964. "How to make a burden of the public debt." In *Public debt and future generations,* ed. James M. Ferguson. Chapel Hill: University of North Carolina Press.

———. 1977. "Economic criteria for intergenerational comparisons." *Futures* (October).

Montesquieu, Baron de. 1949. *The spirit of the laws,* trans. Thomas Nugent. New York: Hafner.

Murray, Charles. 1984. *Losing ground.* New York: Basic Books.

Musgrave, Richard A., and Peggy B. Musgrave. 1989. *Public finance in theory and practice.* 5th ed. New York: McGraw Hill.

Narveson, Jan. 1978. "Future people and us." In *Obligations to future generations,* ed. R. I. Sikora and Brian Barry. Philadelphia: Temple University Press.

Nash, Gerald D., Noel H. Pugach, and Richard F. Tomasson, eds. 1988. *Social Security: The first half-century.* Albuquerque: University of New Mexico Press.

Neikirk, William A. 1987. "Volcker: An appointee is reelected." *Chicago Tribune,* September 24, p. C–1.

Neisser, Hans. 1964. "Is the public debt a burden on future generations?" In *Public debt and future generations,* ed. James M. Ferguson. Chapel Hill: University of North Carolina Press.

Niskanen, William A. 1971. *Bureaucracy and representative government.* Chicago: Aldin.

Noll, Roger. 1971. *Reforming regulation: An evaluation of the Ash Council proposals.* Washington: Brookings Institution.

Nordhaus, William D. "What's wrong with a declining national saving rate?" *Challenge* 32 (July—August): 22, 24.

Nozick, Robert. 1974. *Anarchy, state, and utopia.* New York: Basic Books.

Okun, Arthur. 1970. *The political economy of prosperity.* Washington, D.C.: Brookings Institution Press.

Olson, Mancur. 1965. *The logic of collective action: Public goods and the theory of groups.* Cambridge: Harvard University Press.

Ornstein, Norman J. 1985. "The politics of the deficit." In *Essays in contemporary economic problems,* ed. Philip J. Cagan. Washington, D.C.: American Enterprise Institute.

Palmer, John L., Timothy Smeeding, and Christopher Jencks. 1988. "The uses and limits of income comparisons." In *The vulnerable,* ed. John L. Palmer, Timothy Smeeding, and Barbara Boyle Torrey. Washington, D.C.: Urban Institute Press.

Parfit, Derek. 1984. *Reasons and persons.* New York: Oxford University Press.

Peacock, Alan T., and Jack Wiseman. 1979. "Approaches to the analysis of government expenditure growth." *Public Finance Quarterly* 7 (January): 3.

Pellecchia, Michael. 1992. "This book ought to gladden the hearts of all doomsayers." *Minneapolis Star Tribune,* October 9, p. 2D.

Penner, Rudolph G., and Alan J. Abramson. 1988. *Broken purse strings: Congressional budgeting 1974 to 1988.* Washington, D.C.: Urban Institute Press.

Peterson, Paul E. 1985. "The new politics of deficits." In *The new direction in American politics,* ed. John E. Chubb and Paul E. Peterson. Washington, D.C.: Brookings Institution Press.

Peterson, Paul E., and Mark Rom. 1989. "Macroeconomic policymaking: Who is in control?" In *Can the government govern?* ed. John E. Chubb and Paul E. Peterson. Washington, D.C.: Brookings Institution Press.

Phelps, Edmund S. 1994a. *Structural slumps: The modern equilibrium theory of unemployment, interest, and assets.* Cambridge: Harvard University Press.

———. 1994b. "Economic justice to the working poor through a wage subsidy." In *Aspects of distribution of wealth and income,* ed. Dimitri B. Papadimitrio. New York: St. Martin's Press.

Pigou, Arthur C. 1951. *A study in public finance.* London: Macmillan.

Pimenta, D., et al. 1976. "Land degradation: Effects on food and energy resources." *Science* 194:149–55.

Poterba, James M. 1994. "State responses to fiscal crises: The effects of budgetary institutions and politics." *Journal of Political Economy* 102:799.

Ramsey, Frank. 1928. "A mathematical theory of saving." *Economic Journal* 38:543.

Rawls, John. 1971. *A theory of justice.* Cambridge: Harvard University Press.

Redburn, Tom. 1987. "Volcker goes from villain to hero: But will he stay?" *Los Angeles Times,* April 5, pt. 4, p. 1.

———. 1989. "A look back at the decade in business: Securities and insecurity." *St. Louis Post-Dispatch,* December 31, p. 18.

Reid, Bradford G. 1985. "Aggregate consumption and deficit financing: An attempt to separate permanent from transitory effects." *Economic Inquiry* 23 (July): 475.

Ricardo, David. 1951. *The works and correspondence of David Ricardo.* Vols. 1 and 4, ed. Piero Sraffa. Cambridge: University Press for the Royal Economic Society.

Roberts, Paul Craig. 1978. "Idealism in public choice theory." *Journal of Monetary Economics* 4:603.

Robinson, James W., ed. 1992. *Ross Perot speaks out.* Rocklin, Cal.: Prima.

Rowley, Charles K., William F. Shughart II, and Robert D. Tollison. 1987. "Interest groups and deficits." In *Deficits,* ed. James M. Buchanan, Charles K. Rowley, and Robert D. Tollison. New York: Basil Blackwell.

Samuelson, Paul. 1983. "Comment." In *Keynes and the modern world,* ed. David Worswick and James Trevithick. Cambridge: Cambridge University Press.

Sargent, Thomas. and Neil Wallace. 1975. " 'Rational' expectations, the optimal money instrument, and the optimal money supply rule." *Journal of Political Economy* 83:241.

———. 1976. "Rational expectations and the theory of economic policy." *Journal of Monetary Economics* 4 (April): 169.

Saturno, James. 1989. "Congress and a balanced budget amendment to the U.S. Constitution." Congressional Research Service Report 89–4 GOV (January 3).

Savage, James D. 1988. *Balanced budgets and American politics.* Ithaca, N.Y.: Cornell University Press.

Say, Jean-Baptiste. 1867. *A treatise on political economy; or the production, distribution, and consumption of wealth,* trans. C. R. Prinsep. Philadelphia: J. Lippincott.

Schama, Simon. 1989. *Citizens: A chronicle of the French Revolution.* New York: Alfred A. Knopf.

Scherer, Frederick, and David Ross. 1990. *Industrial market structure and economic performance.* 3rd ed. Boston: Houghton Mifflin.

Schmitt, Eric. 1994. "Study says military bases survive plans to shut them." *New York Times,* October 10, p. A–12.

Schodolski, Vincent J. 1994. "Tax breaks add to breakdown in California." *Chicago Tribune,* June 19, Perspective, p. 1.

Schrag, Peter. 1994. "A shaky economy built upon fees." *San Diego Union Tribune,* September 1, pp. B–10, B–14.

Schumpeter, Joseph. 1934. *The theory of economic development.* Cambridge: Harvard University Press.

Seater, John J. 1981. "The market value of outstanding government debt, 1919–1975." *Journal of Monetary Economics* 8 (July): 85.

———. 1993. "Ricardian equivalence." *Journal of Economic Literature* 31:142.

Seligman, Edwin R. A. 1931. *Essays in taxation.* 10th ed. New York: Macmillan.

Sen, Amartya. 1961. "On optimising the rate of saving." *Economic Journal* 71:479.

Senate Report. 1993. "Balanced budget constitutional amendment." No. 103–163 (October 21).

Shapiro, Carl, and Joseph E. Stiglitz. 1986. "Equilibrium unemployment as a market discipline device." In *Efficiency wage models of the labor market,* ed. George A. Akerlof and Janet L. Yellen. Cambridge: Cambridge University Press.

Shaviro, Daniel N. 1990. "Beyond public choice and public interest: A study of the legislative process as illustrated by tax legislation in the 1980s." *University of Pennsylvania Law Review* 139:1.

———. 1993a. "Commentary: Uneasiness and capital gains." *Tax Law Review* 48:393.

———. 1993b. *Federalism in taxation: The case for greater uniformity.* Washington, D.C.: American Enterprise Institute Press.

Simon, Julian. 1981. *The ultimate resource.* Princeton: Princeton University Press.

Simons, Henry C. 1938. *Personal income taxation: The definition of income as a problem of fiscal policy.* Chicago: University of Chicago Press.

Skidelsky, Robert. 1976. "Keynes and the revolt against the Victorians." *Spectator,* May 1.

Smith, Adam. 1976. *An inquiry into the nature and causes of the wealth of nations.* Vol. 2, ed. Edwin Cannan. Chicago: University of Chicago Press.

Smith, V. Kerry, and John V. Krutilla. 1984. "Economic growth, resource availability, and environmental quality." *American Economic Review* 74:226.

Solow, Robert H. 1957. "Technological change and the aggregate production function." *Review of Economics and Statistics* 39:312.

———. 1974. "Intergenerational equity." *Review of Economic Studies* 41:29.

———. 1986. "Another possible source of wage stickiness." In *Efficiency wage models of the labor market,* ed. George A. Akerlof and Janet L. Yellen. Cambridge: Cambridge University Press.

Stein, Herbert. 1969. *The fiscal revolution in America.* Chicago: University of Chicago Press.

———. 1989a. "Don't worry about the trade deficit." *Wall Street Journal,* May 16, p. A–14.

———. 1989b. *Governing the $5 trillion economy.* New York: Oxford University Press.

———. 1996. "A presidential budget message." *Wall Street Journal,* January 19, p. A–10.

Sterk, Stewart E., and Elizabeth S. Goldman. 1991. "Controlling legislative shortsightedness: The effectiveness of constitutional debt limitations." *Wisconsin Law Review* 1301.

Steuerle, C. Eugene, and Jon M. Bakija. 1994. *Retooling Social Security for the 21st century: Right and wrong approaches to reform.* Washington, D.C.: Urban Institute Press.

Stewart, Richard. 1975. "The reformation of American administrative law." *Harvard Law Review* 88:1667.

Stith, Kate. 1988. "Rewriting the fiscal Constitution: The case of Gramm-Rudman-Hollings." *California Law Review* 76:595.

Stocker, Frederick D. 1991. "Introduction." In *Proposition 13: A ten-year retrospective,* ed. Frederick D. Stocker. Cambridge, Mass: Lincoln Institute of Land Policy.

Sullivan, Kathleen. 1994. "The Constitution wasn't meant to balance the budget." *Chicago Tribune,* February 23, p. 19.

Summers, Lawrence H. 1981. "Capital taxation and accumulation in a life cycle model." *American Economic Review* 71:533.

———. 1990. *Understanding unemployment.* Cambridge: MIT Press.

Sunstein, Cass. 1987. "Lochner's legacy." *Columbia Law Review* 87:873.

Surrey, Stanley. 1973. *Pathways to tax reform.* Cambridge: Harvard University Press.

Thaler, Richard H. 1991. *Quasi-rational economics.* New York: Russell Sage Foundation.

Thuronyi, Victor. 1988. "Tax expenditures: A reassessment." *Duke Law Journal* 1155.

Tiebout, Charles. 1956. "A pure theory of local expenditures." *Journal of Political Economy* 64:416.

Tribe, Laurence H. 1979. "Issues raised by requesting Congress to call a constitutional convention to propose a balanced budget amendment." *Pacific Law Journal* 10:627.

Tsongas, Paul. 1991. *A call to economic arms: Forging a new American mandate.* Boston: Tsongas Committee.

Tullock, Gordon. 1959. "Problems of majority voting." *Journal of Political Economy* 67:571.

———. 1964a. "Public debt: Who bears the burden?" In *Public debt and future generations,* ed. James M. Ferguson. Chapel Hill: University of North Carolina Press.

———. 1964b. "The social rate of discount and the optimal rate of investment: Comment." *Quarterly Journal of Economics* 78:331.

———. 1965. *The politics of bureaucracy.* Washington, D.C.: Public Affairs Press.

———. 1989. *The economics of special privilege and rent seeking.* Boston: Kluwer Academic.

Turner, Robert. 1992. "The passion of Warren Rudman." *Boston Globe,* November 22, Focus, p. 77.

Vaughn, Karen I., and Richard E. Wagner. 1992. "Public debt controversies: An essay in reconciliation." *Kyklos* 45:37.

Vedder, Richard, Lowell Gallaway, and Christopher Frenze. 1987. "Federal tax increases and the budget deficit, 1947–1986: Some empirical evidence." Minority staff, Joint Economic Committee (April 29).

Vickrey, William. 1993. "Today's task for economists." *American Economic Review* 83:1.

Vogel, Thomas T., Jr. 1996. "Americans, notoriously poor savers, are doing better" and "Calculating savings: Should rising home, stock values count?" *Wall Street Journal,* February 9, p. A–2.

Von Furstenberg, George M., R. Jeffery Green, and Jin-ho Jeong. 1986. "Tax and spend, or spend and tax?" *Review of Economics and Statistics* 68:179.

Wang, Nan. 1994. "Why Americans don't save." Xinhua News Agency, June 17.

Weingast, Barry R., and Mark J. Moran. 1983. "Bureaucratic discretion or congressional control? Regulatory policymaking by the Federal Trade Commission." *Journal of Political Economy* 91:765.

Weiss, Deborah. 1991. "Paternalistic pension policy: Psychological evidence and economic theory." *University of Chicago Law Review* 58:1275.

Wells, Roger H. 1924. "The item veto and state budget reform." *American Political Science Review* 18:782.

White, Joseph, and Aaron Wildavsky. 1989. *The deficit and the public interest: The search for responsible budgeting in the 1980s.* Berkeley: University of California Press.

Wines, Michael. 1994. "Taxpayers are angry; they're expensive, too." *New York Times,* November 20, sec. 4, p. 5.

Witte, John F. 1985. *The politics and development of the federal income tax.* Madison: University of Wisconsin Press.

Wood, Gordon. 1969. *The creation of the American republic 1776–1787.* New York: W. W. Norton.

Zodrow, George. 1993. "Economic analyses of capital gains taxation: Realizations, revenues, efficiency, and equity." *Tax Law Review* 48:419.

Zycher, Benjamin. 1984. "An item veto won't work." *Wall Street Journal,* October 24, p. 32.

Index

AARP, 71, 73, 74, 142
Advisory Commission on Intergovernmental Relations, 283
Age Discrimination in Employment Act, 159
agricultural price supports, 226
American Association of Retired Persons. *See* AARP
American Revolution, 17, 18, 90
Americans with Disabilities Act, 102, 240
Articles of Confederation, 90
Auerbach, Alan, 119, 234

Bagwell, Kyle, 74
balance of payments, 186, 192–96
balanced budget amendment
  fiscal policy, effect on, 241
  generational accounting version of, 233–35
  Gramm-Rudman-Hollings Act of 1985 and, 242, 247, 255, 264, 267–68
  Jefferson, proposed by, 20
  more rigorous version of, 268–73
  1995 version
    and countercyclical deficits, 264
    definitions of terms in, 259, 265–66
    effective date, 266–67
    enabling legislation under, need for, 260, 263–65
    enforcement mechanism, lack of, 11, 259–60, 262

    judicial authority in interpreting, 260–61
    likely effectiveness of, 267–68, 307
    likely influence on public sentiment, 267–68, 273
    limit on debt issuance, 262, 274, 277–78
    means of evading, 259, 261–65
    president, effects on, 258, 260, 262–63
    supermajority deficit authorization rule, 11, 257–58, 262
    unauthorized deficits under, 262
    waiver of balanced budget requirement under, 263
  political debate, effect on, 236–38, 267
  in principle, 11, 12, 71, 235–38
  public uncertainty about government policy, effect on, 242
  state government versions of, 242–47
  as structural response to flawed political process, 235–38, 257
  Virginia school theorists, proposed by, 92–94, 221
Ball, Terence, 172
Barro, Robert
  claim of altruism within the household, 68–69, 74–78
  disregard of budget politics by, 8, 71–74

325

compared to monetary policy, 53, 67,
200, 208–10
countercyclical. *See* fiscal policy,
Keynesian
difficulty of defining current policy, 6,
105
dynamic effects of, 134–35
exclusion of in-kind benefits and burdens, 7–8, 136–38
implementation lag, 62, 208
importance of who pays and gets
what, 6–7, 121–22, 144
Keynesian, 10, 44, 53–54, 61–62, 202,
205–11, 221, 241, 306
rational expectations and, 67–68
as vehicle of generational wealth transfer, 74, 147, 221
Fisher, Irving, 36
Fitts, Michael, 296
Flaubert, Gustav, 14
Food and Drug Administration, 229–30
foreign investment, 195–96
French Revolution of 1789, 15
Friedman, Benjamin, 168–69, 172, 178
Friedman, David, 218
Friedman, Milton, 56–58, 62, 67, 200,
202, 204
full employment, 42–43, 107–8, 198, 202,
206–7
functional finance, 23, 42

GDP, 48, 50–51, 106–7
generational accounting
age groups under, 6, 122–23
alternative versions, 128, 130–31, 143,
147
assignment of unfunded tax burden to
future generations, 9–10, 124, 127,
133–34, 234–35
assumed current policy under, 124,
129–31
compared to budget deficit, 7, 122,
128, 140–44, 147–48
and dynamic effects of fiscal policy,
134–36
findings of, 125–28, 147
and in-kind benefits and burdens, 136–
38, 159

and intertemporal budget constraint,
124, 131–33
lifetime income, 6, 123
lifetime net tax payments, 6, 123
lifetime net tax rates, 6, 9, 123, 127,
144, 147
measurement problems, 6–8, 128–40,
307
and policy sustainability, 127–29, 132–
33, 150
political process, likely effects on,
142–43
potential effects on fiscal policy, 128
and Ricardian offsets, 140
and targeted government transfers,
138–39
and tax incidence, 139
use of lifetime perspective, 134
generational equity
budget deficits and, 3
declining marginal utility of wealth
and, 181
defined as, achieving an optimal rate
of saving, 170–76, 180–85
defined as generational balance in lifetime net tax rates, 9, 151, 157–64,
233
defined as implying a no-transfer
norm, 151–57, 164
economic growth and, 9, 178–85,
305–6
modified Rawlsian approach, 172–75,
177, 178, 180–85
overlapping lifespans and, 153–54,
158–59, 179
philosophical literature discussing,
164–66, 171–74
population size and, 173–74
possibility of nuclear war or other
disasters and, 183–84, 306
Rawlsian maximin, 173
Ricardian offsets on, effect of, 153–54,
161–64, 177
tax lag and, 12, 151
uncertainty regarding the future and,
184–85
Gingrich, Newt, 226, 228, 301
Gokhale, Jagadeesh, 119